Lives. Englished by Sir Thomas North in ten volumes

Plutarch Plutarch, Thomas North

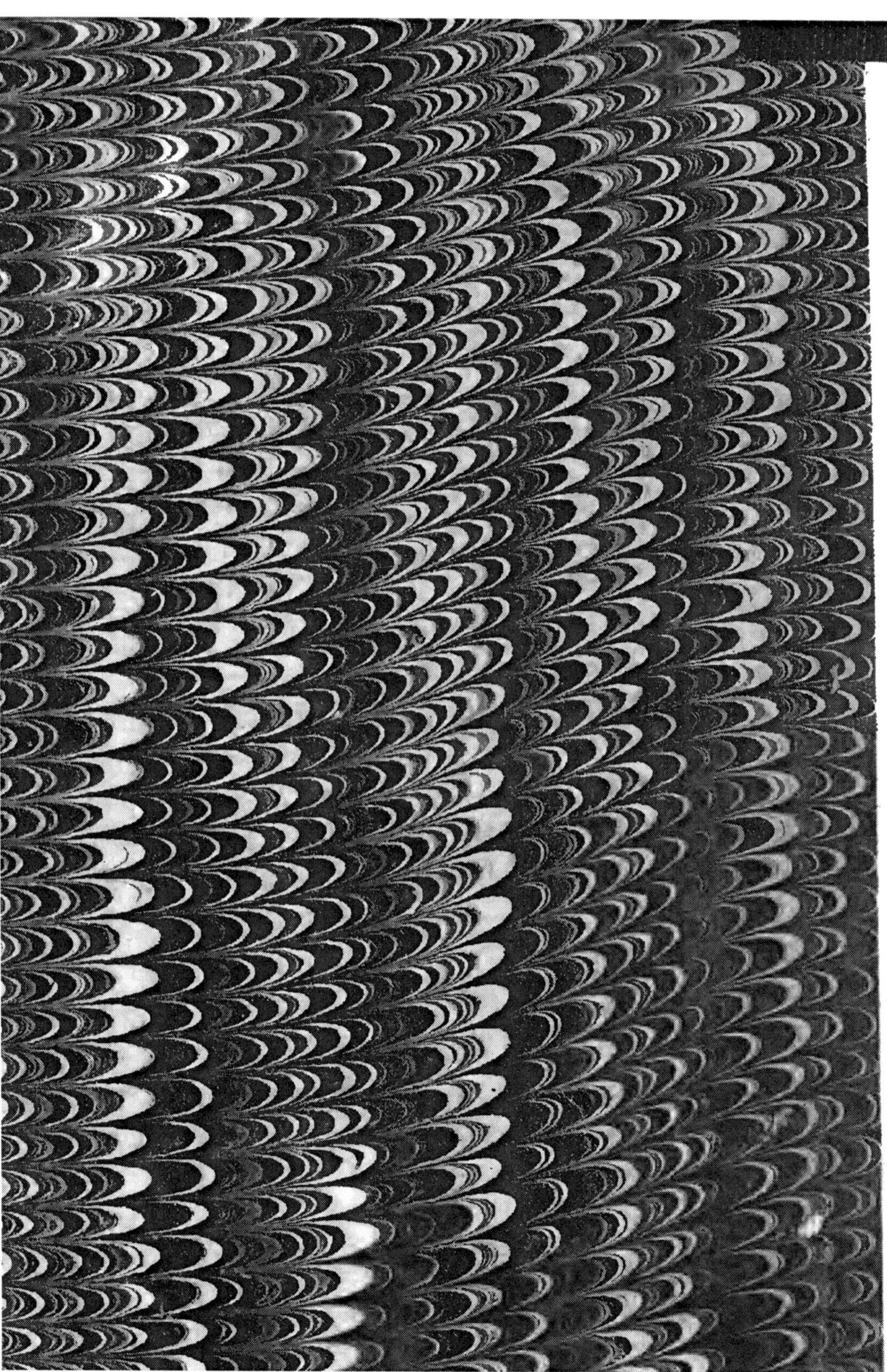

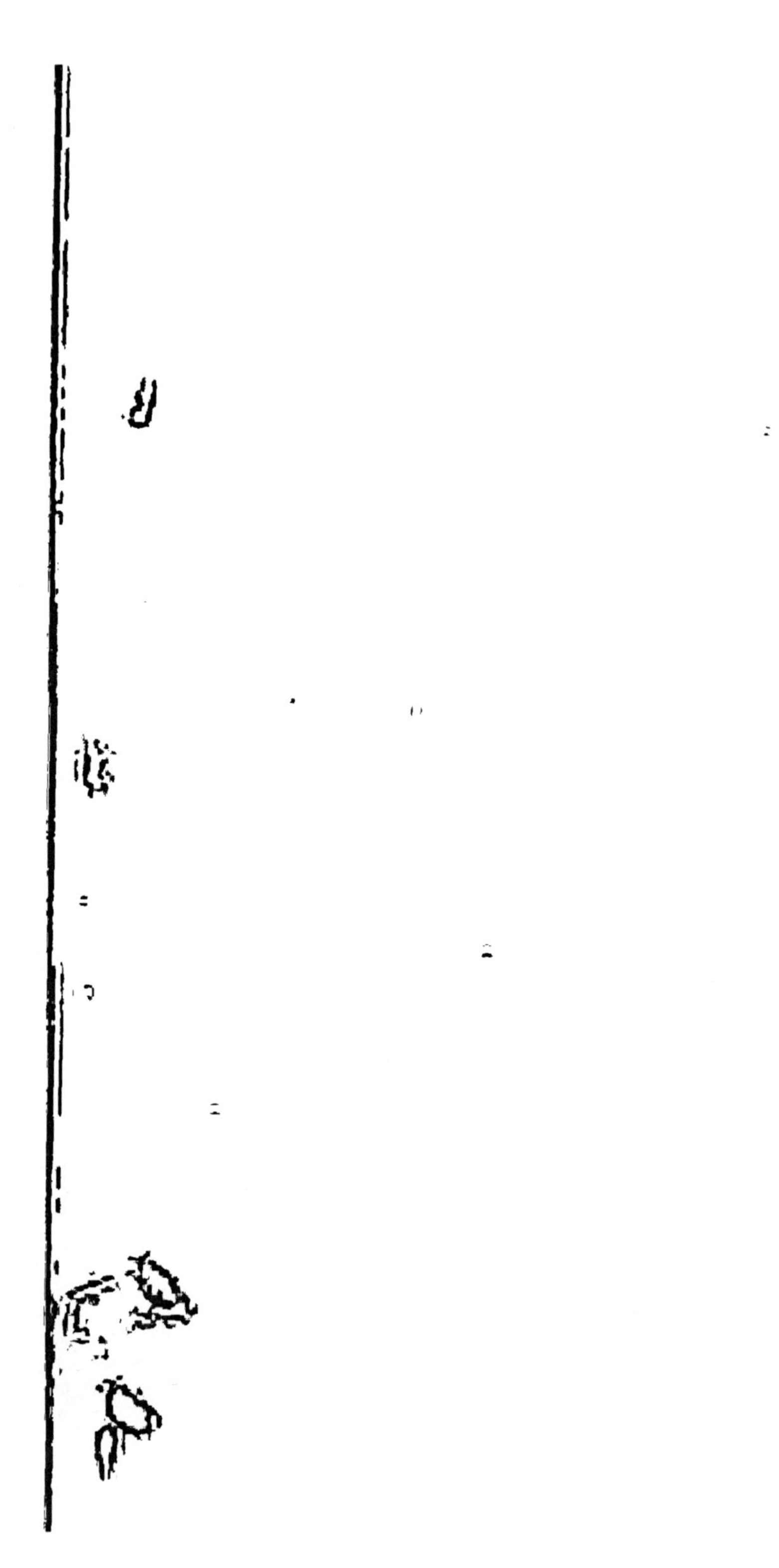

THE TUDOR TRANSLATIONS

EDITED BY

W. E. HENLEY

VIII

PLUTARCH'S

LIVES OF THE NOBLE

GRECIANS AND ROMANS

ENGLISHED BY

SIR THOMAS NORTH

ANNO 1579

With an Introduction by

GEORGE WYNDHAM

SECOND VOLUME

LONDON

Published by DAVID NUTT

IN THE STRAND

1895

Edinburgh: T. and A. CONSTABLE, Printers to Her Majesty

THE TABLE OF THE NOBLE GRECIANS AND ROMANES compared by PLUTARKE of CHÆRONEA

VOLUME II

THE LIFE OF PERICLES

CÆSAR seeing in Rome one daye certen riche and wealthy straungers, having litle dogges and munkeyes in their armes, and that they made marvelous much of them, he asked them if the women in their country had no children: wisely reproving them by his question, for that they bestowed their naturall love and affection upon brute beasts, which they should with all kindnes and love bestowe upon creatures. Nature in like case also, having planted in our minds a naturall desire to learne and understand, we are in reason to reprove those that vainely abuse this good desire, fondly disposing it to learne things vaine and unprofitable: and to cast behinde them in the meane season things honest and necessarie to be learned. For as touching our outward sence, which with passion receaveth impression of the thing it seeth, peradventure it wilbe necessarie to consider indifferently the thing seene, whether it will fall out beneficiall or hurtefull unto him: but so fareth it not with our understanding, for every man maye at his pleasure turne and dispose that to the thinge he taketh delight in, the reason whereof we must allwayes employe to the best parte, and that not only to consider and looke upon the thing, but also to reape the benefit and commoditie of the thing we see. For like as the eye is most delited with the lightest and freshest cullers: even so we must geve our mindes unto those sightes, which by looking upon them doe drawe profit and pleasure unto us. For such effects doth vertue bring: that either to heare or reade them, they doe

Wit allwayes to be employed to good things.

printe in our hartes an earnest love and desire to followe them. But this followeth not in all other things we esteeme, neither are we allwayes disposed to desire to doe the things we see wel done: but contrary oftentimes, when we like the worke, we mislike the worke man, as commonly in making these perfumes and purple cullers. For both the one, and the other doe please us well: but yet we take perfumers and diers to be men of a meane occupation. Therefore Antisthenes aunswered one very wisely, that told him Ismenias was an excellent player of the flute. But yet he is a naughtie man, sayed he: otherwise he could not be so conning at the flute as he is. Even so dyd Philippe king of Macedon saye to his sonne Alexander the great on a time: that at a certen feast had song passing sweetely, and like a master of musicke: Art thou not ashamed, sonne, to singe so well? It is enough for a King to bestowe his leysure somtime to heare musitians singe, and he doth much honour to the muses to heare the masters of the science otherwhile, when one of them singeth to excell another. But he that personally shall bestowe his time, exercising any meane science: bringeth his paynes he hath taken in matters unprofitable, a witnes against him selfe, to prove that he hath bene negligent to learne things honest and profitable. And there was never any young gentleman nobly borne, that seeing the image of Iupiter (which is in the cittie of Pisa) desired to become Phidias: nor Polycletus, for seeing of Iuno in the cittie of Argos: nor that desired to be Anacreon, or Philemon, or Archilochus, for that they tooke pleasure somtime to reade their workes. For it followeth not of necessitie, that though the worke delight, the workeman must needes be praysed. And so in like case, such things doe not profit those which behold them, bicause they doe not move affection in the hartes of the beholders to followe them, neither doe stirre up affection to resemble them, and much lesse to conforme our selves unto them. But vertue hath this singular propertie in all her actions: that she maketh the man that knoweth her to affect her so, that straight he liketh all her doings, and desireth to followe those that are vertuous. For, as for riches, we only desire to have them in possession: but of vertue, we chiefly

Antisthenes saying of a flute player.

The power of vertue.

love the deedes. Wherefore, we are contented to have goodes from other men: but good deedes we would other should have from us. For vertue is of this power, that she allureth a mans minde presently to use her, that wisely considereth of her, and maketh him very desirous in his harte to followe her: and doth not frame his manners that beholdeth her by any imitation, but by the only understanding and knowledge of vertuous deedes, which sodainely bringeth unto him a resolute desire to doe the like. And this is the reason, why me thought I should continew still to write on the lives of noble men, and why I made also this tenthe booke: in the which are conteined the lives of Pericles, and Fabius Maximus, who mainteined warres against Hanniball. For they were both men very like together in many sundry vertues, and specially in curtesie and justice: and for that they could paciently beare the follies of their people, and companions that were in charge of government with them, they were marvelous profitable members for their countrie. But if we have sorted them well together, comparing the one with the other: you shall easely judge that reade our writings of their lives. Pericles was of the tribe of the Acamantides, of the towne of Cholargus, and of one of the best and most auncient families of the cittie of Athens, both by his father and mother. For Xanthippus his father (who overcame in battell the lieutenants of the king of Persia in the jorney of Mycala) maried Agariste that came of Clisthenes, he who drave out of Athens Pisistratus ofspring, and valliantly overthrewe their tyrannie. Afterwards he established lawes, and ordeined a very grave forme of government, to mainteine his cittizens in peace and concorde together. This Agariste dreamed one night, that she was brought a bed of a lyon: and very shortely after she was delivered of Pericles, who was so well proportioned in all the partes of his bodie, that nothing could be mended, saving that his head was somwhat to long and out of proportion to the rest of his bodie. And this is the only cause why all the statues and images of him almost, are made with a helmet of his head: bicause the workemen as it should seeme (and so it is most likely) were willing to hide the bleamishe of his deformitie. But the Attican poets dyd

Pericles stocke.

Pericles mothers dreame.

Pericles had a long head.

call him Schinocephalos, asmuch to saye, as headed like an onyon. For those of Attica doe somtime name that which is called in the vulgar tongue *Scilla*, that is to saye, an onyon of barbarie: *Schinos*. And Cratinus the Comicall poet in his comedie he intituled *Chirones*, sayed:

Olde Saturne he, and dreadfull dyre debate
begotten have, betwene them Carnally,
this tyranne here, this heavy jollting pate,
in courte of goddes so termed worthely.

And againe also in that which he nameth *Nemesis*, speaking of him, he sayeth:

Come Iupiter, come Iupiter,
Come jollthead, and come inkeeper.

And Teleclides mocking him also, sayeth in a place:

Somtimes he standes, amazed when he perceyves,
that harde it were, sufficiently to knowe,
in what estate, his government he leaves.
And then will he, be seldome seene by lowe,
suche heavy heapes, within his braynes doe growe.
But yet somtimes, out of that monstruous pate
he thundreth fast, and threatneth every state.

And Eupolis in a comedie which he intituled *Démi*: being very inquisitive, and asking particularly of every one of the Orators (whom he fayned were returned out of hell) when they named Pericles the last man unto him, he sayed:

Truely thou hast now brought, unto us here that dwell,
the chief of all the captaines, that come from darksome hell.

Pericles studies and teachers.

And as for musicke, the most authors write, that Damon dyd teache him musicke, of whose name (as men saye) they should pronounce the first syllable shorte. Howbeit Aristotle sayeth, that he was taught musicke by Pythoclides. Howsoever it was, it is certaine that this Damon was a man of deepe understanding, and subtill in matters of government: for, to hide from the people his sufficiency therein, he gave it out he was a musitian, and dyd resorte unto Pericles, as a master wrestler, or fenser: but he taught him howe he should deale in matters of state. Notwithstanding, in the ende he could not so conningly convey this matter, but the people sawe his harping and musicke, was only a viser to his other practise: wherefore they dyd banish him Athens for five yeres, as a man that busilie tooke upon him to chaunge the state of things, and that favored tyrannie. And this gave the Comicall poets matter to playe upon him finely: among which Plato in a comedie of his, bringeth in a man that asketh him:

> O Chiron, tell me first: art thou in deede the man,
> which dyd instruct Pericles thus? make aunswer if thou can.

Zenon Eleatean.

He was somtime also scholler to the philosopher Zenon, who was borne in the cittie of Elea, and taught naturall philosophie, as Parmenides dyd: but his profession was to thwarte and contrary all men, and to alledge a world of objections in his disputation, which were so intricate, that his adversarie replying against him, knewe not howe to aunswer him, nor to conclude his argument. The which Timon Philiasius witnesseth in these wordes:

> Zenon was subtill sure, and very eloquent,
> and craftilie could winde a man, by waye of argument,
> if so he were disposed, his cunning to descrie,
> or showe the sharpenes of his witt, to practise pollicie.

But Anaxagoras Clazomenian was he that was most familliar and conversaunt with him, and dyd put in him the majestie and gravity he shewed in all his sayings, and doings, who dyd farre excell the common course of ordinarie Orators that pleaded before the people: and to be shorte, he it was that dyd facion his manners, altogether to carie that grave countenaunce which he dyd. For they called Anaxagoras in his time, Nùs, as much to saye, as understanding. Either bicause they had his singular wit and capacitie in suche great admiration, being growen to searche out the cause of naturall things: or that he was the first man, who dyd ascribe the disposition and government of this world, not unto fortune or fatall necessitie, but unto a pure, simple, and understanding minde, which doth separate at the first moving cause, the

PERICLES substaunce of suche like partes as are medled and compounded of divers substaunces, in all other bodies through the world. Pericles made marvelous muche of Anaxagoras, who had fully instructed him in the knowledge of naturall things, and of those specially that worke above in the ayer and firmament. For he grewe not only to have a great minde and an eloquent tongue, without any affectation, or grosse countrie termes: but to a certen modest countenaunce that scantly smyled, very sober in his gate, having a kynde of sounde in his voyce that he never lost nor altered, and was of very honest behaviour, never troubled in his talke for any thing that crossed him, and many other suche like things, as all that sawe them in him, and considered them, could but wonder at him. But for proofe hereof, the reporte goeth, there was a naughty busy fellowe on a time, that a whole daye together dyd nothing but rayle upon Pericles in the market place, and revile him to his face, with all the villanous wordes he could use. But Pericles put all up quietly, and gave him not a worde againe, dispatching in the meane time matters of importaunce he had in hand, untill night came, that he went softly home to his house, shewing no alteration nor semblaunce of trouble at all, though this lewde varlet followed him at the heeles, with wordes of open defamation. And as he was ready to enter in at his owne doores, being darke night, he commaunded one of his men to take a torche, and to bring this man home to his house. Yet the poet Ion sayeth, that Pericles was a very prowde man, and a stately, and that with his gravity and noble minde, there was mingled a certaine scorne and contempt of other: and contrarilie, he greatly prayseth the civillitie, humanitie, and curtesie of Cimon, bicause he could facion him selfe to all companies. But letting passe that which the poet Ion sayed: who would that vertue should be full of tragicall discipline, bringing in with it, a certaine satyricall discourse to move laughture. Nowe Zennon contrariwise dyd counsell all those, that sayd Pericles gravity was a presumption, and arrogancie: that they should also followe him in his presumption. For, to counterfeate in that sorte things honest and vertuous, doth secretly with time breede an affection and desire to love

Pericles manners and behaviour.

Pericles pacience.

them, and afterwardes with custome even effectually to use and followe them. So Pericles by keeping Anaxagoras company, dyd not onely profit him selfe in these things, but he learned besides to put awaye all superstitious feare, of celestiall signes and impressions seene in the ayer. For to those that are ignoraunte of the causes thereof, suche sights are terrible, and to the godly also feareful, as if they were utterly undone: and all is, bicause they have no certaine knowledge of the reason that naturall philosophy yeldeth, which in steade of a fearefull superstition, would bring a true religion accompanied with assured hope of goodnes. Some saye a man brought Pericles one daye from his farme out of the countrie, a rammes head that had but one horne, and that the prognosticator Lampon considering this head, that had but one strong horne in the middest of his forehead, interpreted, that this was the signification thereof. That being two tribes and severall factions in the cittie of Athens touching government, the one of Pericles, and the other of Thucydides: the power of both should be brought into one, and specially into his parte, in whose house this signe dyd happen. Further, it is sayed that Anaxagoras being present, dyd cause the rammes head to be cloven in two peces, and shewed unto them that stoode by, that the brayne of this ramme dyd not fill the panne of his naturall place, but inclosed it selfe in all partes, being narrowe like the poynte of an egge, in that parte where the horne tooke his first roote of budding out. So Anaxagoras was marvelously esteemed at that present by all those that stoode by: but so was Lampon, sone after that Thucydides was driven awaye, and that the government of the whole common weale fell into the handes of Pericles alone. And it is not to be wondred at (in my opinion) that the naturall philosopher and the prognosticator dyd rightly mete together in trothe: the one directly telling the cause, and the other the ende of the event as it fell out. For the profession of the one, is to knowe howe it commeth: and of the other, wherefore it commeth, and to foretell what it betokeneth. For where some saye, that to shewe the cause, is to take awaye the signification of the signe: they do not consider that in

The benefit of naturall philosophie.

What was signified by the rammes head that had but one horne, and was found in Pericles grounde.

seeking to abolishe by this reason the wonderfull tokens and signes in the ayer, they doe take awaye those also which are done by arte. As the noyse of basons, the lightes of fyre by the sea side, and the shadowes of nedles or pointes of dyalles in the sunne: all which things are done by some cause and handyworke, to be a signe and token of some thing. But this argument peradventure maye serve better in another booke. And nowe againe to Pericles. Whilest he was yet but a young man, the people stoode in awe of him, bicause he somwhat resembled Pisistratus in his countenaunce: and the auncientest men of the cittie also were muche afeard of his softe voyce, his eloquent tongue, and ready utteraunce, bicause in those he was Pisistratus up and downe. Moreover he was very riche and wealthy, and of one of the noblest families of the cittie, and those were his friendes also that caried the only swaye and authoritie in the state: whereupon, fearing least they would banishe him with the banishement of *Ostracismon*, he would not medle with government in any case, although otherwise he shewed him selfe in warres very valliant and forward, and feared not to venter his persone. But after that Aristides was dead, that Themistocles was driven awaye, and that Cimon being ever in service in the warres as generall in forreine countries, was a long time out of Grece: then he came to leane to the tribe of the poore people, preferring the multitude of the poore communaltie, above the small number of Nobilitie and riche men, the which was directly against his nature. For of him selfe he was not popular, nor meanely geven: but he dyd it (as it should seeme) to avoyde suspition, that he should pretend to make him selfe King. And bicause he sawe Cimon was inclined also to take parte with the Nobilitie, and that he was singularly beloved and liked of all the honester sorte: he to the contrarie enclined to the common people, purchasing by this meanes safety to him selfe, and authoritie against Cimon. So he presently beganne a newe course of life, since he had taken upon him to deale in matters of state: for they never sawe him afterwardes at any time goe into the cittie, but to the market place, or to the Senate house. He gave up going to all feastes where he was bidden, and left the entertainment

Pericles likened to Pisistratus.

Pericles first beginning to deale in the common wealth.

of his friendes, their company and familiaritie. So that in all his time wherein he governed the common weale, which was a long time, he never went out to supper to any of his friendes, unles it were that he was once at a feast at his nephew Euryptolemus mariage: and then he taried there no longer, but while the ceremonie was a doing, when they offer wine to the goddes, and so he rose from the table. For these friendly meetings at suche feastes, doe much abase any counterfeate majestie or set countenaunce: and he shall have much a doe to keepe gravity and reputation, shewing familiaritie to every knowen friende in such open places. For in perfect vertue, those things truely are ever most excellent, which be most common: and in good and vertuous men there is nothing more admirable unto straungers, then their dayely conversation is to their friendes. Pericles nowe to prevent that the people should not be glutted with seeing him to ofte, nor that they should come much to him: they dyd see him but at some times, and then he would not talke in every matter, neither came muche abroade among them, but reserved him selfe (as Critolaus sayed they kept the Salaminian galley at Athens) for matters of great importaunce. And in the meane season, in other matters of small moment, he delt by meanes of certaine orators his familliar friendes, amongest whom Ephialtes (as they saye) was one: he who tooke awaye the authoritie and power from the courte of Areopagus, and dyd geve to muche libertie to the people, as Plato sayed. Upon which occasion, as the Comicall poets saye, he became so stowte and head strong, that they could no more holde him backe, then a younge unbrideled colte: and tooke such a corage upon him, that he would obaye no more, but invaded the Ile of Eubœa, and set upon the other Ilandes. Pericles also bicause he would facion a phrase of speache, with a kynde of style altogether agreable to the manner of life and gravitie he had taken upon him: he gave him selfe to all matters which he had learned of Anaxagoras, shadowing his reasons of naturall philosophie, with artificiall rethoricke. For having obteined a deepe understanding by studying of philosophie, and a ready waye effectually to ende any matter, he undertoke to prove (besides that nature

To much familiaritie breedeth contempt.

Ephialtes an orator.

PERICLES

had endued him with an excellent witte and capacitie, as the divine Plato doth write, to bring any thing to serve his purpose) he dyd so artificially compasse it with eloquence, that he farre passed all the orators in his time. And for this cause was he (as they saye) surnamed Olympius, as muche to saye, as heavenly or divine. But some are of opinion he had that surname, by reason of the common buildings and stately workes he raysed up in the cittie of Athens, that dyd muche set forth the same. Other thinke it was geven him for his great authoritie and power he had in government, aswell in warres, as in peace. But it is no marvaill that this glorie was geven him, considering the many other qualities and vertues that were in him. Howbeit the comedies the Poetes caused to be played in those times (in which there were many wordes spoken of him, some in earnest, some in sporte and jeast) doe witnesse that he had that surname geven him, chiefly for his eloquence. For it is reported, that he thundered and lightened in his oration to the people, and that his tongue was a terrible lightning. And touching this matter, they tell of an aunswer Thucydides, Milesius sonne, should pleasauntly make concerning the force of Pericles eloquence. Thucydides was a noble man, and had long time contended against Pericles in matters of the common weale. Archidamus, king of Lacedæmon, asked Thucydides on a time: whether he or Pericles wrestled best. Thucydides made him aunswer: When I have geven him an open fall before the face of the world, he can so excellently deny it, that he maketh the people beleeve he had no fall at all, and persuadeth them the contrarie of that they sawe. Notwithstanding he was ever very grave and wise in speaking. For ever when he went up into the pulpit for orations to speake to the people, he made his prayers unto the goddes, that nothing might escape his mouthe, but that he might consider before whether it would serve the purpose of his matter he treated on: yet are there none of his workes extant in writing, unles it be some fewe lawes he made, and but very fewe of his notable sayings are brought to light, save only these. He sayed on a time that they must take awaye the cittie of Ægina, bicause it was a strawe lying in the

Why Pericles was surnamed Olympius.

Thucydides, Pericles adversarie.

Pericles sayings.

eye of the haven Piræa. And another time, he sayed that he saw the warres a farre of, comming from Peloponnesus. Another time, as he tooke shippe with Sophocles (his companion in commission with him as generall of the armie) who commended a fayer young boye they met as they came to the haven: Sophocles, sayed he, a governour must not only have his handes, but also his eyes cleane. And Stesimbrotus writeth, that in a funerall oration he made in the prayse of those that were slaine in the warre of Samos: he sayed they were immortall as the goddes. For we doe not see the goddes (sayed he) as they be, but for the honour that is done to them, and the great happines they enjoye, we doe conjecture they are immortall: and the same things are in those that dye in service, and defence of their countrie. Nowe where Thucydides doth write the government of the common weale under Pericles to be as a government of Nobilitie, and yet had apparaunce of a popular state: it is true that in effect it was a Kingdome, bicause one alone dyd rule and governe the whole state. And many other saye also, he was the first that brought in the custome to devide the enemies landes wonne by conquest among the people, and of the common money to make the people see playes and pastimes, and that appointed them rewarde for all things. But this custome was ill brought up. For the common people that before were contented with litle, and got their living paynefully with swet of their browes: became nowe to be very vaine, sumptuous, and riotous, by reason of these things brought up then. The cause of the alteration doth easely appeare by those things. For Pericles at his first comming, sought to winne the favour of the people, as we have sayed before, only to get like reputation that Cimon had wonne. But comming farre shorte of his wealthe and abilitie, to carie out the porte and charge that Cimon dyd, entertaining the poore, keeping open house to all commers, clothing poore olde people, breaking open besides all inclosures and pales through all his landes, that every one might with more libertie come in, and take the fruites thereof at their pleasure: and seeing him selfe by these great meanes out gone farre in good will with the common people, by

Pericles common wealthe.

The good deedes of Cimon.

Demonides counsell and procurement (who was borne in the Ile of Ios) he brought in this distribution of the common money, as Aristotle writeth. And having wonne in a shorte time the favour and good will of the common people, by distribution of the common treasure, which he caused to be devided among them, aswell to have place to see these playes, as for that they had rewarde to be present at the judgementes, and by other suche like corruptions: he with the peoples helpe, dyd invey against the courte of the Areopagites, wherof he never was any member. For it never came to be his happe to be yerely governour, nor keeper of the lawes, nor King of the sacrifices, nor master of the warres: all which were offices chosen in auncient time by lot. And further, those on whom the lot fell, if they had behaved them selves well in their office, they were called forwards, and raised to be of the bodie of this courte of the Areopagites. Pericles nowe by these meanes having obteined great credit and authoritie amongest the common people, he troubled the Senate of the Areopagites in suche sorte, that he pluckt many matters from their hearing, by Ephialtes helpe: and in time made Cimon to be banished Athens, as one that favored the Lacedæmonians, and contraried the common wealthe and authoritie of the people. Notwithstanding he was the noblest and richest persone of all the cittie, and one that had wonne so many glorious victories, and had so replenished Athens with the conquered spoyles of their enemies, as we have declared in his life: so great was the authoritie of Pericles amongest the people. Nowe the banishment wherewith he was punished (which they called *Ostracismon*) was limited by the lawe for tenne yeres. In which space the Lacedæmonians being come downe with a great armie into the countrie of Tanagra, the Athenians sent out their power presently against them. There Cimon willing to shewe the Athenians by his deedes, that they had falsely accused him for favoring the Lacedæmonians: dyd arme him self, and went on his country mens side, to fight in the companie of his tribe. But Pericles friends gathered together, and forced Cimon to departe thence as a banished man. And this was the cause that Pericles fought that daye more valliantly then

Pericles large distribution diminished the Areopagit authoritie.

Pericles causeth Cimon to be banished Athens.

The *Ostracismon.*

ever he dyd, and he wanne the honour and name to have done more in the persone of him selfe that daye, then any other of all the armie. At that battell also, all Cimons friends, whom Pericles had burdened likewise to favour the Lacedæmonians doings, dyed every man of them that daye. Then the Athenians repented them much that they had driven Cimon away, and wished he were restored, after they had lost this battell upon the confines of the countrie of Attica: bicause they feared sharpe warres would come upon them againe at the next spring. Which thing when Pericles perceyved, he sought also to further that the common people desired: wherefore he straight caused a decree to be made, that Cimon should be called home againe, which was done accordingly. Now when Cimon was returned, he advised that peace should be made betwene both citties: for the Lacedæmonians dyd love Cimon very well, and contrarily they hated Pericles, and all other governours. Some notwithstanding doe write, that Pericles dyd never passe his consent to call him home againe, before suche time as they had made a secret agreement amongest them selves (by meanes of Elpinice Cimons sister) that Cimon should be sent out with an armie of two hundred galleys, to make warres in the king of Persia his dominions, and that Pericles should remaine at home with the authoritie of government within the cittie. This Elpinice (Cimons sister) had once before intreated Pericles for her brother, at such time as he was accused before the judge of treason. For Pericles was one of the committees, to whom this accusation was referred by the people. Elpinice went unto him, and besought him not to doe his worst unto her brother. Pericles aunswered her merilie: Thou art to old Elpinice, thou art to olde, to goe through with these matters. Yet when his matter came to judgement, and that his cause was pleaded: he rose but once to speake against him (for his owne discharge as it were) and went his waye when he had sayed, doing lesse hurte to Cimon, then any other of his accusers. How is Idomeneus to be credited nowe, who accuseth Pericles that he had caused the orator Ephialtes to be slaine by treason (that was his friende, and dyd allwayes counsell him, and take his parte in all kinde of government

Pericles calleth Cimon from exile.

Pericles moderation unto Cimon.

of the common weale) only for the jealousie and envie he dyd beare to his glorie? I can but muse why Idomeneus should speake so slaunderously against Pericles, unles it were that his melancholy humour procured suche violent speache: who though peradventure he was not altogether blameles, yet he was ever nobly minded, and had a naturall desire of honour, in which kinde of men such furious cruell passions are seldome seene to breede. But this orator Ephialtes being cruell to those that tooke parte with the Nobilitie, bicause he would spare nor pardone no man for any offence whatsoever committed against the peoples authoritie, but dyd followe and persecute them with all rigour to the uttermost: his enemies layed waite for him by meanes of one Aristodicus Tanagrian, and they killed him by treason, as Aristotle writeth. In the meane time Cimon dyed in the Ile of Cyprus, being generall of the armie of the Athenians by sea. Wherefore those that tooke parte with the Nobilitie, seeing Pericles was nowe growen very great, and that he went before all other cittizens of Athens, thincking it good to have some one to sticke on their side against him, and to lessen thereby somewhat his authoritie, that he might not come to rule all as he would: they raised up against him, one Thucydides, of the towne of Alopecia, a grave wise man, and father in lawe to Cimon. This Thucydides had lesse skill of warres then Cimon, but understoode more in civill government then he, for that he remained most parte of his time within the cittie: where continually invaying against Pericles in his pulpit for orations to the people, in shorte time he had stirred up a like companie against the faction of Pericles. For he kept the gentlemen and richer sorte (which they call Nobilitie) from mingling with the common people, as they were before, when through the multitude of the commons their estate and dignitie was abscured, and troden under foote. Moreover he dyd separate them from the people, and dyd assemble them all as it were into one bodie, who came to be of equall power with the other faction, and dyd put (as a man will saye) a counterpease into the ballance. For at the beginning there was but a litle secret grudge only betwene these two factions, as an artificiall flower set in the blade of a sworde, which

The murther of Ephialtes.

Thucydides Pericles adversary in the common wealth.

made those shewe a litle, that dyd leane unto the people: and the other also somwhat that favored the Nobilitie. But the contention betwene these two persones, was as a deepe cut, which devided the cittie wholy in two factions: of the which the one was called the Nobilitie, and the other the communaltie. Therefore Pericles geving yet more libertie unto the people, dyd all things that might be to please them, ordeining continuall playes and games in the cittie, many feastes, banckets, and open pastimes to entertaine the commons with suche honest pleasures and devises: and besides all this, he sent yerely an armie of three score gallyes unto the warres, into the which he put a great number of poore cittizens that tooke paye of the state for nine moneths of the yere, and thereby they dyd learne together, and practise to be good sea men. Furthermore he sent into the countrie of Cherronesus, a thousand free men of the cittie to dwell there, and to devide the landes amongest them: five hundred also into the Ile of Naxos: into the Ile of Andros, two hundred and fiftie: into Thracia, a thousand to dwell with the Bisaltes: and other also into Italie, when the cittie of Sybaris was built againe, which afterwardes was surnamed the cittie of the Thurians. All this he dyd to ryd the cittie of a number of idle people, who through idlenes beganne to be curious, and to desire chaunge of things, as also to provide for the necessitie of the poore townes men that had nothing. For, placing the naturall cittizens of Athens neere unto their subjects and friendes, they served as a garrison to keepe them under, and dyd suppresse them also from attempting any alteration or chaunge. But that which deliteth most, and is the greatest ornament unto the cittie of Athens, which maketh straungers most to wonder, and which alone doth bring sufficient testimonie, to confirme that which is reported of the auncient power, riches, and great wealthe of Grece, to be true and not false: are the stately and sumptuous buildings, which Pericles made to be built in the cittie of Athens. For it is the only acte of all other Pericles dyd, and which made his enemies most to spight him, and which they most accused him for, crying out upon him in all counsailles and assemblies: that the people of Athens were openly

A politicke care for idle persones.

Sumptuous buildings erected by Pericles.

 defamed, for carying awaye the ready money of all Grece, which was left in the Ile of Delos to be safely kept there. And although they could with good honestie have excused this facte, saying that Pericles had taken it from them, for feare of the Barbarous people, to the ende to laye it up in a more stronger place, where it should be in better safetie: yet was this to overgreat an injurie offered unto all the rest of Grece, and to manifest a token of tyrannie also, to beholde before their eyes, howe we doe employe the money, which they were inforced to gather for the maintenaunce of the warres against the barbarous people, in gilding, building, and setting forth our cittie, like a glorious woman, all to be gawded with golde and precious stones, and howe we doe make images, and build up temples of wonderfull and infinite charge. Pericles replied to the contrarie, and declared unto the Athenians that they were not bounde to make any accompt of this money unto their friendes and allies, considering that they fought for their safety, and that they kept the barbarous people farre from Grece, without troubling them to set out any one man, horse, or shippe of theirs, the money only excepted, which is no more theirs that payed it, then theirs that receyved it, so they bestowe it to that use they receyved it for. And their cittie being already very well furnished, and provided of all things necessary for the warres, it was good reason they should employe and bestowe the surplus of the treasure in things, which in time to come (and being throughly finished) would make their fame eternall. Moreover he sayed that whilest they continue building, they should be presently riche, by reason of the diversitie of workes of all sortes, and other things which they should have neede of: and to compasse these things the better, and to set them in hande, all manner of artificers and worke men (that would labour) should be set a worke. So should all the townes men, and inhabitants of the cittie, receyve paye and wages of the common treasure: and the cittie by this meanes should be greatly beawtified, and muche more able to mainteine it selfe. For suche as were stronge, and able men of bodie, and of yeres to carie weapon, had paye and entertainment of the common wealthe, which were sent abroade unto the warres:

and other that were not meete for warres, as craftes men, and labourers: he would also they should have parte of the common treasure, but not without they earned it, and by doing somwhat. And this was his reason, and the cause that made him occupie the common people with great buildings, and devises of works of divers occupations, which could not be finished of long time: to the ende that the cittizens remaining at home, might have a meane and waye to take parte of the common treasure, and enriche them selves, aswell as those that went to the warres, and served on the sea, or els that laye in garrison to keepe any place or forte. For some gayned by bringing stuffe: as stones, brasse, yvory, gold, ebbany, and cypres. Other got, to worke and facion it: as carpinters, gravers, fownders, casters of images, masons, hewers of stone, dyers, goldsmithes, joyners working in yvorie, painters, men that set in sundrie cullers of peces of stone or wodde, and turners. Other gayned to bring stuffe, and to furnishe them: as marchaunts, mariners, and shippemasters, for things they brought them by sea. And by lande other got also: as carte makers, cariers, carters, corde makers, sadlers, coller-makers, and pyoners to make wayes plaine, and miners, and such like. Furthermore, every science and crafte, as a captaine having souldiers, had also their armie of the worke men that served them, labouring truely for their living, who served as prentises and jorney men under the workemasters: so the worke by this meanes dyd disperse abroade a common gayne to all sortes of people and ages, what occupation or trade soever they had. And thus came the buildings to rise in greatnes and sumptuousnes, being of excellent workemanshippe, and for grace and beawtie not comparable: bicause every workeman in his science dyd strive what he could to excell others, to make his worke appeare greatest in sight, and to be most workemanly done in showe. But the greatest thing to be woundred at, was their speede and diligence. For where every man thought those workes were not likely to be finished in many mens lives and ages, and from man to man: they were all done and finished, whilest one only governour continued still in credit and authoritie. And yet they saye, that in the

Divers artificers at Athens.

 same time, as one Agatarchus boasted him self, that he had quickly painted certen beastes: Zeuxis another painter hearing him, aunswered: And I contrarilie doe rejoyce, that I am a long time in drawing of them. For commonly slight and sodaine drawing of any thing, cannot take deepe cullers, nor geve perfect beawty to the worke: but length of time, adding to the painters diligence and labour in making of the worke, maketh the cullers to continue for ever. For this cause therefore the workes Pericles made, are more wonderfull: bicause they were perfectly made in so shorte a time, and have continued so long a season. For every one of those which were finished up at that time, seemed then to be very auncient touching the beawtie thereof: and yet for the grace and continuance of the same, it looketh at this daye as if it were but newly done and finished, there is suche a certaine kynde of florishing freshnes in it, which letteth that the injurie of time cannot impaire the sight thereof: As if every one of those foresaid workes, had some living spirite in it, to make it seeme young and freshe: and a soule that lived ever, which kept them in their good continuing state. Now the chief surveyour generall of all these workes, was Phidias, albeit that there were many other excellent worke masters in every science and occupation. For the temple of Pallas, which is called Parthénon (as a man would saye, the temple of the virgine, and is surnamed Hecatompedon, for that it is a hundred foote every waye) was built by Ictinus, and Callicrates: and the chappell of Eleusin (where the secret ceremonies of the mysteries were made) was first founded by Coræbus, who raised up the first pillers in order, standing beneath on the ground, and dyd set them up unto the master chaptrells. But after he was dead, Metagenes, borne in the towne of Xypeta, turned the arches over, and then dyd set the pillers in order also which are above: and Xenocles of the towne of Cholargea, was he that made the lanterne or toppe of the steeple which covereth the sanctuarie: but the long wall which Socrates heard Pericles him selfe geve order for the building of it, was done by Callicrates, who undertooke the worke. Cratinus the Poet, in a comedie he made, laugheth at this worke, to see how slowly it went forward, and how long it was a doing, saying:

Pericles long a goe, dyd ende this worke begonne:
and build it highe, with glorious wordes, if so it had bene done.
And as for deedes (in dede) he built nothing at all,
but let it stande: as yet it stands, much liker for to fall.

And as for the Theater or place appointed for musicke, where they heare all musitians playe, and is called Odeon: it is very well made within with divers seates and degrees, and many ranges of pillers, but the toppe of the roofe is altogether rounde, which is somwhat hanging downeward round about of it selfe, comming together into one pointe. And it is sayed that this was made after the patterne and facion of king Xerxes royall pavilion, and that Pericles was the first deviser and maker of it. Wherefore Cratinus in another place of his comedie he maketh of the Thracians, doth playe very pretily upon him, saying:

The Odeon.

Pericles here doth come, Dan Iupiter surnamed,
(and onyons hed) which hath in his great noddell finely framed,
The plot of Odeon, when he delivered was
from banishment, and daungers deepe, wherein he long dyd passe.

Pericles was the first that made marvelous earnest labour to the people that they would make an order, that on the daye of the feast called Panathenæa, they would set up games for musicke. And he him selfe being chosen ruler of these games, as judge to rewarde the best deserver: ordained the manner the musitians should ever after keepe in their singing, playing on their flutes, or upon the citherne, or other instruments of musicke. So the first games that ever were for musicke, were kept within the Odeon: and so were the other after them also, ever celebrated there. The gate and entring into the castell was made and finished within the space of five yeres, under the charge of Mnesicles, that was master of the workes. And whilest these gates were a building, there happened a wonderfull chaunce, which declared very well that the goddesse Minerva dyd not mislike the building, but that it pleased her marvelously. For one

Pericles erected games for musicke.

of the most painefullest workemen that wrought there, fell by mischaunce from the height of the castell to the grounde, which fall dyd so sore broose him, and he was so sicke with all, that the phisitians and surgeons had no hope of his life. Pericles being very sorie for his mischaunce, the goddesse appeared to him in his sleepe in the night, and taught him a medicine, with the which he dyd easely heale the poore broosed man, and that in shorte time. And this was the occasion why he caused the image of the goddesse Minerva (otherwise called of healthe) to be cast in brasse, and set up within the temple of the castell, neere unto the altar which was there before, as they saye. But the golden image of Minerva was made by Phidias, and graven round about the base: Who had the charge in manner of all other workes, and by reason of the good will Pericles bare him, he commaunded all the other workemen. And this made the one to be greatly envied, and the other to be very ill spoken of. For their enemies gave it out abroad, that Phidias receyved the gentlewomen of the cittie into his house, under culler to goe see his workes, and dyd convey them to Pericles. Upon this brute, the Comicall poets taking occasion, dyd cast out many slaunderous speaches against Pericles, accusing him that he kept one Menippus wife, who was his friend and lieutenante in the warres: and burdened him further, that Pyrilampes, one of his familiar friends also, brought up fowle, and specially peacoks, which he secretly sent unto the women that Pericles kept. But we must not wonder at these Satyres, that make profession to speake slaunderously against all the worlde, as it were to sacrifice the injuries and wronges they cast upon honorable and good men, to the spight and envie of the people, as unto wicked spirites: considering that Stesimbrotus Thasian durst falsely accuse Pericles of detestable incest, and of abusing his owne sonnes wife. And this is the reason, in my opinion, why it is so hard a matter to come to the perfect knowledge of the trothe of auncient things, by the monuments of historiographers: considering long processe of time, doth utterly obscure the trothe of matters, done in former times. For every written historie speaking of men that are

The Poets raise up slaunders against Pericles.

alive, and of the time of things, whereof it maketh mention: somtime for hate and envie, somtime for favour or flatterie, doth disguise and corrupt the trothe. But Pericles perceyving that the orators of Thucydides faction, in their common orations dyd still crie out upon him, that he dyd vainely waste and consume the common treasure, and that he bestowed upon the workes, all the whole revenue of the cittie: one daye when the people were assembled together, before them all he asked them, if they thought that the coste bestowed were to muche. The people aunswered him: A great deale to muche. Well, said he then, the charges shalbe mine (if you thinke good) and none of yours: provided that no mans name be written upon the workes, but mine onely. When Pericles had sayed so, the people cried out alowde, they would none of that (either bicause that they wondred at the greatnes of his minde, or els for that they would not geve him the only honour and prayse to have done so sumptuous and stately workes) but willed him that he should see them ended at the common charges, without sparing for any coste. But in the end, falling out openly with Thucydides, and putting it to an adventure which of them should banishe other, with the banishment of *Ostracismon*: Pericles got the upper hand, and banished Thucydides out of the cittie, and therewithall also overthrewe the contrarie faction against him. Now when he had rooted out all factions, and brought the cittie againe to unitie and concorde, he founde then the whole power of Athens in his handes, and all the Athenians matters at his disposing. And having all the treasure, armour, gallyes, the Iles, and the sea, and a marvelous seigniorie and Kingdome (that dyd enlarge it selfe partely over the Grecians, and partely over the barbarous people) so well fortified and strengthened with the obedience of nations subject unto them, with the friendshippe of Kings, and with the alliance of divers other Princes and mightie Lords: then from that time forward he beganne to chaunge his manners, and from that he was wont to be toward the people, and not so easely to graunt to all the peoples willes and desires, no more then as it were to contrarie windes. Furthermore he altered his over gentle and popular manner

The noble saying of Pericles.

Thucydides banished by Pericles.

Pericles power.

Pericles somwhat altereth the common weale.

of government which he used untill that time, as to delicate and to effeminate an harmonie of musike, and dyd convert it unto an imperious government, or rather to a kingly authoritie: but yet held still a direct course, and kept him self ever upright without fault, as one that dyd, sayed, and counselled that, which was most expedient for the common weale. He many times brought on the people by persuasions and reasons, to be willing to graunt that he preferred unto them: but many times also, he drave them to it by force, and made them against their willes doe that, which was best for them. Following therein the devise of a wise phisitian: who in a long and chaungeable disease, doth graunt his pacient somtime to take his pleasure of a thing he liketh, but yet after a moderate sorte: and another time also he doth geve him a sharpe or bitter medicine that doth vexe him, though it heale him. For as it falleth out commonly unto people that enjoye so great an empire: many times misfortunes doe chaunce, that fill them full of sundrie passions, the which Pericles alone could finely steere and governe with two principall rudders, feare, and hope: brideling with the one, the fierce and insolent rashenes of the common people in prosperitie, and with the other comforting their grief and discoragement in adversitie. Wherein he manifestly proved, that rethorike and eloquence (as Plato sayeth) is an arte which quickeneth mens spirites at her pleasure, and her chiefest skill is, to knowe howe to move passions and affections throughly, which are as stoppes and soundes of the soule, that would be played upon with a fine fingered hand of a conning master. All which, not the force of his eloquence only brought to passe, as Thucydides witnesseth: but the reputation of his life, and the opinion and confidence they had of his great worthines, bicause he would not any waye be corrupted with gifts, neither had he any covetousnes in him. For, when he had brought his cittie not onely to be great, but exceeding great and wealthy, and had in power and authoritie exceeded many Kings and tyrannes, yea even those which by their willes and testaments might have left great possessions to their children: he never for all that increased his fathers goodes and patrimonie

The force of eloquence.

Pericles commended for his good life and worthines.

left him, the value of a grote in silver. And yet the historiographer Thucydides doth set forth plainely enough, the greatnes of his power. And the Comicall poets also of that time doe reporte it maliciously under covert words, calling his familiar friends, the newe Pisistratides: saying, howe they must make him sweare and protest he would never be King, geving us thereby to understand, that his authoritie was to exceeding great for a popular government. And Teleclides (amongest other) sayeth that the Athenians had put into his hands the revenue of the townes and citties under their obedience, and the townes them selves, to binde the one, and to lose the other, and to pull downe their walles, or to build them againe at his pleasure. They gave him power, to make peace and alliance: they gave all their force, treasure, and authoritie, and all their goodes, wholy into his handes. But this was not for a litle while, nor in a geere of favour, that should continue for a time: but this helde out fortie yeres together, he being allwayes the chief of his cittie amongest the Ephialtes, the Leocrates, the Mironides, the Cimons, the Tolmides, and the Thucydides. For after he had prevailed against Thucydides, and had banished him: he yet remained chief above all other, the space of fifteene yeres. Thus having atteined a regall dignitie to commaunde all, which continued as aforesaid, where no other captaines authoritie endured but one yere: he ever kept him selfe upright from bribes and money, though otherwise he was no ill husband, and could warely looke to his owne. As for his landes and goodes left him by his parents, that they miscaried not by negligence, nor that they should trouble him much, in busying him self to reduce them to a value: he dyd so husband them, as he thought was his best and easiest waye. For he solde in grosse ever the whole yeres profit and commoditie of his landes, and afterwardes sent to the market daylie to buye the cates, and other ordinarie provision of housholde. This dyd not like his sonnes that were men growen, neither were his women contented with it, who would have had him more liberall in his house, for they complained of his overhard and straight ordinarie, bicause in so noble and great a house as his, there

Pericles free from giftes taking.

Pericles good husbandrie.

PERICLES

was never any great remaine left of meate, but all things receyved into the house, ranne under accompt, and were delivered out by proportion. All this good husbandrie of his, was kept upright in this good order, by one Evangelus, Steward of his house, a man very honest and skillfull in ordering his householde provision: and whether Pericles had brought him up to it, or that he had it by nature, it was not knowen. But these things were farre contrarie to Anaxagoras wisedome. For he despising the world, and casting his affection on heavenly things: dyd willingly forsake his house, and suffered all his lande to ronne to layes and to pasture. But (in my opinion) great is the diversitie betwene a contemplative life, and a civill life. For the one employeth all his time upon the speculation of good and honest things: and to attaine to that, he thinketh he hath no neede of any exteriour helpe or instrument. The other applying all his time upon vertue, to the common profit and benefit of men: he thinketh that he needeth riches, as an instrument not only necessarie, but also honest. As, looke upon the example of Pericles: who dyd relieve many poore people. And Anaxagoras specially among other: of whom it is reported, that Pericles being occupied about matters of state at that time, having no leysure to thinke upon Anaxagoras, he seeing him selfe old and forsaken of the world, layed him downe, and covered his head close, determining to starve him selfe to death with hunger. Pericles understanding this, ranne presently to him as a man halfe cast awaye, and prayed him as earnestly as he could, that he would dispose him selfe to live, being not only sorie for him, but for him selfe also, that he should lose so faithfull and wise a counseller, in matters of state and government. Then Anaxagoras shewed his face, and tolde him: O Pericles, those that will see by the light of a lampe, must put oyle to it, to make the light burne. Now beganne the Lacedæmonians to growe jealous, of the greatnes of the Athenians, wherefore Pericles to make the Athenians hartes greater, and to drawe their mindes to great enterprises: set downe an order they should send ambassadours, to persuade all the Grecians (in what part soever they dwelt in Europe, or Asia, aswell the litle

Anaxagoras a mathematician.

Great diversitie betwext contemplative and civill life.

Anaxagoras determined to famish him self to death.

Anaxagoras saying to Pericles.

as the great citties) to send their deputies unto Athens, to the generall assembly that should be holden there, to take order for the temples of the goddes which the barbarous people had burnt, and touching the sacrifices they had vowed for the preservation of Grece, when they gave battell upon them: and touching sea matters also, that every man might sayle in safetie where he would, and that all might live together in good peace and love, one with another. To performe this commission, twenty persones were sent of this embasiate, every one of them being fiftie yeres of age and upward. Whereof five of them went to the Dorians, dwelling in Asia, and to the inhabitants of the Iles, even unto the Iles of Lesbos, and of the Rhodes. Five other went through all the country of Hellespont, and of Thracia, unto the cittie of Bizantium. Other five were commaunded to goe into Bœotia, into Phocides, and through all Peloponnesus, and from thence by the countrie of the Locrians, into the uplande countrie adjoyning to it, untill they came into the country of Acarnania, and of Ambracia. And the other five went first into the Ile of Eubœa, and from thence unto the Œtæians, and through all the gulfe of Malea, unto the Phtiotes, unto the Achaians, and the Thessalians: declaring to all the people where they came, the Athenians commission, persuading them to send unto Athens, and to be present at the councell which should be holden there, for the pacification and union of all Grece. But when all came to all, nothing was done, and the sayed citties of Grece dyd not assemble, by practise of the Lacedæmonians (as it is reported) who were altogether the let: for the first refusall that was made of their summons, was at Peloponnesus. This have I written to make Pericles noble corage to be knowen, and howe profounde a wise man he shewed him selfe unto the world. Furthermore, when he was chosen generall in the warres, he was much esteemed, bicause he ever tooke great regarde to the safetie of his souldiers. For by his good will he would never hazard battell, which he sawe might fall out doubtfull, or in any thing daungerous: and moreover, he never praysed them for good generalls, neither would he followe them that had

Pericles appointeth a generall councell to be holden at Athens.

Pericles loved the safty of his men in warres.

obteined great victories by hazard, howsoever other dyd esteeme or commend them. For he was wont to saye, that if none but him self dyd leade them to the shambles, as much as laye in him, they should be immortall. And when he sawe Tolmides, the sonne of Tolmæus (trusting to his former victories, and the praise and commendation of his good service) dyd prepare upon no occasion, and to no purpose, to enter into the countrie of Bœotia, and had procured also a thousand of the lustiest and most valliant men of the cittie, to be contented to goe with him in that jorney, over and above the rest of the armie he had leavied: he went about to turne him from his purpose, and to keepe him at home, by many persuasions he used to him before the peoples face, and spake certen wordes at that time, that were remembred long after, and these they were. That if he would not beleeve Pericles counsell, yet that he would tarie time at the least, which is the wisest counseller of men. These wordes were pretilie liked at that present time. But with in fewe dayes after, when newes was brought that Tolmides selfe was slaine in a battell he had lost, neere unto the cittie of Coronea, wherein perished also, many other honest and valliant men of Athens: his wordes spoken before, dyd then greatly increase Pericles reputation and good will with the common people, bicause he was taken for a wise man, and one that loved his cittizens. But of all his jorneis he made, being generall over the armie of the Athenians: the jorney of Cherronesus was best thought of and esteemed, bicause it fell out to the great benefit and preservation of all the Grecians inhabiting in that countrie. For besides that he brought thither a thousand cittizens of Athens to dwell there (in which doing he strengthened the citties with so many good men) he dyd fortifie the barre also, which dyd let it from being of an Ile, with a fortification he drue from one sea to another: for that he defended the countrie against all the invasions and piracies of the Thracians inhabiting thereabouts, and delivered it of extreme warre, with the which it was plagued before, by the barbarous people their neighbours, or dwelling amongest them, who only lived upon piracie, and robbing on the seas. So was he likewise much honored and esteemed of

Time, the best counseller.

Tolmides slaine in the field.

Pericles jorneyes.

straungers, when he dyd environne all Peloponnesus, departing out of the haven of Peges, on the coast of Megara, with a fleete of a hundred gallyes. For he dyd not only spoyle the townes all alongest the sea side, as Tolmides had done before him: but going up further into the mayne lande, farre from the sea, with his souldiers he had in the gallyes, he drave some of them to retire within their walles, he made them so affrayed of him: and in the countrie of Nemea, he overcame the Sicyonians in battell, that taried him in the field, and dyd erect a piller for a notable marke of his victorie. And imbarking in his shippes a newe supply of souldiers which he tooke up in Achaia, being friends with the Athenians at that time: he passed over to the firme lande that laye directly against it. And pointing beyond the mouth of the river of Achelous, he invaded the countrie of Acarnania, where he shut up the Œneades within their walles. And after he had layed waste and destroyed all the champion countrie, he returned home againe to Athens: having shewed him selfe in this jorney, a dreadfull captaine to his enemies, and very carefull for the safety of his souldiers. For there fell out no manner of misfortune all this jorney (by chaunce or otherwise) unto the souldiers under his charge. And afterwardes, going with a great navie marvelous well appointed unto the realme of Pontus, he dyd there gentily use and intreate the citties of Grece, and graunted them all that they required of him: making the barbarous people inhabiting thereabouts, and the Kings and Princes of the same also, to know the great force and power of the Athenians, who sailed without feare all about where they thought good, keeping all the coastes of the sea under their obedience. Furthermore, he left with the Sinopians thirteene gallyes, with certen number of souldiers under captaine Lamachus, to defend them against the tyranne Timesileus: who being expulsed, and driven awaye, with those of his faction, Pericles caused proclamation to be made at Athens, that sixe hundred free men of the cittie, that had any desire to goe, without compulsion, might goe dwell at Sinopa, where they should have devided among them, the goodes and landes of the tyranne and his followers. But he dyd not followe the

PERICLES

Achelous fl.

Pericles would not followe the covetousnes of the people.

foolishe vaine humours of his cittizens, nor would not yeld to their unsatiable covetousnes, who being set on a jolitie to see them selves so strong, and of suche a power, and besides, to have good lucke, would needes once againe attempt to conquer Egypt, and to revolte all the countries upon the sea coastes, from the empire of the king of Persia: for there were many of them whose mindes were marvelously bent to attempt the unfortunate enterprise of entering Sicilia, which Alcibiades afterwardes dyd muche pricke forward. And some of them dreamed besides, of the conquest of Thuscan, and the empire of Carthage. But this was not altogether without some likelyhood, nor without occasion of hope, considering the large boundes of their Kingdome, and the fortunate estate of their affayres, which fell out according to their owne desire. But Pericles dyd hinder this going out, and cut of altogether their curious desire, employing the most parte of their power and force, to keepe that they had already gotten: judging it no small matter to keepe downe the Lacedæmonians from growing greater. For he was allwayes an enemie to the Lacedæmonians, as he shewed him selfe in many things, but specially in the warre he made, called the holy warre. For the Lacedæmonians having put the Phocians from the charge of the temple of Apollo, in the cittie of Delphes, which they had usurped, and having restored the Delphians againe unto the same: so sone as they were gone thence, Pericles went also with another armie, and restored the Phocians in again. And where as the Lacedæmonians had caused to be graven in the forehead of a woulfe of brasse, the priviledge the Delphians had graunted them, to be the first that should make their demaundes of the oracle: he having atteined the like priviledge of the Phocians, made his image also to be graven on the right side of the same image, of the brasen woulfe. Nowe howe wisely Pericles dyd governe Grece by the power of the Athenians, his deedes doe plainely shewe. For, first of all, the countrie of Eubœa dyd rebell, against whom he brought the armie of the Athenians. And sodainely in the necke of that, came newes from another coaste, that the Megarians also were in armes against them: and howe that

The enterprise of Sicilia.

Pericles an enemie to the Lacedæmonians.

they were already entered into the countrie of Attica with a great armie, led by Plistonax, king of Lacedæmon. This occasion drewe him homeward againe, and so he marched backe with speede into his countrie, to make preparation to encounter his enemies, that were already entered into the territories of Attica. He durst not offer them battell, being so great a number of valliant souldiers: but hearing that king Plistonax was yet but a young man, and was ruled altogether by Cleandrides counsell and direction (whom the Ephores had placed about him to counsell and direct him) he sought privilie to corrupt Cleandrides. When he had wonne him sone with his money, he persuaded him to drawe backe the Peloponnesians out of their countrie of Attica: and so he dyd. But when the Lacedæmonians sawe their armie cassed, and that the people were gone their waye, every man to his owne cittie or towne: they were so mad at it, that the King was condemned in a great some. The King being unable to aunswer his fine, which was so extreme great: he was driven to absent him self from Lacedæmon. Cleandrides on the other side, if he had not fled in time, even for spight had bene condemned to death. This Cleandrides was Gylippus father, that afterwards overcame the Athenians in Sicilia, in whom it seemed nature bred covetousnes, as a disease inheritable by succession from father to the sonne. For he being shamefully convicted also, for certen vile partes he had played, was likewise banished from Sparta: as we have more amply declared in the life of Lysander. And Pericles delivering up the accompt of his charge, and setting downe an article of the expense of tenne talentes he had employed, or should employe in needefull causes: the people allowed them him, never asking question how, nor which waye, nor whether it was true that they were bestowed. Now there are certen writers (among whom the philosopher Theophrastus is one) who write that Pericles sent yerely unto Sparta tenne talents, with the which he entertained those that were in authoritie there, bicause they should make no warres with them: not to buye peace of them, but time, that he might in the meane season, with better commoditie,

Plistonax king of Lacedæmon.

Cleandrides corrupted by Pericles.

Gylippus overcame the Athenians at Syracusa in Sicile.

Gylippus robbed parte of the treasure Lysander sent him withall to Sparta.

Pericles wise pollicy in forrein entertainement.

Pericles acts in Eubœa.

and that leysure, provide to mainteine the warres. After that, as the armie of the Peloponnesians were out of the countrie of Attica, he returned again against the rebels, and passed into the Ile of Eubœa with fiftie sayle, and five thousand footemen well armed: and there he overcame all the citties that had taken armes against him, and drave away the Hyppobotes, who were the most famous men of all the Chalcidians, aswell for their riches, as for their valliantnes. He drave awaye also all the Hestiæians, whom he chased cleane out of all the countrie, and placed in their cittie, only the cittizens of Athens. And the cause why he delt so rigorously with them was, bicause they having taken a galley of the Athenians prisoner, had put all the men to death that were in her. And peace being concluded afterwards betwene the Athenians and Lacedæmonians for thirtie yeres: he proclaimed open warres against those of the Ile of Samos, burdening them, that they being commaunded by the Athenians, to pacifie the quarrells which they had against the Milesians, they would not obaye. But bicause some hold opinion, that he tooke upon him this warre against Samos, for the love of Aspasia: it shall be no great digression of our storie, to tell you by the waye, what manner of woman she was, and what a marvelous gifte and power she had, that she could entangle with her love the chiefest rulers and governours at that time of the common weale, and that the philosophers them selves dyd so largely speake and write of her. First of all, it is certaine that she was borne in the cittie of Miletum, and was the daughter of one Axiochus: she following the steppes and example of an olde curtisan of Ionia, called Thargelia, gave her selfe only to entertaine the greatest persones and chiefest rulers in her time. For this Thargelia being passing fayer, and carying a comely grace with her, having a sharpe wit and pleasaunt tongue: she had the acquaintaunce and friendshippe of the greatest persones of all Grece, and wanne all those that dyd haunte her company to be at the king of Persiaes commaundement. So that she sowed through all the citties of Grece, great beginnings of the faction of the Medes: for they were the greatest men of power and authoritie of everie cittie that were acquainted with her.

Pericles maketh warre with the Samians.

Aspasia a passing wise woman.

The description of Aspasia.

Thargelia.

But as for Aspasia, some saye that Pericles resorted unto her, bicause she was a wise woman, and had great understanding in matters of state and government. For Socrates him selfe went to see her somtimes with his friends: and those that used her company also, brought their wives many times with them to heare her talke: though her traine about her were to entertaine such as would warme them by their fire. Æschines writeth, that Lysicles a grazier, being before but a meane man, and of a clubbishe nature, came to be the chief man of Athens, by frequenting the companie of Aspasia, after the death of Pericles. And in Platoes booke intituled *Menexenus*, although the beginning of it be but pleasauntly written, yet in that, this storie is written truely: that this Aspasia was repaired unto by divers of the Athenians, to learne the arte of rethorike of her. Yet notwithstanding it seemeth most likely that the affection Pericles dyd beare her, grewe rather of love, then of any other cause. For he was maried unto a kinsewoman of his owne, and that before was Hipponicus wife, by whom she had Callias, surnamed the riche: and had afterwards by Pericles, Xantippus and Paralus. But not liking her companie, he gave her with her owne good will and consent unto another, and maried Aspasia whom he dearely loved. For ever when he went abroad, and came home againe, he saluted her with a kisse. Whereupon in the auncient comedies, she is called in many places, the newe Omphale, and somtimes Deianira, and somtimes Iuno. But Cratinus plainely calleth her whore in these verses:

Callias the riche.

Pericles maried Aspasia the famous curtisan.

> His Iuno she him brought, Aspasia by name,
> which was in deede an open whore, and past all kynde of shame.

And it seemeth that he had a bastard: for Eupolis in a comedie of his called *Demosii*, bringeth him in, asking Pyronides thus:

> I praye thee: is my bastard sonne yet alive?

And then Pyronides aunswered him:

> A perfect man long since, he surely had bene founde,
> if that this lewde, and naughty whore his vertue had not drownde.

PERICLES

To conclude, this Aspasia was so famous, that Cyrus (he that fought against king Artaxerxes his brother, for the empire of Persia) called Aspasia his best beloved of all his concubines, which before was called Milto, and was borne in Phocides, being Hermotimus daughter. And Cyrus being slayne in the field, Aspasia was caried to the King his brother, with whom afterwardes she was in great favour. As I was writing this life, this storie came in my minde: and me thought I should have delt hardly, if I should have left it unwritten. But to our matter againe. Pericles was charged that he made warres against the Samians, on the behalfe of the Milesians, at the request of Aspasia: for these two citties were at warres together, for the cittie of Priena, but the Samians were the stronger. Now the Athenians commaunded them to laye a side their armes, and to come and pleade their matter before them, that the right might be decided: but they refused it utterly. Wherefore Pericles went thither and tooke awaye the government of the small number of Nobilitie, taking for ostages, fiftie of the chiefest men of the cittie, and so many children besides, which he left to be kept in the Ile of Lemnos. Some saye every one of these ostages offered to geve him a talent: and besides those, many other offered him the like, suche as would not have the soveraine authoritie put into the handes of the people. Moreover Pissuthnes the Persian, lieutenant to the king of Persia, for the good will he bare those of Samos, dyd send Pericles tenne thousand crownes to release the ostages. But Pericles never tooke pennie: and having done that he determined at Samos, and established a popular government, he returned againe to Athens. Notwithstanding, the Samians rebelled immediately after, having recovered their ostages againe by meanes of this Pissuthnes that stale them awaye, and dyd furnishe them also with all their munition of warre. Whereupon Pericles returning against them once more, he founde them not idle, nor amazed at his coming, but resolutely determined to receyve him, and to fight for the seigniorie by sea. So there was a great battell fought betwene them, neere the Ile of Tracia. And Pericles wanne the battell: having with foure and fortie sayle only

Pissuthnes the Persian.

A good proofe that Pericles was not covetous.

nobly overcome his enemies, which were three score and tenne in number, wherof twenty of them were shippes of warre. And so following his victorie forthwith, he wanne also the porte of Samos, and kept the Samians besieged within their owne cittie: where they were yet so bolde, as they would make salies out many times, and fight before the walles of the cittie. But when there arrived a newe supplie of shippes bringing a greater ayde unto Pericles: then were they shut up of all sides. Pericles then taking three score gallyes with him, lanched out into the sea, with intent (as some saye) to goe mete certen shippes of the Phoenicians (that came to ayde the Samians) as farre from Samos as he could: or as Stesimbrotus sayeth, to goe into Cyprus, which me thinketh is not true. But whatsoever was his intent, he committed a foule fault. For Melissus (the sonne of Ithagenes, a great philosopher) being at that time generall of the Samians: perceyving that fewe shippes were left behinde at the siege of the cittie, and that the captaines also that had charge of them were no very expert men of warre, persuaded his cittizens to make a salye upon them. Whereupon they fought a battell, and the Samians overcame: the Athenians were taken prisoners, and they suncke many of their shippes. Nowe they being lordes againe of the sea, dyd furnishe their cittie with all manner of munition for warres, whereof before they had great want. Yet Aristotle writeth that Pericles selfe was once overcome in a battell by sea by Melissus. Furthermore the Samians, to be even with the Athenians for the injurie they had receyved of them before: dyd brande them in the forehead with the stampe of an owle, the owle being then the stampe of their coyne at Athens, even as the Athenians had branded the Samian prisoners before with the stampe of Samæna. This Samæna is a kynde of shippe amongest the Samians, lowe afore, and well layed out in the midde shippe, so that it is excellent good to rise with the waves of the sea, and is very swifte under sayle: and it was so called, bicause the first shippe that was made of this facion, was made in the Ile of Samos, by the tyranne Polycrates. It is sayed that the poet Aristophanes, covertly conveying the

Pericles victorie againe of the Samians.

Melissus a philosopher, generall of the Samians.

The owle, the stampe of the coyne at Athens.

Samæna a kinde of a shippe.

PERICLES

stampe of the Samians, speaking merylie in a place of his comedies sayeth:

The wittie saying of Aristophanes of the Samians.

The Samians are great learned men.

Pericles being advertised of the overthrowe of his armie, returned presently to the rescue. Melissus went to mete him, and gave him battell: but he was overthrowen, and driven backe into his cittie, where Pericles walled them in round about the cittie, desiring victorie rather by time and charge, than by daunger, and losse of his souldiers. But when he sawe that they were wearie with tract of time, and that they would bring it to hazard of battell, and that he could by no meanes withholde them: he then devided his armie into eight companies, whom he made to drawe lots, and that companie that lighted on the white beane, they should be quiet and make good cheere, while the other seven fought. And they saye that from thence it came, that when any have made good cheere, and taken pleasure abroade, they doe yet call it a white daye, bicause of the white beane. Ephorus the historiographer writeth, that it was there, where first of all they beganne to use engines of warre to plucke down great walles, and that Pericles used first this wonderfull invention: and that Artemon an enginer was the first deviser of them. He was caried up and downe in a chayer, to set forward these workes, bicause he had a lame legge: and for this cause he was called Periphoretos. But Heraclides Ponticus confuteth Ephorus therein, by the verses of Anacreon, in the which Artemon is called Periphoretos, many yeres before this warre of Samos beganne: and sayeth that this Periphoretos was a marvelous tender man, and so foolishly afeard of his owne shadowe, that the most parte of his time he sturred not out of his house, and did sit allwayes having two of his men by him, that held a copper target over his head, for feare least any thing should fall upon him. And if upon any occasion he were driven, to goe abroade out of his house: he would be caried in a litle bed hanging neere the grounde, and for this cause he was surnamed Periphoretos. At the last, at nine moneths ende the Samians were compelled to yeld. So Pericles tooke the cittie, and rased their walles to the

Artemon Periphoretos a timerous man.

The Samians doe yeld to Pericles.

grounde: he brought their shippes awaye, and made them paye a marvelous great tribute, whereof parte he receyved in hande, and the rest payable at a certen time, taking ostages with him for assurance of payment. But Duris the Samian dilateth these matters marvelous pittiefully, burdening the Athenians, and Pericles self with unnaturall crueltie: whereof neither Thucydides, nor Ephorus, nor Aristotle him selfe maketh mention. And suer I cannot beleeve it is true that is written. That he brought the captaines of the gallyes, and the souldiers them selves of Samia, into the market place of the cittie of Miletum: where he made them to be bound fast unto bordes for the space of tenne dayes, and at the ende of the same, the poore men halfe dead, were beaten downe with clubbes, and their heads passhed in peces: and afterwards they threw out their bodies to the crowes, and would not burie them. So Duris being accustomed to overreach, and to lye many times in things nothing touching him: seemeth in this place out of all reason to aggravate the calamities of his countrie, only to accuse the Athenians, and to make them odious to the world. Pericles having wonne the cittie of Samos, he returned againe to Athens, where he dyd honorably burie the bones of his slaine cittizens in this warre: and him self (according to their manner and custome) made the funerall oration, for the which he was marvelously esteemed. In suche sorte, that after he came downe from the pulpit where he made his oration: the ladies and gentlewomen of the cittie came to salute him, and brought him garlands to put upon his head, as they doe to noble conquerers when they returne from games, where they have wonne the price. But Elpinicé coming to him, sayed: Surely Pericles, thy good service done, deserveth garlands of triumphe: for thou hast lost us many a good and valliant cittizen, not fighting with the Medes, the Phœnicians, and with the barbarous people as my brother Cimon dyd, but for destroying a cittie of our owne nation and kynred. Pericles to these wordes, softely aunswered Elpinicé, with Archilocus verse, smyling:

Elpinicé.

Pericles taunte to an olde woman.

When thou art olde, painte not thy selfe.

But Ion writeth, that he greatly gloried, and stoode muche in his own conceipt, after he had subdued the Samians, saying: Agamemnon was tenne yeres taking of a cittie of the barbarous people: and he in nine moneths only had wonne the strongest cittie of the whole nation of Ionia. In deede he had good cause to glorie in his victorie: for truely (if Thucydides reporte be true) his conquest was no lesse doubtfull, then he founde it daungerous. For the Samians had almost bene lordes of the sea, and taken the seigniorie thereof from the Athenians. After this, the warres of Peloponnesus being whotte againe, the Corinthians invading thilanders of Corphu: Pericles dyd persuade the Athenians to send ayde unto the Corphians, and to joyne in league with that Iland, which was of great power by sea, saying: that the Peloponnesians (before it were long) would have warre with them. The Athenians consented to his motion, to ayde those of Corphu. Whereupon they sent thither Lacedæmonius (Cimons sonne) with tenne gallyes only for a mockery: for all Cimons familie and friendes, were wholy at the Lacedæmonians devotion. Therefore dyd Pericles cause Lacedæmonius to have so fewe shippes delivered him, and further, sent him thither against his will, to the ende that if he dyd so notable exploite in this service, that then they might the more justly suspect his good will to the Lacedæmonians. Moreover whilst he lived, he dyd ever what he could, to keepe Cimons children backe from rysing: bicause that by their names they were no naturall borne Athenians, but straungers. For the one was called Lacedæmonius, the other Thessalus, and the third Elius: and the mother to all them three, was an Arcadian woman borne. But Pericles being blamed for that he sent but tenne gallyes only, which was but a slender ayde for those that had requested them, and a great matter to them that spake ill of them: he sent thither afterwardes a great number of other gallyes, which came when the battell was fought. But the Corinthians were marvelous angrie, and went and complained to the counsell of the Lacedæmonians, where they layed open many grievous complaints and accusations against the Athenians, and so dyd the Megarians also: alledging that the Athenians had forbidden them their

Cimons sonnes.

havens, their staples, and all trafficke of marchaundise in the territories under their obedience, which was directly against the common lawes, and articles of peace, agreed upon by othe among all the Grecians. Moreover the Æginetes finding them selves very ill and cruelly handled, dyd send secretly to make their mone and complaintes to the Lacedæmonians, being afeard openly to complaine of the Athenians. While these things were a doing, the cittie of Potidæa, subject at that time unto the Athenians (and was built in olde time by the Corinthians) did rebell, and was besieged by the Athenians, which did hasten on the warres. Notwithstanding this, ambassadours were first sent unto Athens upon these complaints, and Archidamus, king of the Lacedæmonians, did all that he could to pacifie the most parte of these quarrells and complaints, intreating their friendes and allies. So as the Athenians had had no warres at all, for any other matters wherewith they were burdened, if they would have graunted to have revoked the decree they had made against the Megarians. Whereupon, Pericles, that above all other stood most against the revocation of that decree, and that did sturre up the people, and made them to stand to that they had once decreed, and ordered, against the Megarians: was thought the only original cause and author of the Peloponnesian warres. For it is sayed that the Lacedæmonians sent ambassadours unto Athens for that matter only. And when Pericles alledged a lawe, that dyd forbid them to take away the table, whereupon before time had bene written any common law or edict: Polyarces, one of the Lacedæmon ambassadours, sayed unto him: Well, said he, take it not awaye then, but turne the table onely: your lawe I am suer forbiddeth not that. This was pleasauntly spoken of the ambassadour, but Pericles could never be brought to it for all that. And therefore it seemeth he had some secret occasion of grudge against the Megarians: yet as one that would finely convey it under the common cause and cloke, he tooke from them the holy lands they were breaking up. For to bring this to passe, he made an order, that they should send an herauld to summone the Megarians to let the land alone, and that the same herauld should goe also

The Athenians accused at Lacedæmon.

Pericles, author of the warres against Peloponnesus.

Pericles malice against the Megarians.

unto the Lacedæmonians to accuse the Megarians unto them. It is true that this ordinance was made by Pericles meanes, as also it was most just and reasonable: but it fortuned so, that the messenger they sent thither dyed and not without suspition that the Megarians made him awaye. Wherefore Charinus made a lawe presently against the Megarians: that they should be proclaimed mortall enemies to the Athenians for ever, without any hope of after reconciliation. And also if any Megarian should once put his foote within the territories of Attica, that he should suffer the paynes of death. And moreover, that their captaines taking yerely their ordinary othe, should sweare among other articles, that twise in the yere they should goe with their power, and destroy some parte of the Megarians lande. And lastly, that the heraulde Anthemocritus should be buried by the place called then the gates Thriasienes, and nowe called, Dipylon. But the Megarians stowtely denying, that they were any cause of the death of this Anthemocritus: dyd altogether burden Aspasia and Pericles with the same, alledging for proofe thereof, Aristophanes verses the Poet, in his comedie he intituled the *Acharnes*, which are so common, as every boye hath them at his tongues ende.

> The young men of our lande (to dronken bybbing bent)
> ranne out one daye unrulily, and towards Megara went.
> From whence in their outrage, by force they tooke awaye,
> Simætha noble curtisan, as she dyd sporte and playe.
> Wherewith enraged all (with pepper in the nose)
> the prowde Megarians came to us, as to their mortall foes,
> And tooke by stelthe awaye, of harlots eke a payer,
> attending on Aspasia, which were both young and fayer.

But in very deede, to tell the originall cause of this warre, and to deliver the trothe thereof, it is very harde. But all the historiographers together agree, that Pericles was the chiefest author of the warre: bicause the decree made against the Megarians, was not revoked backe againe. Yet some holde opinion, that Pericles dyd it of a noble minde and judgement, to be constant in that he thought most expedient. For he judged that this commaundement of the Lacedæmonians was but a triall, to prove if the Athenians would graunte them:

and if they yelded to them in that, then they manifestly shewed that they were the weaker. Other contrarilie saye, that it was done of a selfe will and arrogancie, to shewe his authoritie and power, and howe he dyd despise the Lacedæmonians. But the shrowdest profe of all, that bringeth best authoritie with it, is reported after this sorte. Phidias the image maker (as we have tolde you before) had undertaken to make the image of Pallas: and being Pericles friende, was in great estimation about him. But that procured him many ill willers. Then they being desirous to heare by him what the people would judge of Pericles: they intised Menon, one of the worke men that wrought under Phidias, and made him come into the market place to praye assurance of the people that he might openly accuse Phidias, for a faulte he had committed about Pallas image. The people receyved his obedience, and his accusation was heard openly in the market place, but no mention was made of any theft at all: bicause that Phidias (through Pericles counsell and devise) had from the beginning so layed on the gold upon the image, that it might be taken of, and wayed every whitte. Whereupon Pericles openly sayed unto his accusers, Take of the golde and way it. The glorie of his works dyd purchase him this envie. For he having graven upon the scutchion of the goddesse, the battel of the Amazones, had cut out the portraiture of him self marvelous lively, under the persone of an olde balde man, lifting up a great stone with both his handes. Further he had cut out Pericles image, excellently wrought and artificially, seeming in manner to be Pericles self, fighting with an Amazon in this sorte: The Amazones head being lifte up highe, holdeth a darte before Pericles face, so passing cunningly wrought, as it seemed to shadowe the likenes and resemblaunce of Pericles: and yet notwithstanding appeareth plainely to be Pericles self on either side of the portraiture. So Phidias was clapt up in prisone, and there dyed of a sickness, or els of a poyson (as some saye) which his enemies had prepared for him: and all to bring Pericles into further suspition, and to geve them the more cause to accuse him. But howsoever it was, the people gave Menon his freedome, and set him free for payment of all

Phidias the image maker.

subsidies, following the order Glycon made, and gave the captaines charge they should see him safely kept, and that he tooke no hurte. And about the same time also Aspasia was accused, that she dyd not beleeve in the goddes: and her accuser was Hermippus, maker of the comedies. He burdened her further, that she was a bawde to Pericles, and receyved cittizens wives into her house, which Pericles kept. And Diopithes at the same time made a decree, that they should make searche and enquirie for heretickes that dyd not beleeve in the goddes, and that taught certaine newe doctrine and opinion touching the operations of things above in the element, turning the suspition upon Pericles, bicause of Anaxagoras. The people dyd receyve and confirme this inquisition: and it was moved also then by Dracontides, that Pericles should deliver an accompt of the money he had spent, unto the handes of the Prytanes, who were treasorers of the common fines and revenues, and that the judges deputed to geve judgement, should geve sentence within the cittie upon the altar. But Agnon put that worde out of the decree, and placed in stead thereof, that the cause should be judged by the fifteene hundred judges, as they thought good, if any man brought this action for thefte, for batterie, or for injustice. As for Aspasia, he saved her, even for the verie pittie and compassion the judges tooke of him, for the teares he shed in making his humble sute for her, all the time he pleaded her case: as Æschines writeth. But for Anaxagoras, fearing that he could not doe so muche for him: he sent him out of the cittie, and him selfe dyd accompany him. And furthermore, seeing he had incurred the ill will of the people for Phidias facte, and for this cause fearing the issue of the judgement: he set the warres a fyre againe, that alwayes went backeward, and dyd but smoke a litle, hoping by this meanes to weare out the accusations against him, and to roote out the malice some dyd beare him. For the people having waightie matters in hande, and very daungerous also: he knewe they would put all into his handes alone, he having wonne already suche great authoritie and reputation among them. And these be the causes why he would not (as it is sayed) suffer the Athenians to yeld unto the Lacedæmonians

Aspasia accused.

Prytani, treasorers of the common fines.

in any thing: howbeit the trothe cannot certenly be knowen. But the Lacedæmonians knowing well, that if they could wede out Pericles, and overthrowe him, they might then deale as they would with the Athenians: they commaunded them they should purge their cittie of Cylons rebellion, bicause they knew well enough that Pericles kynne by the mothers side were to be touched withall, as Thucydides declareth. But this practise fell out contrarie to their hope, and expectation, that were sent to Athens for this purpose. For, weening to have brought Pericles into further suspition and displeasure, the cittizens honoured him the more, and had a better affiaunce in him then before, bicause they sawe his enemies dyd so much feare and hate him. Wherefore, before king Archidamus entred with the armie of the Peloponnesians into the countrie of Attica, he tolde the Athenians, that if king Archidamus fortuned to waste and destroye all the countrie about, and should spare his landes and goodes for the olde love and familiaritie that was betweene them, or rather to geve his enemies occasion falsely to accuse him: that from thenceforth, he gave all the landes and tenements he had in the countrie, unto the common wealthe. So it fortuned, that the Lacedæmonians with all their friends and confederates, brought a marvelous armie into the countrie of Attica, under the leading of king Archidamus: who burning and spoyling all the countries he came alongest, they came unto the towne of Acharnes, were they incamped, supposing the Athenians would never suffer them approche so neere, but that they would give them battell for the honour and defence of their countrie, and to shewe that they were no cowardes. But Pericles wisely considered howe the daunger was to great to hazard battell, where the losse of the cittie of Athens stoode in perill, seing they were three score thousand footemen of the Peloponnesians, and of the Boeotians together: for so many was their number in the first voyage they made against the Athenians. And as for those that were very desirous to fight, and to put them selves to any hazard, being mad to see their countrie thus wasted and destroyed before their eyes, Pericles dyd comforte and pacific them with these wordes: That trees being cut and

The Lacedæmonians invade Attica.

An excellent comparison to staye the souldiers desier to fight.

hewen downe, dyd spring againe in shorte time: but men being once dead, by no possibilitie could be brought againe. Therefore he never durst assemble the people in counsell, fearing least he should be inforced by the multitude, to doe some thing against his will. But as a wise man of a shippe, when he seeth a storme coming on the sea, doth straight geve order to make all things safe in the shippe, preparing every thing readie to defende the storme, according to his arte and skill, not harkening to the passengers fearefull cries and pittiefull teares, who thinke them selves cast away: even so dyd Pericles rule all things according to his wisedome, having walled the cittie substantially about, and set good watche in every corner: and passed not for those that were angrie and offended with him, neither would be persuaded by his friends earnest requests and intreaties, neither cared for his enemies threates nor accusations against him, nor yet reckoned of all their foolishe scoffing songes they songe of him in the cittie, to his shame and reproche of government, saying that he was a cowardly captaine, and that for dastardlines he let the enemies take all, and spoyle what they would. Of which number Cleon was one that most defamed him, and beganne to enter into some prety credit and favour with the common people, for that they were angrie, and misliked with Pericles: as appeareth by these slaunderous verses of Hermippus, which were then abroade:

Cleon accused Pericles.

O King of Satyres, who with such manly speache
of bloudy warres and doughty dedes, dost daylie to us preache:
Why art thou now afrayed, to take thy launce in hande,
or with thy pike against thy foes, corageously to stande?
Synce Cleon stowte and fierce, doth daylie thee provoke,
With biting wordes, with trenchaunt blades, and deadly daunting stroke.

All these notwithstanding, Pericles was never moved any thing, but with silence dyd paciently beare all injuries and scoffings of his enemies, and dyd send for all that a navie of a hundred sayle unto Peloponnesus, whether he would not go in person, but kept him self at home, to keep the people in quiet: untill such time as the enemies had raised their campe, and were gone awaye. And to entertaine the common people that were offended and angrie at this warre: he comforted the poore people againe, with causing a certain distribution to be made amongest them of the common treasure, and division also of the landes that were got by conquest. For after he had driven all the Æginetes out of their countrie, he caused the whole Ile of Ægina to be divided by lot amongest the cittizens of Athens. And then it was a great comforte to them in this adversitie, to heare of their enemies hurte and losse in suche manner as it dyd fall out. For their armie that was sent by sea unto Peloponnesus, had wasted and destroyed a great parte of the champion countrie there, and had sacked besides many small citties and townes. Pericles selfe also entring into the Megarians countrie by lande, did waste the whole countrie all afore him. So the Peloponnesians receyving by sea asmuche hurte and losse at the Athenians hands, as they before had done by lande unto the Athenians: they had not holden out warres so long with the Athenians, but would sone have geven over (as Pericles had tolde them before) had not the goddes above secretly hindered mans reason and pollicie. For first of all there came such a sore plague among the Athenians, that it took awaye the flower of Athens youth, and weakened the force of the whole cittie besides. Furthermore the bodies of them that were left alive being infected with this disease, their hartes also were so sharpely bent against Pericles, that the sicknes having troubled their braynes, they fell to flat rebellion against him, as the pacient against his physitian, or children against their father, even to the hurting of him, at the provocation of his enemies. Who bruted abroade, that the plague came of no cause els, but of the great multitude of the country men that came into the cittie on heapes, one upon anothers necke in the harte of the sommer, where they were compelled to lye many together, smothred up in litle tentes and cabines, remaining there all daye long, cowring downewardes, and doing nothing, where before they lived in the countrie in a freshe open ayer, and at libertie. And of all this, saye they, Pericles is the only cause, who procuring this warre, hathe pent and shrowded the country men

Note Pericles pollicie to pacifie the peoples anger.

Ægina wonne by the Athenians.

Plague at Athens.

Accusations against Pericles.

PERICLES

together within the walles of a cittie, employing them to no manner of use nor service, but keeping them like sheepe in a pinnefolde, maketh one to poyson another with the infection of their plague sores ronning upon them, and geving them no leave to chaunge ayer, that they might so muche as take breathe abroade. Pericles to remedy this, and to doe their enemies a litle mischief: armed a hundred and fiftie shippes, and shipped into them a great number of armed footemen and horsemen also. Hereby he put the cittizens in good hope, and the enemies in great feare, seeing so great a power. But when he had shipped all his men, and was him self also in the admirall ready to hoyse sayle: sodainely there was a great eclypse of the sunne, and the daye was very darke, that all the armie was striken with a marvelous feare, as of some daungerous and very ill token towardes them. Pericles seeing the master of his gallye in a maze withall, not knowing what to doe: cast his cloke over the masters face, and hid his eyes, asking him whether he thought that any hurte or no. The master aunswered him, he thought it none. Then sayed Pericles againe to him: There is no difference betwene this and that, saving that the bodye which maketh the darknes is greater, then my cloke which hideth thy eyes. These things are thus disputed of in the schooles of the philosophers. But Pericles hoysing sayle notwithstanding, dyd no notable or speciall service, aunswerable to so great an armie and preparation. For he laying seige unto the holy cittie of Epidaurum, when every man looked they should have taken it, was compelled to rayse his seige for the plague that was so vehement: that it dyd not only kill the Athenians them selves, but all other also (were they never so fewe) that came to them, or neere their campe. Wherefore perceyving the Athenians were marvelously offended with him, he dyd what he could to comforte them, and put them in harte againe: but all was in vaine, he could not pacifie them. For by the most parte of voyces, they deprived him of his charge of generall, and condemned him in a marvelous great fine and summe of money, the which those that tell the least doe write, that it was the summe of fifteene talentes: and those that say more, speake of fiftie

An eclypse of the sunne.

Pericles hard fortune.

Pericles deprived of his charge.

talentes. The accuser subscribed in this condemnation, was Cleon, as Idomeneus, or Simmias saye, or as Theophrastus writeth: yet Heraclides Ponticus sayeth, one Lacratidas. Nowe his common grieves were sone blowen over: for the people dyd easely let fall their displeasures towardes him, as the waspe leaveth her stinge behinde her with them she hath stong. But his owne private affayers and household causes were in very ill case: both for that the plague had taken awaye many of his friendes and kinsemen from him, as also for that he and his house had continued a long time in disgrace. For Xanthippus (Pericles sonne and heire) being a man of a very ill disposition and nature, and having married a young woman very prodigall and lavishe of expence, the daughter of Isander, sonne of Epilycus: he grudged much at his fathers hardnes, who scantly gave him money, and but litle at a time. Whereupon he sent on a time to one of his fathers friendes in Pericles name, to praye him to lend him some money, who sent it unto him. But afterwards when he came to demaunde it againe, Pericles dyd not only refuse to paye it him, but further, he put him in sute. But this made the young man Xanthippus so angrie with his father, that he spake very ill of him in every place where he came: and in mockery reported howe his father spent his time when he was at home, and the talke he had with the Sophisters, and the master rethoritians. For a mischaunce fortuning on a time, at the game of throwing the darte, who should throw best, that he that threwe, dyd unfortunately kill one Epitimius a Thessalian: Xanthippus went pratling up and downe the towne, that his father Pericles was a whole daye disputing with Protagoras the Rethoritian, to knowe which of the three by lawe and reason should be condemned for this murther. The darte: he that threwe the darte: or the deviser of that game. Moreover Stesimbrotus writeth, that the brute that ranne abroade through the cittie, howe Pericles dyd keepe his wife, was sowen abroade by Xanthippus him self. But so it is, this quarrell and hate betwext the father and the sonne continued without reconciliation unto the death. For Xanthippus dyed in the great plague, and Pericles own sister

Pericles home troubles.

also: moreover he lost at that time by the plague, the more parte of all his friends and kinsefolkes, and those specially that dyd him greatest pleasure in governing of the state. But all this dyd never pull down his contenaunce, nor anything abate the greatnes of his minde, what misfortunes soever he had susteined. Neither sawe they him weepe at any time, nor mourne at the funeralles of any of his kinsemen or friendes, but at the death of Paralus, his younger and lawful begotten sonne: for, the losse of him alone dyd only melt his harte. Yet he dyd strive to showe his naturall constancie, and to keep his accustomed modestie. But as he would have put a garland of flowers upon his head, sorowe dyd so pierce his harte when he sawe his face, that then he burst out in tears, and cryed a mayne: which they never sawe him doe before, all the dayes of his life. Furthermore the people having proved other captaines and governours, and finding by experience that there was no one of them of judgement and authoritie sufficient, for so great a charge: In the ende, of them selves they called him againe to the pulpit for orations to heare their counsells, and to the state of a captaine also to take charge of the state. But at that time he kept him selfe close in his house, as one bewayling his late grievous losse and sorowe. Howbeit Alcibiades, and other his familiar friendes, persuaded him to shewe him selfe unto the people, who dyd excuse them selves unto him, for their ingratitude towardes him. Pericles then taking the government againe upon him, the first matter he entred into was: that he prayed them to revoke the statute he had made for base borne children, fearing least his lawfull heires would fayle, and so his house and name should fall to the grounde. But as for that lawe, thus it stoode. Pericles when he was in his best authoritie, caused a lawe to be made, that they only should be computed cittizens of Athens, which were naturall Athenians borne by father and mother. Not long after, it fortuned that the king of Egypt having sent a gifte unto the people of Athens, of forty thousand bushells of corne, to be distributed among the cittizens there: many by this lawe were accused to be base borne, and specially men

Pericles constancy.

A lawe at Athens for base borne children.

of the baser sorte of people, which were not knowen before, or at the least had no reckoning made of them, and so some of them were falsely and wrongfully condemned. Whereupon so it fell out, that there were no lesse than five thousand of them convicted and solde for slaves: and they that remained as free men, and were judged to be naturall cittizens, amownted to the number of fourteene thousand and fortie persones. Now this was much misliked of the people, that a lawe enacted, and that had bene of suche force, should by the selfe maker and deviser of the same be againe revoked and called in. Howbeit Pericles late calamitie that fortuned to his house, dyd breake the peoples hardened hartes against him. Who thincking these sorowes smarte, to be punishment enough unto him for his former pryde, and judging that by goddes divine justice and permission, this plague and losse fell upon him, and that his request also was tollerable: they suffered him to enrolle his base borne sonne in the register of the lawfull cittizens of his familie, geving him his owne name, Pericles. It is the self same Pericles, who after he had overcome the Peloponnesians in a great battell by sea, neere unto the Iles Arginuses, was put to death by sentence of the people, with the other captaines his companions. Now was Pericles at that time infected with the plague, but not so vehemently as other were, rather more temperatly: and by long space of time, with many alterations and chaunges, that dyd by litle and litle decaye, and consume the strength of his bodie, and overcame his sences and noble minde. Therefore Theophrastus in his moralles declareth, in a place where he disputeth, whether mens manners doe chaunge with their misfortunes, and whether corporall troubles and afflictions doe so alter men, that they forget vertue, and abandon reason: that Pericles in this sicknes shewed a friende of his that came to see him, I cannot tell what a preserving charme the women had tyed (as a carkanet) about his necke, to let him understand he was very ill, since he suffered them to apply suche a foolishe bable to him. In the ende, Pericles drawing fast unto his death, the Nobilitie of the cittie, and such his friendes as were left alive, standing about his bed, beganne to speake of

Pericles the base borne put to death.

Pericles sicknes.

A philosophicall question touching change of mens manners by misfortunes.

Pericles death.

his vertue, and of the great authoritie he had borne, considering the greatnes of his noble actes, and counting the number of the victories he had wonne (for he had wonne nine foughten battells being generall of the Athenians, and had set up so many tokens and triumphs in honour of his countrie) they reckoned up among them selves all these matters, as if he had not understoode them, imagining his sences had bene gone. But he contrarilie being yet of perfect memorie, heard all what they had sayed, and thus he beganne to speake unto them: That he marveled why they had so highly praysed that in him, which was common to many other captaines, and wherein fortune delt with them in equalitie a like, and all this while they had forgotten to speake of the best and most notable thing that was in him, which was: that no Athenian had ever worne blacke gowne through his occasion. And suer so was he a noble and worthie persone. For he dyd not only shewe him selfe mercifull and curteous, even in most weightie matters of government, among so envious people and hatefull enemies: but he had this judgement also to thincke, that the most noble actes he dyd were these, that he never gave him selfe unto hatred, envie, nor choller, to be revenged of his most mortall enemie, without mercy shewed towardes him, though he had committed unto him suche absolute power and sole government among them. And this made his surname to be Olympius (as to saye, divine or celestiall) which otherwise for him had bene to prowde and arrogant a name, bicause he was of so good and gentle a nature, and for that in so great libertie he had kept cleane handes and undefiled: even as we esteeme the goddes authors of all good, and causers of no ill, and so worthy to governe and rule the whole monarchie of the world. And not as Poets saye, which doe confounde our wittes by their follies, and fonde faynings, and are also contrarie to them selves, considering that they call heaven (which conteineth the goddes) the everlasting seate, which trembleth not, and is not driven nor moved with windes, neither is darkened with clowdes, but is allwayes bright and cleare, and at all times shyning equally with a pure bright light, as being the only habitation and

A notable saying of Pericles at his death.

Pericles deservedly called Olympius.

mansion place of the eternall God, only happy and immortall. And afterwardes they describe it them selves, full of dissentions, of enmities, of anger and passions, which doe nothing become wise and learned men. But this discourse peradventure would be better spoken of in some other booke. Nowe, the troubles the Athenians felt immediatly after Pericles death, made them then lament the losse of so noble a member. For those who unpaciently dyd brooke his great authoritie while he lived, bicause it drowned their owne: when they came after his death to prove other speakers and governours, they were compelled then to confesse, that no mans nature living could be more moderate nor grave, with lenitie and mercie, then his was. And that most hated power, which in his life time they called monarchie, dyd then most plainely appeare unto them, to have bene the manifest ramper and bullwarke of the safetie of their whole state and common weale: suche corruption and vice in government of the state, dyd then spring up immediatly after his death, which when he was alive, he dyd ever suppresse and keepe under in suche sorte, that either it dyd not appeare at all, or at the least it came not to that hed and libertie, that suche faultes were committed, as were unpossible to be remedied.

The Athenians lamented the losse of Pericles being dead.

THE ENDE OF PERICLES LIFE

THE LIFE OF FABIUS MAXIMUS

HAVING already declared unto you such things worthy memorie as we could collect, and gather of the life of Pericles: it is nowe good time we should proceede to write also of the life of Fabius Maximus. It is sayed the first Fabius, from whom the house and familie of the Fabians dyd descend (being the greatest and noblest house of all other in Rome) was begotten by Hercules, whom he gatte of a Nymphe (or as other saye, a woman of the countrie) by the river of Tyber. And some saye, that the first of this house, were called at the beginning Fodians, bicause they dyd hunte wilde beastes, with pittefalles and ditches. For unto this present the Romaines call ditches, *Fossæ*: and to digge *Fodere*. Since that time, the two second letters have bene chaunged, and they have called them Fabians. But howsoever it was, this is certaine, that many noble men have come out of that house: and among other, there was one of that house called Fabius Rullus, whom the Romaines for his noble actes dyd surname Maximus, very great. After him, Fabius Maximus, whose life we have now in hande, was the fourth lineally descended of the same line, and he was surnamed Verrucosus, bicause of a certen birth marke he had upon one of his lippes, like a litle warte. And he was also surnamed Ovicula, a litle lamme, for his softnes, slownes, and gravity of his doings whilest he was a childe. But bicause of nature he was dull, still, and very silent, and that he was seldome seene to playe at any pastime among the boyes, and for that they sawe he was but of slowe capacitie, and hard to learne and conceyve, and withall that the boyes might doe to him what they would, he was so lowly to his fellowes: this made men judge that looked not into him, that he would prove a very foole and nigeot. Yet other were of contrarie opinion of him: who considering more deepely the man, perceyved in his nature a certen secret constancie and the majestie of a lyon. But Fabius selfe when he was called to serve the common weale, dyd quickely shewe to the world, that which they tooke for dullnes in him, was his gravitie, which never altered for no cause or respect: and that which other judged fearefullnes in him, was very wisedome. And where he shewed him selfe not hastie, nor sodaine in any thing: it was found in him an assured and setled constancie. Wherefore when he came to consider the great soveraintie of their common weale, and the continuall warres it was in: he dyd use his bodie to all hardnes, and brought up him selfe therewithall, that he might be the better able to serve in the field: and he gave him selfe much to eloquence also, as a necessary instrument

Fabius Rullus Maximus.

Fabius Maximus called Verrucosus and Ovicula.

to persuade souldiers unto reason. His tongue likewise dyd agree with his conditions, and manner of life. For he had no manner of affectation, nor counterfeate finenes in his speach, but his words were ever very grave and profounde, and his sentences even grafte in him by nature, and (as some saye) were much like Thucydides sayings. As appeareth in a funerall oration he made before the people in the praise of his sonne, who dyed when he came out of his Consulshippe, which is yet extant to be seene. Now as for him, having bene five times chosen Consul, in his first yere of his Consulshippe, he triumphed over the Ligurians (which be people of the mountaines, and upon the coast of Genua) who being overthrowen by him in a great battell, where they had lost many men, they were compelled to goe their waye, and to take the Alpes for their succour, and durst no more appeare upon the borders of Italie, whereupon they dyd confine. Hannibal entring Italy afterwards with a great armie, and having wonne the first battell neere unto the river of Trebia: he passed further, and went through Thuscan, wasting and distroying all the countrie as he passed by. This made Rome quake for feare. Besides they sawe many signes and tokens, some common unto them, as thundering, lightning, and such other like: but other also more straunge, never seene nor heard of before. For it was reported that certen targets were waxen all bloudie of them selves, and that about the cittie of Antium they found wheate eares, which were all bloudie when they were reaped: that there fell from heaven, burning stones all in a flame of fire: and in the countrie of the Phalerians how the element seemed to open, and many litle written scrolles fell downe upon the ground, in one of the which were written these wordes, worde for worde: 'Mars doth now handle his weapons.' But all these signes and wonders dyd nothing appawle nor daunte the boldnes of Caius Flaminius, Consul then: who besides the naturall great corage, and aspiring minde he had to honour, yet was it beyond all reason increased in him, by the wonderfull good successe he had before. For, notwithstanding the Senate called him home againe, and that his fellowe Consul stoode against his intent: he for all that dyd geve

Fabius five times Consul.

Hannibal destroyeth the countrie of Thuscan.

Wonders.

Flaminius rashenes.

battell to the Gaules, in despight of them all, and wanne the victorie. Likewise, though all these signes and wonders in the ayer, dyd greatly trouble, and amaze multitudes of people: yet did they nothing trouble Fabius, for he sawe no apparant cause to be troubled withall. But he understanding the small number of his enemies, and the lacke of money that was among them: gave counsell, and was of opinion they should paciently forbeare a litle, and not to hazard battell against a man, whose armie hadde bene long trained in warres, and by many foughten fields was growen valliant and expert. Moreover, he thought good they should send ayde to their subjects, and other their allies and confederates, as neede required, to keepe their citties still under their obedience: and in the meane season by tract of time, to weare out Hanniballs force and power, which was like strawe set a fire, that straight geveth forth a blase, and yet hath no substaunce to holde fire long. When Fabius had thus sayed enough to persuade Flaminius, yet it would not sincke into Flaminius heade: for, sayeth he, I will not tarie untill the warres come to Rome gates, neither will I be brought to fight upon the walles of the cittie, to defend it, and as Camillus dyd, that fought within the cittie selfe in olde time. Whereupon he commaunded his captaines to set out their bandes to the field, and he him selfe tooke his horse backe: which upon the sodaine, without any cause was so afeard, and tooke so on with him selfe, that he cast the Consul to the grounde with his heade forward. For all this fall he would not chaunge his minde, but helde on his jorney toward Hannibal, and presented him battell in Thuscan, by the lake called Thrasimena, which is the lake of Perusia. This battell was so fiercely fought on both sides, that notwithstanding there was such a terrible earthquake therewhile, that some citties were overthrowen and turned topsi turvey, some rivers had their streames turned against their course, and the foote of the mountaines were torne in sonder, and broken open: yet not one of them that were fighting, heard any such thing at all. Flaminius the Consul selfe was slaine at that battell, after he had in his owne persone done many a valliant acte, and many of the worthiest gentle-

Fabius wise counsell.

The Romaines slaine by the lake of Thrasimena.

Flaminius the Consul slaine.

men and valliantest souldiers of his armie laye dead about him: the residue being fled, the slaughter was great, for the bodies slaine were fifteene thousand, and so many prisoners left alive. After this overthrowe, Hannibal made all the searche he could possible to finde the bodie of Flaminius, to burie him honorably, bicause of his valliantnes: but he could never be founde amongest the dead bodies, neither was it ever hearde what became of it. Now as touching the first overthrowe at Trebia, neither the generall that wrote it, nor the post that brought the first newes to Rome, tolde the trothe of it as it was, but fayned that the ende was doubtfull, and that they could not tell who had the best. But of this battell, so sone as the Prætor Pomponius had receyved the newes, he called all the people to counsell, where without disguising or dissembling at all, he playnely sayed thus unto them: My Lordes, we have lost the battell, our army is overthrowen, and the Consul him selfe is slaine in the field: wherefore consider what you have to doe, and provide for your safety. These wordes spoken to the people, as it had bene a boysterous storme of weather that had fallen on them from the sea, to put them in daunger, dyd so terrifie the multitude, and trouble the whole citie for feare: that they were all in a maze, and knewe not what to determine. Yet in the ende they all agreed, that it stoode them upon to have a chief magistrate, called in Latin *Dictatura*, that should be a man of corage, and could stowtely use it without sparing or fearing any persone. And for this, Fabius Maximus was thought the only man mete to be chosen, as he, whose noble corage and grave behaviour was aunswerable, to the dignitie and soveraintie of the office: and moreover, that to his gravity and wisedome there was joyned (by reasonable age) strength of bodie, and valliantnes with experience. This counsell being confirmed by them all, Fabius was chosen Dictator, who named Lucius Minutius generall of the horsemen. Then he first required the Senate, that they would graunte him he might have his horse in the warres: the which was not lawfull for the Dictator, but expressely forbidden by an auncient order. Either bicause they thought the chiefest force of their armie dyd consist in their foote-

Fabius Dictator.

The Dictator might not ride in the warres.

men, which caused the making of this lawe: whereby the generall should be amongest them in the daye of the battell, and in no wise should forsake them. Or els bicause the authoritie of this magistrate in all other things was so great, that it was in manner after the state of a King: yet all this notwithstanding, they were willing thereunto, and that the Dictator should have absolute power over the people. Fabius at his first comming, bicause he would shewe the majestie and dignitie of his office, and that every man should be the more obedient and readie at his commaundement: when he went abroade, he had foure and twentie sergeants before him, carying the bundells of roddes, and axes. And when one of the Consulls came to him, he sent a sergeant to commaund his bundell of roddes that were caried before him, to be put downe, and all other tokens of dignitie to be layed a side: and that he should come and speake with him, as a private man. And first to make a good foundation, and to beginne with the service of the goddes: he declared unto the people, that the losse they had receyved, came through the rashenes and willfull negligence of their captaine, who made no reckoning of the goddes nor religion: and not through any defaulte and cowardlines of the souldiers. And for this cause he dyd persuade them not to be afrayed of their enemies, but to appease the wrath of the goddes, and to serve and honour them. Not that he made them hereby superstitious, but dyd confirme their valiancy with true religion and godlines: and besides dyd utterly take awaye and aswage their feare of their enemies, by geving them certaine hope and assuraunce of the ayde of the goddes. Then were the holy bookes of the Sibylles prophesies perused, which are kept very secret: and therein they founde certaine auncient prophecies and oracles, which spake of the present misfortunes of the time. But what were conteined therein, it is not lawfull to be uttered to any persone. Afterwards the Dictator, before the open assembly of the people, made a solemne vowe unto the goddes, that he would sacrifice all the profits and fruites that should fall the next yere, of sheepe, of sowes, of milche kyne, and of goates in all the mountaines, champion countrie,

The majestie of Fabius the Dictator.

Fabius religion.

The Sibylles bookes of prophecies.

Fabius vowe.

rivers, or meadowes of Italie. And he would celebrate playes of musike, and shewe other sightes in the honour of the goddes, and would bestowe upon the same the summe of three hundred three and thirtie Sestercians, and three hundred three and thirtie Romaine pence, and a third parte over. All which summe reduced into Græcian money, amownteth to foure score three thousand, five hundred, and foure score, and three silver drachmas, and two obolos. Now it were a hard thing to tell the reason why he doth mention this summe so precisely, and why he dyd devide it by three, unles it were to extolle the power of the number of three: bicause it is a perfect number by the nature, and is the first of the odde numbers, which is the beginning of divers numbers, and conteineth in it self the first differences, and the first elements and principles of all the numbers united and joyned together. So Fabius having brought the people to hope, and trust to have the ayde and favour of the goddes: made them in the ende the better disposed to live well afterwardes. Then Fabius hoping after victorie, and that the goddes would send good lucke and prosperitie unto men, through their valliantnes and wisdome: dyd straight set forwards unto Hannibal, not as minded to fight with him, but fully resolved to weare out his strength and power, by delayes and tract of time: and to increase his povertie by the long spending of his owne money, and to consume the small number of his people, with the great number of his souldiers. Fabius camped allwayes in the strong and highe places of the mountaines, out of all daunger of his enemies horsemen, and coasted still after the enemie: so that when Hannibal stayed in any place, Fabius also stayed: if Hannibal removed, he followed him straight, and would be allwayes neere him, but never forsooke the hilles, neither would he come so neere him, as that he should be inforced to fight against his will. Yet allwayes he followed the enemie at his tayle, and made him ever afeard of him, thincking still that he sought to get the vantage, to geve the charge upon him. Thus by delaying, and prolonging the time in this sorte: he became disliked of every bodye. For every man both in his owne campe, and abroade, spake very ill of him openly: and

Fabius doings against Hannibal.

as for his enemies, they tooke him for no better, then a rancke coward, Hannibal only excepted. But he perceyving his great reache and policie, and foreseeing the manner of fight, sawe there was no remedy, but by playne force or slight to bring him to the fight: for otherwise his delaye would overthrowe the Carthaginians, when they should not come to handy strokes with him, wherein only consisted all their hope and strength, and in the meane time his souldiers should fall away, and dye, and his money was scante, and him selfe should growe the weaker. Thereupon Hannibal beganne to bethinke him, and devise all the stratageames and policies of warre he could imagine: and like a cunning wrestler, to seeke out all the trickes he could to geve his adversarie the falle. For sodainely, he would goe and geve alarom to his campe: by and by againe he would retire. Another time he would remove his campe, from one place to another, and geve him some advantage, to see if he could plucke his lingring devise out of his head, and yet to hazard nothing. But as for Fabius, he continued still resolute in his first determination: that delaye of fight was the best waye so to overthrowe him. Howbeit Minutius, generall of his horsemen, dyd trouble him muche. For he being earnestly bent to fight without discretion, and braving of a lustie corage, crept into opinion with the souldiers, by his whotte furie and desire to fight. Which wrought muche in them, and so sturred up their corages, that they mocked Fabius altogether: and called him Hanniballs schoolemaster: and contrariwise they commended Minutius, for a valliant captaine, and worthie Romaine. This made Minutius looke highe, and have a prowde opinion of him selfe, mocking Fabius bicause he ever lodged on the hilles, with saying, the Dictator would make them goodly sportes, to see their enemies waste and burne Italy before their face. Moreover, he asked Fabius friendes, whether he would in the ende lodge his campe in the skye, that he dyd clyme up so highe upon mountaines, mistrusting the earthe: or els that he was so affrayed, his enemies would finde him out, that he went to hyde him selfe in the clowdes. Fabius friendes made reporte of these jeastes, and advised him

Minutius generall of the horsemen, dispised Fabius counsell.

rather to hazard battell, then to beare suche reproachefull wordes as were spoken of him. But Fabius aunswered them: If I should yeld to that you counsell me, I should shewe my selfe a greater coward then I am taken for now: by leaving my determination, for feare of their mockes and spightfull wordes. For it is no shame for a man to stand fearefull, and jealous, of the welfare and safetie of his countrie: but otherwise to be afeard of the wagging of every strawe, or to regard every common prating, it is not the parte of a worthie man of charge, but rather of a base minded persone, to seeke to please those whom he ought to commaunde and governe, bicause they are but fooles. After this, Hannibal chaunced to fall into a great errour. For intending to leave Fabius to bring his armie into the playnes, where there was plentie of vittells, and store of pasture to feede his horse and cattell: he commaunded his guydes to bring him straight after supper, into the playne of Casinum. They mistaking his wordes, and not understanding well what he sayed, bicause his Italian tongue was but meane: tooke one thing for another, and so brought him and his armie to the ende of a feild neere the cittie of Casilinum, through the middest of the which ronneth a river, the Romaines call Vulturnus. Nowe the countrie lying by it, was a valley compassed in with mountaines round about, saving that the river went to the sea: where leaving his owne banckes, it spreadeth abroade into the marisses, and banckes of sande very deepe, and in the ende fell into that parte of the sea which is most daungerous, and there was neither succour nor covert. Hannibal being now fallen as it were into the bottome of a sacke, Fabius that knewe the countrie, and was very perfect in all the wayes thereaboutes, followed him steppe by steppe, and stopped his passage, where he should have come out of the valley, with foure thousand footemen, which he planted there to keepe the straight, and disposed the rest of his armie upon the hanginges of the hilles, in the most apt and fit places all about. Then with his light horse men he gave a charge, upon the rereward of his enemies battell: which put all Hannibals armie by and by out of order, and so there were

Hannibal fell into great errour.

Casilinum a cittie.

Vulturnus fl.

Hannibal set upon by Fabius.

slaine eight hundred of his men. Whereupon Hannibal would have removed his campe thence immediatly, and knowing then the faulte his guydes had made, taking one place for another, and the daunger wherein they had brought him: he roundely trussed them up, and honge them by the neckes. Now to force his enemies to come downe from the toppes of the hilles, and to winne them from their strength, he sawe it was unpossible, and out of all hope. Wherefore, perceyving his souldiers both afrayed and discouraged, for that they sawe them selves hemmed in on all sides, without any order to escape: Hannibal determined to deceyve Fabius by a devise. He caused straight two thousand oxen to be chosen out of the heard, which they had taken before in their spoyles, and tyed to their hornes light bundells of reedes, and sallowe faggottes, or bunches of the dead cuttings of vines: and commaunded the drovers that had the charge of them, that when they sawe any signall or token lift up in the ayer in the night, they should then straight set fire on those bundels and bunches, and drive up the beastes to the hilles, toward the wayes where the enemies laye. Whilest these things were a preparing, he on the other side ranged his armie in order of battell: and when night came, caused them to marche fayer and softely. Now these beastes, whilest the fyre was but litle that burnt upon their hornes, went but fayer and softly up the hill from the foote of the mountaines from whence they were driven. In so muche as the heard men that were on the toppe of the mountaines, wondred marvelously to see suche flames and fires about the hornes of so many beastes, as if it had bene an armie marching in order of battell with lightes and torches. But when their hornes came to be burnt to the stumpes, and that the force of the fyre dyd frye their very fleshe: then beganne the oxen to fight together, and to shake their heades, wherby they dyd set one another a fyre. Then left they their softe pace, and went no more in order as they dyd before, but for the extreme payne they felt, beganne to runne here and there in the mountaines, carying fyre still about their hornes, and in their tayles, and set fyre of all the boughes and coppesies they passed by. This was a straunge sight to looke upon,

Hannibals stratageame.

and dyd muche amase the Romaines that kept the passages of the mountaines, for they thought they had bene men that ranne here and there with torches in their handes. Whereupon they were in a marvelous feare and trouble, supposing they had bene their enemies that ranne thus towards them, to environne them of all sides: so as they durst no more keepe the passages which they were commaunded, but forsaking the straightes, beganne to flye towards their mayne and great campe. Thereupon Hannibals light horse men immediatly possessed the straights that were kept: by reason whereof, all the rest of his armie marched out at their ease and leysure, without feare or daunger, notwithstanding that they were loden and troubled with marvelous great spoyles, and of all kynde of sortes. Fabius then perceyved very well the same night, that it was but a slight of Hannibal: for some of the oxen that fled here and there fell upon his armie. Whereupon fearing to fall upon some ambushe by reason of the darke night, he kept his men in battell raye, without sturring, or making any noise. The next morning by breake of daye, he beganne to followe his enemie by the tracke, and fell upon the tayle of the rereward, with whom he skirmished within the straites of the mountaines: and so dyd distresse somewhat Hannibals armie. Hannibal thereupon sent out of his vauntgarde a certaine number of Spaniards (very lusty and nymble fellowes, that were used to the mountaines, and acquainted with climing up upon them) who comming downe, and setting upon the Romaines that were heavy armed, slue a great number of them, and made Fabius to retire. Thereupon they despised Fabius the more, and thought worse of him then they dyd before: bicause his pretence and determination was not to be brought to fight with Hannibal, but by wisedome and policie to overthrowe him, where as he him selfe by Hannibal was first finely handled and deceyved. Hannibal then to bring Fabius further in disliking and suspition with the Romaines, commaunded his souldiers when they came neere any of Fabius landes, that they should burne and destroye all round about them, but gave them in charge in no wise to medle with Fabius landes, nor any thing of his, and dyd purposely

Hannibals craftines against Fabius.

appointe a garrison to see that nothing of Fabius should miscarie, nor yet take hurte. This was straight caried to Rome, which dyd thereby the more incense the people against him. And to helpe it forward, the Tribunes never ceased crying out upon him in their orations to the people, and all by Metellus speciall procurement and persuasion: who of him selfe had no cause to mislike with Fabius, but only bicause he was Minutius kinseman (generall of the horsemen) and thought that the ill opinion they bare to Fabius, would turne to the prayse and advauncement of Minutius. The Senate also were muche offended with Fabius, for the composition he made with Hannibal, touching the prisoners taken of either side. For it was articled betweene them, that they should chaunge prisoners, delivering man for man, or els two hundred and fiftie silver drachmas for a man, if the one chaunced to have moe prisoners then the other. When exchaunge was made betweene them, it appeared that Hannibal had left in his handes of Romaine prisoners, two hundred and fortie moe, then Fabius had to exchaunge of his. The Senate commaunded there should be no money sent to redeeme them, and greatly founde faulte with Fabius for making this accorde: bicause it was neither honorable, nor profitable for the common weale to redeeme men that cowardly suffered them selves to be taken prisoners of their enemies. Fabius understanding it, dyd paciently beare this displeasure conceyved against him by the Senate. Howbeit having no money, and meaning to keepe his worde, and not to leave the poore cittizens prisoners behinde him: he sent his sonne to Rome, with commission to sell his landes, and to bring him money immediatly. The young man went his waye to Rome, and sold his fathers farmes, and brought him money forthwith to the campe: Fabius therewith redeemed the prisoners, and sent their ransome unto Hannibal. Many of the prisoners whom he had redeemed, offred to repaye him their ransome: but he would never take any thing againe, and gave them all their ransome freely. Afterwards being called to Rome by the priestes to doe certaine solemne sacrifices, he left the armie in charge with Minutius, to governe the same in his absence, with condition not to set upon the

Fabius chaungeth prisoners with Hannibal.

Fabius redemeth the prisoners with his money.

Fabius leaveth Minutius his lieftenant in the field.

enemie, nor to fight with him at all: the which not only by his authoritie he dyd expressely forbid him, but also as his very friende, he dyd warne and intreate him in no wise to attempt. Howbeit Minutius litle regarding his commaundementes or requestes, so sone as Fabius backe was turned, beganne to be somewhat lustie, and doing with his enemies. So one daye amongest the rest, Minutius perceyving Hannibal had sent a great parte of his armie abroade to forrage and get vittells: came and set upon them that remained behinde, and drave them into their campe, with great slaughter, and dyd put them in a marvelous feare that were saved, as men that looked for no lesse, but to have bene besieged in their campe. Afterwardes also, when their whole armie came together againe: he retired backe in spight of them all, and lost not a man. This exploite set Minutius in a pryde, and brought the souldiers to be more rashe then they were before. The newes of this overthrowe went with speede to Rome, and there they made it a great deale more then it was. Fabius hearing of it, sayed: he was more afeard of Minutius prosperitie, then of his owne adversitie. But the common people rejoyced marvelosly, and made great shewe of joye up and downe the market place. Whereupon Metellus one of the Tribunes going up into the pulpit, made an oration unto the people, in the which he highely magnified Minutius, and commended his corage: and contrarily charged Fabius no more of cowardlines, but with flat treason. Furthermore, he dyd accuse the Nobilitie and greatest men of Rome, saying: that from the first beginning they had layed a platte to drawe these warres out at length, only to destroye the peoples power and authoritie, having brought the whole common weale, to the state of a monarchy, and into the handes of a private persone. Who by his remissenes and delayes, would geve Hannibal leysure to plante him selfe in Italie, and by time geve open passage to the Carthaginians, at their pleasure to send Hannibal a second ayde and armie, to make a full conquest of all Italie. Fabius hearing these wordes, rose up straight, and spake to the people, and taried not about the aunswering of the accusations the Tribune had burdened him withall, but prayed

Minutius rashenes.

Fabius accused of treason by Metellus the Tribune.

them they would dispatche these sacrifices and ceremonies of the goddes, that he might spedilie returne againe to the campe, to punishe Minutius, for breaking his commaundement, in fighting with the enemie. He had no soner spoken these wordes, but there rose a marvelous tumulte and hurly burley presently among the people, for the daunger Minutius stoode in then: bicause the Dictator had absolute power and authoritie to imprisone and put to death, whom he thought good, without ordinary course of lawe or araynement. Moreover, they dyd judge, since Fabius had alate left his accustomed mildnes and affabilitie, that he would growe to such severitie in his anger, that it would be a hard thing to appease him. Wherefore every man held their peace for feare, saving only Metellus the Tribune. He having authoritie by vertue of his office, to saye what he thought good, and who only of all other kept still his place and authoritie, when any Dictator was chosen: then all the officers that were put down, instantly besought the people not to forsake Minutius, nor to suffer the like to be done to him, as Manlius Torquatus dyd alate to his sonne, who strake of his head, after he had valliantly fought with his enemies and overcomed them, for breaking his commaundement. And beganne to persuade them further, to take this tyrannicall power of the Dictatorshippe from Fabius: and to put their affayers into the handes of him, that would and could tell howe to bring them safely to passe. The people were tickled marvelously with these seditious wordes, but yet they durst not force Fabius to resigne his Dictatorshippe, though they bare him great grudge, and were angrie with him in their hartes. Howbeit they ordeined that Minutius thenceforth should have equall power and authoritie with the Dictator in the warres, a thing that was never seene nor heard of before, and yet the very same done in that sorte againe, after the battell of Cannes. For Marcus Iunius being at that time Dictator in the campe, they dyd choose another Dictator at Rome, which was Fabius Buteo, to name and create newe Senators in the place of those that were slaine in the battell. But after he had named them, and restored the full number againe ot the counsell of the Senate: he discharged the selfe same daye the

The crueltie of Manlius Torquatus to his sonne after his victorie.

The Dictator and generall of the horsemen made equall in authoritie.

sergeants that caried the axes before him, and sent awaye the traine that waited upon him, and dyd so put him selfe in prease of the people in the market place, and followed his owne peculiar busines as a private persone. Nowe the Romaines imagined, that when Fabius should see howe they had made Minutius equall in authoritie with him, it would greve him to the harte for very anger: but they came shorte to judge of his nature, for he dyd not thincke that their folly should hurte or dishonour him at all. But as wise Diogenes aunswered one that sayed unto him, Looke, they mocke thee: Tushe (sayd he) they mocke not me. Meaning thereby, that he tooke them to be mocked, that were offended with their mockes. Thus Fabius tooke every thing quietly, that the people offered him, and dyd comfort him selfe with the philosophers rules and examples: who doe mainteine, that an honest and wise man, can no waye be injured nor dishonoured. For all the displeasure he receyved by the peoples follie, was in respect of the common wealth: bicause they had put a sworde into a mad mans hande, in geving Minutius authoritie to followe his rashe humour, and fonde ambition in the warres. Wherefore, fearing least he being blinded with vaine glorie, and presumptuous opinion of him selfe, should rashely (and upon a head) hasten to doe some great hurte before he came to the campe: he departed sodainely out of Rome without any mans knowledge, to returne againe to the campe, where he found Minutius so prowde and stowte, that he was not to be delt with. For he would nedes have the authoritie to commaund the whole armie when it came to his turne. But Fabius would not consent to that, but devided the one halfe of the armie betweene them: thincking it better he should alone commaunde the one halfe, then the whole army by turnes. So he chose for him selfe, the first and third legion: and gave unto him, the seconde and fourth, and devided also betwene them the ayde of their friends. And when Minutius made his boaste, that the majestie of the highest magistrate was brought lower for his sake: Fabius tolde him that he might thincke, if he were wise, he had not to fight with him, but with Hannibal: and if he would nedes contend against his companion, yet he should have a speciall

Diogenes wordes.

Minutius pride.

FABIUS MAXIMUS

regard and consideration, that having wonne nowe the cittizens good willes, by whom he was so much honoured, he should have no lesse care of their healthe and safety, then he had, who was nowe troden under foote, and ill intreated by them. Minutius tooke his lesson, for a counterfeate mocke, after olde mens manners and facion: and so taking the one half of the armie unto him, went and lodged alone by him self. Hannibal hearing of their jarre and squaring together, sought straight oportunitie to make their discord finely to serve his turne. Nowe there was a hill betwene both their campes not very harde to be wonne, and it was an excellent place to lodge a campe safely in, and was very fitte and commodious for all things. The fields that were about it, dyd seeme a farre of to be very playne and even ground, bicause they had no covert of wodde to shadowe them, yet were there many ditches and litle vallies in them: wherefore Hannibal though he might easely have taken it at his pleasure if he had listed, dyd let it alone in the middest betwene them, for a bayte to drawe out his enemies to the battell. Nowe when Hannibal sawe Fabius and Minutius lodged a sonder, he placed certaine bandes in the night, among those ditches and valleyes. Afterwardes the next morning by breake of daye, he sent a small number of men openly to winne this hill: hoping by this pollicie to traine Minutius out to the field, as it fell out in deede. For first Minutius sent thither his light horsemen, and afterwardes all his men at armes: and lastely perceyving that Hannibal him selfe came to relieve his men that were upon the hill, he him self marched forward also with all the rest of his armie in order of battell, and gave a whotte charge upon them that defended the hill, to drive them thence. The fight continued equall a good space betwene them both, untill such time as Hannibal saw his enemie come directly within his daunger, and shewed the rereward of his battell naked unto his men, whom before he had layed in ambushe: he straight raised the signall he had geven them. They upon that discovered all together, and with great cries dyd set upon the rereward of the Romaines, and slue a great number of them at the first charge: and dyd put the reste in suche a feare and disorder, as it is unpossible to expresse it.

Hannibal layed ambush for Minutius.

Then was Minutius rashe braverie and fonde boastes muche cooled, when he looked first upon one captaine, then upon another, and sawe in none of them any corage to tarie by it, but rather that they were all readie to ronne away. Which if they had done, they had bene cast awaye every man: for the Numidians finding they were the stronger, dyd disperse themselves all about the plaine, killing all stragglers that fled. Minutius souldiers being brought to this daunger and distresse, which Fabius foresawe they would fall into, and having upon this occasion his armie readie ranged in order of battell, to see what would be come of Minutius, not by reporte of messengers, but with his owne eyes: he got him to a litle hill before his campe, where when he sawe Minutius and all his men compassed about on every side, and even staggering and ready to flye, and heard besides their cries not like men that had hartes to fight, but as men scared, and ready to flye for feare to save them selves: he clapped his hande on his thighe, and fetched a great sighe, saying to those that were about him: O goddes, howe Minutius is gone to cast him selfe awaye, soner then I looked for, and later then he desired? But in speaking these wordes, he made his ensignes marche on in haste, crying out alowde: O my friends, we must dispatche with speede to succour Minutius: for he is a valliant man of persone, and one that loveth the honour of his countrie. And though with overmuch hardines he hath ventred to farre, and made a faulte, thinking to have put the enemies to flight: time serveth not now to accuse him, we will tell him of it hereafter. So he presently brake the Numides, and dispersed them, that laye waiting in the fields for the Romaines, which they thought would have fled. Afterwardes he went further, and dyd set upon them that had geven charge upon the rereward of Minutius battell, where he slue them that made head against him. The residue, fearing least they should fall into the daunger they had brought the Romaines unto: before they were environned in of all sides, dyd turne taile straight to Fabius. Now Hannibal seeing this chaunge, and considering howe Fabius in persone, with more corage then his age required, dyd make a lane in the middest of those that fought against the

Fabius foresight in the warre.

Fabius rescueth Minutius, generall of the horsemen.

side of the hill, to come to the place where Minutius was: he made the battell to cease, and commaunded to sounde the retreate, and so drue backe his men againe into his campe, the Romaines being very glad also they might retire with safetie. They saye Hannibal in his retiring, sayed merylie to his friends: Have not I tolde you (Sirs) many a time and ofte, of the hanging clowde we sawe on the toppe of the mountaines, howe it would breake out in the ende with a tempest that would fall upon us? After this battell, Fabius having stript those that were left dead in the field, retired againe to his owne campe, and spake not an ill word of Minutius his companion. Minutius then being come to his campe, assembled his souldiers and spake thus to them: 'My friends, not to erre at all, enterprising great matters, it 'is a thing passing mans nature: but to take warning here-'after, by faultes that are paste and done, it is the parte of 'a wise and valliant man. For my selfe, I acknowledge I 'have no lesse occasion to prayse fortune, then I have also 'cause to complaine of her. For that which long time could 'never teach me, I have learned by experience in one litle 'pece of a daye: and that is this. That I am not able to 'commaunde, but am my selfe fitter to be governed and 'commaunded by another: and that I am but a foole to 'stande in mine owne conceipt, thinking to overcome those, 'of whom it is more honour for me to confesse my selfe to be 'overcome. Therefore I tell you, that the Dictator Fabius 'henceforth shalbe he, who alone shall commaund you in all 'things. And to let him knowe that we doe all acknowledge 'the favour which we have presently receyved at his hands: I 'will leade you to geve him thankes, and will my selfe be the 'first man to offer to obey him in all that he shall commaund 'me.' These wordes being spoken, he commaunded his ensigne bearers to followe him, and he him selfe marched formest towards Fabius campe. When he came thither, he went directly to the Dictators tente: whereat every man wondered, not knowing his intent. Fabius came out to mete him. Minutius after he had set downe his ensignes at his feete, sayed with a lowde voyce, O father: and his souldiers unto Fabius souldiers, O masters, which name the bondemen that

The great modestie of Fabius.

Minutius oration to his souldiers.

The wisedom of Minutius acknowledging his fault.

are infranchesed, doe use to them that have manumised them. Afterwards every man being silent, Minutius beganne alowde to saye unto him: 'My lorde Dictator, this daye you have 'wonne two victories. The one of Hannibal, whom valliantly 'you have overcome: the second, of my selfe your companion, 'whom also your wisedome and goodnes hath vanquished. 'By the one, you have saved our lives: and by the other, 'you have wisely taught us. So have we also bene over-'come in two sortes: the one by Hannibal to our shame, 'and the other by your selfe, to our honour and preserva-'tion. And therefore doe I nowe call you my father, 'finding no other name more honorable to call you by, 'wherewith I might honour you: acknowledging my selfe 'more bounde unto you for the present grace and favour I 'have receyved of you, then unto my naturall father that 'begatte me. For by him only I was begotten: but by 'you, mine, and all these honest cittizens lives have bene 'saved.' And having spoken these wordes, he embraced Fabius: and so dyd the souldiers also, hartely embrace together, and kisse one another. Thus the joye was great through the whole campe, and one were so glad of another, that the teares trickled downe their chekes for great joye.

Minutius words to Fabius.

Nowe when Fabius was afterwardes put out of his office of Dictatorshippe, there were new Consuls chosen againe: the two first followed directly Fabius former order he had begonne. For they kept them selves from geving Hannibal any battell, and dyd allwayes send ayde to their subjects and friends, to keepe them from rebellion: untill that Terentius Varro (a man of meane birth, and knowen to be very bold and rashe) by flattering of the people, wanne credit among them to be made Consul. Then they thought that he by his rashnes and lacke of experience, would incontinently hazard battell: bicause he had cried out in all the assemblies before, that this warre would be everlasting, so long as the people dyd chuse any of the Fabians to be their generalles, and vawnted him selfe openly, that the first daye he came to see his enemies, he would overthrowe them. In geving out these brave wordes, he assembled such a power, that the Romaines never sawe so great a number together,

The rashnes of Terentius Varro.

Terentius Varro, Paulus Æmilius Consuls.

FABIUS MAXIMUS

The Romaines campe under Terentius Varro, 88000 men.

Fabius counsell to Paulus Æmilius.

against any enemie that ever they had: for he put into one campe, foure score and eight thousand fighting men. This made Fabius and the other Romaines, men of great wisedome and judgement, greatly affrayed: bicause they sawe no hope for Rome to rise againe, if it fortuned that they should lose so great a number of goodly youth. Therefore Fabius talked with the other Consul, called Paulus Æmilius, a man very skilfull and expert in warres, but ill beloved of the common people, whose furie he yet feared, for that they had condemned him a litle before to paye a great fine to the treasurie: and after he had somewhat comforted him, he beganne to persuade and encorage him to resist the fonde rashnes of his companion, telling him, that he should have asmuch to doe with Terentius Varro for the preservation and safety of his countrie, as to fight with Hannibal for defence of the same. For they were both Marshall men, and had a like desire to fight: the one bicause he knewe not wherein the vantage of his strength consisted, and the other bicause he knewe very well his weaknes. You shall have reason to beleeve me better, for matters touching Hannibal, then Terentius Varro. For I dare warrant you, if you keepe Hannibal from battell but this yere: he shall of necessitie, if he tarie, consume him self, or els for shame be driven to flye with his armie. And the rather, bicause hetherto (though he seeme to be lorde of the field) never one yet of his enemies came to take his parte: and moreover bicause there remaines at this daye in his campe not the third parte of his armie, he brought with him out of his countrie. Unto these persuasions, the Consul (as it is reported) aunswered thus: When I looke into my selfe, my lorde Fabius, me thinkes my best waye were rather to fall upon the enemies pikes, then once againe to light into the hands and voyces of our cittizens. Therefore, sith the estate of the common wealth so requireth it, that it behoveth a man to doe as you have sayed: I will doe my best indevour to shewe my selfe a wise captaine, for your sake only, rather then for all other that should advise me to the contrarie. And so Paulus departed from Rome with this minde. But Terentius his companion would in any case, they should commaund the whole armie by turnes, eche his daye by him selfe: and went to encampe harde by Hannibal, by the river of Aufide, neere unto the village called Cannes. Nowe when it came to his daye to commaund by turnes, early in the mourning he caused the signall of battell to be set out, which was a coate armour of skarlet in graine, that they dyd laye out upon the pavilion of the generall: so that the enemies at the first sight, beganne to be afeard, to see the lustines of this newe come generall, and the great number of souldiers he had also in his hoste, in comparison of them that were not halfe so many. Yet Hannibal of a good corage, commaunded every man to arme, and to put them selves in order of battell: and him selfe in the meane time taking his horse backe, followed with a fewe, gallopped up to the toppe of a litle hill not very steepe, from whence he might plainely discerne all the Romaines campe, and sawe howe they dyd range their men in order of battell. Nowe one Giscon (a man of like state and nobilitie as him selfe) being with him at that time, tolde him, that the enemies seemed a farre of to be a marvelous number. But Hannibal rubbing his forehead, aunswered him: Yea, sayed he, but there is another thing more to be wondered at then you thinke of Giscon. Giscon straight asked him: What? Mary sayeth he this: that of all the great number of souldiers you see yonder, there is not a man of them called Giscon as you are. This mery aunswer delivered contrarie to their expectation that were with him, looking for some great waightie matter, made them all laughe a good. So downe the hill they came laughing alowde, and tolde this prety jeaste to all they met as they rode, which straight from one to another ranne over all the campe, in so much as Hannibal him selfe could not holde from laughing. The Carthaginian souldiers perceyving this, beganne to be of a good corage, imagining that their generall would not be so merylie disposed as to fall a laughing, being so neere daunger, if he had not perceyved him selfe a great deale to be the stronger, and that he had good cause also to make no reckoning of his enemies. Furthermore, he shewed two policies of a skilfull captaine in the battell. The first was,

Aufidius fl.

Hannibals stratagemes at the battell of Cannes.

the situation of the place, where he put his men in order of battell, so as they had the winde on their backes: which raging like a burning lightning, raised a sharpe dust out of the open sandy valley, and passing over the Carthaginians squadron, blewe full in the Romaines faces, with such a violence, that they were compelled to turne their faces, and to trouble their owne rankes. The seconde policie was, the forme and order of his battell. For he placed on either side of his winges, the best and valliantest souldiers he had in all his armie: and dyd fill up the middest of his battell with the worste of his men, which he made like a pointe, and was farder out by a great deale, then the two winges of the fronte of his battell. So he commaunded those of the winges, that when the Romaines had broken his first fronte, and followed those that gave backe, whereby the middest of his battell should leave an hollowe place, and the enemies should come in still increasing within the compasse of the two winges: that then they should set upon them on both sides, and charge their flanks immediatly, and so inclose them in behind. And this was cause of a greater slaughter. For when the midle battell beganne to geve backe, and to receyve the Romaines within it, who pursued the other very whotly, Hannibals battell chaunged her forme: and where at the beginning it was like a pointe, it became nowe in the middest like a cressant or halfe moone. Then the captaines of the chosen bandes that laye out in both the winges, made their men to turne, some on the left hand, and some on the right, and charged the Romaines on the flankes, and behinde, where they were all naked: so they killed all those that could not save them selves by flying, before they were environed. They saye also, that there fell out another mischief by misfortune, unto the horsemen of the Romaines, and by this occasion. The horse of Paulus Æmilius the Consul being hurte, dyd throwe his master on the grounde: whereupon those that were next him, dyd light from their horse backs to helpe him. The residue of the horsemen that were a great waye behinde him, seeing them light, thought they had bene all commaunded to light: hereupon every man forsooke their horse, and fought it out a foote. Hannibal when he sawe

Hannibals order of battell at Cannes.

The slaughter of the Romaines at the battell of Cannes.

that, sayed: Yea marie, I had rather have them so then delivered me bounde hande and foote. But for those matters, the historiographers doe dilate more at large. Furthermore, of the two Consuls, Varro saved him selfe by his horse, with a fewe following him, within the cittie of Venusa. Paulus being in the middest of the throng of all the armie, his bodie full of arrowes that stucke fast in his woundes, and his harte sore loden with grievous sorowe and anguishe to see the overthrowe of his men: was set downe by a rocke, looking for some of his enemies, to come and ryd him out of his payne. But fewe could knowe him, his head and face was of such a gore bloude: insomuch as his friends and servants also passed by him, and knewe him not. And there was but one young gentleman of a noble house of the Patricians, called Cornelius Lentulus, that knewe him, who dyd his best endevour to save him. For he lighted a foote presently, and brought him his horse, praying him to get up upon him, to prove if he could save him selfe for the necessitie of his countrie, which nowe more then ever had neede of a good and wise captaine. But he refused the gentlemans offer and his intreatie, and compelled him to take his horse backe againe, though the teares ranne downe his chekes for pittie: and raising him selfe up to take him by the hande, he sayed unto him: I pray you tell Fabius Maximus from me, and witnesse with me, that Paulus Æmilius even to his last hower hath followed his counsaill, and dyd never swarve from the promise he made him: but that first he was forced to it by Varro, and afterwardes by Hannibal. When he had delivered these wordes, he bad Lentulus farewell: and ronning againe into the furie of the slaughter, there he dyed among his slaine companions. It is thought there were slaine at this battell, fiftie thousand Romaines, and foure thousand taken prisoners: and other tenne thousand that were taken prisoners in two campes after the battell. When this noble victorie was gotten, Hannibals friendes gave him counsaill to followe his good fortune: and to enter Rome after the scattered number that fled thither: so as within fewe dayes following he might suppe in their capitoll. A man cannot easely gesse what was the cause that stayed him,

Paulus Æmilius slaine at the battell of Cannes.

50000 Romaines slaine at the battell of Cannes.

that he went not, unles it was (as I thinke) some good fortune, or favourable God toward the Romaines that withstoode him, and made him afeard and glad to retire. Whereupon they saye, that one Barca a Carthaginian, in his anger sayed to Hannibal: Syr, you have the waye to overcome, but you cannot use victorie. Notwithstanding, this victorie made a marvelous chaunge for him. For hereupon, all Italy in manner came in to submit them selves to him: where before he had no towne at commaundement, nor any storehouse or porte through all Italie, yea he did marvelous hardly, and with much a doe vittell his armie with that he could daylie robbe and spoyle, having no certen place to retire unto, nor grounded hope to entertain these warres, but kept the field with his armie, removing from place to place, as they had bene a great number of murderers and theeves together. For the most parte of the countrie, dyd yeld immediatly unto him: as the cittie of Capua, being the chiefest and greatest cittie of all Italie but Rome, and dyd receyve Hannibal, and were at his devotion. Thus we maye plainely see, that as the poet Euripides sayeth: it is a great mischief not onely to be driven to make triall of friendes, but proofe also of captaines wisdom. For that which before they accompted cowardlines and fainte harte in Fabius, immediatly after the battell, they thought it more then mans reason, and rather a heavenly wisdome and influence, that so long foresawe the things to come, which the parties selves that afterwards felt them, gave litle credit unto before. Upon this occasion, Rome reposed incontinently all their hope and trust in Fabius, and they repaired to him for counsell, as they would have ronne unto some temple or altar for sanctuarie. So as the first and chiefest cause of staying the people together from dispersing them selves abroade, as they dyd when Rome was taken by the Gaules: was the only opinion and confidence they had in Fabius wisedome. For where before he seemed to be a coward, and timerous, when there was no daunger nor misfortune happened: then when every man wept and cried out for sorrowe, which could not helpe, and that all the world was so troubled that there was no order taken for any thing, he contrarily went

All Italy revolted and submitted them selves to Hannibal.

alone up and downe the cittie very modestly, with a bold constant countenaunce, speaking curteously to every one, and dyd appease their womanishe cries and lamentations, and dyd forbid the common assemblies and fonde ceremonies, of lamenting the dead corse at their burialls. Then he persuaded the Senate to assemble in counsell, and dyd comforte up those that were magistrates, and he alone was the only force and power of the cittie: for there was not a man that bare any office, but dyd cast his eye upon Fabius, to knowe what he should doe. He it was that caused the gates of the cittie straight to be warded, and to keepe those in for going their waye, that would have forsaken the cittie. He moreover dyd appointe the time and place of mourning, and dyd commaund whosoever was disposed to mourne, that he should doe it privately in his owne house, and to continue only but thirtie dayes. Then he willed all mourning to be left of, and that the cittie might be cleane from such uncleane things. So the feast of Ceres falling about that time, he thought it better to leave of the sacrifices and procession they were wont to keepe on Ceres daye: then by their small number that were left, and sorowe of those that remained, to let their enemies understand their exceeding great losse. For the goddes delite to be served with glad and rejoycing hartes, and with those that are in prosperitie. But all this notwithstanding, whatsoever the priestes would have done, either to pacifie the wrath of the goddes, or to turne awaye the threatnings of these sinister signes, it was forthwith done. For they dyd sende to the oracle of Apollo, in the cittie of Delphes, one of Fabius kinsemen surnamed Pictor. And two of the Vestall Nunnes being deflowred: the one was buried alive according to the lawe and custome, and the other made her self awaye. But herein the great corage and noble clemency of the Romaines, is marvelously to be noted and regarded. For the Consul Terentius Varro returning backe to Rome, with the shame of his extreme misfortune and overthrowe, that he durste not looke upon any man: the Senate notwithstanding, and all the people following them, went to the gates of the cittie to meete him, and dyd honorably receyve him. Nay furthermore, those that were

Fabius constancie after the overthrow at Cannes.

Fabius order for mourning.

The magnanimitie of the Romaines after the overthrowe at Cannes.

the chief magistrates and Senators, among whom Fabius was one, when silence was made, they commended Varro much: bicause he did not despaire of the preservation of the common weale after so great a calamitie, but dyd returne againe to the cittie, to helpe to reduce things to order, in using the authoritie of the lawe, and the service of the cittizens, as not being altogether under foote, but standing yet in reasonable termes of good recovery. But when they understoode that Hannibal after the battell was gone into other partes of Italie: then they beganne to be of good chere againe, and sent a newe armie and generalles to the field, among which, the two chief generals were, Fabius Maximus, and Claudius Marcellus, both which by contrary meanes in manner, wanne a like glorie and reputation. For Marcellus (as we have declared in his life) was a man of speedy execution, of a quicke hande, of a valliant nature, and a right martiall man, as Homer calleth them, that valliantly put them selves in any daunger: by reason whereof, having to deale with another captaine a like venturous and valliant as him selfe, in all service and execution, he shewed the selfe boldnes and corage that Hannibal dyd. But Fabius persisting still upon his first determination, dyd hope that though he dyd not fight with Hannibal, nor sturre him at all, yet continuall warres would consume him and his armie in the end, and bring them both to nought: as a common wrestler that forceth his bodie above his naturall strength, doth in the ende become a lame and broosed man.

Fabius Maximus, and Claudius Marcellus generalles.

Hereupon Possidonius writeth, that the one was called the Romaines sworde, and the other their target. And that Fabius constancie and resolutnes in warres to fight with securitie, and to commit nothing to hazard and daunger, being mingled with Marcellus heate and furie: was that only, which preserved the Romaines empire. For Hannibal meting allwayes in his waye the one that was furious, as a strong ronning streame, founde that his army was continually turmoyled and overharried: and the other that was slowe as a litle prety river, he founde that his army ranne softely under him without any noyse, but yet continually by litle and litle it dyd still consume and diminishe him, untill he sawe

Possidonius wordes of Fabius and Marcellus.

him selfe at the last brought to that passe, that he was weary with fighting with Marcellus, and affrayed of Fabius bicause he fought not. For during all the time of these warres, he had ever these two captaines almost against him, which were made either Prætors, Consuls, or Proconsuls: for either of them both had bene five times before chosen Consul. Yet as for Marcellus: Hannibal had layed an ambushe for him in the fifte and last yere of his Consulshippe, where he set upon him on a sodaine, and slue him. But as for Fabius, he layed many baytes for him, and dyd what he could by all the skill and reache he had, by ambushes, and other warlike policies to entrappe him: but he could never drawe him within his daunger. Howbeit at one time he put him to a litle trouble, and was in good hope then to have made him falle upon his ambushe he had layed for him: and by this policie. He had counterfeated letters written and sent unto him from the cittie of Metapont, to praye him to come to them, and they would deliver their cittie into his handes: and withall, that such as were privie to the contentes of the same, desired no other thing but his repaire thither. These letters pretily quickned Fabius, insomuch as he was determined one night to have taken parte of his armie, and to have gone to them. But bicause the signes of the birdes dyd promise him no good successe, he left of his purpose. Sone after he understoode they were counterfeate letters, made by Hannibals fine devise to have drawen him out, and to have intrapped him, for whom him selfe laye in persone in ambushe neere the cittie, looking and waiting for his comming: but the goddes who would have him saved, were only to be thanked for his happy scape. Furthermore, concerning the revolte of the citties that were subject unto them, and the rising of their allies and friends against them: Fabius thought it farre better to intreate them curteously, making them ashamed without occasion to rebell against them, rather then openly to suspect them, and to deale straightly with those that were so to be suspected. Now for this matter, it is reported that Fabius had a souldier in his campe that was a Marsian borne by nation, a valliant man of his persone, and also of as noble a house, as any that were of all the allies of the Romaines:

Marcellus slaine by an ambushe of Hannibals.

Hannibals ambush layed for Fabius.

Fabius lenitie in correcting of faultes.

Note how Fabius reclaimed an evill souldier.

who had practised with other his fellowes of the bande he served in, to goe serve the enemie. Fabius hearing of this practise he went about, gave him no ill countenaunce for it, but calling him to him, he sayed: I must confesse there is no reckoning made of you, as your good service doth deserve: wherefore for this time (sayeth he) I blame the pety captaines only, which in such sorte doe bestowe their good will and favour at adventure, and not by deserte. But henceforth it shalbe your owne faulte if you doe not declare your minde unto me, and betweene you and me make me privie of your lacke and necessitie. When he had spoken these wordes to him, he gave him a very good horse for service, and dyd rewarde him with other honorable giftes, as men of good service and desert have commonly bestowed on them: and this dyd so encorage the souldier thenceforth, that he became a very faithfull and serviceable souldier to the Romaines. For Fabius thought it more fit, that hunters, riders of horses, and such like as take upon them to tame brute beastes, should sonner make them leave their savage and churlishe nature, by gentle usage and manning of them: then by beating, and shackling of them. And so a governour of men, should rather correct his souldier by pacience, gentlenes, and clemency: then by rigour, violence, or severitie. Otherwise he should handle them more rudely, and sharpely, then husbandmen doe figge trees, olive trees, and wilde pomegarnets: who by diligent pruning and good handling of them, doe alter their harde and wilde nature, and cause them in the end to bring forth good figges, olives and pomegarnets. Another time certaine captaines of his brought him worde, that there was one of their souldiers which would ever goe out of the campe, and leave his ensigne. He asked them, what manner of man he was. They aunswered him all together, that he was a very good souldier, and that they could hardly finde out suche another, in all their bandes as he: and therewithall they tolde him, of some notable service they had seene him doe in persone. Whereupon Fabius made a diligent enquierie to know what the cause was, that made him goe so oft out of the campe: in the end, he founde he was in love with a young woman, and that to goe see her, was the cause he dyd so ofte

Necessarie rules for a captaine.

leave his ensigne, and dyd put his life in so great daunger, for that she was so farre of. When Fabius understoode this, he sent certaine souldiers (unknowing to the souldier) to bring the woman awaye he loved, and willed them to hyde her in his tente: and then called he the souldier to him, that was a Lucanian borne, and taking him a side, sayed unto him thus: My friend, it hath bene tolde me, how thou hast lyen many nightes out of the campe, against the lawe of armes, and order of the Romaines, but therewithall I understande also that otherwise thou art an honest man, and therefore I pardone thy faultes paste, in consideration of thy good service: but from henceforth I will geve thee in custodie to such a one, as shall make me accompt of thee. The souldier was blancke, when he heard these wordes. Fabius with that, caused the woman he was in love with, to be brought forth, and delivered her into his hands, saying unto him: This woman hereafter shall aunswer me thy bodie to be forth comming in the campe amongest us: and from henceforth thy deedes shall witnesse for the reste, that thy love unto this woman, maye be no cloke of thy departing out of the campe for any wicked practise or intent. Thus much we finde written concerning this matter. Moreover, Fabius after suche a sorte, recovered againe the cittie of Tarentum, and brought it to the obedience of the Romaines, which they had lost by treason. It fortuned there was a young man in his campe, a Tarentine borne, that had a sister within Tarentum, which was very faithfull to him, and loved him marvelous dearely: now there was a captaine, a Brutian borne, that fell in love with her, and was one of those to whom Hannibal had committed the charge of the cittie of Tarentum. This gave the young souldier the Tarentine, very good hope, and waye, to bring his enterprise to good effect: whereupon he revealed his intent to Fabius, and with his privitie fled from his campe, and got into the cittie of Tarentum, geving it out in the cittie, that he would altogether dwell with his sister. Now for a fewe dayes at his first comming, the Brutian captaine laye alone by him selfe, at the request of the mayde his sister, who thought her brother had not knowen of her love: and shortely after the young fellowe tooke his sister aside, and

How Fabius wanne Tarentum againe.

sayed unto her: My good sister, there was a great speache in the Romaines campe, that thou wert kept by one of the chiefest captaines of the garrison: I praye thee if it be so, let me knowe what he is. For so he be a good fellowe, and an honest man (as they saye he is) I care not: for warres that turneth all things topsi turvey, regardeth not of what place or calling he is of, and still maketh vertue of necessitie, without respect of shame. And it is a speciall good fortune, at such time as neither right nor reason rules, to happen yet into the handes of a good and gratious lorde. His sister hearing him speake these wordes, sent for the Brutian captaine to bring him acquainted with her brother, who liked well of both their loves, and indevoured him self to frame his sisters love in better sorte towards him, then it was before: by reason whereof, the captaine also beganne to trust him very muche. So this young Tarentine sawe it was very easie, to winne and turne the minde of this amarous and mercenarie man, with hope of great giftes that were promised him, and Fabius should performe. Thus doe the most parte of writers set downe this storie. Howbeit some writers saye, that this woman who wanne the Brutian captaine, was not a Tarentine, but a Brutian borne, whom Fabius it is sayed, kept afterwards for his concubine: and that she understanding the captaine of the Brutians (who laye in garrison within the cittie of Tarentum) was also a Brutian borne, and of her owne native countrie: made Fabius privie to her intent, and with his consent, she comming to the walles of the cittie, spake with this Brutian captaine, whom she handled in such sorte, that she wanne him. But whilest this geare was a brewing, Fabius, bicause he would traine Hannibal out of those quarters, wrote unto the souldiers of Rhegio: which belonged to the Romaines, that they should enter the borders of the Brutians, and laye seige to the cittie of Caulonia, and rase it to the grounde. These Rhegian souldiers were about the number of eight thousand, and the most of them traitours, and ronneagates, from one campe to another: and the worst sorte of them, and most defamed of life, were those that Marcellus brought thither out of Sicile, so that in losing them all, the losse

Tarentum wonne by a womans meanes.

were nothing to the common weale, and the sorrowe muche lesse. So Fabius thought, that putting these fellowes out for a praye to Hannibal (as a stale to drawe him from those quarters) he should plucke him by this meanes from Tarentum: and so it came to passe. For Hannibal incontinently went thence with his armie to intrappe them: and in the meane time Fabius went to laye seige to Tarentum, where he had not lien six dayes before it, but the young man (who together with his sister had drawen the Brutian captaine to this treason) stale out one night to Fabius, to enforme him of all, having taken very good markes of that side of the walle the Brutian captaine had taken charge of, who had promised him to keepe it secret, and to suffer them to enter, that came to assaulte that side. Yet Fabius would not grounde his hope altogether upon the Brutians executing this treason, but went him self in persone to vewe the place appointed, howbeit without attempting any thing for that time: and in the meane season, he gave a generall assault to all partes of the cittie (aswell by sea as by lande) with great showtes and cries. Then the Brutian captaine seeing all the cittizens and garrison ronne to that parte, where they perceyved the noyse to be greatest: made a signall unto Fabius, that now was the time. Who then caused scaling ladders to be brought a pace, whereupon him selfe with his companie scaled the walles, and so wanne the cittie. But it appeareth here, that ambition overcame him. For first he commaunded they should kill all the Brutians, bicause it should not be knowen he had wonne the cittie by treason. But this bloudie policie failed him: for he missed not only of the glorie he looked for, but most deservedly he had the reproche of crueltie and falsehood. At the taking of this cittie, a marvelous number of the Tarentines were slaine, besides there were solde thirtie thousand of the chiefest of them, and all the cittie was sacked: and of the spoyle thereof was caried to the common store treasure at Rome, three thousand talents. It is reported also, that when they dyd spoyle and carie awaye all other spoyles lefte behinde, the recorder of the cittie asked Fabius, what his pleasure was to doe with the goddes,

Fabius tooke the cittie of Tarentum.

Fabius ambition cause of fowle murder.

meaning the tables, and their images: and to that Fabius aunswered him: Let us leave the Tarentines their goddes that be angrie with them. This notwithstanding, he caried from thence Hercules statue, that was of a monstruous bignes, and caused it to be set up in the Capitoll, and withall dyd set up his owne image in brasse a horse backe by him. But in that act he shewed him self farre harder harted, then Marcellus had done, or to saye more truely, thereby he made the world knowe how muche Marcellus curtesie, clemencie, and bowntie was to be wondred at: as we have written in his life. Newes being brought to Hannibal, that Tarentum was besieged, he marched presently with all speede possible to raise the seige: and they saye he had almost come in time, for he was with in 40 furlonges of the cittie when he understoode the trothe of the taking of it. Then sayed he out alowd, Sure the Romaines have their Hannibal to: for as we wanne Tarentum, so have we lost it. But after that, to his friends he sayed privately (and that was the first time they ever heard him speake it) that he sawe long before, and now appeared plainely, that they could not possibly with this small power keepe Italie. Fabius made his triumphe and entrie into Rome the seconde time, by reason of taking of this cittie: and his seconde triumphe was muche more honorable then the first, as of a valliant captaine that held out still with Hannibal, and easely met with all his fine policies, muche like the slight trickes of a cunning wrestler, which caried not now the former roughenes and strength any more, bicause that his armie was geven to take their ease, and growen to delicacie, partely through the great riches they had gotten, and partely also for that it was sore wasted and diminished, through the sundrie foughten battells and blowes they had bene at. Now there was one Marcus Livius a Romaine, that was governour of Tarentum at that time, when Hannibal tooke it, and nevertheles kept the castell still out of Hannibals handes, and so held it untill the cittie came againe into the handes of the Romaines. This Livius spighted to see suche honour done to Fabius, so that one daye in open Senate, being drowned with envie and

Fabius second triumphe.

ambition, he burst out and sayed: that it was him selfe, not Fabius, that was cause of taking of the cittie of Tarentum againe. Fabius smiling to heare him, aunswered him openly: in deede thou sayest true, for if thou haddest not lost it, I had never wonne it againe. But the Romaines in all other respects dyd greatly honour Fabius, and specially for that they chose his sonne Consul. He having alreadie taken possession of his office, as he was dispatching certen causes touching the warres, his father (whether it was for debilitie of his age, or to prove his sonne) tooke his horse to come to him, and rode through the prease of people that thronged about him, having busines with him. But his sonne seeing him comming a farre of, would not suffer it, but sent an officer of his unto him, to commaund him to light of his horse, and to come a foote if he had any thing to doe with the Consul. This commaundement misliked the people that heard it, and they all looked upon Fabius, but sayed not a worde: thinking with them selves, that the Consul dyd great wronge to his fathers greatnes. So he lighted straight, and went a good rounde pace to embrace his sonne, and sayed unto him: You have reason sonne, and doe well to shewe over whom you commaund, understanding the authoritie of a Consul, which place you have received. For it is the direct course, by the which we and our auncesters have increased the Romaine empire: preferring ever the honour and state of our countrie, above father, mother, or children. And truely they saye, that Fabius great grandfather being the greatest and most noble persone of Rome in his time, having five times bene Consul, and had obteined many triumphes, for divers honorable and sundrie victories he had wonne: was contented after all these, to be his sonnes lieutenaunt, and to goe to the warres with him, he being chosen Consul. And last of all, the Consul his sonne returning home to Rome a conquerour, in his triumphing charret drawen with foure horses, he followed him a horse backe also, in troupe with the rest: thinking it honour to him, that having authoritie over his sonne in the right of a father, and being also the noblest man of all the cittizens, so taken and reputed, nevertheles he willingly submitted

Fabius wittie aunswer.

A straunge commaundment of the sonne to the father.

The father obeyeth his sonnes authoritie and commendeth him.

FABIUS MAXIMUS

him selfe to the lawe and magistrate, who had authoritie of him. Yet besides all this, he had farre more excellent vertues to be had in admiration, then those already spoken of. But it fortuned that this sonne of Fabius died before him, whose death he tooke paciently, like a wise man, and a good father. Now the custome being at that time, that at the death of a noble man, their neerest kinseman should make a funerall oration in their prayse at their obsequies: he him selfe made the same oration in honour of his sonne, and dyd openly speake it in the market place, and moreover wrote it, and delivered it out abroade. About this time, Cornelius Scipio was sent into Spayne, who drave out the Carthaginians from thence, after he had overthrowen them in many battells, and had conquered many great citties, and greately advaunced the honour and estimation of the state of Rome: for the which at his returne, he was asmuche, or rather more honoured, beloved and esteemed, then any other that was in the cittie of Rome. Hereupon Scipio being made Consul, considered that the people of Rome looked for some great matter at his handes, above all other. Therefore he thought, to take upon him to fight against Hannibal in Italie, he should but followe the olde manner, and treade to muche in the steppes of the olde man: whereupon he resolved immediately to make warres in Africke, and to burne and destroye the countrie even unto Carthage gates, and so to transferre the warres out of Italie into Libya, procuring by all possible devise he could, to put it into the peoples heades, and to make them like of it. But Fabius contrarilie, persuading him selfe that the enterprise this young rashe youthe tooke in hande, was utterly to overthrowe the common weale, or to put the state of Rome in great daunger: devised to put Rome in the greatest feare he could possible, without sparing speache or dede he thought might serve for his purpose, to make the people chaunge from that minde. Now he could so cunningly worke his purpose, what with speaking and doing, that he had drawen all the Senate to his opinion. But the people judged, it was the secret envie he bare to Scipioes glorie, that drue him to encounter this devise, only to bleamish Scipioes noble fortune, fearing, least if he should

Scipio Consul.

Fabius was against the counsell and devise of Scipio African.

happen to doe some honorable service (as to make an end altogether of this warre, or otherwise to draw Hannibal out of Italie) that then it would appeare to the world, he had bene to softe, or to negligent, to drawe this warre out to suche a length. For my parte, me thinkes the only matter that moved Fabius from the beginning to be against Scipio, was the great care he had of the safetie of the common weale, by reason of the great daunger depending upon such a resolution. And yet I doe thinke also, that afterwards he went further then he should, contending to sore against him (whether it was through ambition or obstinacie) seeking to hinder and suppresse the greatnes of Scipio: considering also he dyd his best to persuade Crassus, Scipioes companion in the Consulshippe, that he should not graunte unto him the leading of the armie, but if he thought good to goe into Africke, to make warres upon the Carthaginians, that he should rather goe him self. And moreover, he was the let that they gave him no money for maintenaunce of these warres. Scipio hereupon being turned over to his owne credit, to furnish him selfe as he could: he leavied great summes of money in the citties of Thuscan, who for the great love they bare him, made contribution towardes his jorney. And Crassus remained at home, both bicause he was a softe, and no ambitious, nor contentious man of nature: as also, bicause he was the chiefest Prelate and highe bishoppe, who by the lawe of their religion, was constrained to kepe Rome. Fabius seeing his labour lost that waye, tooke againe another course to crosse Scipio, devising to staye the young men at home, that had great desire to goe this jorney with him. For he cried out with open mouth, in all assemblies of the Senate and people, that Scipio was not contented only to flye Hannibal, but that he would carie with him besides the whole force of Italy that remained: alluring the youthe with sweete baytes of vaine hope, and persuading them to leave their wives, their fathers, mothers, and their countrie, even now when their enemie knocked at Rome gates, who dyd ever conquer, and was yet never conquered. These wordes of Fabius dyd so dampe the Romaines, that they appointed Scipio should furnishe his

Crassus, highe bishoppe of Rome.

jorney only with the armie that was in Sicilia, saving that he might supply to them if he would, three hundred of the best souldiers that had served him faithfully in Spayne. And so it doth appeare even to this present, that Fabius both dyd and sayed all things, according to his wonted manner, and naturall disposition. Now Scipio was no sooner arrived in Africke, but newes were brought to Rome incontinently, of wonderfull exploytes, and noble service done beyond measure: and of great spoyles taken by him, which argued the trothe of the newes. As, the king of the Numidians taken prisoner, two campes of the enemies burnt and destroyed at a time, with losse of a great number of people, armour, and horses, that were consumed in the same: letters and postes for life ronning in the necke one of another from Carthage to call Hannibal home, and to praye him to hunte no longer after vayne hope that would never have ende, hasting him selfe with all speede possible to come to the rescue of his countrie. These wonderfull great fortunes of Scipio, made him of suche renowme and fame within Rome, that there was no talke but of Scipio. Fabius notwithstanding desisted not to make a newe request, being of opinion they should send him a successour, alledging no other cause nor reason, but a common speache of every bodie: that it was a daungerous thing to commit to the fortune of one man alone, so great exceeding prosperitie and good successe, bicause it is a rare matter to see one man happie in all things. These wordes dyd so muche mislike the people, that they thought him an envious and troublesome man, or els they thought his age had made him fearefull: and that his corage failed with his strength, fearing Hannibal more doubtfully then he needed. For now though Hannibal was forced to leave Italie, and to returne into Africke, yet Fabius would not graunte, that the peoples joye and securitie they thought they were in, was altogether cleare, and without feare and mistruste: but gave it out that then they were in greatest daunger, and that the common weale was breeding more mischief now, then before. For when Hannibal (sayed he) shall returne home into Africke, and come before Carthage walles, the Romaines shall be lesse able to abide him

The famous actes done in Africke by Scipio Africanus.

there, then they have bene before: and Scipio moreover, shall meete with an armie yet warme, and embrued with the bloude of so many Prætors, Dictators, and Consuls of Rome, which they have overcome, and put to the sword in Italie. With these uncomfortable speaches, he still troubled and disquieted the whole cittie, persuading them that notwithstanding the warre was transferred out of Italie into Africke, yet that the occasion of feare was no less neere unto Rome, then it was ever before. But within shorte space after, Scipio having overcome Hannibal in plaine battell in the field, and troden under foote the glory and pryde of Carthage, he brought a greater joye to Rome, then they ever looked for: and by this noble victorie of his, he shored up again the declining state of the empire of Rome, which a litle before was falling downe right. Howbeit Fabius lived not to the ende of this warre, nor ever heard while he lived the joyfull newes of Hannibals happy overthrowe, neither were his yeres prolonged to see the happy assured prosperitie of his countrie: for about that time that Hannibal departed out of Italie, a sicknes tooke him, whereof he dyed. The stories declare, that the Thebans buried Epaminondas, at the common charges of the people: bicause he dyed in so great povertie, that when he was dead, they founde nothing in the house but a litle iron spit. Now the Romaines buried not Fabius so, at the common charge of the cittie, but every man of benevolence gave towards his funerall charges, a pece of coyne that caried the least value of their currant money: not for that he lacked abillitie to bring him to the grounde, but only to honour his memorie: in making his obsequies at their charges, as of one that had bene their common father. So had his vertuous life, an honorable ende and buriall.

The death of Fabius Max.

The funeralls of Epaminondas.

THE COMPARISON OF PERICLES WITH FABIUS

ERE have you heard what is written, of these two great persones. And forasmuche as they have both left behinde them, many noble examples of vertue, aswell in martiall matters, as in civill government, let us beginne to compare them together. First of all, Pericles beganne to governe the common weale at what time the people of Athens were in their chiefest prosperitie, and of greater power and wealth, then ever they had bene of before or since. The which might seeme to be a cause of the continuall maintenance of the same in securitie without daunger of falling, not so muche for their worthines, as for their common power and felicitie: where contrariwise Fabius acts fell out in the most dishonorable and unfortunate time, that ever happened to his countrie, in the which he dyd not only keepe the cittie in good state from declining, but raised it up, and delivered it from calamitie, and brought it to be better then he found it. Furthermore, Cimons great good fortune and successe, the victories and triumphes of Myronides, and of Leocrates, and many notable valliant dedes of armes of Tolmides, gave good cause to Pericles, to entertaine his cittie in feastes, and playes, whilest he dyd governe the same: and he dyd not finde it in such ill case and distresse, that he was driven to defend it by force of armes, or to conquer that againe which he had lost. But Fabius in contrary manner, when he sawe before him many overthrowes, great flying awaye, muche murder, great slaughters of the generalles of the Romaine armies, the lakes, the playnes, the woddes filled with scattered men, the people overcome, the flouds and rivers ronning all a gore bloude (by reason of the great slaughter)

and the streame carying downe the dead bodies to the mayne sea: dyd take in hande the government of his countrie, and a course farre contrarie to all other: so as he dyd underproppe and shore up the same, that he kept it from flat falling to the grounde, amongest those ruines and overthrowes other had brought it to, before him. Yet a man maye saye also, that it is no great matter of difficultie to rule a cittie already brought lowe by adversitie, and which compelled by necessitie, is contented to be governed by a wise man: as it is to bridle and keepe under the insolencie of a people, pufte up with pryde, and presumption of long prosperitie, as Pericles founde it amongest the Athenians. The great multitude also of so many grievous calamities, as lighted on the Romaines neckes at that time, dyd playnely shewe Fabius to be a grave and a constant man, which would never geve waye unto the importunate cries of the common people, nor could ever be removed from that he had at the first determined. The winning and recovering againe of Tarentum, maye well be compared to the taking of Samos, which Pericles wanne by force: and the citties of Campania, unto the Ile of Euboea: excepting the cittie of Capua, which the Consuls Fulvius and Appius recovered againe. But it seemeth that Fabius never wanne battell, save that only for which he triumphed the first time: where Pericles set up nine triumphes, of battels and victories he had wonne, aswell by sea as by lande. And so also, they cannot alledge such an acte done by Pericles, as Fabius dyd, when he rescued Minutius out of the handes of Hannibal, and saved a whole armie of the Romaines: which doubtles was a famous acte, and proceeded of a noble minde, great wisdome, and an honorable harte. But Pericles, againe dyd never commit so grosse an errour as Fabius dyd when he was outreached, and deceyved by Hannibals fine stratageame of his oxen: who having founde his enemie by chaunce to have shut him selfe up in the straight of a vallye, dyd suffer him to escape in the night by a subtiltie, and in the daye by playne force. For he was prevented by overmuch delaye, and fought withall by him he kept inclosed. Now if it be a requisite, a good captaine doe not only use well that he hath in his handes, but

PERICLES AND FABIUS

The gifte of a good generall.

that he wisely judge also what will followe after, then the warres of the Athenians fell out in suche sorte, as Pericles sayed they would come to passe: for with ambition to imbrace to muche, they overthrewe their estate. But the Romaines contrariwise, having sent Scipio into Africke to make warres with the Carthaginians, wanne all that they tooke in hande: where their generall dyd not overcome the enemie by fortune, but by valliantnes. So that the wisedome of the one is witnessed, by the ruine of his countrie: and the errour of the other testified, by the happy event of that he would have let. Now the faulte is a like in a generall, to fall into daunger, for lacke of forecaste: as for cowardlines to let slippe a fit oportunitie offred, to doe any notable pece of service. For like defaulte and lacke of experience, maketh the one to hardie, and the other to fearefull. And thus muche touching the warres. Now for civill government: it was a fowle blotte to Pericles, to be the author of warres. For it is thought, that he alone was the cause of the same, for that he would not have them yeld to the Lacedæmonians in any respect. And yet me thinkes Fabius Maximus also would no more geve place unto the Carthaginians, but stood firme and bold in all daunger, to mainteine thempire of his countrie against them. But the goodnes and clemency Fabius shewed unto Minutius, doth much condemne Pericles accusations and practises, against Cimon and Thucydides: bothe of them being noble and good men, and taking parte with the Nobilitie, whom he expulsed out of Athens, and banished for a time. So was Pericles power and authoritie in the common weale greater: by reason whereof he dyd ever foresee, that no generall in all his time dyd rashely attempt any thing hurteful unto the common weale, except Tolmides onely: who fled from him, and in despight of him went to fight with the Bœotians where he was slaine. As for all other generals, they wholy put themselves into his hands, and dyd obey him for the greatnes of his authoritie. But Fabius, although for his parte he never committed any faulte, and that he went orderly to worke in all government: yet bicause he was not of power to keepe other from doing ill, it seemeth in

The faultes of generalles.

The comparison betwext Pericles and Fabius for civill government.

this respect he was defective. For if Fabius had caried like authoritie in Rome, as Pericles dyd in Athens: the Romaines had not fallen into so great miserie as they dyd. And for liberalitie: the one shewed it, in refusing the money offred him: and the other, in geving unto those that needed, and redeeming his poore captive contry men. And yet Fabius might dispend no great revenue: for his whole receiptes came only to sixe talents. But for Pericles, it is hard to saye howe riche he was, who had comming in to him, great presents by his authoritie, aswel of the subjects, as of the friends and allies of the Athenians, as also of Kings and straunge Princes: yet he never tooke bribe for all that, of any persone living. And to conclude, as for the sumptuous building of temples, the stately workes and common buildings: put all the ornaments together that ever were in Rome, before the times of the Cæsars, they are not to be compared with those, wherewith Pericles dyd beawtifie and adorne the cittie of Athens. For neither in qualitie nor quantitie was there any proportion or like comparison betweene the exceeding sumptuousnes of the one, and of the other.

PERICLES AND FABIUS

Fabius revenue.

The buildings of Rome nothing comparable to Pericles workes.

THE ENDE OF FABIUS MAXIMUS LIFE

THE LIFE OF ALCIBIADES

ALCIBIADES by his fathers side, was aunciently descended of Eurysaces, that was the sonne of Ajax, and by his mothers side, of Alcmæon: for his mother Dinomacha, was the daughter of Megacles. His father Clinias having armed, and set forth a gallye, at his owne proper costes and charges, dyd winne great honour in the battell by sea, that was fought alongest the coaste of Artemisium, and he was slaine afterwardes in another battell fought at Coronea, against the

Alcibiades stocke.

ALCIBIADES

Alcibiades tutours.

Bœotians. His sonne Alcibiades tutours, were Pericles, and Ariphron Xanthippus sonnes: who were also his neere kinsemen. They saye, and truely: that Socrates good will and friendshippe dyd greatly further Alcibiades honour. For it appeareth not, neither was it ever written, what were the names of the mothers of Nicias, of Demosthenes, of Lemachus, of Phormion, of Thrasibulus, and of Theramenes: all which were notable famous men in their time. And to the contrarie, we finde the nource of Alcibiades, that she was a Lacedæmonian borne, and was called Amicla, and that his schoolemaster was called Zopyrus: of the which, Antisthenes mentioneth the one, and Plato the other. Now for Alcibiades beawtie, it made no matter if we speake not of it, yet I will a litle touche it by the waye: for he was wonderfull fayer, being a child, a boye, and a man, and that at all times, which made him marvelous amiable, and beloved of every man. For where Euripides sayeth, that of all the fayer times of the yere, the Autumne or latter season is the fayrest: that commonly falleth not out true. And yet it proved true in Alcibiades, though in fewe other: for he was passing fayer even to his latter time, and of good temperature of bodie. They write of him also, that his tongue was somewhat fatte, and it dyd not become him ill, but gave him a certen naturall pleasaunt grace in his talke: which Aristophanes mentioneth, mocking one Theorus that dyd counterfeat a lisping grace with his tongue.

The mothers of famous men never knowen what they were.

Alcibiades beawtie.

Alcibiades lisped by nature.

*The equivocation of these two Greeke wordes Κορα and Κολα, is harde to be expressed in Inglishe, in stead whereof I have set flatling blowes, for flattering browes, observing the grace of lisping, as neere as I could, like to the Latin and French translations, likewise Theolus for Theorus.

This Alcibiades, with his fat lisping tongue,
into mine eares, this trusty tale, and songe full often songe.
Looke upon Theolus (quoth he) lo there he bowes,
beholde his comely crowebright face with fat and *flatling blowes.
The sonne of Clinias, would lispe it thus somewhiles,
and sure he lisped never a lye, but rightly hyt his wiles.

And Archippus another poet also, mocking the sonne of Alcibiades, sayeth thus:

Bicause he would be like his father everie waye
in his long trayling gowne he would goe jetting daye by daye.
And counterfeate his speache, his countenaunce and face:
as though dame nature had him geven, therein a perfect grace.
To lispe and looke aside, and holde his head awrye,
even as his father lookt and lispt, so would he prate and prye.

For his manners they altered and chaunged very oft with time, which is not to be wondred at, seing his marvelous great prosperitie, as also adversitie that followed him afterwards. But of all the great desiers he had, and that by nature he was most inclined to, was ambition, seeking to have the upper hand in all things, and to be taken for the best persone: as appeareth by certaine of his dedes, and notable sayings in his youthe, extant in writing. One daye wrestling with a companion of his, that handled him hardly, and thereby was likely to have geven him the fall: he got his fellowes arme in his mouth, and bit so harde, as he would have eaten it of. The other feeling him bite so harde, let goe his holde straight, and sayed unto him: What Alcibiades, bitest thou like a woman? No mary doe I not (quoth he) but like a lyon. Another time being but a litle boye, he played at skayles in the middest of the streete with other of his companions, and when his turne came about to throwe, there came a carte loden by chaunce that waye: Alcibiades prayed the carter to staye a while, untill he had played out his game, bicause the skailes were set right in the high way where the carte should passe over. The carter was a stubborne knave, and would not staye for any request the boye could make, but drave his horse on still, in so much as other boyes gave backe to let him goe on: but Alcibiades fell flat to the grounde before the carte, and bad the carter drive over and he durste. The carter being afeard, plucked backe his horse to staye them: the neighbours flighted to see the daunger, ranne to the boye in all hast crying out. Afterwards when he was put to schoole to learne, he was very obedient to all his masters that taught him any thing, saving that he disdained to learne to playe of the flute or recorder: saying, that it was no gentlemanly qualitie. For, sayed he, to playe on the vyoll with a sticke, doth not alter mans favour, nor disgraceth any gentleman: but otherwise, to playe on the flute, his countenaunce altereth and chaungeth so ofte, that his familliar friends can scant knowe him. Moreover, the harpe or vyoll doth not let him that playeth on them, from speaking, or singing as he playeth: where he that playeth on the flute, holdeth his mouth so harde to it,

ALCIBIADES

Alcibiades ambitious.

Alcibiades studies.

A vile thing to playe of a flute.

that it taketh not only his wordes from him, but his voyce. Therefore, sayed he, let the children of the Thebans playe on the flute, that cannot tell howe to speake: as for us Athenians, we have (as our forefathers tell us) for protectours and patrones of our countrie, the goddesse Pallas, and the god Apollo: of the which the one in olde time (as it is sayed) brake the flute, and the other pulled his skinne over his eares, that played upon the flute. Thus Alcibiades alledging these reasons, partely in sporte, and partely in good earnest: dyd not only him selfe leave to learne to playe on the flute, but he turned his companions mindes also quite from it. For these wordes of Alcibiades, ranne from boye to boye incontinently: that Alcibiades had reason to despise playing of the flute, and that he mocked all those that learned to play of it. So afterwards, it fell out at Athens, that teaching to playe of the flute, was put out of the number of honest and liberall exercises, and the flute it selfe was thought a vile instrument, and of no reputation. Furthermore, in the accusations Antiphon wrote against Alcibiades, it is declared: that when he was a boye, he fled out of his tutours house, into the house of Democrates one of his lovers, and howe Ariphron one of his tutours thought to have made a beadle crie him through the cittie. But Pericles would not suffer him, saying: that if he were dead, they should knowe it but one daye sooner by crying of him: and if he were alive, that it would be such a shame to him while he lived, that he had bene better he had never bene heard of againe. The same Antiphon accuseth him further, that he had killed a servaunt of his that attended on him, in the wrestling place of Sibyrtius, with a blowe of a staffe. But there is no reason to credit his writing, who confesseth he speaketh all the ill he can of him, for the ill will he dyd beare him. Now straight there were many great and riche men that made muche of Alcibiades, and were glad to get his good will. But Socrates love unto him had another ende and cause, which witnessed that Alcibiades had a naturall inclination to vertue. Who perceyving that vertue dyd appeare in him, and was joyned with the other beawtie of his face and bodye, and fearing the corruption of riches,

Socrates love to Alcibiades.

dignitie and authoritie, and the great number of his companions, aswell of the chiefest of the cittie, as of straungers, seeking to entise him by flatterie, and by many other pleasures: he tooke upon him to protect him from them all, and not to suffer so goodly an ympe to lose the hope of the good fruite of his youthe. For fortune doth never so intangle nor snare a man without, with that which they commonly call riches, as to let and hinder him so, that philosophie should not take holde on him with her free, severe, and quicke reasons. So Alcibiades was at the beginning, assayed with all delightes, and shut up as it were in their companie that feasted him with all pleasures, only to turne him that he should not hearken to Socrates wordes, who sought to bring him up at his charge, and to teach him. But Alcibiades notwithstanding, having a good naturall wit, knewe what Socrates was, and went to him, refusing the companie of all his riche friendes and their flatteries, and fell in a kinde of familliar friendshippe with Socrates. Whom when he had heard speake, he noted his wordes very well, that they were no persuasions of a man seeking his dishonesty, but one that gave him good counsell, and went about to reforme his faultes and imperfections, and to plucke downe the pride and presumption that was in him: then, as the common proverbe sayeth,

> Like to the craven cocke, he drowped downe his winges,
> which cowardly doth ronne awaye, or from the pit out flinges.

And dyd thinke with selfe, that all Socrates love and following of young men, was in dede a thing sent from the goddes, and ordeined above for them, whom they would have preserved, and put into the pathe waye of honour. Therefore he beganne to despise him selfe, and greatly to reverence Socrates, taking pleasure of his good using of him, and much imbraced his vertue: so as he had (he wist not howe) an image of love graven in his harte, or rather (as Plato sayeth) a mutuall love, to wit, an holy and honest affection towards Socrates. Insomuch as all the world wondred at Alcibiades, to see him commonly at Socrates borde, to playe, to wrestle, and to lodge in the warres with Socrates: and

ALCIBIADES

contrarily to chide his other well willers, who could not so much as have a good looke at his handes, and besides became daungerous to some, as it is sayed he was unto Anytus, the sonne of Anthemion, being one of those that loved him well. Anytus making good cheere to certen straungers his friendes that were come to see him, went and prayed Alcibiades to come and make merie with them: but he refused to goe. For he went to make merie with certen of his companions at his own house, and after he had well taken in his cuppes, he went to Anytus house to counterfeate the foole amongest them, and staying at the halle doore, and seeing Anytus table and cubberd full of plate of silver and gold, he commaunded his servants to take awaye half of it, and carie it home to his house. But when he had thus taken his pleasure, he would come no neerer into the house, but went his waye home. Anytus friendes and guestes misliking this straunge parte of Alcibiades, sayed it was shamefully and boldly done so to abuse Anytus. Nay, gently done of him, sayed Anytus: for he hath left us some, where he might have taken all. All other also that made much of him, he served after that sorte. Saving a straunger that came to dwell in Athens: who being but a poore man as the voyce went, sold all that he had, whereof he made about a hundred stateres which he brought unto Alcibiades, and prayed him to take it at his handes. Alcibiades beganne to be merie, and being very glad to understand his good will towards him, tooke his honest offer, and prayed him to come to supper to him: so he welcomed him very hartely, and made him good cheere. When supper was done, he gave him his money againe, and commaunded him not to faile the next morning to meete him where the farmes and landes of the cittie are wont to be let out to those that byd most, and charged him he should out byd all. The poore man would fayne have excused him self, saying, the farmes were to great for him to hyre: but Alcibiades threatned to whippe him, if he would not doe it. For besides the desire he had to pleasure him, he bare a private grudge against the ordinary farmers of the cittie. The next morning the straunger was ready in the market place, where they dyd

Alcibiades insolencie unto Anytus.

Alcibiades liberall facte.

crie out the letting of their farmes, and he raised one to a talent more, then all other dyd offer. The other farmers were as mad with him as they could be, that they all dyd set upon him, crying out: Let him put in suertie straight, supposing he could have founde none. The straunger was marvelous blancke thereat, and beganne to shrincke backe. Then cried Alcibiades out alowde to the officers that sate there to take the best offers: I will be his suertie, sayeth he, put me in the booke, for he is a friend of mine. The farmers hearing him saye so, were at their wittes ende, and wiste not what to doe. For they being allwayes accustomed to paye their yerely rent as it went before, by the helpe of the rest of the yeres that followed after: perceyving now that they should not be able to paye the arrerages of the rentes due to the common weale, and seeing no other remedie, they prayed him to take a pece of money, and to leave the bargaine. Then Alcibiades would in no wise he should take lesse then a talent, which they gave him willingly. So Alcibiades suffered the straunger then to departe, and made him gaine by his devise. Now Socrates love which he bare him, though it had many mightie and great adversaries, yet it dyd staye much Alcibiades, somtime by his gentle nature, somtime by his grave counsell and advise: so as the reason thereof tooke so deepe roote in him, and dyd so pearce his harte, that many times the teares ranne downe his cheekes. Another time also being caried awaye with the intisement of flatterers, that held up his humour with all pleasure and delightes, he stale awaye from Socrates, and made him ronne after him to fetche him againe, as if he had bene a slave that had ronne awaye from his masters house: for Alcibiades stoode in awe of no man but of Socrates only, and in deede he dyd reverence him, and dyd despise all other. And therefore Cleanthes was wont to saye, that Alcibiades was held of Socrates by the eares: but that he gave his other lovers holde, which Socrates never sought for: for to saye truely, Alcibiades was muche geven over to lust and pleasure. And peradventure it was that Thucydides ment of him, when he wrote that he was incontinent of bodie, and dissolute of life. Those that marred Alcibiades quite, dyd still pricke forward his ambi-

Alcibiades ranne from Socrates.

Alcibiades geven to pleasure.

tion and desire of honour, and dyd put him in the head to thrust him selfe into great matters betimes, making him beleeve that if he dyd but once beginne to shewe him selfe to deale in matters of state, he would not only bleamishe and deface all other governours, but farre excell Pericles, in authoritie and power among the Græcians. For like as iron by fire is made softe, to be wrought in to any forme, and by colde also doth shut and harden in againe: even so Alcibiades being puffed up with vanitie and opinion of him self, as ofte as Socrates tooke him in hande, was made faste and firme againe by his good persuasions, insomuch that when he sawe his owne faulte and follie, and how farre wide he had strayed from vertue, he became sodainely very humble and lowly againe. Now on a time when he was growen to mans state, he went into a grammer schoole, and asked the schoolemaster for one of Homers bookes. The schoolemaster aunswered him, he had none of them: Alcibiades up with his fiste, and gave him a good boxe on the eare, and went his waye. Another grammarian tolde him on a time he had Homer which he had corrected. Alcibiades replied, Why what meanest thou, to stand teaching litle children their abce, when thou art able to correct Homer, and to teache young men, not boyes? Another time he came and knocked at Pericles gate, desirous to speake with him: aunswer was made him, he was not at leysure now, for that he was busilie occupied by him self, thinking on his reckonings he had to make with the Athenians. Why, sayed he, going his waye: it were better he were occupied, thinking how to make no accompt at all. Moreover, being but a young boye, he was at the jorney of Potidæa, where he laye still with Socrates, who would never let him be from him in all battells and skirmishes he was in: among which there was one, very whotte and bloody, where they both fought valliantly, and Alcibiades was hurte. But Socrates stepped before him, and dyd defend him so valliantly before them all, that he saved him and his weapon out of the enemies handes. So the honour of this fight out of doubt, in equitie and reason, was due unto Socrates: but yet the captaines would faine have judged it on Alcibiades side, bicause he was of a noble house. But Socrates, bicause he

Alcibiades strake a schoolemaster, bicause he had not Homer in his schoole.

Alcibiades first souldier fare with Socrates.

Alcibiades saved by Socrates.

would increase his desire of honour, and would pricke him forward to honest and commendable things, was the very first that witnessed Alcibiades had deserved it: and therefore prayed the captaines to judge him the crowne and complet armour. Afterwards, in the battell of Delion, the Athenians having receyved the overthrowe, Socrates retired with a fewe other a foote. Alcibiades being a horse backe, and overtaking him, would not goe from him, but kept him company, and defended him against a troupe of his enemies that followed him, and slue many of his company. But that was a prety while after, and before he gave a boxe of the eare unto Hipponicus, Callias father: who was one of the greatest men of power in the cittie, being a noble man borne, and of great possessions, which was done upon a bravery and certaine lustines, as having layed a wager with his companions he would doe it, and for no malice or quarrell that he bare the man. This light parte was straight over all the cittie, and every one that heard it, sayed it was lewdly done. But Alcibiades the next morning went to his house, and knocking at his gate was let in: so he stripping him selfe before him, delivered him his bodie to be whipped, and punished at his pleasure. Hipponicus pardoned him, and was friends with him, and gave him his daughter Hipparete afterwards in mariage. Howbeit some saye, it was not Hipponicus that gave her to him: but Callias sonne, with tenne talents of gold with her. Afterwards at the birth of his first child he had by her, he asked tenne talents more, saying: they were promised him upon the contract, if his wife had children. But Callias fearing least this was an occasion sought of him to lye in wayte to kill him for his goodes: declared openly to the people, that he made him his heire generall, if he dyed without heires speciall of his bodie. This gentlewoman Hipparete, being an honest true wife to Alcibiades, misliking her husband dyd so muche misuse her, as to entertaine common light strumpets, aswell cittizens as straungers: she went abroad one day to her brothers house, and tolde him of it. Alcibiades passed not for it, and made no further reckoning of the matter: but only bad his wife, if she would, present her cause of divorse before the judge.

Alcibiades saved Socrates life after the overthrow at the battaill of Delion.

Alcibiades maried.

Hipparete sueth to be divorced from Alcibiades.

So she went thither her selfe, to sue the divorce betwene them, according to the lawe: but Alcibiades being there also, tooke her by the hande, and caried her through the market place home to his house, and no man durst medle betwene them, to take her from him. And so she continued with him all the dayes of her life, which was not long after for she died, when Alcibiades was in his jorney he made to Ephesus. This force Alcibiades used, was not thought altogether unlawfull, nor uncivill, bicause it seemeth that the lawe was grounded upon this cause: that the wife which would be divorced from her husband, should goe her selfe openly before the judge to put up her complainte, to the ende, that by this meanes, the husband might come to speake with his wife, and seeke to staye her if he could. Alcibiades had a marvelous fayer great dogge, that cost him three score and tenne minas, and he cut of his taile that was his chief beawtie. When his friendes reproved him, and tolde him how every man blamed him for it: he fell a laughing, and tolde them he had that he sought. For, sayeth he, I would have the Athenians rather prate upon that, then they should saye worse of me. Moreover, it is sayed, the first time that Alcibiades spake openly in the common weale, and beganne to deale in matters, was upon a gifte of money he gave to the people, and not of any pretence, or former purpose he had to doe it. One daye as he came through the market place, hearing the people very lowde, he asked what the matter was: they tolde him it was about money certen men had geven to the people. Then Alcibiades went to them, and gave them money out of his owne purse. The people were so glad at that, as they fell to showting and clapping of their handes, in token of thankfullnes: and him selfe was so glad for companie, that he forgat a quayle he had under his gowne, which was so afeard of the noyse, that she tooke her flight away. The people seeing the quayle, made a greater noyse then before, and many rose out of their places to runne after her: so that in the ende, it was taken up by a master of a shippe called Antiochus, who brought him the quayle againe, and for that cause Alcibiades dyd love him ever after. Now albeit the nobilitie of his house, his goodes,

Alcibiades great dogge.

Alcibiades largesse.

his worthines, and the great number of his kinsemen and friends made his waye open to take upon him government in the common weale. Yet the only waye he desired to winne the favour of the common people by, was the grace of his eloquence. To prove he was eloquent, all the Comicall poets doe testifie it: and besides them, Demosthenes the prince of orators also doth saye, in an oration he made against Midias, that Alcibiades above all other qualities he had, was most eloquent. And if we maye beleeve Theophrastus, the greatest searcher of antiquities, and best historiographer above any other philosopher: he hath written, that Alcibiades had as good a witte to devise and consider what he would saye, as any man that was in his time. Howbeit somtimes studying what he should saye, as also to deliver good wordes, not having them very readilie at his tongues ende: he many times tooke breath by the waye, and paused in the middest of his tale, not speaking a worde, untill he had called it to minde, that he would saye. His charge was great, and muche spoken of also, for keeping of ronning horses at games: not only bicause they were the best and swiftest, but for the number of coches he had besides. For never private persone, no nor any prince, that ever sent seven so well appointed coches, in all furniture, unto the games Olympicall, as he dyd: nor that at one course hath borne awaye the first, the second, and the fourth prise, as Thucydides sayeth: or as Euripides reporteth, the third. For in that game, he excelled all men in honour and name that ever strived for victorie therein. For Euripides pronounced his praise, in a songe he made of him, as followeth:

Alcibiades comming into the common wealth.

Alcibiades marvelous eloquent.

Alcibiades witte and imperfection.

Alcibiades victorie at the games Olympicall.

O sonne of Clinias, I will resounde thy praise:
for thou art bold in martiall dedes, and overcommest allwayes.
Thy victories therewith, doe farre exceede the rest,
that ever were in Greece ygot, therefore I compt them best.
For at thOlympike games, thou hast with chariots wonne,
the first price, seconde, thirde and all, which there in race were ronne.
With praise and litle payne, thy head hath twise bene crownde,
with olive boughes for victorie, and twise by trumpets sounde,
The herаulds have proclaimed thee victor by thy name:
above all those, which ranne with thee, in hope to get the game.

Howbeit the good affection divers citties did beare him, contending which should gratifie him best, dyd muche increase his fame and honour. For the Ephesians dyd set up a tente for him, very sumptuously and richely furnished. Those of the cittie of Chio, furnished him with provinder for his horse, and gave him muttons besides, and other beastes to sacrifice withall. They of Lesbos also sent him in wine and other provision for vittells, to helpe him to defraye the great charges he was at in keeping open house, and feeding such a number of mouthes daylie. Yet the spite they dyd beare him, or rather his breache of promise which he often made, with this magnificence and state he shewed, gave the people more cause to speak of him then before. For they saye there was one Diomedes at Athens, a friend of Alcibiades, and no ill man, who desired once in his life to winne a game at the playes Olympicall. This man being enformed that the Argives had a coche excellently furnished, belonging to their common weale, and knowing that Alcibiades could doe very much in the cittie of Argos, bicause he had many friends in the same: he came to intreate Alcibiades to buye this coche for him. Alcibiades thereupon bought it, but kept it to him selfe, not regarding Diomedes request he had made. Diomedes seeing that fell starke mad for anger, and called the goddes and men to witnesses, that Alcibiades did him open wrong: and it seemeth, that there fell out sute in lawe upon the same. For Isocrates wrote an oration, and drue a plea in defence of Alcibiades, being yet but a childe, touching a couple of horses: yet in this plea, his adversarie was called Tisias, and not Diomedes. Furthermore, Alcibiades being yet but a young man, when he came to practise and pleade publikly, he put all other Oratours to silence, but only two that were ever against him: the one was Phæax the sonne of Erasistratus, and the other Nicias, the sonne of Niceratus. Of these two, Nicias was a man growen, and had wonne the name and reputation of a good captaine. And Phæax beganne also to come forward as he dyd, being of a good and honorable house: but he lacked many things, and among other, eloquence specially. For, he could more properly talke and discourse among his friends privately, then he had any

Alcibiades a breaker of promise.

Alcibiades adversaries in the common wealth when he came to pleade.

Phæax lacked eloquence.

good grace to open a matter openly before the people. For he had, as Eupolis sayeth:

Wordes enowe, but no eloquence.

There is a certen oration extant in writing, against Alcibiades and Phæax: where among other accusations is brought in, howe Alcibiades was ordinarily served in his house, with gold and silver plate that belonged to the common weale, and which were used to be borne for state and magnificence, in solemne processions before them, and how he used them as boldly, as if they had bene his owne. Now there was one Hyperbolus in Athens at that time borne in the village of Perithoide: of whom Thucydides maketh mencion, as of a naughty wicked man, whose tongue was a fit instrument to deliver matter to all the Comicall poets of that time, to poore out all their tawnts and mockes against men. Howbeit he was so impudent a persone, and cared so litle what men sayed of him, that he passed not though he were defamed, neither dyd any thing greve him, whatsoever they reported of him: which some doe call boldnes, and corage, being no better in deede then plaine impudencie, extreme madnes, and desperate follie. He would never please any man: and if the common people had any grudge to any noble man or magistrate, whom they would any waye accuse, Hyperbolus wicked tongue was their instrument to utter their spyte. Now the people (by Hyperbolus procurement) being assembled, were ready to proceede to the banishment of *Ostracismon* by most voyces. The manner and custome of this kynde of banishment was for a time to banish out of their cittie such a one, as seemed to have to great authoritie and credit in the cittie: and that was, rather to satisfie their envie, then for to remedy their feare. And bicause it was manifest it would fall out to one of them three to be banished (to wit, Alcibiades, Nicias, or Phæax) Alcibiades found meanes to joyne all their three factions in one, becomming friends one to another: and having conferred with Nicias about it, he made Hyperbolus self to be banished, who was the chief instrument to prepare the waye of their banishment. Howbeit other saye, he spake not with Nicias about

Hyperbolus banished for 10 years.

The manner of the punishment of the *Ostracismon.*

ALCIBIADES

it, but with Phæax, and joyning his parte with Phæax, he caused Hyperbolus to be banished, who feared nothing lesse: for it was never seene before, that a man of meane countenaunce, and of small authoritie, fell into the happe of this banishment. As Plato the Comical poet testifieth, speaking of Hyperbolus:

> Although for his deserts, this payne to him is due,
> or greater punishment prepard, the which might make him rue:
> Yet since he was by birth, a persone meane and base,
> such punishment therefore dyd seeme (for him) to great of grace.
> Since *Ostracismon* was, not made at first to be,
> nor yet devisde as punishment, for suche meane folke as he.

But of this matter, we have spoken more at large before: and now to returne againe to Alcibiades. Nicias had great reputation among straungers, and his enemies greved at it no lesse, then at the honour the cittizens selves dyd unto him. For his house was the common inne for all Lacedæmonians when they came to Athens, and they ever laye with him: moreover he had very well entertained the Lacadæmon prisoners that were taken at the forte of Pyle. And afterwards when peace was concluded betweene Lacedæmon and Athens, and their prisoners redelivered home againe by Nicias meanes only and procurement: they loved him more then ever they dyd before. This was blowen abroade through Greece, that Pericles had kindled the warres amongest them, and Nicias quenched it: so some called this peace Nicium, as one would saye, Nicias worke. But Alcibiades stomaking this, and envying Nicias glorie, determined to breake the peace whatsoever came of it. Wherefore to compasse this matter, knowing first of all that the Argives had no liking of the Lacedæmonians, but were their mortall enemies; and that they dyd but seeke matter to fall out with them: he secretly put them in hope of peace and league with the Athenians. Moreover he dyd persuade them to it, both by letters and worde of mouthe, speaking with the magistrates, and suche as had greatest authoritie and credit amongest the people: declaring unto them, that they should not feare the Lacedæmonians, nor yeld to them at all, but to sticke to the Athenians, who would sone repent them of the peace they had made, and

Nicias peace.

Alcibiades breaketh the peace of the Græcians.

breake it with them. Afterwardes when the Lacedæmonians had made league with the Bœotians, and had redelivered the cittie of Panactum to the Athenians, all defaced and spoyled, contrarie to the league: Alcibiades perceyving how the people were muche offended thereat, made them more earnest against them, and therewithall brought Nicias in disgrace with the people, and charged him with many matters of great likelyhood. As at that time, when he was generall: that he would never take any of the Lacedæmonians, when they were shut up within the Ile of Sphacteria, and muche lesse distresse them when he might: and moreover that when other had taken them prisoners by force, that he had founde the meanes to deliver them, and send them home againe, to gratifie the Lacedæmonians. Furthermore, that being their friende, he dyd not his duety to disswade the people from making of league offensive, and defensive with the Bœotians and the Corinthians: and againe also, if there were any people of Greece that had a desire to become friendes and allies with the Athenians, that he dyd the best he could to let them, if the Lacedæmonians had no liking of the matter. Now as Nicias was thus in disgrace with the people, for the causes above sayd: in the middest of this sturre, ambassadours came by chaunce from Lacedæmon to Athens, who at their comming gave very good wordes, saying they had full power and commission to compound all controversies, under reasonable and equall conditions. The Senate heard them, and receaved them very curteously, and the people the next daye should assemble in counsell to geve them audience: which Alcibiades fearing muche, he went to labour the ambassadours, and spake with them aparte in this sorte. What meane you, my Lordes of Sparta: doe ye not knowe that the Senate hath allwayes accustomed to be gracious and favorable unto those that sue unto them for any matter, and that the people contrarilie are of a prowde nature, and desirous to imbrace all great matters? If therefore at the first sight, ye doe geve them to understand that you are come hither with full power, to treate freely with them in all manner of causes: doe you not thinke that they make you stretche your authoritie farre, to graunte them all that they will demaunde. Therefore, my

Alcibiades beguileth the Lacedæmonians.

ALCIBIADES

Lordes ambassadours, if you looke for indifferencie at the Athenians handes, and that they shall not prease you to farre against your willes, to graunte them any thing of advantage: I would wishe you a litle to cover your full commission, and in open manner to propound certen articles, and reasonable capitulations of peace, not acquainting them otherwise with your full power to agree in all things: and for my parte, I will assure you of my good will in favour of the Lacedæmonians. When he had tolde them this tale, he gave them his faithfull promise, and vowed as it were to performe his worde. Hereupon Alcibiades turned the Ambassadours from the trust they reposed in Nicias, and wanne them on his side: in so muche as they gave credit to no man but to him, wondering muche at his great wisedome and readye wit, and they thought him a rare and notable man. The next morning the people were assembled to geve the ambassadours audience. They were sent for, and brought into the market place. There Alcibiades gently asked them, what was the cause of their comming. They aunswered: that they were come to treate of peace, but they had no power to determine any thing. Then beganne Alcibiades to be angrie with them, as if they had done him wrong, and not he any to them: calling them unfaithfull, unconstant, and fickle men, that were come neither to doe, nor saye any thing worth the hearing. The Senate also were offended with them, and the people rated them very roughely: whereat Nicias was so ashamed and amased withall, that he could not tell what to saye, to see so sodaine a chaunge, knowing nothing of Alcibiades malice and subtill practise with the ambassadours. So the ambassadours of Lacedæmon were dispatched, without any thing done, and Alcibiades chosen generall: who presently brought the Argives, the Elians, and the Mantinians in league with the Athenians. Though no man dyd commend this practise of his, in working it after this sorte: yet was it a marvelous thing of him to devise to put all Peloponnesus in armes, and to procure such a number of souldiers against the Lacedæmonians, as he dyd before the cittie of Mantinea, and to shifte of the miseries of warre and hazard of battell, so farre from Athens. Which if the Lacedæmonians dyd winne, could

Alcibiades chosen generall.

not profit them muche: and if they lost it, they could hardely save their cittie of Sparta. After this battell of Mantinea, the thousand men whom the cittie by an auncient order dyd keepe continually in paye, aswell in peace as in warre, within the cittie of Argos, thinking now oportunitie served them very trimly: attempted to take the soveraine authoritie from the common people, and to make them selves Lords of the cittie. And to bring this to passe, the Lacedæmonians comming in the meane time, dyd ayde them in their purpose, and so dyd put downe the government of the people: notwithstanding, immediatly after the people tooke armes againe, and became the stronger. Alcibiades comming thither even at that time, dyd warrant them the victorie, and to set up againe the authoritie of the people. Then he persuaded them to make their walles longer to joyne their cittie to the sea, to the ende they might more easely be ayded by sea, by the Athenians. He brought them also from Athens, many carpinters, masons, stone hewers, and other workemen: and to conclude, he shewed them by all the meanes and wayes he could, that he dyd beare good will unto them, and thereby wanne him selfe no lesse favour particularly emong them, then generally he dyd good unto his countrie. He dyd persuade also the cittizens of Patras to joyne their towne to the sea, by making long walles, which they built out even to the clyffes of the sea. And when one sayed unto them, Alas, poore people of Patras, what doe ye meane? the Athenians will eate you out. Alcibiades aunswered him, It maye well be, but it shalbe by litle and litle, beginning first at the feete: but the Lacedæmonians will devoure you all at once, and beginne at the head. Now although Alcibiades dyd make the cittie of Athens strong by sea, yet he dyd not leave to persuade the Athenians also, to make them selves strong by lande. For he dyd put the young men oftentimes in minde of the othe they were made to sweare in Agraulos, and dyd advise them to accomplishe it in deede. Which was, that they should take all corne fields, vines, and olyve trees, to be the borders and confines of Attica, whereby they were taught to reckon all lande theirs, that was manured, and dyd bring forth fruite. Yet with all these goodly dedes and fayer

The walles brought to the sea by the Argives.

Alcibiades ryot.

wordes of Alcibiades, and with this great corage and quicknes of understanding, he had many great faultes and imperfections. For he was to daintie in his fare, wantonly geven unto light women, riotous in bankets, vaine and womanishe in apparell: he ware ever a long purple gowne that swept the market place as he walked up and downe, it had suche a traine, and was to riche and costely for him to weare. And following these vaine pleasures and delightes, when he was in his galley, he caused the planckes of the poope thereof to be cutte and broken up, that he might lye the softer: for his bed was not layed apon the overloppe, but laye upon girthes strained over the hole, cut out and fastened to the sides, and he caried to the warres with him a gilded scutchion, wherein he had no cognizaunce nor ordinary devise of the Athenians, but only had the image of Cupide in it, holding lightning in his hande. The noble men, and best cittizens of Athens perceyving this, they hated his facions and conditions, and were muche offended at him, and were afeard withall of his rashnes and insolencie: he dyd so contemne the lawes and customes of their countrie, being manifest tokens of a man that aspired to be King, and would subvert and turne all over hand. And as for the good will of the common people towards him, the poet Aristophanes doth plainely expresse it in these wordes:

The people most desire, what most they hate to have:
and what their minde abhorres, even that they seeme to crave.

And in another place he sayed also, aggravating the suspition they had of him:

For state or common weale, muche better should it be,
to keepe within the countrie none suche lyons lookes as he.
But if they nedes will keepe, a lyon to their cost,
then must they nedes obeye his will, for he will rule the roste.

For to saye truely: his curtesies, his liberallities, and noble expences to shewe the people so great pleasure and pastime as nothing could be more: the glorious memorie of his auncesters, the grace of his eloquence, the beawtie of his persone, the strength and valliantnes of his bodie, joyned together with his wisedome and experience in marshall affayers: were the very causes that made them to beare with him in all things, and that the Athenians dyd paciently endure all his light partes, and dyd cover his faultes, with the best wordes and termes they could, calling them youthfull, and gentlemens sportes. As when he kept Agartharchus the painter prisoner in his house by force, untill he had painted all his walles within: and when he had done, dyd let him goe, and rewarded him very honestly for his paines. Againe when he gave a boxe of the eare to Taureas, who dyd paye the whole charges of a companie of common players, in spite of him, to carie awaye the honour of the games. Also when he tooke awaye a young woman of Melia by his authoritie, that was taken among certaine prisoners in the warres, and kept her for his concubine: by whom he had a childe, which he caused to be brought up. Which they called a worke of charitie, albeit afterwards they burdened him, that he was the only cause of murdering of the poore Melians, saving the litle children, bicause he had favored and persuaded that unnaturall and wicked decree, which another had propounded. Likewise where one Aristophon a painter, had painted a curtisan named Nemea, holding Alcibiades in her armes, and sitting in her lappe, which all the people ranne to see, and tooke great pleasure to behold it: the grave and auncient men, were angrie at these foolishe partes, accompting them impudent things, and done against all civill modestie and temperancie. Wherefore it seemed Archestratus words were spoken to good purpose, when he sayed, that Greece could not abide two Alcibiades at once. And on a daye as he came from the counsaill and assembly of the cittie, where he had made an excellent oration, to the great good liking and acceptation of all the hearers, and by meanes thereof had obteined the thing he desired, and was accompanied with a great traine that followed him to his honour: Timon, surnamed Misanthropus (as who would saye, Loup-garou, or the manhater) meeting Alcibiades thus accompanied, dyd not passe by him, nor gave him waye (as he was wont to doe to all other men) but went straight to him, and tooke him by the hande, and sayed: O, thou dost well my sonne, I can thee thancke, that thou goest on, and climest up still: for if

Alcibiades dishonestie and wantonnes.

Archestratus saying.

ever thou be in authoritie, woe be unto those that followe thee, for they are utterly undone. When they had heard these wordes, those that stoode by fell a laughing: other reviled Timon, other againe marked well his wordes, and thought of them many a time after, suche sundry opinions they had of him for the unconstancie of his life, and waywardnes of his nature and conditions. Now for the taking of Sicile, the Athenians dyd marvelosly covet it in Pericles life, but yet they dyd not medle withall, untill after his death: and then they dyd it at the first under culler of friendshippe, as ayding those citties which were oppressed, and spoyled by the Syracusans. This was in manner a plaine bridge made, to passe afterwardes a greater power and armie thither. Howbeit the only procurer of the Athenians, and persuader of them, to send small companies thither no more, but to enter with a great armie at once to conquer all the countrie together, was Alcibiades: who had so allured the people with his pleasaunt tongue, that upon his persuasion, they built castells in the ayer, and thought to doe greater wonders, by winning only of Sicilia. For where other dyd set their mindes apon the conquest of Sicile, being that they only hoped after: it was to Alcibiades, but a beginning of further enterprises. And where Nicias commonly in all his persuasions, dyd turne the Athenians from their purpose to make warres against the Syracusans, as being to great a matter for them to take the cittie of Syracusa: Alcibiades againe had a further reache in his head, to goe conquer Libya, and Carthage, and that being conquered, to passe from thence into Italie, and so to Peloponnesus: so that Sicilia should serve but to furnishe them with vittells, and to paye the souldiers for their conquestes which he had imagined. Thus the young men were incontinently caried awaye with a marvelous hope and opinion of this jorney, and gave good eare to olde mens tales that tolde them wonders of the countries: insomuche as there was no other pastime nor exercise among the youth in their meetings, but companies of men to set rounde together, drawe plattes of Sicile, and describe the situation of Libya and Carthage. And yet they saye, that neither Socrates the philosopher,

Alcibiades the author of the warres in Sicilia.

nor Meton the astronomer dyd ever hope to see any good successe of this jorney. For the one by the revealing of his familliar spirite, who tolde him all things to come, as was thought, had no great opinion of it: and Meton, whether it was for the feare of the successe of the jorney he had by reason, or that he knew by divination of his arte what would followe, he counterfeated the mad man, and holding a burning torche in his hand, made as though he would have set his house a fyer. Other saye, that he dyd not counterfeate, but like a mad man in deede dyd set his house a fyre one night, and that the next morning betimes he went into the market place to praye the people, that in consideration of his great losse and his grievous calamitie so late happened him, it would please them to discharge his sonne for going this voyage. So by this mad devise, he obteined his request of the people for his sonne, whom he abused much. But Nicias against his will was chosen captaine, to take charge of men in these warres: who misliked this jorney, aswell for his companion and associate in the charge of these warres, as for other misfortunes he foresawe therein. Howbeit the Athenians thought the warre would fall out well, if they dyd not commit it wholy to Alcibiades rashnes and hardines, but dyd joyne with him the wisedome of Nicias: and appointed Lamachus also for their third captaine, whom they sent thither, though he were waxen now somewhat olde, as one that had shewed him selfe no lesse venturous and hardie in some battells, then Alcibiades him selfe. Now when they came to resolve of the number of souldiers, the furniture and order of these warres, Nicias sought crookedly to thwart this jorney, and to breake it of altogether: but Alcibiades withstoode him, and gate the better hande of him. There was an orator called Demostratus, who moved the people also that the captaines whom they had chosen for these warres, might have full power and authoritie to leavy men at their discretion, and to make suche preparation as they thought good: whereunto the people condescended, and dyd authorise them. But when they were even readie to goe their waye, many signes of ill successe lighted in the necke one of another: and amongest the rest this was one.

The divination of Socrates and Meton.

ALCIBIADES

That they were commaunded to take shippe, on the daye of the celebration of the feast of Adonia, on the which the custome is, that women doe set up in divers places of the cittie, in the middest of the streates, images, like to dead corses which they carie to buriall, and they represent the mourning and lamentations made at the funeralles of the dead, with blubbering, and beating them selves, in token of the sorowe the goddesse Venus made, for the death of her friend Adonis. Moreover, the Hermes (which are the images of Mercurie, and were wont to be set up in every lane and streete) were found in a night all hacked and hewed, and mangled specially in their faces: but this put divers in great feare and trouble, yea even those that made no accompt of suche toyes. Whereupon it was alledged that it might be the Corinthians that dyd it, or procured that lewde acte to be done, favoring the Syracusans, who were their neere kynsemen, and had bene the first fownders of them, imagining upon this ill token, it might be a cause to breake of the enterprise, and to make the people repent them, that they had taken this warre in hande. Nevertheles, the people would not allow this excuse, neither hearken to their wordes that sayed, they should not reckon of any such signes or tokens, and that they were but some light brained youthes, that being tippled, had played this shamefull parte in their braverie or for sporte. But for all these reasons, they tooke these signes very grevously, and were in deede not a litle afeard, as thinking undoutedly that no man durst have bene so bolde to have done suche an abhominable facte, but that there was some conspiracie in the matter. Hereupon, they looked apon every suspition and conjecture that might be (how litle or unlikely soever it were) and that very severely: and both Senate and people also met in counsell upon it, very ofte, and in a fewe dayes. Now whilest they were busilie searching out the matter, Androcles a common counseller, and orator in the common wealth, brought before the counsell certaine slaves and straungers that dwelt in Athens: who deposed that Alcibiades, and other of his friends and companions, had hacked and mangled other images after that sorte, and in a mockerie had counter-

Images hewen and mangled at Athens.

feated also in a banket that he made, the ceremonies of the holy mysteries, declaring these matters particularly. How one Theodorus counterfeated the herauld, that is wonte to make the proclamations: Polytion the torche bearer, and Alcibiades the priest, who sheweth the holy signes and mysteries: and that his other companions were the assistantes, as those that make sute to be receyved into their religion and order, and into the brotherhood of their holy mysteries, whom for this cause they call Mystes. These very wordes are written in the accusation Thessalus (Cimons sonne) made against Alcibiades, charging him that he had wickedly mocked the two goddesses, Ceres, and Proserpina. Whereat the people being marvelously moved and offended, and the orator Androcles his mortall enemie aggravating and stirring them up the more against him: Alcibiades a litle at the first beganne to be amased at it. But afterwards, hearing that the mariners which were prepared for the voyage of Sicilia, and the souldiers also that were gathered, dyd beare him great good will, and specially how the ayde, and that bande that came from Argos, and Mantinea (being a thousand footemen, well armed and appointed) dyd saye openly, how it was for Alcibiades sake they dyd take upon them so long a voyage beyond sea, and that if they went about to doe him any hurte or wrong, they would presently returne home againe from whence they came: he beganne to be of a good corage againe, and determined with this good favorable oportunitie of time, to come before the counsell, to aunswer to all suche articles and accusations as should be layed against him. Thereupon his enemies were a litle cooled, fearing least the people in this judgement would have shewed him more favour, bicause they stoode in nede of him. Wherefore to prevent this daunger, they had fed other Oratours who set a good face on the matter, as they had bene Alcibiades friends, and yet bare him no lesse good will, then the ranckest enemies he had. These fine fellowes rose up in open assembly, and sayed: it was no reason, that he that was now chosen one of the generalles of so mightie and puissant an armie (being ready to hoyse sayle and the ayde also of their allies and friendes) should

Alcibiades accused for prophaning the holy mysteries.

The crafte of Alcibiades enemies.

be driven to staye now, and to lose time and occasion of well doing, whilest they should goe about to choose judges, and appointe him his howres and time of aunswer. Therefore, they sayed, it was fit he should take his jorney betimes, and when warres were done, that he should present him selfe to requier justice, and to purge him selfe of suche matters as should be objected against him. But Alcibiades smelling streight their fetche, and perceyving the practise of his staye, stept up, and declared how they dyd him great wrong, to make him departe with the charge of a generall of so great an armie, his minde being troubled with continuall feare of so grievous curses, as he should leave apon him: and that he deserved death, if he could not purge and justifie him selfe, of all the unjust and surmised accusations against him. And if he had once clered him selfe of all thinges, and had published his innocencie: he should then have nothing in his head to trouble him, nor to thinke upon, but to goe on lustely to fight with his enemies, and to cast behinde him the daunger of all his slaunderous detracters. But all this could not persuade them. And so he was presently commaunded in the behalfe of the people, to imbarke, and shippe awaye his men. Thus he was compelled to take the seas with his other companions, having in their navie about a hundred and forty gallyes, all having three owers to a bancke: and five thousand one hundred footemen very well armed and appointed, and throwers with slinges, archers, and other light armed men to the number of thirteene hundred, sufficiently furnished of all warlicke and necessarie munition. Now after they were arrived on the coaste of Italie, they landed in the cittie of Rhegio: where, holding counsell in what sorte they should direct these warres, it was resolved in the ende that they should goe straight unto Sicilia. This opinion was followed, although Nicias dyd contrarie it, when Lamachus gave his consent thereunto: and at his first comming, he was the occasion of winning the cittie of Catana. But he never after dyd any exployte, for he was called home immediatly by the Athenians, to come and aunswer certaine accusations layed to his charge. For as we tolde you before, there was at the beginning, certaine light suspitions and ac-

Alcibiades jorney into Sicile.

cusations put up against him, by some slaves and straungers. But afterwards when he was gone, his enemies enforced them, and burdened him more cruelly, adding to his former faulte, that he had broken the images of Mercurie: and had committed sacriledge in counterfeating in jeast and mockery the holy ceremonies of the mysteries: and blue into the eares of the people, that both the one and the other proceeded of one set conspiracie, to chaunge and alter the government of the state of the cittie. Upon these informations, the people tooke it in so ill parte, that they committed all to prisone, that were in any sorte accused or suspected thereof, and would never let them come to their aunswer: and moreover dyd much repent them that they had not condemned Alcibiades, upon so great complaintes and informations as were exhibited against him, while his offense was in question before them. And the furie and hatred of the people was such towards him, that if any of Alcibiades friends and acquaintance came within their daunger, they were the worse handled for his sake. Thucydides dyd not name his accusers, but some other doe name Dioclides and Teucer: amongest whom, Phrynicus the Comicall poet is one, who discovereth it in his verses, by bringing in one that speaketh thus to the image of Mercury:

ALCIBIADES

Phrynicus the Comicall poet.

My good friend Mercury, I praye thee take good heede,
that thou fall not, and breake thy necke: for so thou mightst me breede,
both daunger and distrust, and though I giltles be,
some Dioclides falsely might accuse and trouble me.

Mercury aunswereth:

Take thou no thought for me, my selfe I shall well save:
and will foresee full well therewith that Teucer (that false knave)
shall not the money get, which he by lawe hath wonne,
for his promowters bribing parte, and accusation.

And yet for all this, these tokens doe showe no certaintie of any thing. For one of them being asked, howe he could knowe them by their faces in the night, that had broken and defaced these images? he aunswered, that he knewe them well enough by the brightnes of the moone. And

ALCIBIADES

hereby it appeareth playnely that he was perjured, bicause that the same night, on the which this fact was committed, there was a conjunction of the moone. This dyd a litle trouble and staye men of judgement: howbeit the common sorte of people this notwithstanding, dyd not leave to be as sharpe set, to receyve all accusations and informations, that were brought in against him, as ever they were before. Now there was among the prisoners whose cause was hanging before them, the orator Andocides (whom Hellanicus the historiographer describeth to descend of the race of Ulysses) whom they tooke to be a man that hated the government of the common people, and bent altogether to favour the small number of the nobilitie. But one of the chiefest occasions why he was suspected to be one of them that had broken the images, was: for that hard by his house there was a fayer great image set up in olde time, by the familie or tribe of the Ægeides, and that alone amongest all the rest of so many famous images, was lefte whole and unbroken: whereupon it is called at this daye, the Mercury of Andocides, and is so called generally of every bodye, albeit the inscription sheweth the contrarie. Andocides being in prisone, chaunced to fall in acquaintaunce with one Timæus, with whom he was more familliar then with all the rest, who was also prisoner with him for the self cause. This Timæus was a man not so well knowen as he, but besides, a wise man, and very hardie. He persuaded him, and put into his head, that he should accuse him selfe, and certaine other with him: for taking the matter upon him, and confessing it, he should receyve grace and pardone, according to the course and promise of the lawe. Where contrarilie, if he should stande upon the curtesie of the judges sentence, he might easely endaunger him self: bicause judgements in such cases are uncertaine to all people, and most to be doubted and feared toward the riche. And therefore he told him it were his best waye, if he looked into the matter wisely, by lying to save his life, rather then to suffer death with shame, and to be condemned upon this false accusation. Also he sayed if he would have regarde to the common wealth, that it

Andocides the orator cast into prison.

should in like case be wisely done of him, to put in daunger a fewe of those (which stood doubtfull whether in trothe they were any of them or not) to save from the furie of the people, and terrour of death, many honest men, who in deede were innocent of this lewde fact. Timæus wordes and persuasions wrought such effect with Andocides, that they made him yeld unto them, and brought him to accuse him selfe, and certaine other with him: by meanes whereof Alcibiades according to the lawe had his pardone. But all suche as he named and accused, were every man put to death, saving suche as saved them selves by ronning awaye. Furthermore, to shadowe his accusation with some apparaunce of trothe, Andocides among those that were accused, dyd accuse also certen of his owne servaunts. Now though the people had no more occasion to occupie their busie heades about the breakers of these images, yet was not their malice thus appeased against Alcibiades, untill they sent the galley called Salaminiana, commaunding those they sent by a speciall commission to seeke him out, in no case to attempt to take him by force, nor to laye holde on him by violence: but to use him with all the good wordes and curteous manner that they possibly could, and to will him only to appeare in persone before the people, to aunswer to certaine accusations put up against him. If otherwise they should have used force, they feared muche least the armie would have mutined on his behalfe within the countrie of their enemies, and that there would have growen some sedition amongest their souldiers. This might Alcibiades have easely done, if he had bene disposed. For the souldiers were very sorie to see him departe, perceyving that the warres should be drawen out now in length, and be much prolonged under Nicias, seeing Alcibiades was taken from them, who was the only spurre that pricked Nicias forward to doe any service: and that Lamachus also, though he were a valliant man of his handes, yet he lacked honour and authoritie in the armie, bicause he was but a meane man borne, and poore besides. Now Alcibiades for a farewell, disapointed the Athenians of winning the cittie of Messina: for they having intelligence by certaine private persones within the cittie, that it

Alcibiades sent for to aunswer to his accusation.

would yeld up into their handes, Alcibiades knowing them very well by their names, bewrayed them unto those that were the Syracusans friendes: whereupon all this practise was broken utterly. Afterwards when he came to the cittie of Thuries, so sone as he had landed, he went and hid him selfe incontinently in suche sorte, that such as sought for him, could not finde him. Yet there was one that knewe him where he was, and sayed: Why, how now Alcibiades, darest thou not trust the justice of thy countrie? Yes very well (quoth he) and it were in another matter: but my life standing upon it, I would not trust mine own mother, fearing least negligently she should put in the blacke beane, where she should cast in the white. For by the first, condemnation of death was signified: and by the other, pardone of life. But afterwards, hearing that the Athenians for malice had condemned him to death: Well, quoth he, they shall knowe I am yet alive. Now the manner of his accusation and inditement framed against him, was found written in this sorte: Thessalus the sonne of Cimon, of the village of Laciades, hath accused, and doth accuse Alcibiades, the sonne of Clinias, of the village of Scambonides, to have offended against the goddesses, Ceres and Proserpina, counterfeating in mockery their holy mysteries, and shewing them to his familliar friends in his house, him selfe apparrelled and arrayed in a long vestement or cope, like unto the vestement the priest weareth when he sheweth these holy sacred mysteries: and naming him selfe the priest, Polytion the torche bearer, and Theodorus of the village of Phygea the verger, and the other lookers on, brethern, and fellowe scorners with them, and all done in manifest contempt and derision, of holy ceremonies and mysteries of the Eumolpides, the religious priests and ministers of the sacred temple of the cittie of Eleusin. So Alcibiades for his contempt and not appearing, was condemned, and his goodes confiscate. Besides this condemnation, they decreed also, that all the religious priestes and women should banne and accurse him. But hereunto aunswered, one of the Nunnes called Theano, the daughter of Menon, of the village of Agraula, saying: that she was professed religious, to praye and to blesse, not

Alcibiades accusation.

Alcibiades condemned being absent.

to curse and banne. After this most grievous sentence and condemnation passed against him, Alcibiades departed out of the cittie of Thuries, and went into the countrie of Peloponnesus, where he continued a good season in the cittie of Argos. But in the ende fearing his enemies, and having no hope to returne againe to his owne countrie with any safety: he sent unto Sparta to have safe conduct and licence of the Lacedæmonians, that he might come and dwell in their countrie, promising them he would doe them more good being now their friend, then he ever dyd them hurte, while he was their enemie. The Lacedæmonians graunted his request, and receyved him very willingly into their cittie: where even upon his first comming, he dyd three things. The first was: That the Lacedæmonians by his persuasion and procurement, dyd determine speedily to send ayde to the Syracusans, whom they had long before delayed: and so they sent Gylippus their captaine, to overthrowe the Athenians armie, which they had sent thither. The second thing he did for them, was: That he made them of Greece to beginne warre apon the Athenians. The third, and greatest matter of importance, was: That he dyd counsell them to fortifie the cittie of Decelea, which was within the territories of Attica selfe: which consumed, and brought the power of the Athenians lower, then any other thing whatsoever he could have done. And if he were welcome, and well esteemed in Sparta, for the service he dyd to the common wealth: muche more he wanne the love and good willes of private men, for that he lived after the Laconian manner. So as they that sawe his skinne scraped to the fleshe, and sawe him washe him selfe in cold water, and howe he dyd eate browne bread, and suppe of their blacke brothe: would have doubted (or to saye better, never have beleeved) that suche a man had ever kept cooke in his house, nor that he ever had seene so muche as a perfuming panne, or had touched clothe of tissue made at Miletum. For among other qualities and properties he had (wherof he was full) this as they saye was one, whereby he most robbed mens hartes: that he could frame altogether with their manners and facions of life, transforming him selfe more easely to all

Alcibiades flyeth to Sparta.

Alcibiades more chaungeable then the camelion.

manner of shapes, then the Camelion. For it is reported, that the Camelion cannot take white culler: but Alcibiades could put apon him any manners, customes or facions, of what nation soever, and could followe, exercise, and counterfeate them when he would, aswell the good as the bad. For in Sparta, he was very paynefull, and in continuall exercise: he lived sparingly with litle, and led a straight life. In Ionia, to the contrary: there he lived daintely and superfluously, and gave him self to all mirthe and pleasure. In Thracia, he dranke ever, or was allwayes a horse backe. If he came to Tissaphernes, lieutenaunt of the mightie king of Persia: he farre exceeded the magnificence of Persia in pompe and sumptuousnes. And these things notwithstanding, never altered his naturall condition from one facion to another, neither dyd his manners (to saye truely) receyve all sortes of chaunges. But bicause peradventure, if he had shewed his naturall disposition, he might in divers places where he came, have offended those whose companie he kept, he dyd with such a viser and cloke disguise him selfe, to fit their manners, whom he companied with, by transforming him selfe into their naturall countenaunce. As he that had seene him when he was at Sparta, to have looked apon the outward man, would have sayed as the common proverbe sayeth:

It is not the sonne of Achilles, but Achilles selfe:

Even so it is even he, whom Lycurgus brought up. But he that had inwardly seene his naturall doings, and good will in deede lye naked before him: would have sayed contrarilie, as they saye commonly in another language:

This woman is no chaungeling.

For he entertained Queene Timæa, King Agis wife of Sparta, so well in his absence, he being abroade in the warres: that he got her with childe, and she her selfe denied it not. For she being brought a bed of a sonne, who was named Leotychides, openly to the world called him by that name: but when she was amongest her familliars and very friends, she called him sofetly Alcibiades, she was so farre in love with him. And Alcibiades jeasting out the matter, sayed he had done it for no hurte, nor for any lust of fleshe to satisfie

Alcibiades got Timæa, king Agis wife with childe.

his desire: but only to leave of his race, to reigne amongest the Lacedæmonians. This matter was brought by divers unto king Agis eares, who at the length beleeved it: but specially when he beganne to make a reckoning of the time, how long it was sence he laye with his wife. For lying with his wife one night when there was a terrible earthquake, he ranne out of his chamber for feare the house would fall on his head: so that it was tenne moneths after ere he laye again with her. Whereupon, her sonne Leotychides being borne at the ende of tenne moneths, he sayed he was none of his: and this was the cause that Leotychides dyd not succede afterwards in the Kingdome, bicause he was not of the bloude royall. After the utter overthrowe of the Athenians in Sicilia, those of the Iles of Chio and Lesbos, with the Cyzicenians, dyd send all about a tenne ambassadours to Sparta: to let the Lacedæmonians understand, they had good will to leave the Athenians, so they would send them ayde to defend them. The Bœotians favored those of Lesbos: Pharnabazus, the king of Persiaes lieutenaunt, favored the Cyzicenians. This notwithstanding, the Lacedæmonians were better affected to helpe those of Chio first, by the persuasion of Alcibiades, who tooke their matters in hande. And he tooke sea him self and went into Asia, where he almost turned the countrie of Ionia against the Athenians: and keeping allwayes with the generalles of the Lacedæmonians, he dyd muche hurte the Athenians. Yet notwithstanding, king Agis dyd beare him ill will, partely for the injurie he dyd him in dishonoring and defiling his wife, and partely also, for that he envied his glorie: bicause the rumour ranne about, that the most parte of the goodly exploytes of these warres dyd happen well, by Alcibiades meanes. Other also of the greatest authoritie among the Spartans, that were most ambitious emong them, beganne in their mindes to be angrie with Alcibiades, for the envie they bare him: who were of so great power, that they procured their governours to write their letters to their captaines in the field, to kill him. Alcibiades hearing of this, dyd no whit desist to doe all he could for the benefit of the Lacedæmonians: yet he had an eye behind him, flying all occasions to fall into their handes. So in the

Leotychides Alcibiades bastarde.

The Lacedæmonians practise to kill Alcibiades.

Alcibiades flying the Lacedæmonians goeth to Tisaphernes.

ende, for more suerty of his persone, he went unto Tisaphernes, one of the king of Persiaes lieutenantes, with whom he wanne incontinently suche credit, that he was the first and chiefest persone he had about him. For this barbarous man being no simple persone, but rather malicious, and subtill of nature, and that loved fine and crafty men: dyd wonder how he could so easely turne from one manner of living to another, and also at his quicke witte and understanding. Moreover, his company and manner to passe the time awaye, was commonly marvelous full of mirthe and pleasure, and he had suche pleasaunt comely devises with him, that no man was of so sullen a nature, but he would make him merie, nor so churlishe, but he would make him gentle. So that both those that feared him, and also envied him: they were yet glad to see him, and it did them good to be in his companie, and use talke with him. In so muche as this Tisaphernes (that otherwise was a churlishe man, and naturally hated the Grecians) dyd geve him selfe so muche unto Alcibiades flatteries, and they pleased him so well: that he him selfe dyd studie to flatter Alcibiades againe, and make muche of him. For he called Alcibiades his fayer house of pleasure, and goodly prospect: notwithstanding he had many goodly gardens, sweete springes, grene arbours and pleasaunt meadowes, and those in all royall and magnificent manner. Alcibiades despairing utterly to finde any safetie or friendshippe emong the Spartans, and fearing on thother side king Agis also: he beganne to speake ill of them, and to disgrace all that they dyd, to Tisaphernes. By this practise he stayed Tisaphernes from ayding them so friendly as he might: moreover, he dyd not utterly destroye the Athenians. For he persuaded him that he should furnishe the Lacedæmonians but with litle money, to let them diminishe and consume by litle and litle: to the ende that after one had troubled and weakned the other, they both at the length should be the easier for the King to overcome. This barbarous man dyd easely consent to this devise. All the world then sawe he loved Alcibiades, and esteemed of him very muche: in so muche as he was sought to, and regarded of all handes of the Grecians. Then were the

Alcibiades called a pleasaunt place and goodly prospect.

Athenians sorie, and repented them when they had receyved so great losse and hurte, for that they had decreed so severely against Alcibiades, who in like manner was very sorowfull, to see them brought to so harde termes, fearing, if the cittie of Athens came to destruction, that he him selfe should fall in the ende into the handes of the Lacedæmonians, who maliced him to the death. Now about that time, all the power of the Athenians were almost in the Ile of Samos, from whence with their armie by sea, they sought to suppresse the rebelles that were up against them, and to keepe all that which yet remained. For they were yet pretily strong to resist their enemies, at the least by sea: but they stoode in great feare of the power of Tisaphernes, and of the hundred and fiftie gallyes which were reported to be comming out of the countrie of Phenicia, to the ayde of their enemies, which if they had come, the cittie of Athens had bene utterly spoyled, and for ever without hope of recovery. The which Alcibiades understanding, sent secretly unto the chiefest men that were in the armie of the Athenians at Samos, to geve them hope he would make Tisaphernes their friende: howbeit not of any desire he had to gratifie the people, nor that he trusted to the communaltie of Athens, but only to the honorable, and honest cittizens, and that conditionally so as they had the harte and corage, to bridell a litle the over licentiousnes and insolencie of the common people, and that they would take upon them the authoritie to governe, and to redresse their state, and to preserve the cittie of Athens, from finall and utter destruction. Upon this advertisement, all the heades and chief men dyd geve very good eare unto it: saving only Phrynichus, one of the captaines, and of the towne of Dirades. Who mistrusting (that was true in deede) that Alcibiades cared not which ende went forward, nor who had the chief government of Athens, the nobilitie, or the communaltie, and dyd but seeke all the devises and wayes he could, to returne againe if it might be possible, in any manner of sorte, and that he dyd but currie favour with the Nobilitie, blaming and accusing the people: he stoode altogether against the motion, whereupon Alcibiades devise was not followed.

The inconstancie of the common people.

And having now shewed him selfe open enemie to Alcibiades, he dyd secretly advertise Astiochus then admirall to the Lacedæmonians, of Alcibiades practise, and warned him to take heede of him, and to laye him up safe, as a double dealer, and one that had intelligence with both sides: but he understoode not how it was but one traitour to speake to another. For this Astiochus was a follower of Tisaphernes for his private commoditie: and perceyving Alcibiades in suche credit with him, he dyd discover to Alcibiades all that Phrynichus had advertised him. Alcibiades straight sent men of purpose to Samos, unto the captains there, to accuse Phrynichus of the treason he had revealed against them. Those of the counsaill there, receyving this intelligence: were highly offended with Phrynichus. So, he seeing no better waye to save him selfe for making of this faulte, went about to make amends with committing a worse faulte. Thereupon he sent againe to Astiochus, complaining muche he had disclosed him: and yet nevertheles he promised him, if he would keepe his counsaill, that he would deliver the whole fleete and armie of the Athenians into his handes. Howbeit this treason of Phrynichus dyd the Athenians no hurte at all, by reason of Astiochus counter treason: for he dyd let Alcibiades againe understand what offer Phrynichus had made him. Phrynichus looking to be charged with this againe, the second time before the counsell, by meanes of Alcibiades: dyd first advertise the chief of the armie of the Athenians: That their enemies would come and set upon them, and where, and howe: and gave them therefore warning to keepe neere their shippes, to make a strong watche, and to fortifie them selves with all speede, the which forthwith they dyd. And as they were about it, there came other letters from Alcibiades, by the which he dyd warne them againe to take heede of Phrynichus, bicause he had practised againe with their enemies, to deliver the whole armie of Athens into their handes. But they gave no credit to his second letters: for they thought that he knowing the preparations and mindes of the enemies, would serve his own turne with the false accusing of Phrynichus. Notwithstanding this, there was some falsehood in fellowshippe:

for one Hermon, openly in the market place, stabbed Phrynichus in with a dagger, and killed him. The facte being pleaded in lawe, and throughly considered of: the dead bodie by the sentence of the people was condemned for a traitour: and Hermon the murtherer, and his fellowes, were crowned in recompence of their facte they had done to kill a traitour to the common wealth. Wherefore those that were Alcibiades friends, being at that time the stronger, and greatest men of the counsell in the armie at Samos: they sent one Pisander to Athens, to attempt to alter the government, and to encorage the noble men to take upon them the authoritie, and to plucke it from the people: assuring them that Tisaphernes would give them ayde to doe it, by meanes of Alcibiades, who would make him their friende. This was the culler and cloke wherewith they served their turnes, that dyd chaunge the government of Athens, and that brought it into the handes of a small number of nobilitie: for they were in all but foure hundred, and yet they called them selves five thousand. But so sone as they felt them selves strong, and that they had the whole authoritie of government, without contradiction in their handes: they made then no more reckoning of Alcibiades, and so they made warres more coldly and slackly then before. Partely bicause they mistrusted their cittizens, who founde the chaunge of government very strange: and partely also bicause they were of opinion that the Lacedæmonians (who at all times dyd most favour the government of Nobilitie) would be better inclined to make peace with them. Now the common people that remained still in the cittie, sturred not, but were quiet against their willes, for feare of daunger, bicause there were many of them slaine, that boldely tooke apon them in open presence to resist these foure hundred. But those that were in the campe, in the Ile of Samos, hearing these newes, were so grievously offended: that they resolved to returne incontinently againe, unto the haven of Piræa. First of all, they sent for Alcibiades, whom they chose their captaine: then they commaunded him straightly to leade them against these tyrantes, who had usurped the libertie of the people of Athens. But nevertheles he dyd

The murder of Phrynichus and his condemnation.

Alcibiades called home from exile.

not therein, as another would have done in this case, seeing him selfe so sodainely crept againe in favour with the common people: for he dyd not thinke he should incontinently please and gratifie them in all things, though they had made him now their generall over all their shippes and so great an armie, being before but a banished man, a vacabond, and a fugitive. But to the contrarie, as it became a generall worthie of suche a charge, he considered with him selfe, that it was his parte wisely to staye those, who would in a rage and furie carelesly cast them selves awaye, and not suffer them to doe it. And truely Alcibiades was the cause of the preserving of the cittie of Athens at that time, from utter destruction. For if they had sodainly (according to their determination) departed from Samos to goe to Athens: the enemies finding no man to let them, might easely have wonne all the countrie of Ionia, of Hellespont, and of all the other Iles without stroke striking, whilest the Athenians were busie fighting one against another in civill warres, and within the compasse of their owne walles. This Alcibiades alone, and no other, dyd prevent, not only by persuading the whole armie, and declaring the inconvenience thereof, which would fall out apon their sodaine departure: but also by intreating some particularly aparte, and keeping a number backe by very force. To bring this about, one Thrasibulus of the towne of Stira, dyd helpe him muche: who went through the armie, and cried out apon them that were bent to enterprise this jorney. For he had the biggest and lowdest voyce as they saye, of any man that was in all the cittie of Athens. This was a notable acte, and a great pece of service done by Alcibiades: that he promised five hundred saile of the Phenicians (which the Lacedæmonians assuredly looked for, in their ayde from the king of Persia) should not come at all, or els if they came, it should be in the favour of the Athenians. For he departed immediatly, and went with great speede to Tisaphernes: whom he handled in suche sorte, that he brought not the shippes that laye at rode before the cittie of Aspenda, and so he brake promise with the Lacedæmonians. Therefore Alcibiades was marvelously blamed and accused, both of the one and the other side, to have altered Tisaphernes minde,

Thrasibulus a man of the biggest voyce of all the Athenians.

but chiefly of the Lacedæmonians: who sayed that he had persuaded this barbarous captaine, he should neither ayde the one nor the other, but rather to suffer them one to devoure and destroye eache other. For it had bene out of doubt, if this great fleete and navy of the Kings had come, to joyne their force with either partie: that they had taken from the one of them, the signiorie and domination of the sea. Shortely after, the foure hundred noble men that had usurped the authoritie and government of Athens, were utterly driven awaye and overthrowen, by meanes of the friendly ayde, and assistaunce that Alcibiades friends gave those that tooke the peoples parte. So the cittizens were very well pleased with Alcibiades, in so muche as they sent for him to returne when he thought good. But he judging with him selfe it would be no honour nor grace unto him to returne without some well deserving, and before he had done some greater exployte, as only upon the peoples favour and good will, whereas otherwise his returne might be both glorious and triumphant: departed first from Samos with a small number of gallyes, and went sailing up and downe the Iles of Cos and of Gnidos. There he was advertised, that Mindarus, the admirall of the Lacedæmonians, was gone with all his fleete unto the straight of Hellespont, and that the captaines of the Athenians gave chase unto him. Thereupon he went also and sayled thither with speede, to ayde the Athenians: and by very good fortune came with eighteene gallyes even at the very instant, when they were both in the middest of their fight, with all their shippes before the cittie of Abydos. The battell was cruelly foughten betwene them from morning till night, both the one and the other having the better in one parte of the battell, and the worst in another place. Now at the first discoverie of Alcibiades comming, both partes had in deede contrarie imaginations of him. For the enemies tooke harte unto them: and the Athenians beganne to be afeard. But Alcibiades set up straight his flagge in the toppe of the galley of his admirall, to shewe what he was. Wherewithall, he set upon the Peloponnesians that had the better, and had certen gallyes of the Athenians in chase: whereupon the Peloponnesians gave over their chase, and fled. But Alci-

The cittizens of Athens sent for Alcibiades to return.

Battell by sea before the cittie of Abydos, betweene the Athenians and Lacedæmonians.

Alcibiades victorie of the Lacedæmonians by sea.

biades followed them so lustely, that he ranne divers of them a ground, and brake their shippes, and slue a great number of men that lept into the sea, in hope to save them selves by swimming a lande. So notwithstanding that Pharnabazus was come thither to ayde the Lacedæmonians, and dyd his best indevour to save their gallyes by the sea shore: yet the Athenians in the end wanne thirtie gallyes of their enemies, and saved all their owne, and so dyd set up certaine flagges of triumphe and victorie. Alcibiades having now happely gotten this glorious victorie, would nedes goe shewe him selfe in triumphe unto Tisaphernes. So having prepared to present him with goodly riche presents, and appointed also a convenient traine and number of sayle mete for a generall, he tooke his course directly to him. But he found not that entertainment he hoped for. For Tisaphernes standing in great hazard of displeasure, and feare of punishment at the Kings handes, having long time before bene defamed by the Lacedæmonians, who had complained of him, that he dyd not fulfill the Kings commaundement, thought that Alcibiades was arrived in very happy hower: whereupon he kept him prisoner in the cittie of Sardis, supposing the wrong he had done, would by this meanes easely discharge, and purge him to the King. Yet at the ende of thirtie dayes, Alcibiades by fortune got a horse, and stealing from his keepers, fled unto the cittie of Clazomenes: and this dyd more increase the suspition they had of Tisaphernes, bicause they thought that under hand he had wrought his libertie. Alcibiades toke then sea again, and went to seeke out the armie of the Athenians. Which when he had founde, and heard newes that Mindarus and Pharnabazus were together in the cittie of Cizicum: he made an oration to his souldiers, and declared unto them how it was very requisite they should fight with their enemies, both by sea and by lande, and moreover that they should assault them within their fortes and castells, bicause otherwise they could have no money to defraye their charges. His oration ended, he made them immediatly hoyse sayle, and so to goe lye at anker in the Ile of Proconesus: where he tooke order that they should keepe in all the pinnases and brigantines emong the shippes of warre, that the

Alcibiades taken prisoner at Sardis, flyeth from Tisaphernes.

enemie might have no manner of intelligence of his comming. The great showers of rayne also, with thunder and darke weather that fell out sodainely upon it, dyd greatly further him in his attempt and enterprise: in so muche as not only his enemies, but the Athenians that were there before, knewe nothing of his comming. So some made their reckoning, that they could doe litle or nothing all that daye: yet he made them sodainely imbarke, and hoyse sayle. They were no sooner in the mayne sea, but they discried a farre of the gallyes of their enemies, which laye at rode before the haven of Cyzicum. And fearing least the great number of his fleete would make them flye, and take lande before he could come to them: he commaunded certaine captaines to staye behinde, and to rowe softely after him, and him selfe with fortie gallyes with him, went towards the enemies to provoke them to fight. The enemies supposing there had bene no more shippes, then those that were in sight: dyd set out presently to fight with them. They were no sooner joyned together, but Alcibiades shippes that came behinde, were also descried: the enemies were so afeard thereat, that they cast about, and fled straight. Alcibiades leaving his fleete, followed the chase with twentie of the best gallyes he had, and drave them a lande. Thereupon he landed also, and pursued them so corageously at their heeles, that he slue a great number of them on the mayne lande, who thought by flying to have saved them selves. Moreover, Mindarus, and Pharnabazus, being come out of the cittie to rescue their people, were overthrowen both. He slue Mindarus in the field, fighting valliantly: as for Pharnabazus, he cowardly fled away. So the Athenians spoyled the dead bodies (which were a great number) of a great deale of armour and riches, and tooke besides all their enemies shippes. After they tooke the cittie of Cizycum, Pharnabazus having left it. Then the Peloponnesians being slaine, they had not only the possession of the whole countrie of Hellespont, which they kept: but they drave their enemies by force, out of all partes of the sea. There were at that time certaine letters intercepted, whereby a secretarie gave advertissement unto the Ephori at Sparta, of the overthrowe in this sorte: All is

Alcibiades victorie at Cyzicum.

ALCIBIADES

lost, Mindarus is slaine, our people dye for hunger, and we knowe not what to doe. Now the souldiers of Athens that had bene at this jorney and overthrowe, grewe to suche a pryde and reputation of them selves, that they would not, and disdained also to serve with the other souldiers that had bene beaten many times, and went away with the worse. Where they to the contrarie had never bene overcome, as a litle before it happened, that the captaine Thrasyllus had bene overthrowen by the cittie of Ephesus. And for this overthrowe, the Ephesians had set up a triumphe, and token of brasse, to the utter shame and ignominie of the Athenians. For the which Alcibiades souldiers did very muche rebuke Thrasyllus men, and dyd exceedingly extoll their captaine and them selves, and would neither encampe with them, neither have to doe with them, nor yet keepe them companie. Untill suche time as Pharnabazus came with a great armie against them, aswell of footemen as horsemen, when they ranne a foraging upon the Abydenians: and then Alcibiades went to the rescue of them, and gave Pharnabazus battell, and overthrewe him once againe, and dyd together with Thrasyllus chase him even untill darke night. Then both Alcibiades and Thrasyllus souldiers dyd companie together, one rejoycing with another: and so returned all with great joye into one campe. The next morning Alcibiades set up a triumphe for the victorie he had the daye before, and then went to spoyle and destroye Pharnabazus countrie, where he was governour, and no man durst once come out to meete him. In this rode there were taken prisoners, certaine priestes and Nunnes of the countrie: but Alcibiades freely delivered them afterwards without ransome. And preparing to make warres against the Chalcedonians, who were revolted from the Athenians, and had receyved a garrison and governour of the Lacedæmonians into their cittie: he was advertissed that they had brought in all their goods and cattells out of the fieldes, and had delivered them to the safe custodie of the Bithynians, who were their neighbours and friends. Hereupon he led his armie into their borders, and sent a herauld before to summone the Bithynians, to make amends for the wrong they had done the

Athenians. The Bithynians fearing least Alcibiades would set apon them, dyd straight deliver him the goodes they had as afore in their custodie, and moreover, made a league with the Athenians besides. That done, he went and layed seige to the cittie of Chalcedon, the which he environned all about from the one side of the sea to the other. Pharnabazus came thither, thincking to have raised the seige. And Hippocrates, a captain of the Lacedæmonians, that was governour of the cittie, assembled all the force he was able to make within the same, and made a salye out also upon the Athenians at the very same time. Whereupon Alcibiades putting his men in order of battell, so as they might geve a charge upon them both at one instant: he fought so valliantly, that he forced Pharnabazus to runne his waye with shame enough, and slue Hippocrates in the field, with a great number of his men. Then tooke he the seas againe, to goe towardes the countrie of Hellespont, to get some money, where upon the sodaine he did take the cittie of Selybrea: bicause he valliantly put him selfe in hazard before the time appointed him. For certain of his friends within, with whom he had secret practise, had geven him a token, that when time served, they would shewe a burning torche in the ayer at midnight: but they were compelled to shew this fyer in the ayer before they were readie, for feare least one of their confederacie would bewraye the matter, who sodainly repented him. Now this torche burning in the ayer, was set up before Alcibiades was readie with his companie. But he perceyving the signe set, tooke about thirtie men with him in his companie, and ranne with them to the walles of the cittie, having commaunded the rest of his armie to followe him with all speede possible. The gate was opened to him, and to his thirtie men: besides them there followed twentie other light armed men. Howbeit they were no soner entered the cittie, but they heard the cittizens armed come against them: so that there was no hope to scape, if he dyd tarie their comming. Nevertheles, considering that untill that present time he was never overcome in battell, where he had taken charge, it greved him very muche to flye: wherefore it straight came in his head t

Alcibiades victorie at Chalcedonia.

Alcibiades tooke the cittie of Selybrea.

The present wit of Alcibiades.

make silence by sound of trumpet, and after silence made, he caused one of them that were about him to make proclamation with a lowde voyce, that the Selybrianians should not take armes against the Athenians. This cooled them a litle that would fayne have bene doing, bicause they supposed that all the armie of the Athenians had bene already in the cittie: the other on the contrarie side, were very glad to talke of peace, without any further daunger. And as they beganne to parle upon composition, the rest of Alcibiades armie was come on. Now he thincking in deede (which was true) that the Selybrianians sought nothing but peace, and fearing least the Thracians which were many in number (and came with good will to serve him in that jorney) would sacke and spoyle the cittie, he made them all to goe out againe: and so concluding peace with the chiefe of the Selybrianians, he dyd them no more hurte, apon their humble submission, but made them paye him a summe of money, and so leaving a garrison of the Athenians within the cittie, he departed thence. Whilest Alcibiades was in treatie with the Selybrianians, the other Athenian captaines that laye at the siege of Chalcedon, made an agreement with Pharnabazus, that he should geve them a summe of money, and give up the towne into the Athenians handes, to enjoye it as they had before. And with expresse condition also, that the Athenians should make no rodes into Pharnabazus dominions, to hurte or spoyle any of his: and likewise should be bounde to geve good safe conduyte unto the ambassadours of the Athenians, to goe and come safe from time to time, to the king of Persia. The other captaines being sworn to this peace, Pharnabazus conditioned also, that Alcibiades at his returne should likewise be sworne to the peace and conditions thereof. But Alcibiades sayed, he would not be sworne at all, unles Pharnabazus were first sworne for his parte. Thus when othes were taken of either side, Alcibiades went also against those of Byzantium, who in like case had rebelled against the Athenians. At his first comming thither, he environned the cittie round about with a walle. Afterwards he practised with two secret friends of his, Anaxilaus, and Lycurgus, and certen other within the

The Chalcedonians receyve the Athenians.

cittie, who promised him to deliver it into his handes, so they might be assured he would doe them no hurte. To culler this practise, he gave it out, that he must nedes leave the siege, and departe with speede, for certain newes that were come out of Ionia: and thereupon he imbarked presently, and went out of the haven at none dayes with all his shippes, howbeit he returned again the same night. And going a lande with the choycest and best armed men he had, he approched the walles of the cittie, without any manner of noyse, having left order with them that remained in the shippes, that in the meane season they should rowe with all force into the haven, with as great cries and showtes as might be, to feare and trouble the enemies: partely to feare the Bizantines the more with their sodaine comming among them, and partely that his confederates within the cittie, might with better oportunitie receyve him and his companie, into the towne with the more assured safety, whilest every man ranne to the haven, to resist them that were upon the gallyes. Nevertheles they went not away unfought with. For those that laye in garrison within the cittie, some of them Peloponnesians, other Bœotians, and other Megarians, dyd so valliantly repulse them that came out of their gallyes, that they drave them to retire abord againe. Afterwardes hearing how the Athenians were entred: the cittie on thother side, they put them selves in battell raye, and went to mete them. The battell was terrible of both partes: but Alcibiades in the ende obtained victorie, leading the right winge of his battell, and Theramenes the lefte. The victorie being gotten, he tooke 300 of his enemies prisoners, who had escaped the furie of the battell. But after the battell, there was not a Byzantine put to death, neither banished, nor his good confiscated: bicause it was capitulated by Alcibiades with his confederats, that neither he, nor his, should hurt any of the Bizantines either in persone or goodes, nor any way should rifle them. And Anaxilaus being afterwards accused of treason in Lacedæmon, for this practise: he aunswered, and justified him self in suche sorte, that they could not finde he had committed the faulte layed unto his charge. For he sayed, that he was no Lacedæmonian, but a Byzantine: and that

Alcibiades stratageame at Bizantium.

Alcibiades winneth Bizantium.

he sawe not Lacedæmon in daunger, but Byzantium, which the enemies had compassed about with a walle they had built, that it was unpossible to bring any thing into the cittie. Moreover he alleaged, that they having very smal store of corne within the cittie (as was true in dede) the Peloponnesians, and Bœotians, that laye there in garrison dyd eate it up, while the poore Byzantines them selves, their wives and children, dyed for very hunger. Therefore it could not be sayed of him, that he had betrayed his countrie, but rather that he had delivered it from the miseries and calamities the warres brought upon it: wherein he had followed the example of the honestest men of Lacedæmon, who dyd acknowledge nothing honest and juste, but that which was necessarie and profitable for their countrie. The Lacedæmonians hearing his reasons he alleaged for his purgation, were ashamed to condemne him, and therefore they let him goe. Now Alcibiades desirous in the ende to see his native countrie againe (or to speake more truely, that his contry men should see him) after he had so many times overthrowen their enemies in battell: he hoysed saile, and directed his course towardes Athens, bringing with him all the gallyes of the Athenians richely furnished, and decked all about, with skutchines and targettes, and other armour and weapon gotten amongest the spoyles of his enemies. Moreover, he brought with him many other shippes, which he had wonne and broken in the warres, besides many ensignes and other ornaments: all which being compted together one with the other, made up the number of two hundred shippes. Furthermore, where Duris Samian writeth (who challengeth that he came of his house) that at his returne one Chrysogonus, an excellent player of the flute (that had wonne certaine of the Pythian games) dyd playe suche a note, that at the sounde thereof the galley slaves would keepe stroke with their owers, and that Callipides another excellent player of tragedies, playing the parte of a comedie, dyd sturre them to rowe, being in suche players garments as every master of suche science useth commonly to weare, presenting him selfe in Theater or stage before the people to shewe his arte: and that the admirall galley wherein him self was, entred the

Alcibiades honorable returne into his countrie.

haven with a purple saile, as if some maske had come into a mans house after some great banket made: neither Ephorus, nor Theopompus, nor Xenophon, make any mention of this at all. Furthermore, me thinkes it should not be true, that he returning from exile after so long a banishment, and having passed over such sorowes and calamities as he had susteined, would so prowdly and presumptuously shewe him selfe unto the Athenians. But merely contrarie, it is most certain, that he returned in great feare and doubt. For when he was arrived in the haven of Piræa, he would not set foote a lande, before he first sawe his nephewe Eury-ptolemus, and divers other of his friendes from the hatches of his shippe, standing apon the sandes in the haven mouthe. Who were come thither to receyve and welcome him, and tolde him that he might be bolde to lande, without feare of any thing. He was no soner landed, but all the people ranne out of every corner to see him, with so great love and affection, that they tooke no heede of the other captaines that came with him, but clustred all to him only, and cried out for joye to see him. Those that could come neere him, dyd welcome and imbrace him: but all the people wholy followed him. And some that came to him, put garlands of flowers upon his head: and those that could not come neere him, sawe him a farre of, and the olde folkes dyd pointe him out to the yonger sorte. But this common joye was mingled notwithstanding, with teares and sorowe, when they came to thinke upon their former misfortunes and calamities, and to compare them with their present prosperitie: waying with them selves also how they had not lost Sicilia, nor their hope in all things els had failed them, if they had delivered them selves and the charge of their armie into Alcibiades hands, when they sent for him to appeare in persone before them. Considering also how he found the cittie of Athens in manner put from their seigniorie and commandement on the sea, and on the other side how their force by lande was brought unto such extremitie, that Athens scantly could defend her suburbes, the cittie self being so devided and turmoiled with civill dissention: yet he gathered together those fewe, and small force that remained, and had now not only restored

ALCIBIADES

Athens to her former power and soveraintie on the sea, but had made her also a conquerer by lande. Now the decree for his repaire home againe, was past before by the people, at the instant request of Callias, the sonne of Callæschrus, who dyd preferre it: as he him selfe dyd testifie in his elegies, putting Alcibiades in remembraunce of the good turne he had done him, saying:

I was the first that moved in open conference,
  the peoples voyce to call thee home, when thou wert banisht hence.
So was I eke the first, which thereto gave consent,
  and therefore maye I boldly saye, by truthe of suche intent:
I was the only meane, to call thee home againe,
  by suche request so rightly made, to move the peoples vayne.
And this maye serve for pledge, what friendshippe I thee beare:
  fast sealed with a faithfull tongue, as plainely shall appeare.

But notwithstanding, the people being assembled all in counsaill, Alcibiades came before them, and made an oration: wherein he first lamented all his mishappes, and founde him selfe grieved a litle with the wronges they had offred him, yet he imputed all in the ende to his cursed fortune, and some spightfull god that envied his glorie and prosperitie. Then he dilated at large the great hope their enemies had to have advantage of them: and therewithall persuaded the people to be of good corage, and afeard of nothing that was to come. And to conclude, the people crowned him with crownes of golde, and chose him generall againe of Athens, with soveraine power and authoritie both by lande as by sea. And at that very instant it was decreed by the people, that he should be restored againe to all his goodes, and that the priestes Eumolpides should absolve him of all their curses, and that the herauldes should with open proclamation revoke the execrations and cursinges they had thundered out against him before, by commaundement of the people. Whereto they all agreed, and were very willing, saving Theodorus the bishoppe, who sayed: I dyd neither excommunicate him, nor curse him, if he hath done no hurte to the common wealth. Now Alcibiades florished in his chiefest prosperitie, yet were there some notwithstanding that misliked very muche the time of his landing: saying it was very unluckie and unfor-

Alcibiades oration to the people.

Alcibiades chosen generall with soveraine authoritie.

tunate. For the very daye of his returne and arrivall, fell out by chaunce on the feast which they call Plynteria, as you would saye, the washing daye, which they celebrate in honour of Minerva: on the which daye, the priestes that they call Praxiergides, doe make certen secret and hidden sacrifices and ceremonies, being the five and twenty daye of the moneth of September, and doe take from the image of this goddesse, all her rayment and juells, and keepe the image close covered over. Hereupon the Athenians doe ascribe that daye, for a most unfortunate daye, and are very circumspect to doe any matter of importance on it. Moreover, it was commonly scanned abroade of every bodye, that it seemed the goddesse was not content, nor glad of Alcibiades returne: and that she dyd hide her selfe, bicause she would not see him, nor have him come neere her. Notwithstanding all these toyes and ceremonies, when Alcibiades found every thing fall out well at his returne, and as he would have wished it: he armed a hundred gallyes presently, to returne againe to the warres. Howbeit he wisely regarded the time and solemnitie of celebration of these mysteries, and considerately stayed untill they had finished all. And it fell out, that after the Lacedæmonians had taken and fortified the cittie of Decelea, within the territorie of Attica, and that the enemies being the stronger in the field, dyd keepe the waye going from Athens to Eleusin, so as by no possible meanes they could make their solemne procession by lande, with suche honour and devotion as they were before accustomed to doe: and thereby all the sacrifices, dawnces, and many other holy devowte ceremonies they were wonte to doe by the waye, in singing the holy songe of Iacchus, came of very necessitie to be left of, and cleane layed a side. Then Alcibiades thought he should doe a meritorious dede to the godds, and an acceptable to men, to bring the olde ceremonies up againe upon the said feast: and thereupon purposed to accompanie the procession, and defend it by power, against all invasion and disturbaunce by the enemies. As one that foresawe one of those two things would come to passe. Either that Agis king of the Lacedæmonians would not sturre at all against the sacred ceremonies, and by this

Plynteria

Alcibiades restored the olde ceremonies.

meanes should much imbase and diminishe his reputation and glorie: or if he dyd come out to the field, that he would make the battell very gratefull to the goddes, considering it should be in defence of their most holy feast and worshippe, and in the sight of his countrie, where the people should see and witnesse both, his valliantnes, and also his corage. Alcibiades being fully resolved upon this procession, went and made the priestes Eumolpides, their vergers, and other their ministers and officers of these mysteries, privie to his determination. Then he sent out skowtes to watche on the side of the hilles thereabouts, and to viewe the waye of their perambulation. The next morning very early he sent out light horsemen also to scowre the countrie. Then he made the priestes, the professed, and all the ministers of religion, goe in procession, together with those that followed the same: and he him selfe compassed them about with his armie on every side, marching in battell raye, and very good order, and with great silence. This was an honorable and devoute leading of an armie, and suche as if his greatest enemies would confesse a trothe, they could not but saye, Alcibiades had as muche shewed the office of a highe bishoppe, as of a noble souldier and good captaine. So he ended this procession, returning to Athens in all safe order againe, and not an enemie that durst once looke out into the field to set upon him. Now this dyd more increase the greatnes of his minde, and therewith the peoples good opinion of his sufficiencie, and wise conduction of an armie: in so much as they thought him unvincible, having the soveraine power and authoritie of a generall. Furthermore, he spake so fayer to the poore people, and meaner sorte, that they chiefly wished and desired he would take upon him like a King: yea, and many went to him to persuade him in it, as though he should thereby withstand all envie, and drive awaye the lawes and customes of trying of matters by the voyces of the people, and all suche fond devises, as dyd destroye the state of the common weale. And furthermore, they sayed it was very needefull that he alone should take upon him the whole rule and government of the cittie, that he might dispose all things according to his will, and not stande in feare of slaunderous and wicked tongues. Now, whether Alcibiades ever had any minde to usurpe the Kingdome, the matter is somewhat doubtfull. But this is certaine, the greatest men of the cittie, fearing least in deede he ment some suche thing, dyd hasten his departure as sone as they could possible, doing all other things according to his minde: and dyd assigne him suche associates in his charge of generall, as he him selfe best liked. So in the ende, he departed with a fleete of a hundred gallyes, and first of all he fell with the Ile of Andros, where he overcame by fight, the inhabitantes of the said Ile, and certaine Lacedæmonians that were amongest them: but he tooke not the cittie, which was one of the first matters his enemies dyd accuse him for. For if ever man was overthrowen and envied, for the estimation they had of his vallure and sufficiency, truely Alcibiades was the man. For the notable and sundry services he had done, wanne him suche estimation of wisedome and valliantnes, that where he slacked in any service whatsoever, he was presently suspected, judging the ill successe not in that he could not, but for that he would not: and that where he undertooke any enterprise, nothing could withstand or lye in his waye. Hereupon the people persuading them selves, that immediatly after his departure, they should heare that the Ile of Chio was taken, with all the countrie of Ionia: they were angrie they could have no newes so sodainely from him as they looked for. Moreover, they dyd not consider the lacke of money he had, and specially making warre with suche enemies, as were ever relieved with the great king of Persiaes ayde, and that for necessities sake he was sundrie times driven to leave his campe, to seeke money where he could get it, to paye his souldiers, and to mainteine his armie. Now for testimony hereof, the last accusation that was against him, was only for this matter. Lysander being sent by the Lacedæmonians for admirall and generall of their armie by sea, used suche policie with Cyrus, the king of Persiaes brother, that he got into his handes a great some of money: by meanes whereof he gave unto his mariners foure oboles a daye for their wages, where before they were

Alcibiades second jorney.

Lacke of money, the occasion of the overthrowe of the Athenians armie by sea.

wont to have but three, and yet Alcibiades had muche a doe to furnishe his with three only a daye. For this cause, to get money, Alcibiades sailed into Caria. But in the meane time Antiochus, whom Alcibiades had left his lieutenaunt behind him, and had geven him charge of all the shippes in his absence, being a very skilfull sea man, but otherwise a hastie harebraynd foole, and of small capacitie: he being expressely commaunded by Alcibiades not to fight in any case, though the enemies offred him battell, was so foolishe rashe, and made so litle reckoning of his straight commaundement, that he armed his owne gallye, whereof him selfe was captaine, and another besides, and went to the cittie of Ephesus, passing all alonge his enemies gallyes, reviling and offering villany to those that stoode apon the hatches of their gallyes. Lysander being marvelously provoked by those wordes, went and encountered him at the first with a fewe shippes. The other captaines of the gallyes of the Athenians, seeing Antiochus in daunger, went to ayde him, one after another. Then Lysander of his parte also set out all his whole fleete against him, and in the end overcame them, Antiochus self was killed in the conflict, and many gallyes and men were taken prisoners: wherefore Lysander set up shewes of triumphe in token of victorie. Alcibiades hearing these ill favored newes, returned presently with all possible speede to Samos: and when he came thither, he went with all the rest of his fleete to offer Lysander battell. But Lysander quietly contenting him selfe with his first victorie: went not out against him. Now this victorie was no soner wonne, but one Thrasybulus the sonne of Thrason, Alcibiades enemie, went incontinently from the campe, and got him to Athens, to accuse Alcibiades to the people: whom he informed how all went to wracke, and that he had lost many shippes, for that he regarded not his charge, carelesly putting men in truste, whom he gave to great credit to, bicause they were good fellowes, and would drincke droncke with him, and were full of mariners mockes and knavishe jeastes, such as they use commonly amongest them selves. And that he in the meane time tooke his pleasure abroade, here, and

Antiochus rashnes, procured his owne death, and the overthrowe of the Athenians armie.

Lysander beinggenerall of the Lacedæmonians, overcame the Athenians.

Alcibiades accused again by Thrasybulus.

there, scraping money together where he could come by it, keeping good cheere, and feasting of the Abydenian and Ionian courtisans, when the enemies armie was so neere theirs as it was. Moreover, they layed to his charge, that he dyd fortifie a castell in the countrie of Thracia, neere unto the cittie of Bisanthe, for a place to retire him selfe unto, either bicause he could not, or rather that he would not, live any lenger in his owne countrie. Upon those accusations, the Athenians geving over credit to the reporte: dyd immediatly choose newe captaines, and thereby declared their misliking. Alcibiades hearing of this, and fearing least they would doe him some worse harme, dyd leave straight the Athenians campe, and gathering a certaine number of straungers together, went of him selfe to make warre apon certaine free people of the Thracians, who were subject to no prince nor state: where he got a marvelous masse of money together, by meanes whereof he dyd assure the Græcians inhabiting those marches, from all invasion of forreine enemies. Now Tydeus, Menander, and Adimanthus the Athenians captaines, being afterwards in a place commonly called the goates river, with all the gallyes the cittie of Athens had at that time apon that coast: used every morning commonly to goe to the sea, to offer battell to Lysander, who rode at an ancker before the cittie of Lampsacus, with all the Lacedæmonians armie by sea, and commonly returned againe to the place from whence they came, in very ill order, without either watche or warde, as men that were careles of their enemies. Alcibiades being on the lande not farre of, and finding their great faulte and negligence: tooke his horse, and went to them, and told them that they laye on an ill shore, where there was no good rode, nor towne, and where they were driven to seeke their vittells, as farre as to the cittie of Sestos, and that they suffered their mariners to leave their shippes, and goe a lande when they laye at ancker, straggling up and downe the countrie as they would them selves, without regarde that there laye a great armie of their enemies before them, readie to be set out at their generalles commaundement: and therefore he advised them to remove thence, and to goe cast ancker before the cittie of Sestos. How-

Alcibiades put from his authoritie of generall.

Lysander rode at ancker before Lampsacus.

The Athenians regarded not Alcibiades good counsell.

ALCIBIADES

beit the captaines would not be advised by him: and that which was worst of all, Tydeus, one of the captaines, stowtely commaunded him to get him awaye, as one that had nothing to doe with the matter, and that other had charge of the armie. Whereupon Alcibiades fearing they would purpose some treason against him, dyd departe presently from them. And as he went his waye, he sayed to some of his friendes which accompanied him out of the campe at his returne: that if the captaines of the Athenians had not bene so rounde with him, he would have forced the Lacedæmonians to have come to the battell in despight of their beardes, or els he would have driven them to forsake their shippes. Some tooke this for a glorious bragge: other thought he was like enough to have done it, bicause he could have brought from lande a great number of Thracians, both archers and horsemen, with whom he might have geven a charge upon the Lacedæmonians, and done great mischief unto their campe. But now, how wisely Alcibiades dyd foresee the faultes he tolde the Athenians captaines of: their great misfortune and losse that followed incontinently, did to plainely witnesse it to the worlde. For Lysander came so fiercely apon them on a sodaine, that of all the shippes they had in their whole fleete, only eight gallyes were saved, with whom Conon fled: and the other being not much lesse then two hundred in number, were every one of them taken and caried awaye, with three thousand prisoners whom Lysander put to death. Shortely after, he tooke the cittie self of Athens, and rased their long walles even to the ground. After this great and notable victorie, Alcibiades fearing sore the Lacedæmonians, who then without let or interruption of any, were only Lords and Princes by sea and by lande: he went into the countrie of Bithynia, and caused great good to be brought after him, and tooke a marvelous summe of money with him, besides great riches he left also in the castells of Thracia, where he dyd remaine before. Howbeit he lost much of his goodes in Bithynia, which certaine Thracians dwelling in that countrie had robbed him of, and taken from him. So he determined to repaire forthwith unto king Artaxerxes, hoping that when the King had once

The Athenians overcome by Lysander.

Athens taken by Lysander.

Alcibiades flieth into the countrie of Bithynia.

proved him, he should finde him a man of no lesse service, then he had found Themistocles before him: besides that the occasion of his going thither, should be muche juster then his was. For he dyd not goe thither, to make warre against the cittie of Athens and his countrie, as Themistocles did: but of a contrarie intent, to make intercession to the King, that it would please him to ayde them. Now Alcibiades thinking he could use no better meane, then Pharnabazus helpe only, to see him safely conducted to the Kings courte: he proposed his jorney to him, into the countrie of Phrygia, where he abode a certaine time to attend upon him, and was very honorably entertained and receyved of Pharnabazus. All this while the Athenians founde them selves desolate, and in miserable state to see their empire lost: but then much more, when Lysander had taken all their liberties, and dyd set thirtie governours over their cittie. Now to late, after all was lost (where they might have recovered againe, if they had been wise) they beganne together to bewaile and lament their miseries and wretched state, looking backe apon all their wilfull faultes and follies committed: emong which, they dyd reckon their second time of falling out with Alcibiades, was their greatest faulte. So they banished him only of malice and displeasure, not for any offense him selfe in persone had committed against them, saving that his lieutenaunt in his absence had shamefully lost a fewe of their shippes: and they them selves more shamefully had driven out of their cittie, the noblest souldier, and most skilfull captaine that they had. And yet they had some litle poore hope lefte, that they were not altogether cast awaye, so long as Alcibiades lived, and had his health. For before, when he was a forsaken man, and led a banished life: yet he could not live idely, and doe nothing. Wherefore now much more, sayed they to them selves: if there be any helpe at all, he will not suffer out of doubt the insolencie and pryde of the Lacedæmonians, nor yet abyde the cruelties and outrages of these thirtie tyrauntes. And surely the common people had some reason to have these thoughts in their heades, considering that the thirtie governours them selves dyd what they could possiblie to spye out Alcibiades doinges, and

Lysander appointed 30 tyrannes over the cittizens of Athens.

To late repentaunce of the Athenians.

what he went about. In so muche as Critias at the last, declared to Lysander, that so long the Lacedæmonians might reckon them selves Lordes over all Greece, as they kept from the common people the rule and authoritie of the cittie of Athens. And further he added, that notwithstanding the people of Athens could well awaye to live like subjects under the government of a fewe: yet Alcibiades whilest he lived, would never suffer them so to be reigned over, but would attempt by all devise he could to bring a chaunge and innovation emong them. Yet Lysander would not credit these persuasions, before speciall commandement was sent to him from the Senate of Lacedæmon, upon his allegiaunce, that he should devise to kill Alcibiades by all meanes he could procure: either bicause in trothe they feared the subtiltie of his wit, and the greatnes of his corage, to enterprise matters of great weight and daunger, or els that they sought to gratifie king Agis by it. Lysander being thus straightly commaunded, dyd send and practise incontinently with Pharnabazus to execute the facte: who gave his brother Magæus, and his uncle Susamithres, commission to attempt the matter. Now was Alcibiades in a certen village of Phrygia, with a concubine of his called Timandra. So he thought he dreamed one night that he had put on his concubines apparell, and how she dandling him in her armes, had dressed his head, friseling his heare, and painted his face, as he had bene a woman. Other saye, that he thought Magæus strake his head, and made his bodie to be burnt: and the voyce goeth, this vision was but a litle before his death. Those that were sent to kill him, durst not enter the house where he was, but set it a fire round about. Alcibiades spying the fire, got suche apparell and hanginges as he had, and threwe it on the fire, thincking to have put it out: and so casting his cloke about his left arme, tooke his naked sworde in his other hande, and ranne out of the house, him selfe not once touched with fyer, saving his clothes were a litle singed. These murderers so sone as they spied him, drewe backe, and stoode a sonder, and durst not one of them come neere him, to stande and fight with him: but a farre of, they bestowed so many arrowes and dartes

The Lacedæmonians will Lysander to kill Alcibiades.

Alcibiades dreame in Phrygia before his death.

Alcibiades death.

of him, that they killed him there. Now when they had left him, Timandra went and tooke his bodie which she wrapped up in the best linnen she had, and buried him as honorably as she could possible, with suche things as she had, and could get together. Some holde opinion that Lais, the only famous curtisan, which they saye was of Corinthe (though in deede she was borne in a litle towne of Sicilia, called Hyccara, where she was taken) was his doughter. Notwithstanding, touching the death of Alcibiades, there are some that agree to all the rest I have written, saving that they saye, it was neither Pharnabazus, nor Lysander, nor the Lacedæmonians, which caused him to be slaine: but that he keeping with him a young gentlewoman of a noble house, whom he had stolen awaye, and intised to follie; her brethern to revenge this injurie, went to set fire upon the house where he was, and that they killed him as we have tolde you, thinking to leape out of the fyre.

Timandra the curtisan buried Alcibiades.

Lais a curtisan of Corinthe.

THE ENDE OF ALCIBIADES LIFE

THE LIFE OF CAIUS MARTIUS CORIOLANUS

THE house of the Martians at Rome was of the number of the Patricians, out of the which hath sprong many noble personages: whereof Ancus Martius was one, king Numaes daughters sonne, who was king of Rome after Tullus Hostilius. Of the same house were Publius, and Quintus, who brought Rome their best water they had by conducts. Censorinus also came of that familie, that was so surnamed, bicause the people had chosen him Censor twise. Through whose persuasion they made a lawe, that no man from thenceforth might require, or enjoye the Censorshippe twise. Caius Martius, whose life we intend now to

The familie of the Martians.

Publius and Quintus Martius, brought the water by conducts to Rome.

Censorinus lawe.

CORIOLANUS

write, being left an orphan by his father, was brought up under his mother a widowe, who taught us by experience, that orphanage bringeth many discommodities to a childe, but doth not hinder him to become an honest man, and to excell in vertue above the common sorte: as they are meanely borne, wrongfully doe complayne, that it is the occasion of their casting awaye, for that no man in their youth taketh any care of them to see them well brought up, and taught that were meete. This man also is a good proofe to confirme some mens opinions. That a rare and excellent witte untaught, doth bring forth many good and evill things together: like as a fat soile bringeth forth herbes and weedes that lieth unmanured. For this Martius naturall wit and great harte dyd marvelously sturre up his corage, to doe and attempt notable actes. But on the other side for lacke of education, he was so chollericke and impacient, that he would yeld to no living creature: which made him churlishe, uncivill, and altogether unfit for any mans conversation. Yet men marveling much at his constancy, that he was never overcome with pleasure, nor money, and howe he would endure easely all manner of paynes and travailles: thereupon they well liked and commended his stowtnes and temperancie. But for all that, they could not be acquainted with him, as one cittizen useth to be with another in the cittie. His behaviour was so unpleasaunt to them, by reason of a certaine insolent and sterne manner he had, which bicause it was to lordly, was disliked. And to saye truely, the greatest benefit that learning bringeth men unto, is this: that it teacheth men that be rude and rough of nature, by compasse and rule of reason, to be civill and curteous, and to like better the meane state, then the higher. Now in those dayes, valliantnes was honoured in Rome above all other vertues: which they called *Virtus*, by the name of vertue selfe, as including in that generall name, all other speciall vertues besides. So that *Virtus* in the Latin, was asmuche as valliantnes. But Martius being more inclined to the warres, then any other gentleman of his time: beganne from his Childehood to geve him self to handle weapons, and daylie dyd exercise him selfe therein. And

Coriolanus wit.

The benefit of learning.

What this worde Virtus signifieth.

outward he esteemed armour to no purpose, unles one were naturally armed within. Moreover he dyd so exercise his bodie to hardnes, and all kynde of activitie, that he was very swift in ronning, strong in wrestling, and mightie in griping, so that no man could ever cast him. In so much as those that would trye masteries with him for strength and nimblenes, would saye when they were overcome: that all was by reason of his naturall strength, and hardnes of warde, that never yelded to any payne or toyle he tooke apon him. The first time he went to the warres, being but a strippling, was when Tarquine surnamed the prowde (that had bene king of Rome, and was driven out for his pride, after many attemptes made by sundrie battells to come in againe, wherein he was ever overcome) dyd come to Rome with all the ayde of the Latines, and many other people of Italie: even as it were to set up his whole rest apon a battell by them, who with a great and mightie armie had undertaken to put him into his Kingdome againe, not so much to pleasure him, as to overthrowe the power of the Romaines, whose greatnes they both feared and envied. In this battell, wherein were many hotte and sharpe encounters of either partie, Martius valliantly fought in the sight of the Dictator: and a Romaine souldier being throwen to the ground even hard by him, Martius straight bestrid him, and slue the enemie with his owne handes that had before overthrowen the Romaine. Hereupon, after the battell was wonne, the Dictator dyd not forget so noble an acte, and therefore first of all he crowned Martius with a garland of oken boughs. For whosoever saveth the life a Romaine, it is a manner among them, to honour him with such a garland. This was, either bicause the lawe dyd this honour to the oke, in favour of the Arcadians, who by the oracle of Apollo were in very olde time called eaters of akornes; or els bicause the souldiers might easely in every place come by oken boughes: or lastely, bicause they thought it very necessarie to geve him that had saved a cittizens life, a crowne of this tree to honour him, being properly dedicated unto Iupiter, the patron and protectour of their citties, and thought amongest other wilde trees to bring forth a profitable fruite,

Coriolanus first going to the warres.

Coriolanus crowned with a garland of oken boughes.

CORIO-
LANUS

The goodnes of the oke.

and of plantes to be the strongest. Moreover, men at the first beginning dyd use akornes for their bread, and honie for their drincke: and further, the oke dyd feede their beastes, and geve them birdes, by taking glue from the okes, with the which they made birdlime to catche seely birdes. They saye that Castor, and Pollux, appeared in this battell, and how incontinently after the battell, men sawe them in the market place at Rome, all their horses being on a white fome: and they were the first that brought newes of the victorie, even in the same place, where remaineth at this present a temple built in the honour of them neere unto the fountaine. And this is the cause, why the daye of this victorie (which was the fiftenth of Iulye) is consecrated yet to this daye unto Castor and Pollux. Moreover it is daylie seene, that honour and reputation lighting on young men before their time, and before they have no great corage by nature: the desire to winne more, dieth straight in them, which easely happeneth, the same having no deepe roote in them before. Where contrariwise, the first honour that valliant mindes doe come unto, doth quicken up their appetite, hasting them forward as with force of winde, to enterprise things of highe deserving praise. For they esteeme, not to receave reward for service done, but rather take it for a remembraunce and encoragement, to make them doe better in time to come: and be ashamed also to cast their honour at their heeles, not seeking to increase it still by like deserte of worthie valliant dedes. This desire being bred in Martius, he strained still to passe him selfe in manlines: and being desirous to shewe a daylie increase of his valliantnes, his noble service dyd still advaunce his fame, bringing in spoyles apon spoyles from the enemie. Whereupon, the captaines that came afterwards (for envie of them that went before) dyd contend who should most honour him, and who should beare most honorable testimonie of his valliantnes. In so much the Romaines having many warres and battells in those dayes, Coriolanus was at them all: and there was not a battell fought, from whence he returned not without some rewarde of honour. And as for other, the only respect that made them valliant, was they hoped

To soden honor in youth killeth further desier of fame.

Coriolanus noble endevour to continue well deserving.

to have honour: but touching Martius, the only thing that made him to love honour, was the joye he sawe his mother dyd take of him. For he thought nothing made him so happie and honorable, as that his mother might heare every bodie praise and commend him, that she might allwayes see him returne with a crowne upon his head, and that she might still embrace him with teares ronning downe her cheekes for joye. Which desire they saye Epaminondas dyd avowe, and confesse to have bene in him: as to thinke him selfe a most happie and blessed man, that his father and mother in their life time had seene the victorie he wanne in the plaine of Leuctres. Now as for Epaminondas, he had this good happe, to have his father and mother living, to be partakers of his joye and prosperitie. But Martius thinking all due to his mother, that had bene also due to his father if he had lived: dyd not only content him selfe to rejoyce and honour her, but at her desire tooke a wife also, by whom he had two children, and yet never left his mothers house therefore. Now he being growen to great credit and authoritie in Rome for his valliantnes, it fortuned there grewe sedition in the cittie, bicause the Senate dyd favour the riche against the people, who dyd complaine of the sore oppression of userers, of whom they borowed money. For those that had litle, were yet spoyled of that litle they had by their creditours, for lacke of abilitie to paye the userie: who offered their goodes to be solde, to them that would geve most. And suche as had nothing left, their bodies were layed holde of, and they were made their bonde men, notwithstanding all the woundes and cuttes they shewed, which they had receyved in many battells, fighting for defence of their countrie and common wealth: of the which, the last warre they made, was against the Sabynes, wherein they fought apon the promise the riche men had made them, that from thenceforth they would intreate them more gently, and also upon the worde of Marcus Valerius chief of the Senate, who by authoritie of the counsell, and in the behalfe of the riche, sayed they should performe that they had promised. But after that they had faithfully served in this last battell of all, where they overcame their enemies, seeing

Coriolanus and Epaminondas did both place their desire of honour alike.

The obedience of Coriolanus to his mother.

Extremitie of userers complained of at Rome by the people.

Counsellers promises make men valliant, in hope of just performance.

they were never a whit the better, nor more gently intreated, and that the Senate would geve no eare to them, but make as though they had forgotten their former promise, and suffered them to be made slaves and bonde men to their creditours, and besides, to be turned out of all that ever they had: they fell then even to flat rebellion and mutine, and to sturre up daungerous tumultes within the cittie. The Romaines enemies hearing of this rebellion, dyd straight enter the territories of Rome with a marvelous great power, spoyling and burning all as they came. Whereupon the Senate immediatly made open proclamation by sounde of trumpet, that all those which were of lawfull age to carie weapon, should come and enter their names into the muster masters booke, to goe to the warres: but no man obeyed their commaundement. Whereupon their chief magistrates, and many of the Senate, beganne to be of divers opinions emong them selves. For some thought it was reason, they should somewhat yeld to the poore peoples request, and that they should a litle qualifie the severitie of the lawe. Other held hard against that opinion, and that was Martius for one. For he alleaged, that the creditours losing their money they had lent, was not the worst thing that was thereby: but that the lenitie that was favored, was a beginning of disobedience, and that the prowde attempt of the communaltie, was to abolish lawe, and to bring all to confusion. Therefore he sayed, if the Senate were wise, they should betimes prevent, and quenche this ill favored and worse ment beginning. The Senate met many dayes in consultation about it: but in the end they concluded nothing. The poore common people seeing no redresse, gathered them selves one daye together, and one encorag-ing another, they all forsooke the cittie, and encamped them selves upon a hill, called at this daye the holy hill, alongest the river of Tyber, offering no creature any hurte or violence, or making any shewe of actuall rebellion: saving that they cried as they went up and down, that the riche men had driven them out of the cittie, and that all Italie through they should finde ayer, water, and ground to burie them in. Moreover, they sayed, to dwell at Rome was

Ingratitude, and good service unrewarded, provoketh rebellion.

Martius Coriolanus against the people.

The people leave the cittie and doe goe to the holy hill.

nothing els but to be slaine, or hurte with continuall warres, and fighting for defence of the riche mens goodes. The Senate being afeard of their departure, dyd send unto them certaine of the pleasauntest olde men, and the most acceptable to the people among them. Of those, Menenius Agrippa was he, who was sent for chief man of the message from the Senate. He, after many good persuasions and gentle requestes made to the people, on the behalfe of the Senate: knit up his oration in the ende, with a notable tale, in this manner. That on a time all the members of mans bodie, dyd rebell against the bellie, complaining of it, that it only remained in the middest of the bodie, without doing any thing, neither dyd beare any labour to the maintenaunce of the rest: whereas all other partes and members dyd labour paynefully, and was very carefull to satisfie the appetites and desiers of the bodie. And so the bellie, all this notwithstanding, laughed at their follie, and sayed: It is true, I first receyve all meates that norishe mans bodie: but afterwardes I send it againe to the norishement of other partes of the same. Even so (quoth he) O you, my masters, and cittizens of Rome: the reason is a like betweene the Senate, and you. For matters being well digested, and their counsells throughly examined, touching the benefit of the common wealth: the Senatours are cause of the common commoditie that commeth unto every one of you. These persuasions pacified the people, conditionally, that the Senate would graunte there should be yerely chosen five magistrates, which they now call *Tribuni Plebis*, whose office should be to defend the poore people from violence and oppression. So Iunius Brutus, and Sicinius Vellutus, were the first Tribunes of the people that were chosen, who had only bene the causers and procurers of this sedition. Hereupon the cittie being growen againe to good quiet and unitie, the people immediatly went to the warres, shewing that they had a good will to doe better then ever they dyd, and to be very willing to obey the magistrates in that they would commaund, concerning the warres. Martius also, though it liked him nothing to see the greatnes of the people thus increased, considering it was to the prejudice, and imbasing

An excellent tale tolde by Menenius Agrippa to pacifie the people.

The first beginning of *Tribuni plebis.*

Iunius Brutus, Sicinius Vellutus, the 2 first tribunes.

of the nobilitie, and also sawe that other noble Patricians were troubled as well as him selfe: he dyd persuade the Patricians, to shew them selves no lesse forward and willing to fight for their countrie, then the common people were: and to let them knowe by their dedes and actes, that they dyd not so muche passe the people in power and riches, as they dyd exceede them in true nobilitie and valliantnes. In the countrie of the Volsces, against whom the Romaines made warre at that time, there was a principall cittie and of most fame, that was called Corioles, before the which the Consul Cominius dyd laye seige. Wherefore all the other Volsces fearing least that cittie should be taken by assault, they came from all partes of the countrie to save it, entending to geve the Romaines battell before the cittie, and to geve an onset on them in two severall places. The Consul Cominius understanding this, devided his armie also in two partes, and taking the one parte with him selfe, he marched towards them that were drawing to the cittie, out of the countrie: and the other parte of his armie he left in the campe with Titus Lartius (one of the valliantest men the Romaines had at that time) to resist those that would make any salye out of the cittie apon them. So the Coriolans making small accompt of them that laye in campe before the cittie, made a salye out apon them, in the which at the first the Coriolans had the better, and drave the Romaines backe againe into the trenches of their campe. But Martius being there at that time, ronning out of the campe with a fewe men with him, he slue the first enemies he met withall, and made the rest of them staye upon a sodaine, crying out to the Romaines that had turned their backes, and calling them againe to fight with a lowde voyce. For he was even such another, as Cato would have a souldier and a captaine to be: not only terrible, and fierce to laye about him, but to make the enemie afeard with the sounde of his voyce, and grimnes of his countenaunce. Then there flocked about him immediatly, a great number of Romaines: whereat the enemies were so afeard, that they gave backe presently. But Martius not staying so, dyd chase and followe them to their owne gates, that fled for life. And there, perceyving

The cittie of Corioles besieged by the Consul Cominius.

Titus Lartius, a valliant Romaine.

The propertie of a souldier.

that the Romaines retired backe, for the great number of dartes and arrowes which flewe about their eares from the walles of the cittie, and that there was not one man amongest them that durst venter him selfe to followe the flying enemies into the cittie, for that it was full of men of warre, very well armed, and appointed: he dyd encorage his fellowes with wordes and dedes, crying out to them, that fortune had opened the gates of the cittie, more for the followers, then the flyers. But all this notwithstanding, fewe had the hartes to followe him. Howbeit Martius being in the throng emong the enemies, thrust him selfe into the gates of the cittie, and entred the same emong them that fled, without that any one of them durst at the first turne their face upon him, or els offer to staye him. But he looking about him, and seeing he was entred the cittie with very fewe men to helpe him, and perceyving he was environned by his enemies that gathered round about to set apon him: dyd things then as it is written, wonderfull and incredible, aswell for the force of his hande, as also for the agillitie of his bodie, and with a wonderfull corage and valliantnes, he made a lane through the middest of them, and overthrewe also those he layed at: that some he made ronne to the furthest parte of the cittie, and other for feare he made yeld them selves, and to let fall their weapons before him. By this meanes, Lartius that was gotten out, had some leysure to bring the Romaines with more safety into the cittie. The cittie being taken in this sorte, the most parte of the souldiers beganne incontinently to spoyle, to carie awaye, and to looke up the bootie they had wonne. But Martius was marvelous angry with them, and cried out on them, that it was no time now to looke after spoyle, and to ronne straggling here and there to enriche them selves, whilest the other Consul and their fellowe cittizens peradventure were fighting with their enemies: and howe that leaving the spoyle they should seeke to winde them selves out of daunger and perill. Howbeit, crie, and saye to them what he could, very fewe of them would hearken to him. Wherefore taking those that willingly offered them selves to followe him, he went out of the cittie, and tooke his waye towardes that parte, where he

The cittie of Corioles taken.

understoode the rest of the armie was: exhorting and intreating them by the waye that followed him, not to be fainte harted, and ofte holding up his handes to heaven, he besought the goddes to be so gracious and favorable unto him, that he might come in time to the battell, and in good hower to hazarde his life in defence of his country men. Now the Romaines when they were put in battell raye, and ready to take their targettes on their armes, and to guirde them upon their arming coates, had a custome to make their willes at that very instant, without any manner of writing, naming him only whom they would make their heire, in the presence of three or foure witnesses. Martius came just to that reckoning, whilest the souldiers were a doing after that sorte, and that the enemies were approched so neere, as one stoode in viewe of the other. When they sawe him at his first comming, all bloody, and in a swet, and but with a fewe men following him: some thereupon beganne to be afeard. But sone after, when they sawe him ronne with a lively cheere to the Consul and to take him by the hande, declaring howe he had taken the cittie of Corioles, and that they sawe the Consul Cominius also kisse and embrace him: then there was not a man but tooke harte againe to him, and beganne to be of a good corage, some hearing him reporte from poynte to poynte, the happy successe of this exployte, and other also conjecturing it by seeing their gestures a farre of. Then they all beganne to call upon the Consul to marche forward, and to delaye no lenger, but to geve charge upon the enemie. Martius asked him howe the order of their enemies battell was, and on which side they had placed their best fighting men. The Consul made him aunswer, that he thought the bandes which were in the voward of their battell, were those of the Antiates, whom they esteemed to be the warlikest men, and which for valliant corage would geve no place, to any of the hoste of their enemies. Then prayed Martius, to be set directly against them. The Consul graunted him, greatly praysing his corage. Then Martius, when both armies came almost to joyne, advaunced him selfe a good space before his companie, and went so fiercely to geve charge on the voward that came right against

Souldiers testaments.

By Coriolanus meanes, the Volsci were overcome in battell.

him, that they could stande no lenger in his handes: he made suche a lane through them, and opened a passage into the battell of the enemies. But the two winges of either side turned one to the other, to compasse him in betweene them: which the Consul Cominius perceyving, he sent thither straight of the best souldiers he had about him. So the battell was marvelous bloudie about Martius, and in a very shorte space many were slaine in the place. But in the ende the Romaines were so strong, that they distressed the enemies, and brake their arraye: and scattering them, made them flye. Then they prayed Martius that he would retire to the campe, bicause they sawe he was able to doe no more, he was already so wearied with the great payne he had taken, and so fainte with the great woundes he had apon him. But Martius aunswered them, that it was not for conquerours to yeld, nor to be fainte harted: and thereupon beganne a freshe to chase those that fled, untill suche time as the armie of the enemies was utterly overthrowen, and numbers of them slaine, and taken prisoners. The next morning betimes, Martius went to the Consul, and the other Romaines with him. There the Consul Cominius going up to his chayer of state, in the presence of the whole armie, gave thankes to the goddes for so great, glorious, and prosperous a victorie: then he spake to Martius, whose valliantnes he commended beyond the moone, both for that he him selfe sawe him doe with his eyes, as also for that Martius had reported unto him. So in the ende he willed Martius, he should choose out of all the horses they had taken of their enemies, and of all the goodes they had wonne (whereof there was great store) tenne of every sorte which he liked best, before any distribution should be made to other. Besides this great honorable offer he had made him, he gave him in testimonie that he had wonne that daye the price of prowes above all other, a goodly horse with a capparison, and all furniture to him: which the whole armie beholding, dyd marvelously praise and commend. But Martius stepping forth, tolde the Consul, he most thanckefully accepted the gifte of his horse, and was a glad man besides, that his service had deserved his generalls

The tenth parte of the enemies goods offered Martius for rewarde of his service, by Cominius the Consul.

Valiancie rewarded with honour in the fielde.

commendation: and as for his other offer, which was rather a mercenary reward, then an honorable recompence, he would none of it, but was contented to have his equall parte with other souldiers. Only, this grace (sayed he) I crave, and beseeche you to graunt me. Among the Volsces there is an olde friende and hoste of mine, an honest wealthie man, and now a prisoner, who living before in great wealth in his owne countrie, liveth now a poore prisoner in the handes of his enemies: and yet notwithstanding all this his miserie and misfortune, it would doe me great pleasure if I could save him from this one daunger: to keepe him from being solde as a slave. The souldiers hearing Martius wordes, made a marvelous great showte among them: and they were moe that wondred at his great contentation and abstinence, when they sawe so litle covetousnes in him, then they were that highely praised and extolled his valliantnes. For even they them selves, that dyd somewhat malice and envie his glorie, to see him thus honoured, and passingly praysed, dyd thincke him so muche the more worthy of an honorable recompence for his valliant service, as the more carelesly he refused the great offer made him for his profit: and they esteemed more the vertue that was in him, that made him refuse suche rewards, then that which made them to be offred him, as unto a worthie persone. For it is farre more commendable, to use riches well, then to be valliant: and yet it is better not to desire them, then to use them well. After this showte and noyse of the assembly was somewhat appeased, the Consul Cominius beganne to speake in this sorte: We cannot compell Martius to take these giftes we offer him, if he will not receave them: but we will geve him suche a rewarde for the noble service he hath done, as he cannot refuse. Therefore we doe order and decree, that henceforth he be called Coriolanus, onles his valliant acts have wonne him that name before our nomination. And so ever since, he stil bare the third name of Coriolanus. And thereby it appeareth, that the first name the Romaines have, as Caius: was our Christian name now. The second, as Martius: was the name of the house and familie they came of. The third, was some addition geven, either for

Martius noble aunswer and refusall.

Martius surnamed Coriolanus by the Consul.

How the Romaines came to three names.

some acte or notable service, or for some marke on their face, or of some shape of their bodie, or els for some speciall vertue they had. Even so dyd the Græcians in olde time give additions to Princes, by reason of some notable acte worthie memorie. As when they have called some, Soter, and Callinicos: as muche to saye, saviour and conquerour. Or els for some notable apparaunt marke on ones face, or on his bodie, they have called him Phiscon, and Grypos: as ye would saye, gorebelley, and hooke nosed: or els for some vertue, as Euergetes, and Phyladelphos: to wit, a Benefactour, and lover of his brethern. Or otherwise for ones great felicitie, as Eudæmon: as muche to saye, as fortunate. For so was the second of the * Battes surnamed. And some Kings have had surnames of jeast and mockery. As one of the Antigones that was called Doson, to saye, the Gever: who was ever promising, and never geving. And one of the Ptolomees was called Lamyros: to saye, conceitive. The Romaines use more then any other nation, to give names of mockerie in this sorte. As there was one Metellus surnamed Diadematus, the banded: bicause he caried a bande about his heade of longe time, by reason of a sore he had in his forehead. One other of his owne familie was called Celer: the quicke flye. Bicause a fewe dayes after the death of his father, he shewed the people the cruell fight of fensers at unrebated swordes, which they founde wonderfull for the shortnes of time. Other had their surnames derived of some accident of their birthe. As to this daye they call him Proculeius, that is borne, his father being in some farre voyage: and him Posthumius, that is borne after the deathe of his father. And when of two brethern twinnes, the one doth dye, and thother surviveth: they call the survivor, Vopiscus. Somtimes also they geve surnames derived of some marke or misfortune of the bodie. As Sylla, to saye, crooked nosed: Niger, blacke: Rufus, red: Cæcus, blinde: Claudus, lame. They dyd wisely in this thing to accustome men to thincke, that neither the losse of their sight, nor other such misfortunes as maye chaunce to men, are any shame or disgrace unto them, but the manner was to aunswer boldly to suche names, as if they were called by their proper

Why the Græcians gave Kings surnames.

* These were the princes that built the cittie of Cyrene.

Names of mockery among the Romaines.

names. Howbeit these matters would be better amplified in other stories then this. Now when this warre was ended, the flatterers of the people beganne to sturre up sedition againe, without any newe occasion, or just matter offered of complainte. For they dyd grounde this seconde insurrection against the Nobilitie and Patricians, apon the peoples miserie and misfortune, that could not but fall out, by reason of the former discorde and sedition betweene them and the Nobilitie. Bicause the most parte of the errable lande within the territorie of Rome, was become heathie and barren for lacke of plowing, for that they had no time nor meane to cause corne, to be brought them out of other countries to sowe, by reason of their warres which made the extreme dearth they had emong them. Now those busie pratlers that sought the peoples good will, by suche flattering wordes, perceyving great scarsitie of corne to be within the cittie, and though there had bene plenty enough, yet the common people had no money to buye it: they spread abroad false tales and rumours against the Nobilitie, that they in revenge of the people, had practised and procured the extreme dearthe emong them. Furthermore, in the middest of this sturre, there came ambassadours to Rome from the cittie of Velitres, that offered up their cittie to the Romaines, and prayed them they would send newe inhabitants to replenishe the same: bicause the plague had bene so extreme among them, and had killed such a number of them, as there was not left alive the tenth persone of the people that had bene there before. So the wise men of Rome beganne to thincke, that the necessitie of the Velitrians fell out in a most happy hower, and howe by this occasion it was very mete in so great a scarsitie of vittailes, to disburden Rome of a great number of cittizens: and by this meanes as well to take awaye this newe sedition, and utterly to ryd it out of the cittie, as also to cleare the same of many mutinous and seditious persones, being the superfluous ill humours that grevously fedde this disease. Hereupon the Consuls prickt out all those by a bill, whom they intended to sende to Velitres, to goe dwell there as in forme of a colonie: and they leavied out of all the rest that remained in the cittie of

Sedition at Rome, by reason of famine.

Velitres made a colonie to Rome.

Rome, a great number to goe against the Volsces, hoping by the meanes of forreine warre, to pacifie their sedition at home. Moreover they imagined, when the poore with the riche, and the meane sorte with the nobilitie, should by this devise be abroad in the warres, and in one campe, and in one service, and in one like daunger: that then they would be more quiet and loving together. But Sicinius and Brutus, two seditious Tribunes, spake against either of these devises, and cried out apon the noble men, that under the gentle name of a colonie, they would cloke and culler the most cruell and unnaturall facte as might be: bicause they sent their poore cittizens into a sore infected cittie and pestilent ayer, full of dead bodies unburied, and there also to dwell under the tuytion of a straunge god, that had so cruelly persecuted his people. This were (said they) even as muche, as if the Senate should hedlong cast downe the people into a most bottomles pyt. And are not yet contented to have famished some of the poore cittizens hertofore to death, and to put other of them even to the mercie of the plague: but a freshe, they have procured a voluntarie warre, to the ende they would leave behind no kynde of miserie and ill, wherewith the poore syllie people should not be plagued, and only bicause they are werie to serve the riche. The common people being set on a broyle and braverie with these wordes, would not appeare when the Consuls called their names by a bill, to prest them for the warres, neither would they be sent out to this newe colonie: in so muche as the Senate knewe not well what to saye, or doe in the matter. Martius then, who was now growen to great credit, and a stowte man besides, and of great reputation with the noblest men of Rome, rose up, and openly spake against these flattering Tribunes. And for the replenishing of the cittie of Velitres, he dyd compell those that were chosen, to goe thither, and to departe the cittie, apon great penalties to him that should disobey: but to the warres, the people by no meanes would be brought or constrained. So Martius taking his friendes and followers with him, and such as he could by fayer wordes intreate to goe with him, dyd ronne certen forreyes into the dominion of the Antiates, where he met with great plenty

Two practises to remove the sedition in Rome.

Sicinius and Brutus Tribunes of the people, against both those devises.

Coriolanus offendeth the people.

Coriolanus invadeth the Antiates, and bringeth rich spoyles home.

of corne, and had a marvelous great spoyle, aswell of cattell, as of men he had taken prisoners, whom he brought awaye with him, and reserved nothing for him selfe. Afterwardes having brought backe againe all his men that went out with him, safe and sounde to Rome, and every man riche and loden with spoyle: then the hometarriers and housedoves that kept Rome still, beganne to repent them that it was not their happe to goe with him, and so envied both them that had sped so well in this jorney, and also of malice to Martius, they spited to see his credit and estimation increase still more and more, bicause they accompted him to be a great hinderer of the people. Shortely after this, Martius stoode for the Consulshippe: and the common people favored his sute, thinking it would be a shame to them to denie, and refuse, the chiefest noble man of bloude, and most worthie persone of Rome, and specially him that had done so great service and good to the common wealth. For the custome of Rome was at that time, that suche as dyd sue for any office, should for certen dayes before be in the market place, only with a poore gowne on their backes, and without any coate underneath, to praye the cittizens to remember them at the daye of election: which was thus devised, either to move the people the more, by requesting them in suche meane apparell, or els bicause they might shewe them their woundes they had gotten in the warres in the service of the common wealth, as manifest markes and testimonie of their valliantnes. Now it is not to be thought that the suters went thus lose in a simple gowne in the market place, without any coate under it, for feare, and suspition of the common people: for offices of dignitie in the cittie were not then geven by favour or corruption. It was but of late time, and long after this, that buying and selling fell out in election of officers, and that the voyces of the electours were bought for money. But after corruption had once gotten waye into the election of offices, it hath ronne from man to man, even to the very sentence of judges, and also emong captaines in the warres: so as in the ende, that only turned common wealthes into Kingdomes, by making armes subject to money. Therefore me thinckes he

The manner of suyng for office at Rome.

Whereupon this manner of suyng was so devised.

Offices geven then by desert, without favour or corruption.

had reason that sayed: He that first made banckets, and gave money to the common people, was the first that tooke awaye authoritie, and destroyed common wealth. But this pestilence crept in by litle and litle, and dyd secretly winne ground still, continuing a long time in Rome, before it was openly knowen and discovered. For no man can tell who was the first man that bought the peoples voyces for money, nor that corrupted the sentence of the judges. Howbeit at Athens some holde opinion, that Anytus, the sonne of Anthemion, was the first man that fedde the judges with money, about the ende of the warres of Peloponnesus, being accused of treason for yelding up the forte of Pyle, at that time, when the golden and unfoiled age remained yet whole in judgement at Rome. Now Martius following this custome, shewed many woundes and cuttes apon his bodie, which he had receyved in seventeene yeres service at the warres, and in many sundrie battells, being ever the formest man that dyd set out feete to fight. So that there was not a man emong the people, but was ashamed of him selfe, to refuse so valliant a man: and one of them sayed to another, We must needes chuse him Consul, there is no remedie. But when the daye of election was come, and that Martius came to the market place with great pompe, accompanied with all the Senate, and the whole Nobilitie of the cittie about him, who sought to make him Consul, with the greatest instance and intreatie they could, or ever attempted for any man or matter: then the love and good will of the common people, turned straight to an hate and envie toward him, fearing to put this office of soveraine authoritie into his handes, being a man somewhat partiall toward the nobilitie, and of great credit and authoritie amongest the Patricians, and as one they might doubt would take away alltogether the libertie from the people. Whereupon for these considerations, they refused Martius in the ende, and made two other that were suters, Consuls. The Senate being marvelously offended with the people, dyd accompt the shame of this refusall, rather to redownd to them selves, then to Martius: but Martius tooke it in farre worse parte then the Senate, and was out of all pacience. For he was a man to

Bankets and money geven: only destroyers of common wealth.

Anytus the Athenian, the first that with money corrupted the sentence of the judge, and voyces of the people.

See the fickle mindes of common people.

CORIOLANUS

full of passion and choller, and to muche geven to over selfe will and opinion, as one of a highe minde and great corage, that lacked the gravity, and affabilitie that is gotten with judgment of learning and reason, which only is to be looked for in a governour of state: and that remembred not how wilfulnes is the thing of the world, which a governour of a common wealth for pleasing should shonne, being that which Plato called solitarines. As in the ende, all men that are wilfully geven to a selfe opinion and obstinate minde, and who will never yeld to others reason, but to their owne: remaine without companie, and forsaken of all men. For a man that will live in the world, must nedes have patience, which lusty bloudes make but a mocke at. So Martius being a stowte man of nature, that never yelded in any respect, as one thincking that to overcome allwayes, and to have the upper hande in all matters, was a token of magnanimitie, and of no base and fainte corage, which spitteth out anger from the most weake and passioned parte of the harte, much like the matter of an impostume: went home to his house, full fraighted with spite and malice against the people, being accompanied with all the lustiest young gentlemen, whose mindes were nobly bent, as those that came of noble race, and commonly used for to followe and honour him. But then specially they floct about him, and kept him companie, to his muche harme: for they dyd but kyndle and inflame his choller more and more, being sorie with him for the injurie the people offred him, bicause he was their captaine and leader to the warres, that taught them all marshall discipline, and stirred up in them a noble emulation of honour and valliantnes, and yet without envie, praising them that deserved best. In the meane season, there came great plenty of corne to Rome, that had bene bought, parte in Italie, and parte was sent out of Sicile, as geven by Gelon the tyranne of Syracusa: so that many stoode in great hope, that the dearthe of vittells being holpen, the civill dissention would also cease. The Senate sate in counsell upon it immediatly, the common people stoode also about the palice where the counsell was kept, gaping what resolution would fall out: persuading them selves, that the corne they had

The fruites of selfe will and obstinacie.

Great store of corne brought to Rome.

bought should be solde good cheape, and that which was geven, should be devided by the polle, without paying any pennie, and the rather, bicause certaine of the Senatours amongest them dyd so wishe and persuade the same. But Martius standing up on his feete, dyd somewhat sharpely take up those, who went about to gratifie the people therein: and called them people pleasers, and traitours to the nobilitie. ‘Moreover he sayed they nourrished against them selves, the ‘naughty seede and cockle, of insolencie and sedition, which ‘had bene sowed and scattered abroade emongest the people, ‘whom they should have cut of, if they had bene wise, and ‘have prevented their greatnes: and not to their owne de-‘struction to have suffered the people, to stablishe a magis-‘trate for them selves, of so great power and authoritie, as ‘that man had, to whom they had graunted it. Who was ‘also to be feared, bicause he obtained what he would, and ‘dyd nothing but what he listed, neither passed for any ‘obedience to the Consuls, but lived in all libertie, acknow-‘ledging no superiour to commaund him, saving the only ‘heades and authours of their faction, whom he called his ‘magistrates. Therefore sayed he, they that gave counsell, ‘and persuaded that the corne should be geven out to the ‘common people *gratis*, as they used to doe in citties of ‘Græce, where the people had more absolute power: dyd ‘but only nourishe their disobedience, which would breake ‘out in the ende, to the utter ruine and overthrowe of the ‘whole state. For they will not thincke it is done in re-‘compense of their service past, sithence they know well ‘enough they have so ofte refused to goe to the warres, ‘when they were commaunded: neither for their mutinies ‘when they went with us, whereby they have rebelled and ‘forsaken their countrie: neither for their accusations which ‘their flatterers have preferred unto them, and they have ‘receyved, and made good against the Senate: but they will ‘rather judge we geve and graunt them this, as abasing our ‘selves, and standing in feare of them, and glad to flatter ‘them every waye. By this meanes, their disobedience will ‘still growe worse and worse: and they will never leave to ‘practise newe sedition, and uprores. Therefore it were a

Coriolanus oration against the insolencie of the people.

'great follie for us, me thinckes to doe it: yea, shall I saye 'more? we should if we were wise, take from them their 'Tribuneshippe, which most manifestly is the embasing of 'the Consulshippe, and the cause of the division of the 'cittie. The state whereof as it standeth, is not now as it 'was wont to be, but becommeth dismembred in two factions, 'which mainteines allwayes civill dissention and discorde be- 'twene us, and will never suffer us againe to be united into 'one bodie.' Martius dilating the matter with many such like reasons, wanne all the young men, and almost all the riche men to his opinion: in so much they range it out, that he was the only man, and alone in the cittie, who stoode out against the people, and never flattered them. There were only a fewe olde men that spake against him, fearing least some mischief might fall out apon it, as in dede there followed no great good afterward. For the Tribunes of the people, being present at this consultation of the Senate, when they sawe that the opinion of Martius was confirmed with the more voyces, they left the Senate, and went downe to the people, crying out for helpe, and that they would assemble to save their Tribunes. Hereupon the people ranne on head in tumult together, before whom the wordes that Martius spake in the Senate were openly reported: which the people so stomaked, that even in that furie they were readie to flye apon the whole Senate. But the Tribunes layed all the faulte and burden wholy upon Martius, and sent their sergeantes forthwith to arrest him, presently to appeare in persone before the people, to aunswer the wordes he had spoken in the Senate. Martius stowtely withstoode these officers that came to arrest him. Then the Tribunes in their owne persones, accompanied with the Ædiles, went to fetche him by force, and so layed violent hands upon him. Howbeit the noble Patricians gathering together about him, made the Tribunes geve backe, and layed it sore apon the Ædiles: so for that time, the night parted them, and the tumult appeased. The next morning betimes, the Consuls seing the people in an uprore, ronning to the market place out of all partes of the cittie, they were affrayed least all the cittie would together by the eares: wherefore assembling the

Sedition at Rome for Coriolanus.

Senate in all hast, they declared how it stoode them upon, to appease the furie of the people, with some gentle wordes, or gratefull decrees in their favour: and moreover, like wise men they should consider, it was now no time to stande at defence and in contention, nor yet to fight for honour against the communaltie: they being fallen to so great an extremitie, and offering such imminent daunger. Wherefore they were to consider temperately of things, and to deliver some present and gentle pacification. The most parte of the Senatours that were present at this counsaill, thought this opinion best, and gave their consents unto it. Whereupon the Consuls rising out of counsaill, went to speake unto the people as gently as they could, and they dyd pacific their furie and anger, purging the Senate of all the unjust accusations layed upon them, and used great modestie in persuading them, and also in reproving the faultes they had committed. And as for the rest, that touched the sale of corne: they promised there should be no disliking offred them in the price. So the most parte of the people being pacified, and appearing so plainely by the great silence and still that was among them, as yelding to the Consuls, and liking well of their wordes: the Tribunes then of the people rose out of their seates, and sayed: Forasmuche as the Senate yelded unto reason, the people also for their parte, as became them, dyd likewise geve place unto them: but notwithstanding, they would that Martius should come in persone to aunswer to the articles they had devised. First, whether he had not solicited and procured the Senate to chaunge the present state of the common weale, and to take the soveraine authoritie out of the peoples handes. Next, when he was sent for by authoritie of their officers, why he dyd contemptuously resist and disobey. Lastely, seeing he had driven and beaten the Ædiles into the market place before all the worlde: if in doing this, he had not done as muche as in him laye, to raise civill warres, and to set one cittizen against another. All this was spoken to one of these two endes, either that Martius against his nature should be constrained to humble him selfe, and to abase his hawty and fierce minde: or els if he continued still in his stowtnes, he should incurre the peoples

Articles against Coriolanus.

displeasure and ill will so farre, that he should never possibly winne them againe. Which they hoped would rather fall out so, then otherwise: as in deede they gest unhappely, considering Martius nature and disposition. So Martius came, and presented him selfe, to aunswer their accusations against him, and the people held their peace, and gave attentive eare, to heare what he would saye. But where they thought to have heard very humble and lowly wordes come from him, he beganne not only to use his wonted boldnes of speaking (which of it selfe was very rough and unpleasaunt, and dyd more aggravate his accusation, then purge his innocencie) but also gave him selfe in his wordes to thunder, and looke therewithall so grimly, as though he made no reckoning of the matter. This stirred coales emong the people, who were in wonderfull furie at it, and their hate and malice grewe so toward him, that they could holde no lenger, beare, nor indure his bravery and careles boldnes. Whereupon Sicinius, the cruellest and stowtest of the Tribunes, after he had whispered a litle with his companions, dyd openly pronounce in the face of all the people, Martius as condemned by the Tribunes to dye. Then presently he commaunded the Ædiles to apprehend him, and carie him straight to the rocke Tarpeian, and to cast him hedlong downe the same. When the Ædiles came to laye handes upon Martius to doe that they were commaunded, divers of the people them selves thought it to cruell, and violent a dede. The noble men also being muche troubled to see such force and rigour used, beganne to crie alowde, Helpe Martius: so those that layed handes of him being repulsed, they compassed him in rounde emong them selves, and some of them holding up their handes to the people, besought them not to handle him thus cruelly. But neither their wordes, nor crying out could ought prevaile, the tumulte and hurly burley was so great, untill suche time as the Tribunes owne friendes and kinsemen weying with them selves the impossiblenes to convey Martius to execution, without great slaughter and murder of the nobilitie: dyd persuade and advise not to proceede in so violent and extraordinary a sorte, as to put such a man to death, without

Coriolanus stowtnes in defence of him selfe.

Sicinius the Tribune, pronounceth sentence of death upon Martius.

lawfull processe in lawe, but that they should referre the sentence of his death, to the free voyce of the people. Then Sicinius bethinking him self a litle, dyd aske the Patricians, for what cause they tooke Martius out of the officers handes that went to doe execution? The Patricians asked him againe, why they would of them selves, so cruelly and wickedly put to death, so noble and valliant a Romaine, as Martius was, and that without lawe or justice? Well, then sayed Sicinius, if that be the matter, let there be no more quarrell or dissention against the people: for they doe graunt your demaunde, that his cause shalbe heard according to the law. Therfore sayed he to Martius, We doe will and charge you to appeare before the people, the third daye of our next sitting and assembly here, to make your purgation for such articles as shalbe objected against you, that by free voyce the people maye geve sentence apon you as shall please them. The noble men were glad then of the adjornment, and were muche pleased they had gotten Martius out of this daunger. In the meane space, before the third day of their next cession came about, the same being kept every nineth daye continually at Rome, whereupon they call it now in Latin, *Nundinæ*: there fell out warre against the Antiates, which gave some hope to the nobilitie, that this adjornment would come to litle effect, thinking that this warre would hold them so longe, as that the furie of the people against him would be well swaged or utterly forgotten, by reason of the trouble of the warres. But contrarie to expectation, the peace was concluded presently with the Antiates, and the people returned again to Rome. Then the Patricians assembled oftentimes together, to consult how they might stande to Martius, and keepe the Tribunes from occasion to cause the people to mutine againe, and rise against the nobilitie. And there Appius Clodius (one that was taken ever as an heavy enemie to the people) dyd avowe and protest, that they would utterly abase the authoritie of the Senate, and destroye the common weale, if they would suffer the common people to have authoritie by voyces to geve judgment against the nobilitie. On thother side againe, the most auncient Senatours, and suche as were geven to

Coriolanus hath daye geven him to aunswer the people.

favour the common people sayed: that when the people should see they had authoritie of life and death in their handes, they would not be so cruell and fierce, but gentle and civill. More also, that it was not for contempt of nobilitie or the Senate, that they sought to have the authoritie of justice in their handes, as a preheminence and prerogative of honour: but bicause they feared, that them selves should be contemned and hated of the nobilitie. So as they were persuaded, that so sone as they gave them authoritie to judge by voyces: so sone would they leave all envie and malice to condemne anye. Martius seeing the Senate in great doubt how to resolve, partely for the love and good will the nobilitie dyd beare him, and partely for the feare they stoode in of the people: asked alowde of the Tribunes, what matter they would burden him with? The Tribunes aunswered him, that they would shewe howe he dyd aspire to be King, and would prove that all his actions tended to usurpe tyrannicall power over Rome. Martius with that, rising up on his feete, sayed: that thereupon he dyd willingly offer him self to the people, to be tried apon that accusation. And that if it were proved by him, he had so muche as once thought of any suche matter, that he would then refuse no kinde of punishment they would offer him: conditionally (quoth he) that you charge me with nothing els besides, and that ye doe not also abuse the Senate. They promised they would not. Under these conditions the judgement was agreed upon, and the people assembled. And first of all the Tribunes would in any case (whatsoever became of it) that the people would proceede to geve their voyces by Tribes, and not by hundreds: for by this meanes the multitude of the poore needy people (and all suche rable as had nothing to lose, and had lesse regard of honestie before their eyes) came to be of greater force (bicause their voyces were numbred by the polle) then the noble honest cittizens, whose persones and purse dyd duetifully serve the common wealth in their warres. And then when the Tribunes sawe they could not prove he went about to make him self King: they beganne to broache a freshe the former wordes that Martius had spoken in the Senate, in hindering the distribution of

Coriolanus accused that he sought to be King.

the corne at meane price unto the common people, and persuading also to take the office of Tribuneshippe from them. And for the third, they charged him a newe, that he had not made the common distribution of the spoyle he had gotten in the invading the territories of the Antiates: but had of his owne authoritie devided it among them, who were with him in that jorney. But this matter was most straunge of all to Martius, looking least to have bene burdened with that, as with any matter of offence. Wherupon being burdened on the sodaine, and having no ready excuse to make even at that instant: he beganne to fall a praising of the souldiers that had served with him in that jorney. But those that were not with him, being the greater number, cried out so lowde, and made suche a noyse, that he could not be heard. To conclude, when they came to tell the voyces of the Tribes, there were three voyces odde, which condemned him to be banished for life. After declaration of the sentence, the people made suche joye, as they never rejoyced more for any battell they had wonne upon their enemies, they were so brave and lively, and went home so jocondly from the assembly, for triumphe of this sentence. The Senate againe in contrary manner were as sad and heavie, repenting them selves beyond measure, that they had not rather determined to have done and suffered any thing whatsoever, before the common people should so arrogantly, and outrageously have abused their authoritie. There needed no difference of garments I warrant you, nor outward showes to know a Plebeian from a Patrician, for they were easely decerned by their lookes. For he that was on the peoples side, looked cheerely on the matter: but he that was sad, and honge downe his head, he was sure of the noble mens side. Saving Martius alone, who neither in his countenaunce, nor in his gate, dyd ever showe him selfe abashed, or once let fall his great corage: but he only of all other gentlemen that were angrie at his fortune, dyd outwardly shewe no manner of passion, nor care at all of him selfe. Not that he dyd paciently beare and temper his good happe, in respect of any reason he had, or by his quiet condition: but bicause he was so caried awaye with the vehemencie of anger, and desire of

Coriolanus banished for life.

Coriolanus constant minde in adversitie.

CORIOLANUS

The force of anger.

revenge, that he had no sence nor feeling of the hard state he was in, which the common people judge, not to be sorow, although in dede it be the very same. For when sorow (as you would saye) is set a fyre, then it is converted into spite and malice, and driveth awaye for that time all faintnes of harte and naturall feare. And this is the cause why the chollericke man is so altered, and mad in his actions, as a man set a fyre with a burning agewe: for when a mans harte is troubled within, his pulse will beate marvelous strongely. Now that Martius was even in that taking, it appeared true sone after by his doinges. For when he was come home to his house againe, and had taken his leave of his mother and wife, finding them weeping, and shreeking out for sorrowe, and had also comforted and persuaded them to be content with his chaunce: he went immediatly to the gate of the cittie, accompanied with a great number of Patricians that brought him thither, from whence he went on his waye with three or foure of his friendes only, taking nothing with him, nor requesting any thing of any man. So he remained a fewe dayes in the countrie at his houses, turmoyled with sundry sortes and kynde of thoughtes, suche as the fyer of his choller dyd sturre up. In the ende, seeing he could resolve no waye, to take a profitable or honorable course, but only was pricked forward still to be revenged of the Romaines: he thought to raise up some great warres against them, by their neerest neighbours. Whereupon, he thought it his best waye, first to stirre up the Volsces against them, knowing they were yet able enough in strength and riches to encounter them, notwithstanding their former losses they had receyved not long before, and that their power was not so muche impaired, as their malice and desire was increased, to be revenged of the Romaines. Now in the cittie of Antium, there was one called Tullus Aufidius, who for his riches, as also for his nobilitie and valliantnes, was honoured emong the Volsces as a King. Martius knewe very well, that Tullus dyd more malice and envie him, then he dyd all the Romaines besides: bicause that many times in battells where they met, they were ever at the encounter one against another, like lustie coragious youthes, striving in all emula-

Tullus Aufidius, a greate persone emong the Volsces.

tion of honour, and had encountered many times together. In so muche, as besides the common quarrell betweene them, there was bred a marvelous private hate one against another. Yet notwithstanding, considering that Tullus Aufidius was a man of a great minde, and that he above all other of the Volsces, most desired revenge of the Romaines, for the injuries they had done unto them: he dyd an acte that confirmed the true wordes of an auncient Poet, who sayed:

> It is a thing full harde, mans anger to withstand,
> if it be stiffely bent to take an enterprise in hande.
> For then most men will have, the thing that they desire,
> although it cost their lives therefore, suche force hath wicked ire.

And so dyd he. For he disguised him selfe in suche arraye and attire, as he thought no man could ever have knowen him for the persone he was, seeing him in that apparell he had upon his backe: and as Homer sayed of Ulysses,

> So dyd he enter into the enemies towne.

Coriolanus disguised, goeth to Antium, a cittie of the Volsces.

It was even twy light when he entred the cittie of Antium, and many people met him in the streetes, but no man knewe him. So he went directly to Tullus Aufidius house, and when he came thither, he got him up straight to the chimney harthe, and sat him downe, and spake not a worde to any man, his face all muffled over. They of the house spying him, wondered what he should be, and yet they durst not byd him rise. For ill favoredly muffled and disguised as he was, yet there appeared a certaine majestie in his countenance, and in his silence: whereupon they went to Tullus who was at supper, to tell him of the straunge disguising of this man. Tullus rose presently from the borde, and comming towards him, asked him what he was, and wherefore he came. Then Martius unmuffled him selfe, and after he had paused a while, making no aunswer, he sayed unto him: 'If thou knowest 'me not yet, Tullus, and seeing me, dost not perhappes 'beleeve me to be the man I am in dede, I must of necessitie 'bewraye my selfe to be that I am. I am Caius Martius, who 'hath done to thy self particularly, and to all the Volsces 'generally, great hurte and mischief, which I cannot denie for

Coriolanus oration to Tullus Aufidius.

CORIOLANUS

'my surname of Coriolanus that I beare. For I never had 'other benefit nor recompence, of all the true and paynefull 'service I have done, and the extreme daungers I have bene 'in, but this only surname: a good memorie and witnes, of 'the malice and displeasure thou showldest beare me. In 'deede the name only remaineth with me: for the rest, the 'envie and crueltie of the people of Rome have taken from 'me, by the sufferance of the dastardly nobilitie and magis-'trates, who have forsaken me, and let me be banished by the 'people. This extremitie hath now driven me to come as a 'poore suter, to take thy chimney harthe, not of any hope I 'have to save my life thereby. For if I had feared death, I 'would not have come hither to have put my life in hazard: 'but prickt forward with spite and desire I have to be revenged 'of them that thus have banished me, whom now I beginne to 'be avenged on, putting my persone betweene thy enemies. 'Wherefore, if thou hast any harte to be wrecked of the 'injuries thy enemies have done thee, spede thee now, and let 'my miserie serve thy turne, and so use it, as my service maye 'be a benefit to the Volsces; promising thee, that I will fight 'with better good will for all you, then ever I dyd when I 'was against you, knowing that they fight more valliantly, 'who knowe the force of their enemie, then such as have 'never proved it. And if it be so that thou dare not, and 'that thou art wearye to prove fortune any more: then am 'I also weary to live any lenger. And it were no wisedome 'in thee, to save the life of him, who hath bene heretofore 'thy mortall enemie, and whose service now can nothing 'helpe nor pleasure thee.' Tullus hearing what he sayed, was a marvelous glad man, and taking him by the hande, he sayed unto him: Stande up, O Martius, and bee of good chere, for in profering thy selfe unto us, thou dost us great honour: and by this meanes thou mayest hope also of greater things, at all the Volsces handes. So he feasted him for that time, and entertained him in the honorablest manner he could, talking with him in no other matters at that present: but within fewe dayes after, they fell to consultation together, in what sorte they should beginne their warres. Now on thother side, the cittie of Rome was in marvelous

Great dissention at Rome about Martius banishment.

uprore, and discord, the nobilitie against the communaltie, and chiefly for Martius condemnation and banishment. Moreover the priestes, the Soothesayers, and private men also, came and declared to the Senate certaine sightes and wonders in the ayer, which they had seene, and were to be considered of: amongest the which, such a vision happened. There was a cittizen of Rome called Titus Latinus, a man of meane qualitie and condition, but otherwise an honest sober man, geven to a quiet life, without superstition, and much lesse to vanitie or lying. This man had a vision in his dreame, in the which he thought that Iupiter appeared unto him, and commaunded him to signifie to the Senate, that they had caused a very vile lewde daunser to goe before the procession: and sayed, the first time this vision had appeared unto him, he made no reckoning of it: and comming againe another time into his minde, he made not muche more accompt of the matter then before. In the ende, he sawe one of his sonnes dye, who had the best nature and condition of all his brethern: and sodainely he him selfe was so taken in all his limmes, that he became lame and impotent. Hereupon he tolde the whole circumstance of this vision before the Senate, sitting upon his litle couche or bedde, whereon he was caried on mens armes: and he had no sooner reported this vision to the Senate, but he presently felt his bodie and limmes restored again, to their former strength and use. So raising up him self upon his couche, he got up on his feete at that instant, and walked home to his house, without helpe of any man. The Senate being amazed at this matter, made diligent enquierie to understand the trothe: and in the ende they found there was such a thing. There was one that had delivered a bondman of his that had offended him, into the hands of other slaves and bondemen, and had commanded them to whippe him up and down the market place, and afterwards to kill him: and as they had him in execution, whipping him cruelly, they dyd so martyre the poore wretch, that for the cruell smarte and payne he felt, he turned and writhed his bodie, in straunge and pittiefull sorte. The procession by chaunce came by even at the same time, and many that followed it, were hartely moved and offended with the sight, saying: that this was no good sight to behold, nor mete to be met in procession time. But for all this, there was nothing done: saving they blamed and rebuked him, that punished his slave so cruelly. For the Romaines at that time, dyd use their bondemen very gently, bicause they them selves dyd labour with their owne hands, and lived with them, and emong them: and therefore they dyd use them the more gently and familliarly. For the greatest punishment they gave a slave that had offended, was this. They made him carie a limmer on his showlders that is fastened to the axeltree of a coche, and compelled him to goe up and downe in that sorte amongest all their neighbours. He that had once abidden this punishement, and was seene in that manner, was proclaimed and cried in every market towne: so that no man would ever trust him after, and they called him Furcifer, bicause the Latines call the wodd that ronneth into the axeltree of the coche, *Furca*, as muche to saye, as a forke. Now when Latinus had made reporte to the Senate of the vision that had happened to him, they were devising whom this unpleasaunt daunser should be, that went before the procession. Thereupon certain that stoode by, remembred the poore slave that was so cruelly whipped through the market place, whom they afterwardes put to death: and the thing that made them remember it, was the straunge and rare manner of his punishment. The priestes hereupon were repaired unto for advise: they were wholy of opinion, that it was the whipping of the slave. So they caused the slaves master to be punished, and beganne againe a newe procession, and all other showes and sightes in honour of Iupiter. But hereby appeareth plainely, how king Numa dyd wisely ordaine all other ceremonies concerning devotion to the goddes, and specially this custome which he stablished, to bring the people to religion. For when the magistrates, bishoppes, priests, or other religious ministers goe about any divine service, or matter of religion, an herauld ever goeth before them, crying out alowde, *Hoc age*: as to saye, doe this, or minde this. Hereby they are specially commaunded, wholy to dispose them selves to serve God, leaving all other

The Romaines manner of punishing their slaves.

Whereof Furcifer came.

A ceremonie instituted by king Numa, touching religion.

busines and matters a side: knowing well enough, that whatsoever most men doe, they doe it as in a manner constrained unto it. But the Romaines dyd ever use to beginne againe their sacrifices, processions, playes, and suche like showes done in honour of the goddes, not only upon suche an occasion, but apon lighter causes then that. As when they went a procession through the cittie, and dyd carie the images of their goddes, and suche other like holy relikes upon open hallowed coches or charrets, called in Latin *Thensæ*: one of the coche horses that drue them stoode still, and would drawe no more: and bicause also the coche man tooke the raynes of the bridle with the left hande, they ordained that the procession should be begonne againe a newe. Of later time also, they dyd renewe and beginne a sacrifice thirtie times one after another, bicause they thought still there fell out one faulte or other in the same, so holy and devout were they to the goddes. Now Tullus and Martius had secret conference with the greatest personages of the cittie of Antium, declaring unto them, that now they had good time offered them to make warre with the Romaines, while they were in dissention one with another. They aunswered them, they were ashamed to breake the league, considering that they were sworne to keepe peace for two yeres. Howbeit shortely after, the Romaines gave them great occasion to make warre with them. For on a holy daye common playes being kept in Rome, apon some suspition, or false reporte, they made proclamation by sound of trumpet, that all the Volsces should avoyde out of Rome before sunne set. Some thincke this was a crafte and deceipt of Martius, who sent one to Rome to the Consuls, to accuse the Volsces falsely, advertising them howe they had made a conspiracie to set apon them, whilest they were busie in seeing these games, and also to set their cittie a fyre. This open proclamation made all the Volsces more offended with the Romaines, then ever they were before: and Tullus agravating the matter, dyd so inflame the Volsces against them, that in the ende they sent their ambassadours to Rome, to summone them to deliver their landes and townes againe, which they had taken from them in times past, or to looke for present warres.

The superstition of the Romaines.

Thensæ.

The Romaines gave the Volsces occasion of warres.

Martius Coriolanus craftie accusation of the Volsces.

The Romaines hearing this, were marvelously netled: and made no other aunswer but thus: If the Volsces be the first that beginne warre: the Romaines will be the last that will ende it. Incontinently upon returne of the Volsces ambassadours, and deliverie of the Romaines aunswer: Tullus caused an assembly generall to be made of the Volsces, and concluded to make warre apon the Romaines. This done, Tullus dyd counsell them to take Martius into their service, and not to mistrust him for the remembraunce of any thing past, but boldely to trust him in any matter to come: for he would doe them more service in fighting for them, then ever he dyd them displeasure in fighting against them. So Martius was called forth, who spake so excellently in the presence of them all, that he was thought no lesse eloquent in tongue, then warlike in showe: and declared him selfe both expert in warres, and wise with valliantnes. Thus he was joyned in commission with Tullus as generall of the Volsces, having absolute authoritie betwene them to follow and pursue the warres. But Martius fearing least tract of time to bring this armie togither with all the munition and furniture of the Volsces, would robbe him of the meane he had to execute his purpose and intent: left order with the rulers and chief of the cittie, to assemble the rest of their power, and to prepare all necessary provision for the campe. Then he with the lightest souldiers he had, and that were willing to followe him, stale awaye upon the sodaine, and marched with all speede, and entred the territories of Rome, before the Romaines heard any newes of his comming. In so much the Volsces found such spoyle in the fields, as they had more then they could spend in their campe, and were wearie to drive and carie awaye that they had. Howbeit the gayne of the spoyle and the hurte they dyd to the Romaines in this invasion, was the least parte of his intent. For his chiefest purpose was, to increase still the malice and dissention betweene the nobilitie, and the communaltie: and to drawe that on, he was very carefull to keepe the noble mens landes and goods safe from harme and burning, but spoyled all the whole countrie besides, and would suffer no man to take or hurte any thing of the noble mens. This

Coriolanus chosen generall of the Volsces, with Tullus Aufidius against the Romaines.

Coriolanus invadeth the territories of the Romaines.

A fine devise to make the communaltie suspect the nobilitie.

Great harte burning betwext the nobilitie and people.

made greater sturre and broyle betweene the nobilitie and people, then was before. For the noble men fell out with the people, bicause they had so unjustly banished a man of so great valure and power. The people on thother side, accused the nobilitie, how they had procured Martius to make these warres, to be revenged of them: bicause it pleased them to see their goodes burnt and spoyled before their eyes, whilest them selves were well at ease, and dyd behold the peoples losses and misfortunes, and knowing their owne goodes safe and out of daunger: and howe the warre was not made against the noble men, that had the enemie abroad, to keepe that they had in safety. Now Martius having done this first exploite (which made the Volsces bolder, and lesse fearefull of the Romaines) brought home all the armie againe, without losse of any man. After their whole armie (which was marvelous great, and very forward to service) was assembled in one campe: they agreed to leave parte of it for garrison in the countrie about, and the other parte should goe on, and make the warre apon the Romaines. So Martius bad Tullus choose, and take which of the two charges he liked best. Tullus made him aunswer, he knewe by experience that Martius was no lesse valliant then him selfe, and howe he ever had better fortune and good happe in all battells, then him selfe had. Therefore he thought it best for him to have the leading of those that should make the warres abroade: and him selfe would keepe home, to provide for the safety of the citties and of his countrie, and to furnishe the campe also of all necessary provision abroade. So Martius being stronger then before, went first of all unto the cittie of Circees, inhabited by the Romaines, who willingly yelded them selves, and therefore had no hurte. From thence, he entred the countrie of the Latines, imagining the Romaines would fight with him there, to defend the Latines, who were their confederates, and had many times sent unto the Romaines for their ayde. But on the one side, the people of Rome were very ill willing to goe: and on the other side the Consuls being apon their going out of their office, would not hazard them selves for so small a time: so that the ambassadours of the Latines returned home againe,

CORIOLANUS

and dyd no good. Then Martius dyd besiege their citties, and having taken by force the townes of the Tolerinians, Vicanians, Pedanians, and the Bolanians, who made resistaunce: he sacked all their goodes, and tooke them prisoners. Suche as dyd yeld them selves willingly unto him, he was as carefull as possible might be to defend them from hurte: and bicause they should receyve no damage by his will, he removed his campe as farre from their confines as he could. Afterwards, he tooke the cittie of Boles by assault, being about an hundred furlonge from Rome, where he had a marvelous great spoyle, and put every man to the sword that was able to carie weapon. The other Volsces that were appointed to remaine in garrison for defence of their countrie, hearing this good newes, would tary no lenger at home, but armed them selves, and ranne to Martius campe, saying they dyd acknowledge no other captaine but him. Hereupon his fame ranne through all Italie, and every one praised him for a valliant captaine, for that by chaunge of one man for another, suche and so straunge events fell out in the state. In this while, all went still to wracke at Rome. For, to come into the field to fight with the enemie, they could not abyde to heare of it, they were one so muche against another, and full of seditious wordes, the nobilitie against the people, and the people against the nobilitie. Untill they had intelligence at the length that the enemies had layed seige to the cittie of Lavinium, in the which were all the temples and images of the goddes their protectours, and from whence came first their auncient originall, for that Æneas at his first arrivall into Italie dyd build that cittie. Then fell there out a marvelous sodain chaunge of minde among the people, and farre more straunge and contrarie in the nobilitie. For the people thought good to repeale the condemnation and exile of Martius. The Senate assembled upon it, would in no case yeld to that. Who either dyd it of a selfe will to be contrarie to the peoples desire: or bicause Martius should not returne through the grace and favour of the people. Or els, bicause they were throughly angrie and offended with him, that he would set apon the whole, being offended but by a fewe, and in his doings would shewe him selfe an

Lavinium built by Æneas.

open enemie besides unto his countrie: notwithstanding the most parte of them tooke the wrong they had done him, in marvelous ill parte, and as if the injurie had bene done unto them selves. Reporte being made of the Senates resolution, the people founde them selves in a straight: for they could authorise and confirme nothing by their voyces, unles it had bene first propounded and ordeined by the Senate. But Martius hearing this sturre about him, was in a greater rage with them then before: in so muche as he raised his seige incontinently before the cittie of Lavinium, and going towardes Rome, lodged his campe within fortie furlonge of the cittie, at the ditches called Cluiliæ. His incamping so neere Rome, dyd put all the whole cittie in a wonderfull feare: howbeit for the present time it appeased the sedition and dissention betwext the Nobilitie and the people. For there was no Consul, Senatour, nor Magistrate, that durst once contrarie the opinion of the people, for the calling home againe of Martius. When they sawe the women in a marvelous feare, ronning up and downe the cittie: the temples of the goddes full of olde people, weeping bitterly in their prayers to the goddes: and finally, not a man either wise or hardie to provide for their safetie: then they were all of opinion, that the people had reason to call home Martius againe, to reconcile them selves to him, and that the Senate on the contrary parte, were in marvelous great faulte to be angrie and in choller with him, when it stoode them upon rather to have gone out and intreated him. So they all agreed together to send ambassadours unto him, to let him understand howe his countrymen dyd call him home againe, and restored him to all his goodes, and besought him to deliver them from this warre. The ambassadours that were sent, were Martius familliar friendes, and acquaintaunce, who looked at the least for a curteous welcome of him, as of their familliar friende and kynseman. Howbeit they founde nothing lesse. For at their comming, they were brought through the campe, to the place where he was set in his chayer of state, with a marvelous and an unspeakable majestie, having the chiefest men of the Volsces about him: so he commaunded them to declare openly the

The Romaines send ambassadours to Coriolanus to treate of peace.

CORIOLANUS

cause of their comming. Which they delivered in the most humble and lowly wordes they possiblie could devise, and with all modest countenaunce and behaviour agreable for the same. When they had done their message: for the injurie they had done him, he aunswered them very hottely, and in great choller. But as generall of the Volsces, he willed them to restore unto the Volsces, all their landes and citties they had taken from them in former warres: and moreover, that they should geve them the like honour and freedome of Rome, as they had before geven to the Latines. For otherwise they had no other meane to ende this warre, if they dyd not graunte these honest and just conditions of peace. Thereupon he gave them thirtie dayes respit to make him aunswer. So the ambassadours returned straight to Rome, and Martius forthwith departed with his armie out of the territories of the Romaines. This was the first matter wherewith the Volsces (that most envied Martius glorie and authoritie) dyd charge Martius with. Among those, Tullus was chief: who though he had receyved no private injurie or displeasure of Martius, yet the common faulte and imperfection of mans nature wrought in him, and it grieved him to see his owne reputation bleamished, through Martius great fame and honour, and so him selfe to be lesse esteemed of the Volsces, then he was before. This fell out the more, bicause every man honoured Martius, and thought he only could doe all, and that all other governours and captaines must be content with suche credit and authoritie, as he would please to countenaunce them with. From hence they derived all their first accusations and secret murmurings against Martius. For private captaines conspiring against him, were very angrie with him: and gave it out, that the removing of the campe was a manifest treason, not of the townes, nor fortes, nor of armes, but of time and occasion, which was a losse of great importaunce, bicause it was that which in treason might both lose and binde all, and preserve the whole. Now Martius having geven the Romaines thirtie dayes respit for their aunswer, and specially bicause the warres have not accustomed to make any great chaunges, in lesse space of time then that: he thought it good yet, not

The first occasion of the Volsces envy to Coriolanus.

to lye a sleepe idle all the while, but went and destroyed the landes of the enemies allies, and tooke seven citties of theirs well inhabited, and the Romaines durst not once put them selves into the field, to come to their ayde and helpe: they were so fainte harted, so mistrustfull, and lothe besides to make warres. In so muche as they properly ressembled the bodyes paralyticke, and losed of their limmes and members: as those which through the palsey have lost all their sence and feeling. Wherefore, the time of peace expired, Martius being returned into the dominions of the Romaines againe with all his armie, they sent another ambassade unto him, to praye peace, and the remove of the Volsces out of their countrie: that afterwardes they might with better leysure fall to suche agreementes together, as should be thought most mete and necessarie. For the Romaines were no men that would ever yeld for feare. But if he thought the Volsces had any grounde to demaunde reasonable articles and conditions, all that they would reasonably aske should be graunted unto, by the Romaines, who of them selves would willingly yeld to reason, conditionally, that they dyd laye downe armes. Martius to that aunswered: that as generall of the Volsces he would replie nothing unto it. But yet as a Romaine cittizen, he would counsell them to let fall their pride, and to be conformable to reason, if they were wise: and that they should returne againe within three dayes, delivering up the articles agreed upon, which he had first delivered them. Or otherwise, that he would no more geve them assuraunce or safe conduite to returne againe into his campe, with suche vaine and frivolous messages. When the ambassadours were returned to Rome, and had reported Martius aunswer to the Senate: their cittie being in extreme daunger, and as it were in a terrible storme or tempest, they threw out (as the common proverbe sayeth) their holy ancker. For then they appointed all the bishoppes, priestes, ministers of the goddes, and keepers of holy things, and all the augures or soothesayers, which foreshowe things to come by observation of the flying of birdes (which is an olde auncient kynde of prophecying and divination amongest the Romaines) to goe to Martius apparelled, as when they

Another ambassade sent to Coriolanus.

The priestes and soothesayers sent to Coriolanus.

CORIO-
LANUS

doe their sacrifices: and first to intreate him to leave of warre, and then that he would speake to his contrymen, and conclude peace with the Volsces. Martius suffered them to come into his campe, but yet he graunted them nothing the more, neither dyd he entertaine them or speake more curteously to them, then he dyd the first time that they came unto him, saving only that he willed them to take the one of the two: either to accept peace under the first conditions offered, or els to receyve warre. When all this goodly rable of superstition and priestes were returned, it was determined in counsell that none should goe out of the gates of the cittie, and that they should watche and warde upon the walles, to repulse their enemies if they came to assault them: referring them selves and all their hope to time, and fortunes uncertaine favour, not knowing otherwise howe to remedie the daunger. Now all the cittie was full of tumult, feare, and marvelous doubt what would happen: untill at length there fell out suche a like matter, as Homer oftetimes sayed they would least have thought of. For in great matters, that happen seldome, Homer sayeth, and crieth out in this sorte,

The goddesse Pallas she, with her fayer glistering eyes,
dyd put into his minde suche thoughts, and made him so devise.

And in an other place:

But sure some god hath ta'ne, out of the peoples minde,
both wit and understanding eke, and have therewith assynde
some other simple spirite, in steede thereof to byde,
that so they might their doings all, for lacke of wit misguyde.

And in an other place:

The people of them selves, did either it consider,
or else some god instructed them, and so they joynde together.

Many reckon not of Homer, as referring matters unpossible, and fables of no likelyhoode or trothe, unto mans reason, free will, or judgement: which in deede is not his meaning. But things true and likely, he maketh to depend of our owne free wil and reason. For he oft speaketh these wordes:

I have thought it in my noble harte.

And in an other place:

Achilles angrie was, and sorie for to heare
him so to say, his heavy brest was fraught with pensive feare.

And againe in an other place:

Bellerophon (she) could not move with her fayer tongue,
so honest and so vertuous, he was the rest among.

But in wonderous and extraordinarie thinges, which are done by secret inspirations and motions, he doth not say that God taketh away, from man his choyce and freedom of will, but that he doth move it: neither that he doth worke desire in us, but objecteth to our mindes certaine imaginations whereby we are lead to desire, and thereby doth not make this our action forced, but openeth the way to our will, and addeth thereto courage, and hope of successe. For, either we must say, that the goddes meddle not with the causes and beginninges of our actions: or else what other meanes have they to helpe and further men? It is apparaunt that they handle not our bodies, nor move not our feete and handes, when there is occasion to use them: but that parte of our minde from which these motions proceede, is induced thereto, or caried away by such objectes and reasons, as God offereth unto it. Now the Romaine Ladies and gentlewomen did visite all the temples and goddes of the same, to make their prayers unto them: but the greatest Ladies (and more parte of them) were continuallie about the aulter of Jupiter Capitolin, emonge which troupe by name, was Valeria, Publicolaes owne sister. The selfe same Publicola, who did such notable service to the Romaines, both in peace and warres: and was dead also certaine yeares before, as we have declared in his life. His sister Valeria was greatly honoured and reverenced amonge all the Romaines: and did so modestlie and wiselie behave her selfe, that she did not shame nor dishonour the house she came of. So she sodainely fell into suche a fansie, as we have rehearsed before, and had (by some god as I thinke) taken holde of a noble devise. Whereuppon she rose, and thother Ladies with her, and they all together

Valeria Publicolaes sister.

CORIOLANUS

Volumnia, Martius mother.

The wordes of Valeria, unto Volumnia and Virgilia.

The aunswere of Volumnia to the Romaine ladies.

went straight to the house of Volumnia, Martius mother: and comming into her, founde her, and Martius wife her daughter in lawe set together, and havinge her husbande Martius young children in her lappe. Now all the traine of these Ladies sittinge in a ringe rounde about her: Valeria first beganne to speake in this sorte unto her: 'We Ladies, 'are come to visite you Ladies (my Ladie Volumnia and 'Virgilia) by no direction from the Senate, nor commaunde-'ment of other magistrate: but through the inspiration (as 'I take it) of some god above. Who havinge taken com-'passion and pitie of our prayers, hath moved us to come 'unto you, to intreate you in a matter, as well beneficiall 'for us, as also for the whole citizens in generall: but to 'your selves in especiall (if it please you to credit me) and 'shall redounde to our more fame and glorie, then the 'daughters of the Sabynes obteined in former age, when 'they procured lovinge peace, in stead of hatefull warre, 'betwene their fathers and their husbands. Come on good 'ladies, and let us goe all together unto Martius, to intreate 'him to take pitie uppon us, and also to reporte the trothe 'unto him, howe muche you are bounde unto the citizens: 'who notwithstandinge they have susteined greate hurte 'and losses by him, yet they have not hetherto sought re-'venge apon your persons by any discurteous usage, neither 'ever conceyved any suche thought or intent against you, 'but doe deliver ye safe into his handes, though thereby 'they looke for no better grace or clemency from him.' When Valeria had spoken this unto them, all thother ladyes together with one voyce confirmed that she had sayed. Then Volumnia in this sorte did aunswer her: 'My good ladies, we are partakers with you of the common 'miserie and calamitie of our countrie, and yet our griefe 'exceedeth yours the more, by reason of our particular 'misfortune: to feele the losse of my sonne Martius former 'valiancie and glorie, and to see his persone environned 'nowe with our enemies in armes, rather to see him foorth 'comminge and safe kept, then of any love to defende his 'persone. But yet the greatest griefe of our heaped mis-'happes is, to see our poore countrie brought to suche 'extremitie, that all hope of the safetie and preservation 'thereof, is nowe unfortunately cast uppon us simple women: 'bicause we knowe not what accompt he will make of us, 'sence he hath cast from him all care of his naturall countrie 'and common weale, which heretofore he hath holden more 'deere and precious, then either his mother, wife, or children. 'Notwithstandinge, if ye thinke we can doe good, we will 'willingly doe what you will have us: bringe us to him I 'pray you. For if we can not prevaile, we maye yet dye 'at his feete, as humble suters for the safetie of our countrie.' Her aunswere ended, she tooke her daughter in lawe, and Martius children with her, and being accompanied with all the other Romaine ladies, they went in troupe together unto the Volsces campe: whome when they sawe, they of them selves did both pitie and reverence her, and there was not a man amonge them that once durst say a worde unto her. Nowe was Martius set then in his chayer of state, with all the honours of a generall, and when he had spied the women comming a farre of, he marveled what the matter ment: but afterwardes knowing his wife which came formest, he determined at the first to persist in his obstinate and inflexible rancker. But overcomen in the ende with naturall affection, and being altogether altered to see them: his harte would not serve him to tarie their comming to his chayer, but comming downe in hast, he went to meete them, and first he kissed his mother, and imbraced her a pretie while, then his wife and litle children. And nature so wrought with him, that the teares fell from his eyes, and he coulde not keepe him selfe from making much of them, but yeelded to the affection of his bloode, as if he had bene violently caried with the furie of a most swift running streame. After he had thus lovingly received them, and perceivinge that his mother Volumnia would beginne to speake to him, he called the chiefest of the counsell of the Volsces to heare what she would say. Then she spake in this sorte: 'If we helde our peace (my sonne) and determined 'not to speake, the state of our poore bodies, and present 'sight of our rayment, would easely bewray to thee what 'life we have led at home, since thy exile and abode abroad.

The oration of Volumnia, unto her sonne Coriolanus.

CORIOLANUS

'But thinke now with thy selfe, howe much more unfortunatly, then all the women livinge we are come hether, 'considering that the sight which should be most pleasaunt 'to all other to beholde, spitefull fortune hath made most 'fearefull to us: making my selfe to see my sonne, and my 'daughter here, her husband, besieging the walles of his 'native countrie. So as that which is thonly comforte to 'all other in their adversitie and miserie, to pray unto the 'goddes, and to call to them for aide: is the onely thinge 'which plongeth us into most deepe perplexitie. For we 'can not (alas) together pray, both for victorie, for our 'countrie, and for safety of thy life also: but a worlde of 'grievous curses, yea more then any mortall enemie can heape 'uppon us, are forcibly wrapt up in our prayers. For the 'bitter soppe of most harde choyce is offered thy wife and 'children, to forgoe the one of the two: either to lose the 'persone of thy selfe, or the nurse of their native contrie. For 'my selfe (my sonne) I am determined not to tarie, till fortune 'in my life time doe make an ende of this warre. For if I 'cannot persuade thee, rather to doe good unto both parties, 'then to overthrowe and destroye the one, preferring love 'and nature, before the malice and calamitie of warres: thou 'shalt see, my sonne, and trust unto it, thou shalt no soner 'marche forward to assault thy countrie, but thy foote shall 'treade upon thy mothers wombe, that brought thee first 'into this world. And I maye not deferre to see the daye, 'either that my sonne be led prisoner in triumphe by his 'naturall country men, or that he him selfe doe triumphe 'of them, and of his naturall countrie. For if it were so, 'that my request tended to save thy countrie, in destroying 'the Volsces: I must confesse, thou wouldest hardly and 'doubtfully resolve on that. For as to destroye thy naturall 'countrie, it is altogether unmete and unlawfull: so were it 'not just, and lesse honorable, to betraye those that put 'their trust in thee. But my only demaunde consisteth, to 'make a gayle deliverie of all evills, which delivereth equall 'benefit and safety, both to the one and the other, but most 'honorable for the Volsces. For it shall appeare, that having 'victorie in their handes, they have of speciall favour graunted 'us singular graces: peace, and amitie, albeit them selves have 'no lesse parte of both, then we. Of which good, if so it 'came to passe, thy selfe is thonly authour, and so hast thou 'thonly honour. But if it faile, and fall out contrarie: thy 'selfe alone deservedly shall carie the shamefull reproche and 'burden of either partie. So, though the ende of warre be 'uncertaine, yet this notwithstanding is most certaine: that 'if it be thy chaunce to conquer, this benefit shalt thou reape 'of thy goodly conquest, to be chronicled the plague and 'destroyer of thy countrie. And if fortune also overthrowe 'thee, then the world will saye, that through desire to re-'venge thy private injuries, thou hast for ever undone thy 'good friendes, who dyd most lovingly and curteously receyve 'thee.' Martius gave good eare unto his mothers wordes, without interrupting her speache at all: and after she had sayed what she would, he held his peace a prety while, and aunswered not a worde. Hereupon she beganne againe to speake unto him, and sayed: 'My sonne, why doest thou 'not aunswer me? doest thou thinke it good altogether to 'geve place unto thy choller and desire of revenge, and 'thinkest thou it not honestie for thee to graunt thy 'mothers request, in so weighty a cause? doest thou take 'it honorable for a noble man, to remember the wronges 'and injuries done him: and doest not in like case thinke 'it an honest noble mans parte, to be thankefull for the 'goodnes that parents doe shewe to their children, acknow-'ledging the duety and reverence they ought to beare unto 'them? No man living is more bounde to shewe him selfe 'thankefull in all partes and respects, then thy selfe: who 'so unnaturally sheweth all ingratitude. Moreover (my 'sonne) thou hast sorely taken of thy countrie, exacting 'grievous payments apon them, in revenge of the injuries 'offered thee: besides, thou hast not hitherto shewed thy 'poore mother any curtesie. And therefore, it is not only 'honest, but due unto me, that without compulsion I should 'obtaine my so just and reasonable request of thee. But 'since by reason I cannot persuade thee to it, to what pur-'pose doe I deferre my last hope?' And with these wordes, her selfe, his wife and children, fell downe upon their knees

CORIO-
LANUS

Coriolanus compassion of his mother.

before him. Martius seeing that, could refraine no lenger, but went straight and lifte her up, crying out: Oh mother, what have you done to me? And holding her hard by the right hande, oh mother, sayed he, you have wonne a happy victorie for your countrie, but mortall and unhappy for your sonne: for I see my self vanquished by you alone. These wordes being spoken openly, he spake a litle a parte with his mother and wife, and then let them returne againe to Rome, for so they dyd request him: and so remaining in campe that night, the next morning he dislodged, and marched homewardes into the Volsces countrie againe, who were not all of one minde, nor all alike contented. For some misliked him, and that he had done. Other being well pleased that peace should be made, sayed: that neither the one, nor the other, deserved blame nor reproche. Other, though they misliked that was done, dyd not thincke him an ill man for that he dyd, but sayed: he was not to be blamed, though he yelded to suche a forcible extremitie. Howbeit no man contraried his departure, but all obeyed his commaundement, more for respect of his worthines and valiancie, then for feare of his authoritie. Now the cittizens of Rome plainely shewed, in what feare and daunger their cittie stoode of this warre, when they were delivered. For so sone as the watche upon the walles of the cittie perceyved the Volsces campe to remove, there was not a temple in the cittie but was presently set open, and full of men, wearing garlands of flowers upon their heads, sacrificing to the goddes, as they were wont to doe upon the newes of some great obteined victorie. And this common joye was yet more manifestly shewed, by the honorable curtesies the whole Senate, and people dyd bestowe on their ladyes. For they were all throughly persuaded, and dyd certenly beleeve, that the ladyes only were cause of the saving of the cittie, and delivering them selves from the instant daunger of the warre. Whereupon the Senate ordeined, that the magistrates to gratifie and honour these ladyes, should graunte them all that they would require. And they only requested that they would build a temple of Fortune of the women, for the building whereof they offered them selves to defraye the

Coriolanus withdraweth his armie from Rome.

whole charge of the sacrifices, and other ceremonies belonging to the service of the goddes. Nevertheles, the Senate commending their good will and forwardnes, ordeined, that the temple and image should be made at the common charge of the cittie. Notwithstanding that, the ladyes gathered money emong them, and made with the same a second image of Fortune, which the Romaines saye dyd speake as they offred her up in the temple, and dyd set her in her place: and they affirme, that she spake these wordes: Ladyes, ye have devoutely offered me up. Moreover, that she spake that twise together, making us to beleeve things that never were, and are not to be credited. For to see images that seeme to sweate or weepe, or to put forth any humour red or blowdie, it is not a thing unpossible. For wodde and stone doe commonly receyve certaine moysture, whereof is ingendred an humour, which doe yeld of them selves, or doe take of the ayer, many sortes and kyndes of spottes and cullers: by which signes and tokens it is not amisse we thincke, that the goddes sometimes doe warne men of things to come. And it is possible also, that these images and statues doe somtimes put forth soundes, like unto sighes or mourning, when in the middest or bottome of the same, there is made some violent separation, or breaking a sonder of things, blowen or devised therein: but that a bodie which hath neither life nor soule, should have any direct or exquisite worde formed in it by expresse voyce, that is altogether unpossible. For the soule, nor god him selfe can distinctly speake without a bodie, having necessarie organes and instrumentes mete for the partes of the same, to forme and utter distinct wordes. But where stories many times doe force us to beleeve a thing reported to be true, by many grave testimonies: there we must saye, that it is some passion contrarie to our five naturall sences, which being begotten in the imaginative parte or understanding, draweth an opinion unto it selfe, even as we doe in our sleeping. For many times we thinke we heare, that we doe not heare: and we imagine we see, that we see not. Yet notwithstanding, such as are godly bent, and zealously geven to thinke apon heavenly things, so as they can no waye be drawen from be-

The temple of Fortune built for the women.

The image of Fortune spake to the ladyes at Rome.

miracles

Of the sweating and voyces of images.

Of the omnipotencie of God.

leeving that which is spoken of them, they have this reason to grounde the foundation of their beleefe upon. That is, the omnipotencie of God which is wonderfull, and hath no manner of resemblaunce or likelines of proportion unto ours, but is altogether contrarie as touching our nature, our moving, our arte, and our force: and therefore if he doe any thing unpossible to us, or doe bring forth and devise things, without mans common reache and understanding, we must not therefore thinke it unpossible at all. For if in other things he is farre contrarie to us, muche more in his workes and secret operations, he farre passeth all the rest: but the most parte of goddes doings, as Heraclitus sayeth, for lacke of faith, are hidden and unknowen unto us. Now when Martius was returned againe into the cittie of Antium from his voyage, Tullus that hated and could no lenger abide him for the feare he had of his authoritie: sought divers meanes to make him out of the waye, thinking that if he let slippe that present time, he should never recover the like and fit occasion againe. Wherefore Tullus having procured many other of his confederacy, required Martius might be deposed from his estate, to render up accompt to the Volsces of his charge and government. Martius fearing to become a private man againe under Tullus being generall (whose authoritie was greater otherwise, then any other emong all the Volsces) aunswered: he was willing to geve up his charge, and would resigne it into the handes of the lordes of the Volsces, if they dyd all commaund him, as by all their commaundement he receyved it. And moreover, that he would not refuse even at that present to geve up an accompt unto the people, if they would tarie the hearing of it. The people hereupon called a common counsaill, in which assembly there were certen oratours appointed, that stirred up the common people against him: and when they had tolde their tales, Martius rose up to make them aunswer. Now, notwithstanding the mutinous people made a marvelous great noyse, yet when they sawe him, for the reverence they bare unto his valliantnes, they quieted them selves, and gave still audience to alledge with leysure what he could for his purgation. Moreover, the honestest men of the Antiates, and who most re-

Tullus Aufidius seeketh to kill Coriolanus.

joyced in peace, shewed by their countenaunce that they would heare him willingly, and judge also according to their conscience. Whereupon Tullus fearing that if he dyd let him speake, he would prove his innocencie to the people, bicause emongest other things he had an eloquent tongue, besides that the first good service he had done to the people of the Volsces, dyd winne him more favour, then these last accusations could purchase him displeasure: and furthermore, the offence they layed to his charge, was a testimonie of the good will they ought him, for they would never have thought he had done them wrong for that they tooke not the cittie of Rome, if they had not bene very neere taking of it, by meanes of his approche and conduction. For these causes Tullus thought he might no lenger delaye his pretence and enterprise, neither to tarie for the mutining and rising of the common people against him: wherefore, those that were of the conspiracie, beganne to crie out that he was not to be heard, nor that they would not suffer a traytour to usurpe tyrannicall power over the tribe of the Volsces, who would not yeld up his estate and authoritie. And in saying these wordes, they all fell upon him, and killed him in the market place, none of the people once offering to rescue him. Howbeit it is a clere case, that this murder was not generally consented unto, of the most parte of the Volsces: for men came out of all partes to honour his bodie, and dyd honorably burie him, setting out his tombe with great store of armour and spoyles, as the tombe of a worthie persone and great captaine. The Romaines understanding of his death, shewed no other honour or malice, saving that they graunted the ladyes the request they made: that they might mourne tenne moneths for him, and that was the full time they used to weare blackes for the death of their fathers, brethern, or husbands, according to Numa Pompilius order, who stablished the same, as we have enlarged more amplie in the description of his life. Now Martius being dead, the whole state of the Volsces hartely wished him alive againe. For first of all they fell out with the Æques (who were their friendes and confederates) touching preheminence and place: and this quarrell grew on so farre betwene them, and frayes and

Coriolanus murdered in the cittie of Antium.

Coriolanus funeralles.

The time of mourning appointed by Numa.

CORIOLANUS

murders fell out apon it one with another. After that, the Romaines overcame them in battell, in which Tullus was slaine in the field, and the flower of all their force was put to the sworde: so that they were compelled to accept most shamefull conditions of peace, in yelding them selves subject unto the conquerers, and promising to be obedient at their commandement.

Tullus Aufidius slaine in battell.

THE COMPARISON OF ALCIBIADES WITH MARTIUS CORIOLANUS

The acts done by both.

NOW that we have written all the dedes of worthie memorie, done by either of them both: we maye presently discerne, that in matters of warre, the one hath not greatly exceeded the other. For both of them in their charge, were a like hardie and valliant for their persones, as also wise and politike in the warres: unles they will saye, that Alcibiades was the better captaine, as he that had foughten more battells with his enemies, both by sea and lande, then ever Coriolanus had done, and had allwayes the victorie of his enemies. For otherwise, in this they were much a like: that where they were both present, and had charge and power to commaund, all things prospered notably, and with good successe on the parte they were of: and also when they tooke the contrary side, they made the first have the worse every waye. Now for matters of government, the noble men and honest cittizens dyd hate Alcibiades manner of rule in the common weale, as of a man most dissolute, and geven to flatterie: bicause he ever studied by all devise he could, to currie favour with the common people. So dyd the Romaines malice also Coriolanus government, for that it was to arrogant, prowde, and tyrannicall: whereby neither the one nor the other was to be commended. Notwithstanding, he is lesse to be blamed, that seeketh to please and gratifie his common people: then he that despiseth and disdaineth them, and therefore offereth them wrong and injurie, bicause he would not seeme to flatter them, to winne the more authoritie. For as it is an evill thing to flatter the common people to winne credit: even so is it besides dishonesty, and injustice also, to atteine to credit and authoritie, for one to make him selfe terrible to the people, by offering them wrong and violence. It is true that Martius was ever counted an honest natured man, plaine and simple, without arte or cunning: Howbeit Alcibiades merely contrarie, for he was fine, subtill, and deceiptfull. And the greatest faulte they ever burdened Alcibiades for, was his malice and deceipt, wherewith he abused the ambassadours of the Lacedæmonians, and that he was a let that peace was not concluded, as Thucydides reporteth. Now, though by this acte he sodainly brought the cittie of Athens into warres, yet he brought it thereby to be of greater power, and more fearefull to the enemies, by making alliance with the Mantinians and the Argives, who by Alcibiades practise entred into league with the Athenians. And Martius, as Dionysius the historiographer writeth: dyd by craft and deceipt bring the Romaines into warres against the Volsces, causing the Volsces maliciously, and wrongfully to be suspected, that went to Rome to see the games played. But the cause why he dyd it, made the fact so much more fowle and wicked. For it was not done for any civill dissention, nor for any jelouzy and contention in matters of government, as Alcibiades dyd: but only following his cholerike moode, that would be pleased with no thing, as Dion sayed, he would needes trouble and turmoile the most parte of Italie, and so beinge angrie with his countrie, he destroyed many other townes and cities that could not helpe it, nor doe with all. This is true also, that Alcibiades spite and malice did worke great mischiefe and miserie to his countrie: but when he saw they repented them of the injurie they had done him, he came to him selfe, and did withdrawe his armie. An other time also, when they had banished Alcibiades, he would not yet suffer the captaines of the Athenians to runne into great errours, neither would he see them cast away, by followinge ill counsell which they

The manners of Alcibiades and Coriolanus.

tooke, neither would he forsake them in any daunger they put them selves into. But he did the very same that Aristides had done in olde time unto Themistocles, for which he was then, and is yet so greatly praised. For he went unto the captaines that had charge then of the armie of the Athenians, although they were not his friendes, and tolde them wherein they did amisse, and what they had further to doe. Where Martius to the contrarie, did first great hurte unto the whole citie of Rome, though all in Rome had not generally offended him: yea, and when the best and chiefest parte of the citie were grieved for his sake, and were very sorie and angrie for the injurie done him. Furthermore, the Romaines sought to appease one onely displeasure and despite they had done him, by many ambassades, petitions and requestes they made, whereunto he never yelded, while his mother, wife, and children came, his harte was so hardned. And hereby it appeared he was entred into this cruell warre (when he would harken to no peace) of an intent utterly to destroy and spoyle his countrie, and not as though he ment to recover it, or to returne thither againe. Here was in deede the difference betwene them: that spialls being layed by the Lacedæmonians to kill Alcibiades, for the malice they did beare him, as also for that they were affrayed of him, he was compelled to returne home againe to Athens. Where Martius contrariwise, having bene so honorably received and entertained by the Volsces, he could not with honestie forsake them, consideringe they had done him that honour, as to choose him their generall, and trusted him so farre, as they put all their whole armie and power into his handes: and not as thother, whome the Lacedæmonians rather abused, then used him, suffering him to goe up and downe their citie (and afterwardes in the middest of their campe) without honour or place at all. So that in the ende Alcibiades was compelled to put him selfe into the handes of Tisaphernes: unlesse they will say that he went thither of purpose to him, with intent to save the citie of Athens from utter destruction, for the desire he had to returne home againe. Moreover, we read of Alcibiades, that he was a great taker, and would be corrupted with money: and when he had it, he would

Alcibiades and Coriolanus manner for money.

ALCIBIADES AND CORIOLANUS

most licentiously and dishonestly spend it. Where Martius in contrarie maner would not so much as accept giftes lawefully offered him by his Captaines, to honour him for his valliantnesse. And the cause why the people did beare him such ill will, for the controversie they had with the Nobilitie about clearing of dettes, grew: for that they knewe well enough it was not for any gayne or benefit he had gotten thereby, so much as it was for spite and displeasure he thought to doe them. Antipater in a letter of his, writing of the death of Aristotle the philosopher, doth not without cause commend the singular giftes that were in Alcibiades, and this inespecially: that he passed all other for winning mens good willes. Wheras all Martius noble actes and vertues, wanting that affabilitie, became hatefull even to those that received benefit by them, who could not abide his severitie and selfe will: which causeth desolation (as Plato sayeth) and men to be ill followed, or altogether forsaken. Contrariwise, seeing Alcibiades had a trimme enterteinment, and a very good grace with him, and could facion him selfe in all companies: it was no marvell if his well doing were gloriously commended, and him selfe much honoured and beloved of the people, considering that some faultes he did, were oftetimes taken for matters of sporte, and toyes of pleasure. And this was the cause, that though many times he did great hurte to the common wealth, yet they did ofte make him their generall, and trusted him with the charge of the whole citie. Where Martius suing for an office of honour that was due to him, for the sundrie good services he had done to the state, was notwithstanding repulsed, and put by. Thus doe we see, that they to whome the one did hurte, had no power to hate him: and thother that honoured his vertue, had no liking to love his persone. Martius also did never any great exployte, beinge generall of his contry men, but when he was generall of their enemies against his naturall contrie: whereas Alcibiades, being both a private persone, and a generall, did notable service unto the Athenians. By reason whereof, Alcibiades wheresoever he was present, had the upper hande ever of his accusers, even as he would him selfe, and their accusations tooke no place

Alcibiades and Coriolanus love unto their contrie.

ALCIBIADES AND CORIOLANUS

against him: onlesse it were in his abscence. Where Martius being present, was condemned by the Romaines: and in his person murdered, and slaine by the Volsces. But here I can not say they have done well, nor justly, albeit him selfe gave them some colour to doe it, when he openly denied the Romaine Ambassadors peace, which after he privatly graunted, at the request of women. So by this dede of his, he tooke not away the enmity that was betwene both people: but leaving warre still betwene them, he made the Volsces (of whome he was generall) to lose the oportunity of noble victory. Where in deede he should (if he had done as he ought) have withdrawen his armie with their counsaill and consent, that had reposed so great affiance in him, in making him their generall: if he had made that accompt of them, as their good will towards him did in duety binde him. Or else, if he did not care for the Volsces in the enterprise of this warre, but had only procured it of intent to be revenged, and afterwards to leave it of, when his anger was blowen over: yet he had no reason for the love of his mother to pardone his contrie, but rather he should in pardoning his contrie, have spared his mother, bicause his mother and wife were members of the bodie of his contrie and city, which he did besiege. For in that he uncurteously rejected all publike petitions, requestes of Ambassadors, intreaties of the bishoppes and priestes, to gratifie only the request of his mother with his departure: that was no acte so much to honour his mother with, as to dishonour his contrie by, the which was preserved for the pitie and intercession of a woman, and not for the love of it selfe, as if it had not bene worthie of it. And so was this departure a grace, to say truly, very odious and cruell, and deserved no thankes of either partie, to him that did it. For he withdrew his army, not at the request of the Romaines, against whom he made warre: nor with their consent, at whose charge the warre was made. And of all his misfortune and ill happe, the austeritie of his nature, and his hawtie obstinate minde, was the onely cause: the which of it selfe being hatefull to the worlde, when it is joyned with ambition, it groweth then much more churlish, fierce, and intollerable. For men that have that fault in

ALCIBIADES AND CORIOLANUS

nature, are not affable to the people, seeming thereby as though they made no estimacion or regard of the people: and yet on thother side, if the people should not geve them honour and reverence, they would straight take it in scorne, and litle care for the matter. For so did Metellus, Aristides, and Epaminondas, all used this manner: not to seeke the good will of the common people by flatterie and dissimulation: which was in deede, bicause they despised that which the people coulde geve or take awaye. Yet would they not be offended with their citizens, when they were amerced, and set at any fines, or that they banished them, or gave them any other repulse: but they loved them as wel as they did before, so soone as they shewed any token of repentaunce, and that they were sorie for the wrong they had done them, and were easely made frendes againe with them, after they were restored from their banishment. For he that disdaineth to make much of the people, and to have their favour, shoulde much more scorne to seeke to be revenged, when he is repulsed. For, to take a repulse and deniall of honour, so inwardly to the hart: commeth of no other cause, but that he did too earnestly desire it. Therefore Alcibiades did not dissemble at all, that he was not very glad to see him selfe honored, and sory to be rejected and denied any honour: but also he sought all the meanes he could to make him selfe beloved of those amongest whome he lived. Whereas Martius stowtnes, and hawty stomake, did stay him from making much of those, that might advaunce and honour him: and yet his ambition made him gnawe him selfe for spite and anger, when he sawe he was despised. And this is all that reasonably may be reproved in him: for otherwise he lacked no good commendable vertues and qualities. For his temperaunce, and cleane handes from taking of bribes and money, he may be compared with the most perfect, vertuous, and honest men of all Græce: but not with Alcibiades, who was in that undoutedly alwayes too licentious and losely geven, and had too small regard of his credit and honestie.

Coriolanus notable abstinence from bribes.

THE END OF CAIUS MARTIUS CORIOLANUS LIFE

THE LIFE OF PAULUS ÆMILIUS

HEN I first beganne to write these lines, my intent was to profit other: but since, continuing and going on, I have muche profited my self by looking into these histories, as if I looked into a glasse, to frame and facion my life, to the mowld and patterne of these vertuous noble men. For ronning over their manners in this sorte, and seeking also to describe their lives: me thinkes I am still conversaunt and familliar with them, and doe as it were lodge them with me, one after another. And when I come to peruse their histories, and to waye the vertues and qualities they have had, and what singularitie eche of them possessed: and to choose and culle out the chiefest things of note in them, and their best speaches and doings most worthie of memorie: Then I crie out,

O godds, can there be more passing pleasure in the worlde?

Or is there any thing of more force, to teach man civill manners, and a ruled life, or to reforme the vice in man? Democritus the philosopher writeth, that we should praye we might ever see happy images and sightes in the ayer, and that the good which is meete and proper to our nature, maye rather come to us, then that is evill and unfortunate: presupposing a false opinion and doctrine in philosophie, which allureth men to infinite superstitions. That there are good and bad images flying in the ayer, which geve a good or ill impression unto men, and incline men to vice, or to vertue. But as for me, by continuall reading of auncient histories, and gathering these lives together which now I leave before you, and by keeping allwayes in minde the actes of the most noble, vertuous, and best geven men of former age, and worthie memorie: I doe teache and prepare my selfe to shake of and banishe from me, all lewde and dishonest condition, if by chaunce the companie and conversation of them whose companie I keepe, and must of necessitie haunte, doe acquainte me with some unhappie or ungratious touche. This is easie unto me, that doe dispose my quiet minde, and not troubled with any passion, unto the deepe consideration of so many noble examples. As I doe present unto you now in this volume, the lives of Timoleon the Corinthian, and of Paulus Æmilius the Romaine, who had not only a good and an upright minde with them, but were also fortunate and happie, in all the matters they both did take in hand. So as you shall hardly judge, when you have red over their lives, whether wisedome, or good fortune brought them to atchieve to suche honorable actes and exploytes as they dyd. Many (and the most parte of historiographers) doe write, that the house and familie of the Æmilians in Rome, was allwayes of the most auncient of the nobilitie, which they call *Patricians.* Some writers affirme also, that the first of the house that gave name to all the posteritie after, was Marcus, the sonne of Pythagoras, the wise, whom king Numa for the sweetnes and pleasaunt grace of his tongue, surnamed Marcus Æmilius: and those specially affirme it, that saye king Numa was Pythagoras scholler. Howsoever it was, the most parte of this familie that obteined honour and estimation for their vertue, were ever fortunate also in all their doings, saving Lucius Paulus only, who dyed in the battell of Cannes. But his misfortune doth beare manifest testimonie of his wisedome and valliancy together. For he was forced to fight against his will, when he sawe he could not bridle the rashnes of his fellowe Consul that would nedes joyne battell, and to doe as he dyd, saving that he fled not as the other, who being first procurer of the battell, was the first that ranne awaye: where he to the contrarie, to his power dyd what he could to let him, and dyd sticke by it, and fought it valliantly unto the last gaspe. This Æmylius left a daughter behind him called Æmylia, which was maried unto Scipio the great: and a sonne, Paulus Æmylius, being the same man whose life we presently treate of. His youth fortunately fell out in a florishing time of glorie and honour, through the sundrie vertues of many

The house of the Æmylians came of Pythagoras sonne.

Lucius Paulus Æmylius Consul, slaine at the battell of Cannes.

Æmylia, the daughter of Lucius Æmylius, maried to Scipio the great.

great and noble persones living in those dayes, emong whom he made his name famous also: and it was not by that ordinarie arte and course, which the best esteemed young men of that age dyd take and followe. For he dyd not use to pleade private mens causes in lawe, neither would creepe into mens favour by fawning upon any of them: though he sawe it a common practise, and policie of men, to seeke the peoples favour and good willes by suche meanes. Moreover, he refused not that common course which other tooke, for that it was contrarie to his nature, or that he could not frame with either of both, if he had bene so disposed: but he rather sought to winne reputation by his honestie, his valliantnes, and upright dealing, as choosing that the better waye, then either of thother two, in so much as in marvelous shorte time he passed all those that were of his age. The first office of honour he sued for, was the office of Ædilis, in which sute he was preferred before twelve other that sued for the selfe same office: who were men of no small qualitie, for they all came afterwardes to be Consuls. After this, he was chosen to be one of the number of the priestes, whom the Romaines call Augures: who have the charge of all the divinations and soothesayings, in telling of things to come by flying of byrdes, and signes in the ayer. He was so carefull, and tooke suche paynes to understand how the Romaines dyd use the same, and with suche diligence sought the observation of the auncient religion of Romaines in all holie matters: that where that priesthood was before esteemed but a title of honour, and desired for the name only: he brought it to passe, that it was the most honorable science, and best reputed of in Rome. Wherein he confirmed the philosophers opinion: that religion is the knowledge how to serve God. For when he dyd any thing belonging to his office of priesthood, he dyd it with great experience, judgment, and diligence, leaving all other thoughtes, and without omitting any auncient ceremonie, or adding to any newe, contending oftentimes with his companions, in things which seemed light, and of small moment: declaring unto them, that though we doe presume the goddes are easie to be pacified, and that they readilie pardone all faultes and

The vertues of Paulus Æmylius.

Paulus Æmylius made Ædilis and Augure.

The philosophers opinion of religion.

Paulus diligence in the common wealth, even in trifles.

scapes committed by negligence, yet if it were no more but for respect of common wealths sake, they should not slightly, nor carelesly dissemble or passe over faultes committed in those matters. For no man (sayeth he) at the first that committeth any faulte, doth alone trouble the state of the common wealth: but withall, we must thincke he leaveth the groundes of civill government, that is not as carefull to keepe the institutions of small matters, as also of the great. So was he also a severe captaine, and strict observer of all marshall discipline, not seeking to winne the souldiers love by flatterie, when he was generall in the field, as many dyd in that time: neither corrupting them for a second charge, by shewing him selfe gentle and curteous in the first, unto those that served under him: but him selfe dyd orderly shewe them the very rules and preceptes of the discipline of warres, even as a priest that should expresse the names and ceremonies of some holy sacrifice wherein were daunger to omit any parte or parcell. Howbeit, being terrible to execute the lawe of armes apon rebellious and disobedient souldiers, he kept up thereby the state of the common weale the better: judging, to overcome the enemie by force, was but an accessorie as a man maye terme it, in respect of well training and ordering his cittizens by good discipline. While the Romaines were in warres against king Antiochus surnamed the great, in the South partes: all the chiefest captaines of Rome being employed that wayes, there fell out another in the necke of that, in the West partes towardes Spayne, where they were all up in armes. Thither they sent Æmylius Prætor, not with sixe axes as the other Prætors had borne before them, but with twelve: so that under the name of Prætor, he had the authoritie and dignitie of a Consul. He twise overcame the barbarous people in mayne battell, and slue a thirtie thousand of them, and got this victorie through his great skill and wisedome, in choosing the advantage of place and time, to fight with his enemies, even as they passed over a river: which easely gave his souldiers the victorie. Moreover he tooke there, two hundred and fiftie citties, all which dyd open, and gladly receyve him in. So, leaving that countrie quiet and in good peace, and

The discipline of warres.

Paulus Æmylius sent Prætor into Spayne.

Æmylius skilful to choose place and time to fight.

having receaved their fealtie by othe made betweene his handes, he returned againe to Rome, not enriched the value of a Drachma more then before. For then he tooke litle regard to his expences, he spent so franckly, neither was his purse his master, though his revenue was not great to beare it out: as it appeared to the world after his death, for all that he had, was litle enough to satisfie his wifes joynter. His first wife was Papyria, the daughter of a noble Consul Papyrius Masso, and after they had lived a long time together, he was divorsed from her, notwithstanding he had goodly children by her. For by her he had that famous Scipio the second, and Fabius Maximus. The just cause of the divorse betweene them, appeareth not to us in writing: but me thinckes the tale that is tolde concerning the separation of a certaine mariage is true. That a certen Romaine having forsaken his wife, her friendes fell out with him, and asked him: What fault dost thou finde in her? is she not honest of her bodie? is she not fayer? doth she not bring thee goodly children? But he putting forth his foote, shewed them his shooe, and aunswered them. Is not this a goodly shooe? is it not finely made? and is it not newe? yet I dare saye there is never a one of you can tell where it wringeth me. For to saye truely, great and open faultes are commonly occasions to make husbands put awaye their wives: but yet oftentimes household wordes ronne so betweene them (proceeding of crooked conditions, or of diversitie of natures, which straungers are not privie unto) that in processe of time they doe beget suche a straunge alteration of love and mindes in them, as one house can no lenger holde them. So Æmylius, having put awaye Papyria his first wife, he maried another that brought him two sonnes, which he brought up with him selfe in his house, and gave his two first sonnes (to wit, Scipio the second, and Fabius Maximus) in adoption, to two of the noblest and richest families of the cittie of Rome. The elder of the twaine, unto Fabius Maximus, he that was five times Consul: and the younger unto the house of the Cornelians, whom the sonne of the great Scipio the African dyd adopt, being his cosin germaine, and named him Scipio. Concerning his daughters, the sonne of Cato maried the one,

Scipio the seconde, and Fabius Maximus, were the sonnes of P. Æmylius, by Papyria his first wife.

A prety tale of a Romaine that forsooke his wife.

and Ælius Tubero the other, who was a marvelous honest man, and dyd more nobly mainteine him selfe in his povertie, then any other Romaine: for they were sixteene persones all of one name, and of the house of the Ælians, very neere a kynne one to the other, who had all but one litle house in the cittie, and a small farme in the countrie, wherewith they enterteined them selves, and lived all together in one house, with their wives, and many litle children. Amongest their wives, one of them was the daughter of Paulus Æmylius, after he had bene twise Consul, and had triumphed twise, not being ashamed of her husbands povertie, but wondering at his vertue that made him poore. Whereas brethern and kynsemen, as the world goeth now, if they dwell not farre a sonder, and in other countries, not one neere another, and that rivers parte them not, or walles devide their landes, leaving great large wastes betweene them: they are never quiet, but still in quarrell one with another. Goodly examples doth this storie laye before the wise, and well advised readers, to learne thereby howe to frame their life, and wisely to behave them selves. Now Æmylius being chosen Consul, went to make warre with the Ligurians, who dwelled in the Alpes, and which otherwise are called Ligustines. These are very valliant and warlike men, and were very good souldiers at that time, by reason of their continual warres against the Romaines, whose neere neighbours they were. For they dwelt in the furdest parte of Italie, that bordereth upon the great Alpes, and the rowe of Alpes, whereof the foote joyneth to the Thuscan sea, and pointeth towards Africke, and are mingled with the Gaules, and Spanyards, neighbours unto that sea coast: who scowring all the Mediterranian sea at that time, unto the straight of Hercules pillars, dyd with their litle light pinnases of pirats, let all the trafficke and entercourse of marchaundise. Æmylius being gone to seeke them in their countrie, they taried his comming with an armie of forty thousand men: nevertheles, though he had but eight thousand men in all, and that they were five to one of his, yet he gave the onset apon them, and overthrew them, and drave them into their citties. Then he sent to offer them peace, for the Romaines would not altogether destroye the Ligurians,

The vertue of Ælius Tubero, his povertie and quiet life.

Innaturalitie emongest kinred infamous.

Æmylius Consul.

Æmylius overcommeth the Ligurians.

bicause their countrie was a rampeyr or bullwarke against the invasion of the Gaules, who laye lurking for oportunitie and occasion to invade Italie : whereupon these Ligurians yelded them selves unto him, and put all their fortes and shippes into his handes. Æmylius delivered unto them their holdes againe, without other hurte done unto them, saving that he rased the walles of their fortifications: howbeit he tooke all their shippes from them, leaving them litle botes of three owers only, and no greater, and set all the prisoners at libertie they had taken, both by sea and by lande, aswell Romaines as other, which were a marvelous number. These were all the notable acts he dyd worthie memorie, in the first yere of his Consulshippe. Afterwards, he oftentimes shewed him self very desirous to be Consul againe, and dyd put forth him selfe to sue for it : but when he was denied it, he never after made sute for it againe, but gave him selfe only to studie divine things, and to see his children vertuously brought up, not only in the Romaine tongue which him selfe was taught, but also a litle more curiously in the Græke tongue. For he dyd not only retaine Grammarians, Rethoricians, and Logitians, but also painters, gravers of images, riders of horses, and huntes of Græce about his children : and he him selfe also (if no matters of common wealth troubled him) was ever with them in the schoole when they were at their bookes, and also when they otherwise dyd exercise them selves. For he loved his children as much, or more, then any other Romaine. Now concerning the state of the common wealth, the Romaines were at warres with king Perseus, and they much blamed the captaines they had sent thither before, for that for lacke of skill and corage, they had so cowardly behaved them selves, as their enemies laughed them to scorne: and they receyved more hurte of them, then they dyd unto the King. For not long before, they had driven king Antiochus beyound mount Taurus, and had made him forsake the rest of Asia, and had shut him up within the borders of Syria: who was glad that he had bought that contrie with fifteene thousand talents, which he payed for a fine. A litle before also, they had overcome Philip, king of Macedon, in Thessaly, and had delivered the Græcians from the bondage of the Macedonians. And more-

The cowardlines of the Romaines in Spayne.

over, having overcome Hannibal (unto whom no Prince nor King that ever was in the worlde was comparable, either for his power or valliantnes) they thought this to great a dishonour to them, that this warre they had against king Perseus, should hold so long of even hande with them, as if he had bene an enemie equall with the people of Rome: considering also that they fought not against them, but with the refuse and scattered people of the overthrowen armie his father had lost before, and knew not that Philip had left his armie stronger, and more experte by reason of his overthrowe, then it was before. As I will briefly reherse the storie from the beginning. Antigonus, who was of the greatest power of all the captaines and successours of Alexander the great, having obteined for him self and his posteritie the title of a King, had a sonne called Demetrius, of whom came Antigonus the second, that was surnamed Gonatas, whose sonne was also called Demetrius, that raigned no long time, but dyed, and left a young sonne called Philippe. By reason whereof, the Princes and Nobilitie of Macedon, fearing that the Realme should be left without heire: they preferred one Antigonus, cosin to the last deceased King, and made him marie the mother of Philip the lesse, geving him the name at the first of the Kings protectour only, and lieutenaunt generall of his majestie. But after, when they had founde he was a good and wise prince, and a good husband for the Realme, they then gave him the absolute name of a King, and surnamed him Doson, to saye, the giver: for he promised muche, and gave litle. After him reigned Philip, who in his grene youth gave more hope of him selfe, then any other of the Kings before: in so much they thought that one daye he would restore Macedon her auncient fame and glorie, and that he alone would plucke downe the pride and power of the Romaines, who rose against all the world. But after that he had lost a great battell, and was overthrowen by Titus Quintus Flaminius neere unto the cittie of Scotusa: then he beganne to quake for feare, and to leave all to the mercie of the Romaines, thinking he escaped good cheape, for any light ransome or tribute the Romaines should impose apon him. Yet afterwards comming to understand

The succession of Antigonus king of Macedon.

Antigonus Doson, king of Macedon.

Philip king of Macedon was overcome in battell, by Titus Quintus Flaminius at the cittie of Scotusa.

him selfe, he grewe to disdaine it much, thinking that to reigne through the favour of the Romaines, was but to make him selfe a slave, to seeke to live in pleasure at his ease, and not for a valliant and noble prince borne. Whereupon he set all his minde, to studie the discipline of warres, and made his preparations as wisely and closely, as possiblie he could. For he left all his townes alongest the sea coast, and standing upon any high wayes, without any fortification at all, and in manner desolate without people, to the ende there might appeare no occasion of doubt or mistrust in him: and in the meane time, in the highe countries of his Realme farre from great beaten wayes, he leavied a great number of men of warre, and replenished his townes and strong holdes that laye scatteringly abroad, with armour and weapon, money, and men, providing for warre, which he kept as secretly as he could. For he had provision of armour in his armorie, to arme thirtie thousand men, and eight million busshels of corne safely lokt up in his fortes and stronger places, and ready money, as much as would serve to entertaine tenne thousand straungers in paye, to defend his countrie for the space of tenne yeres. But before he could bring that to passe he had purposed, he dyed for grief and sorowe, after he knewe he had unjustly put Demetrius the best of his sonnes to death, apon the false accusation of the worst, that was Perseus: who as he dyd inherite the Kingdom of his father by succession, so dyd he also inherite his fathers malice against the Romaines. But he had no shoulders to beare so heavy a burden, and especially being as he was, a man of so vile and wicked nature: for among many lewde and naughty conditions he had, he was extreme covetous and miserable. They saye also, that he was not legitimate, bicause Philippes wife had taken him from Gnathainia (a tailours wife borne at Argos) immediatly after he was borne, and dyd adopt the child to be hers. And some thinke that this was the chiefest cause why he practised to put Demetrius to death, fearing least this lawful sonne would seeke occasion to prove him a bastard. Notwithstanding, simple though he was, and of vile and base nature, he found the strength of his Kingdom

Philipssecond preparation for warres in Macedon.

Philips armorie.

The death of king Philip.

Perseus extreme covetous.

so great, that he was contented to take upon him to make warre against the Romaines, which he mainteined a long time, and fought against their Consuls, that were their generalles, and repulsed great armies of theirs both by sea and lande, and overcame some. As Publius Licinius among other, the first that invaded Macedon, was overthrowen by him in a battell of horsemen, where he slewe at that time two thousand five hundred good men of his, and tooke sixe hundred prisoners. And their armie by sea, riding at ancker before the cittie of Oreum, he dyd sodainly set apon, and tooke twenty great shippes of burden, and all that was in them, and soncke the rest, which were all loden with corne: and tooke of all sortes besides, about foure and fiftie foystes, and galliots of fiftie owers a pece. The second Consul and generall he fought with all, was Hostilius, whom he repulsed, attempting by force to invade Macedon, by waye of the cittie of Elumia. Another time again, when he entred in by stelth upon the coast of Thessaly, he offred him battel, but the other durst not abide it. Furthermore, as though the warre troubled him nothing at all, and that he had cared litle for the Romaines: he went and fought a battell in the meane time with the Dardanians, where he slue tenne thousand of those barbarous people, and brought a marvelous great spoyle awaye with him. Moreover he procured the nation of the Gaules dwelling upon the river of Danubie, which they call Bastarnæ (men very warlike, and excellent good horsemen) and did practise with the Illyrians also by meane of their king Gentius, to make them joyne with him in these warres: so that there ranne a rumour all about, that for money he had gotten these Gaules to come downe into Italie, from the highe contrie of Gaule, all alongest the Adriatick sea. The Romaines being advertised of these newes, thought the time served not now to dispose their offices in warres any more by grace and favour unto those that sued for them: but contrariwise, that they should call some noble man that were very skilfull, and a wise captaine, and could discretly governe and performe things of great charge. As Paulus Æmylius, a man well stepped on in yeres, being three score yere olde: and yet of good power,

King Perseus maketh warre with the Romaines.

Publius Licinius Consul, overthrowen by Perseus.

Hostilius Consul repulsed out of Macedon.

Bastarnæ, the Gaules dwelling apon the river of Danubie.

by reason of the lusty young men his sonnes, and sonnes in lawe, besides a great number of his friends and kinsefolke. So all that bare great authoritie, dyd altogether with one consent counsaill him to obey the people, which called him to the Consulshippe. At the beginning, in deede he delayed the people muche that came to importune him, and utterly denied them: saying, he was no meete man neither to desire, nor yet to take upon him any charge. Howbeit in the ende, seeing the people dyd urge it apon him, by knocking continually at his gates, and calling him alowde in the streetes, willing him to come into the market place, and perceyving they were angrie with him, bicause he refused it: he was content to be persuaded. And when he stoode among them that sued for the Consulshippe, the people thought straight that he stoode not there so muche for desire of the office, as for that he put them in hope of assured victorie, and happie successe of this begonne warre: so great was their love towardes him, and the good hope they had of him, that they chose him Consul againe the second time. Wherefore so sone as he was chosen, they would not proceede to drawing of lottes according to their custome, which of the two Consuls should happen to goe into Macedon: but presently with a full and whole consent of them all, they gave him the whole charge of the warres of Macedon. So being Consul now, and appointed to make warre upon king Perseus, all the people dyd honorably companie him home unto his house: where a litle girle (a daughter of his) called Tertia, being yet an infant, came weeping unto her father. He making muche of her: asked her why she wept. The poore girle aunswered, colling him about the necke, and kissing him: Alas, father, wote you what? our Perseus is dead. She ment it by a litle whelpe so called, which was her playe fellowe. In good hower, my girle, sayed he, I like the signe well. Thus doth Cicero the orator reporte it in his booke of divinations. The Romaines had a custome at that time, that suche as were elected Consuls (after that they were openly proclaimed) should make an oration of thanckes unto the people, for the honour and favour they had shewed him. The people then (according to the custome) being

Æmylius chosen Consul the second time, taketh charge of the warres of Macedon.

Good lucke pronounced by Tertia, a litle girle.

gathered together to heare Æmylius speake, he made this oration unto them: 'That the first time he sued to be 'Consul, was in respect of him selfe, standing at that time 'in neede of suche honour: now he offred him selfe the 'second time unto it, for the good love he bare unto them, 'who stoode in nede of a generall, wherefore he thought him 'selfe nothing bounde nor beholding unto them now. And 'if they dyd thincke also this warre might be better followed 'by any other, then by him selfe, he would presently with all 'his harte resigne the place. Furthermore, if they had any 'trust or confidence in him, that they thought him a man 'sufficient to discharge it: then that they would not speake 'nor medle in any matter that concerned his duetie, and the 'office of a generall, saving only, that they would be diligent '(without any wordes) to doe whatsoever he commaunded, 'and should be necessarie for the warre and service they 'tooke in hand. For if every man would be a commaunder, 'as they had bene heretofore, of those by whom they should 'be commaunded: then the world would more laughe them 'to scorne in this service, then ever before had bene accus- 'tomed.' These wordes made the Romaines very obedient to him, and conceyved good hope to come, being all of them very glad that they had refused those ambitious flatterers that sued for the charge, and had geven it unto a man, that durst boldly and franckly tell them the troth. Marke how the Romaines by yelding unto reason and vertue, came to command all other, and to make them selves the mightiest people of the world. Now that Paulus Æmylius setting forward to this warre, had winde at will, and fayer passage to bring him at his jorneis ende: I impute it to good fortune, that so quickly and safely conveyed him to his campe. But for the rest of his exploytes, he dyd in all this warre, when parte of them were performed by his owne hardines, other by his wisedome and good counsell, other by the diligence of his friendes in serving him with good will, other by his owne resolute constancy and corage in extremest daunger, and last, by his marvelous skill in determining at an instant what was to be done: I cannot attribute any notable acte or worthy service unto this his good fortune,

Paulus Æmylius oration of thanckes to the Romaines when he was Consul, observing the custome.

See what fruite souldiers reape, by obedience and reason.

Perseus covetousnes and miserie, was the destruction of him selfe, and his realme of Macedon.

Bastarnæ, a mercenary people.

they talke of so much, as they maye doe in other captaines doings. Onles they will saye peradventure, that Perseus covetousnes and miserie was Æmilius good fortune: for his miserable feare of spending money, was the only cause and destruction of the whole realme of Macedon, which was in good state and hope of continuing in prosperitie. For there came downe into the countrie of Macedon at king Perseus request, tenne thousand Bastarnæ a horse backe, and as many footemen to them, who allwayes joyned with them in battell, all mercenary souldiers, depending upon paye and enterteinment of warres, as men that could not plowe nor sowe, nor trafficke marchandise by sea, nor skill of grasing to gaine their living with: and to be shorte, that had no other occupation or marchandise, but to serve in the warres, and to overcome those with whom they fought. Furthermore, when they came to incampe and lodge in the Medica, neere to the Macedonians, who sawe them so goodly great men, and so well trained and exercised in handling all kinde of weapons, so brave and lustie in wordes and threates against their enemies: they beganne to plucke up their hartes, and to looke bigge, imagining that the Romaines would never abide them, but would be afeard to looke them in the face, and only to see their marche, it was so terrible and fearefull. But Perseus, after he had incoraged his men in this sorte, and had put them in suche a hope and jollitie, when this barbarous supply came to aske him a thousand crownes in hande for every captaine, he was so damped and troubled withall in his minde, casting up the summe it came to, that his only covetousnes and miserie made him returne them backe, and refuse their service: not as one that ment to fight with the Romaines, but rather to spare his treasure, and to be a husband for them, as if he should have geven up a straight accompt unto them of his charges in this warre, against whom he made it. And notwithstanding also his enemies dyd teache him what he had to doe, considering that besides all other their warlike furniture and munition, they had no lesse then a hundred thousand fighting men lying in campe together, ready to execute the Consuls commaundement. Yet he taking upon him to resist so puissant

Note, what became of Perseus husbandry.

Æmylius army against Perseus, was a hundred thousand men.

an armie, and to mainteine the warres, which forced his enemies to be at extreme charge in enterteining such multitudes of men, and more then needed: hardly would depart with his gold and silver, but kept it safe locked up in his treasurie, as if he had bene affrayed to touche it, and had bene none of his. And he dyd not shewe that he came of the noble race of these kings of Lydia, and of Phœnicia, who gloried to be riche: but shewed howe by inheritaunce of bloude he chalenged some parte of the vertue of Philip, and of Alexander, who both bicause they esteemed to buye victorie with money, not money with victorie, dyd many notable things, and thereby conquered the world. Hereof came the common saying in olde time, that it was not Philip, but his gold and silver that wanne the citties of Græce. And Alexander when he went to conquer the Indes, seeing the Macedonians carie with them all the wealth of Persia, which made his campe very heavie, and slowe to marche: he him selfe first of all set fire of his owne cariage that conveyed all his necessaries, and persuaded other to doe the like, that they might marche more lightly, and easelier goe on the jorney. But Perseus contrarilie would not spend any parte of his goodes, to save him selfe, his children and Realme, but rather yelded to be led prisoner in triumphe with a great ransome, to shewe the Romaines howe good a husband he had bene for them. For he dyd not only send away the Gaules without geving them paye as he had promised, but moreover having persuaded Gentius king of Illyria to take his parte in these warres, for the summe of three hundred talents which he had promised to furnish him with: he caused the money to be told, and put up in bagges by those whom Gentius sent to receive it. Whereupon Gentius thinking him selfe sure of the money promised, committed a fond and fowle parte: for he stayed the ambassadours the Romaines sent unto him, and committed them to prisone. This parte being come to Perseus eares, he thought now he needed not hier him with money to be an enemie to the Romaines, considering he had waded so farre, as that he had already done, was as a manifest signe of his ill will towards them, and that it was to late to looke backe and repent him, now that his

Gentius king of the Illyrians, ayded Perseus.

Perseus double dealing with king Gentius.

King Gentius overcome by Lucius Anicius Prætor.

Perseus laye at the foote of the mount Olympus, with 4000 horsemen, and 40000 footemen.

Æmylius admonition to his souldiers.

Paulus Æmylius would have the watch to have no speares nor pikes.

fowle parte had plonged him into certen warres, for an uncerten hope. So dyd he abuse the unfortunate King, and defrauded him of the three hundred talents he had promised him. And worse then this, shortely after he suffered Lucius Anicius the Romaine Prætor, whom they sent against him with an armie, to plucke king Gentius, his wife, and children, out of his Realme and Kingdome, and to carie them prisoners with him. Now when Æmylius was arrived in Macedon, to make warre against such an enemie: he made no manner of reckoning of his persone, but of the great preparation and power he had. For in one campe he had foure thousand horsemen, and no lesse then forty thousand footemen, with the which armie he had planted him selfe alongest the sea side, by the foote of the mount Olympus, in a place unpossible to be approched: and there he had so well fortified all the straites and passages unto him with fortifications of woode, that he thought him selfe to lye safe out of all daunger, and imagined to dalie with Æmylius, and by tract of time to eate him out with charge. Æmylius in the meane season laye not idle, but occupied his wittes throughly, and left no meanes unattempted, to put some thing in proofe. And perceyving that his souldiers by overmuche licentious libertie (wherein by sufferaunce they lived before) were angrie with delaying and lying still, and that they dyd busilie occupie them selves in the generalles office, saying this, and suche a thing would be done that is not done: he tooke them up roundely, and commaunded them they should medle no more to curiously in matters that perteined not to them, and that they should take care for nothing els, but to see their armour and weapon ready to serve valliantly, and to use their swordes after the Romaines facion, when their generall should appoint and commaund them. Wherefore, to make them more carefull to looke to them selves, he commaunded those that watched should have no speares nor pykes, bicause they should be more wakefull, having no long weapon to resist the enemie, if they were assaulted. The greatest trouble his army had, was lacke of freshe water, bicause the water that ranne to the sea was very litle, and marvelous fowle by the sea side. But Æmylius considering they were at the foote of the mount Olympus (which is of a marvelous height, and full of wodde withall) conjectured, seeing the trees so freshe and grene, that there should be some litle pretie springes among them, which ranne under the grounde. So he made them digge many holes and welles alongest the mountaine, which were straight filled with fayer water, being pent within ground before for lacke of breaking open the heades, which then ranne downe in streames, and met together in sundrie places. And yet some doe denie, that there is any meeting of waters within the grounde, from whence the springes doe come. For they saye, that ronning out of the earth as they doe, it is not for that, that the water breaketh out by any violence, or openeth in any place, as meeting together in one place of long time: but that it ingendreth and riseth, at the same time and place where it ronneth out, turning the substaunce into water, which is a moist vapour, thickneth and waxeth cold by the coldnes of the earth, and so becommeth a streame, and ronneth downe. Even so, saye they, as womens brestes are not allwayes full of milke, as milke pannes are that continually keepe milke, but doe of them selves convert the nutriment women take into milke, and after commeth forth at their nipples: the very like are springes and watery places of the earth, from whence the fountaines come, which have no meeting of hidden waters, nor hollowe places capable, readily to deliver water from them, as one would drawe it out of a pompe, or sesterne, from so many great brookes, and deepe rivers. But by their naturall coldnes and moisture, they waxe thicke, and put forth the vapour and ayer so strong, that they turne it into water. And this is the reason why the places where they digge and open the earth, doe put forth more abundaunce of water by opening the grounde: like as womens brestes doe geve more milke, when they are most drawen and suckt, bicause in a sorte they doe better feede the vapour within them, and convert it thereby into a ronning humour. Where, to the contrarie, those partes of the earth that are not digged, nor have no vent outward, are the more unable, and lesse mete to ingender water, having not that provocation and course to ronne, that causeth the bringing forth of moisture. Yet

The originall of springes.

Fountaines compared to womens brests.

such as mainteine this opinion, doe geve them occasion that love argument, to contrarie them thus. Then we maye saye by like reason also, that in the bodies of beastes there is no bloud long before, and that it ingendreth upon a sodaine, when they are hurte, by transferring of some spirite or fleshe that readilie chaungeth into some ronning licoure. And moreover, they are confuted by the common experience of these mine men, that digge in the mines for mettell, or that undermine castells to winne them: who when they digge any great depth, doe many times meete in the bowells of the earth with ronning rivers, the water whereof is not ingendred by litle and litle, as of necessitie it should be, if it were true, that upon the present opening of the ground, the humour should immediatly be created, but it falleth vehemently all at one time. And we see oftentimes that in cutting through a mountaine or rocke, sodainely there ronneth out a great quantitie of water. And thus much for this matter. Now to returne to our historie againe. Æmylius laye there a convenient time, and stirred not: and it is sayed there were never seene two so great armies one so neere to the other, and to be so quiet. In the ende, casting many things with him selfe, and devising sundrie practises, he was enformed of another waye to enter into Macedon, through the countrie of Perræbia, over against the temple called Pythion, and the rocke upon which it is built, where there laye no garrison: which gave him better hope to passe that waye, for that it was not kept, then that he feared the narrownes and hardnes of the waye unto it. So, he brake the matter to his counsaill.

Scipio Nasica, and Fabius Maximus, offer them selves to take the straights.

Thereupon Scipio called Nasica (the sonne adopted of that great Scipio the African, who became afterwards a great man, and was president of the Senate or counsell) was the first man that offred him self to leade them, whom it would please him to send to take that passage, and to assault their enemies behind. The second was Fabius Maximus, the eldest sonne of Æmylius, who being but a very young man, rose notwithstanding, and offred him self very willingly. Æmylius was very glad of their offers, and gave them not so many men as Polybius writeth, but so many as Nasica him self declareth, in a letter of his he wrote to a King, where he reporteth all the storie of this jorney. There were 3000 Italians leavied in Italie, by the confederats of the Romaines, who were not of the Romaine legions, and in the left winge about 5000. Besides those, Nasica tooke also 120 men at armes, and about 200 Cretans and Thracians mingled together, of those Harpalus had sent thither. With this number Nasica departed from the campe, and tooke his waye toward the sea side, and lodged by the temple of Hercules, as if he had determined to doe this feate by sea, to environne the campe of the enemies behind. But when the souldiers had supped, and that it was darke night, he made the captaines of every bande privie to his enterprise, and so marched all night a contrary waye from the sea, untill at the length they came under the temple of Pythion, where he lodged to rest the souldiers that were sore travelled all night. In this place, the mount Olympus is above tenne furlonge highe, as appeareth in a place ingraven by him that measured it.

The height of the mount Olympus.

Olympus mounte is just, by measure made with line,
twelve hundred seventie paces trodde, as measure can assigne.
The measure being made, right ore against the place,
whereas Apolloes temple stands, ybuilt with stately grace.
Even from the leavell plott, of that same countries plaine,
unto the toppe which all on highe, doth on the hill remaine.
And so Xenagoras the sonne of Eumelus,
in olden dayes by measure made, the same dyd finde for us.
And dyd engrave it here in writing for to see,
when as he tooke his latest leave (Apollo god) of thee.

Yet the Geometricians saye, that there is no mountaine higher, nor sea deeper, then the length of tenne furlonges: so that I thinke this Xenagoras (in my opinion) dyd not take his measure at aventure, and by gesse, but by true rules of the arte, and instrumentes Geometricall. There Nasica rested all night. King Perseus perceyving in the meane time that Æmylius stirred not from the place where he laye, mistrusted nothing his practise, and the comming of Nasica who was at hande: untill such time as a traitour of Creta (stealing from Nasica) dyd reveale unto him the pretended practise, as also the Romaines compassing of him about. He wondred muche at these newes, howbeit he removed not his campe from the place he laye in, but dispatched one of his captaines called Milon, with tenne thousand straungers, and two thousand Macedonians: and straightly commanded him with all the possible speede he could, to get the toppe of the hill before them. Polybius sayeth, that the Romaines came and gave them an alarom, when they were sleeping. But Nasica writeth, that there was a marvelous sharpe and terrible battell on the toppe of the mountaine: and sayed plainely, that a Thracian souldier comming towards him, he threwe his darte at him, and hitting him right in the brest, slue him starke dead: and having repulsed their enemies, Milon their captaine shamefully ronning awaye in his coate without armour or weapon, he followed him without any daunger, and so went downe to the valley, with the safety of all his companie. This conflict fortuning thus, Perseus raised his campe in great haste from the place where he was, and being disapointed of his hope, he retired in great feare, as one at his wittes ende, and not knowing howe to determine. Yet was he constrained either to staye, and incampe before the cittie of Pydne, there to take the hazard of battell: or els to devide his armie into his citties and strong holdes, and to receyve the warres within his owne countrie, the which being once crept in, could never be driven out againe, without great murder and bloudeshed. Hereupon his friends dyd counsell him, to choose rather the fortune of battell: alledging unto him, that he was the stronger in men a great waye, and that the Macedonians would fight lustely with all the corage they could, considering that they fought for the safety of their wives and children, and also in the presence of their King, who should both see every mans doing, and fight him selfe in persone also for them. The King moved by these persuasions, determined to venter the chaunce of battell. So he pitched his campe, and viewed the situation of the places all about, and devided the companies amongest his captaines, purposing to geve a whotte charge upon the enemies when they should drawe nere. The place and countrie was suche, as being all champion, there was a goodly valley to raunge a battell of footemen

Nisica wanne the straights of Macedon.

Perseus pitched his campe before the cittie of Pydne.

in, and litle prety hilles also one depending upon another, which were very commodious for archers, naked men, and such as were lightly armed, to retire them selves unto being distressed, and also to environne their enemies behind. There were two small rivers also, Æson and Leucus that ranne through the same, the which though they were not very deepe, being about the later ende of the sommer, yet they would annoye the Romaines notwithstanding. Now when Æmylius was joyned with Nasica, he marched on straight in battell raye towards his enemies. But perceyving a farre of their battell marched in very good order, and the great multitude of men placed in the same: he wondred to behold it, and sodainly stayed his armie, considering with him selfe what he had to doe. Then the young captaines having charge under him, desirous to fight it out presently, went unto him to praye him to geve the onset: but Nasica specially above the rest, having good hope in the former good lucke he had at his first encounter. Æmylius smiling, aunswered him: So would I doe, if I were as young as thou. But the sundry victories I have wonne heretofore, having taught me by experience the faultes the vanquished doe commit: doe forbid me to goe so whottely to worke (before my souldiers have rested, which dyd returne but now) to assault an armie set in suche order of battell. When he had aunswered him thus, he commaunded the first bands that were now in viewe of the enemies, should imbattell them selves, shewing a countenaunce to the enemie as though they would fight: and that those in the rereward should lodge in the meane time, and fortifie the campe. So, bringing the foremost men to be hindemost, by chaunging from man to man before the enemies were ware of it: he had broken his battell by litle and litle, and lodged his men, fortified within the campe without any tumult or noyse, and the enemies never perceyving it. But when night came, and every man had supped, as they were going to sleepe and take their rest: the moone which was at the full, and of a great height, beganne to darken, and to chaunge into many sortes of cullers, losing her light, untill suche time as she vanished awaye, and was eclipsed altogether. Then the Romaines beganne

The rivers of Æson and Leucus.

Æmylius aunswer to Scipio Nasica, for geving charge apon the enemies.

The skill and foresight of a wise captaine.

The eclipse of the moone.

The superstition of the Romaines when the moone is eclipsed.

to make a noyse with basons and pannes, as their facion is to doe in suche a chaunce, thinking by this sound to call her againe, and to make her come to her light, lifting up many torches lighted, and firebrands into the ayer. The Macedonians on thother side dyd no suche matter within their campe, but were all together striken with an horrible feare: and there ranne straight a whispering rumour through the people, that this signe in the element signified the eclipse of the King. For Æmylius was not ignoraunt of the diversities of the eclipses, and he had heard saye the cause is, by reason that the moone making her ordinarie course about the world (after certen revolutions of time) doth come to enter into the round shadowe of the earth, within the which she remaineth hidden: untill suche time as having past the darke region of the shadow, she commeth afterwards to recover her light which she taketh of the sunne. Nevertheles, he being a godly devout man, so sone as he perceyved the moone had recovered her former brightnes againe, he sacrificed eleven calves. And the next morning also by the breake of daye, making sacrifice to Hercules, he could never have any signes or tokens that promised him good lucke, in sacrificing twenty oxen one after another: but at the one and twenteth, he had signes that promised him victorie, so he defended him self. Wherfore, after he had vowed a solemne sacrifice of a hundred oxen to Hercules, and also games of prices at the weapons, he commaunded his captaines to put their men in readines to fight: and so sought to winne time, tarying till the sunne came about in the after noone towardes the West, to the ende that the Romaines which were turned towardes the East, should not have it in their faces when they were fighting. In the meane time, he reposed him selfe in his tent, which was all open behind towardes the side that looked into the valley, where the campe of his enemies laye. When it grewe towards night, to make the enemies set apon his men: some saye he used this policie. He made a horse be driven towards them without a bridell, and certen Romaines followed him, as they would have taken him againe: and this was the cause of procuring the skirmishe. Other saye, that the

The cause of an eclipse of the moone.

Æmylius policie to procure skirmishe.

Thracians serving under the charge of captaine Alexander, dyd set apon certen forragers of the Romaines, that brought forage into the campe: out of the which, seven hundred of the Ligurians ranne sodainly to the rescue, and relief comming still from both armies, at the last the mayne battell followed after. Wherefore Æmilius like a wise generall foreseeing by the daunger of this skirmishe, and the stirring of both campes, what the furie of the battell would come to: came out of his tent, and passing by the bandes, dyd encorage them, and prayed them to sticke to it like men. In the meane time, Nasica thrusting him selfe into the place where the skirmishe was whottest, perceyved the army of the enemies marching in battell, ready to joyne. The first that marched in the voward, were the Thracians, who seemed terrible to looke apon, as he writeth him self: for they were mightie made men, and caried marvelous bright targets of steele before them, their legges were armed with greaves, and their thighes with tases, their coates were blacke, and marched shaking heavy halberds upon their shoulders. Next unto these Thracians, there followed them all the other straungers and souldiers whom the King had hiered, diversely armed and set forth: for they were people of sundrie nations gathered together, emong whom the Pæonians were mingled. The third squadron was of Macedonians, and all of them chosen men, aswell for the flower of their youthe, as for the valliantnes of their persones: and they were all in goodly gilt armours, and brave purple cassocks apon them, spicke, and spanne newe. And at their backes came after them, the olde bandes to shewe them selves out of the campe, with targets of copper, that made all the plaine to shine with the brightnes of their steele and copper. And all the hilles and mountaines thereabouts dyd ringe againe like an Eccho, with the crie and noyse of so many fighting men, one incoraging another. In this order they marched so fiercely, with so great harte burning, and such swiftnes: that the first which were slaine at the incounter, fell dead two furlonges from the campe of the Romaines. The charge being geven, and the battell begonne, Æmylius galloping to the voward of his battell,

The army of the Macedonians, marching against the Romaines in battell.

The battell betwext Perseus and Æmylius.

perceyved that the captaines of the Macedonians which were in the first ranckes, had already thrust their pikes into the Romaines targets, so as they could not come neere them with their swordes: and that the other Macedonians carying their targets behinde them, had now plucked them before them, and dyd base their pikes all at one time, and made a violent thrust into the targets of the Romaines. Which when he had considered, and of what strength and force his walle and rancke of targets was, one joyning so neere another, and what a terrour it was to see a fronte of a battell with so many armed pikes and steele heades: he was more afeard and amazed withall, then with any sight he ever sawe before. Nevertheles he could wisely dissemble it at that time. And so passing by the companies of his horsemen, without either curaces or helmet upon his head, he shewed a noble cherefull countenaunce unto them that fought. But on the contrarie side, Perseus the king of Macedon, as Polybius writeth, so sone as the battell was begonne, withdrewe him self, and got into the cittie of Pydne, under pretence to goe to doe sacrifice unto Hercules: who doth not accept the fainte sacrifice of cowards, neither doth receyve their prayers, bicause they be unreasonable. For it is no reason, that he that shooteth not, should hyt the white: nor that he should winne the victorie, that bideth not the battell: neither that he should have any good, that doeth nothing toward it: nor that a naughty man should be fortunate, and prosper. The goddes dyd favour Æmylius prayers, bicause he prayed for victorie with his sworde in his hande, and fighting dyd call to them for ayde. Howbeit there is one Posidonius a writer, who sayeth he was in that time, and moreover, that he was at the battell: and he hath written an historie conteining many bookes of the actes of king Perseus, where he sayeth that it was not for fainte harte, nor under culler to sacrifice unto Hercules, that Perseus went from the battell: but bicause he had a stripe of a horse on the thighe the daye before. Who though he could not very well helpe him self, and that all his friends sought to persuade him not to goe to the battell: yet he caused one of his horse to be brought to him notwithstanding (which he

Perseus goeth out of the battell unto Pydne.

Victorie wonne by labour, not by slothe.

commonly used to ryde up and downe on) and taking his backe, rode into the battell unarmed, where an infinite number of dartes were throwen at him from both sides. And emong those, he had a blowe with a darte that hurte him somwhat, but it was overthwart, and not with the pointe, and dyd hit him on the left side glawnsing wise, with suche a force, that it rent his coate, and rased his skinne underneath, so as it left a marke behinde a long time after. And this is all that Posidonius writeth to defend and excuse Perseus. The Romaines having their hands full, and being stayed by the battell of the Macedonians that they could make no breache into them: there was a captaine of the Pelignians called Salius, who tooke the ensigne of his band, and cast it among the prease of his enemies. Then all the Pelignians brake in apon them, with a marvelous force and furie into that place: for all Italians thinke it to great a shame and dishonour for souldiers, to lose, or forsake their ensigne. Thus was there marvelous force of both sides used in that place: for the Pelignians proved to cut the Macedonians pikes with their swordes, or els to make them geve backe with their great targets, or to make a breache into them, and to take the pikes with their handes. But the Macedonians to the contrarie, holding their pikes fast with both hands, ranne them thorow that came neere unto them: so that neither target nor corselet could hold out the force and violence of the pushe of their pikes, in so muche as they turned up the heeles of the Pelignians and Terracinians, who like desperate beastes without reason, shutting in them selves emong their enemies, ranne wilfully upon their owne deathes, and their first rancke were slaine every man of them. Thereupon those that were behind, gave backe a litle, but fled not turning their backes, and only retired geving backe, towardes the mountaine Olocrus. Æmylius seeing that (as Posidonius writeth) rent his arming coate from his backe for anger, bicause that some of his men gave backe: other durst not fronte the battell of the Macedonians, which was so strongly imbattelled of every side, and so mured in with a wall of pikes, presenting their armed heades on everie side a man

Salius a captaine of the Pelignians tooke the ensigne, and threwe it among the enemies.

could come, that it was impossible to breake into them, no not so muche as to come neere them only. Yet notwithstanding, bicause the field was not altogether plaine and even, the battell that was large in the fronte, could not allwayes keepe that walle, continuing their targets close one to another, but they were driven of necessitie to breake and open in many places, as it happeneth oft in great battells, according to the great force of the souldiers: that in one place they thrust forward, and in another they geve backe, and leave a hole. Wherefore Æmylius sodainly taken the vauntage of this occasion, devided his men into small companies, and commaunded them they should quickly thrust in betwene their enemies, and occupie the places they sawe voyde in the fronte of their enemies, and that they should set on them in that sorte, and not with one whole continuall charge, but occupying them here and there with divers companies, in sundry places. Æmylius gave this charge unto the private captaines of every band and their lieutenaunts, and the captaines also gave the like charge unto their souldiers that could skilfully execute their commaundement. For they went presently into those partes where they sawe the places open, and being once entred in among them, some gave charge upon the flanckes of the Macedonians, where they were all naked and unarmed: other set upon them behind: so that the strength of all the corpes of the battell (which consisteth in keeping close together) being opened in this sorte, was straight overthrowen. Furthermore, when they came to fight man for man, or a fewe against a fewe: the Macedonians with their litle shorte swordes, came to strike upon the great sheldes of the Romaines, which were very strong, and covered all their bodies downe to the foote. And they to the contrarie, were driven of necessitie to receave the blowes of the strong heavy swordes of the Romaines, upon their litle weake targettes: so that what with their heavines, and the vehement force wherewith the blowes lighted upon them, there was no target nor corselet, but they passed it through, and ranne them in. By reason whereof they could make no long resistance, whereupon they turned their backes, and ranne awaye. But when they came to the squadron of the olde beaten souldiers of the Macedonians, there was the cruellest fight and most desperate service, where they saye that Marcus Cato (sonne of great Cato, and sonne in lawe of Æmylius) shewing all the valliantnes in his persone that a noble minde could possibly performe, lost his sword which fell out of his hande. But he like a young man of noble corage, that had bene valliantly brought up in all discipline, and knew how to follow the steppes of his father (the noblest persone that ever man sawe) was to shewe then his value and worthines: and thought it more honour for him there to dye, then living to suffer his enemies to enjoye any spoyle of his. So, by and by he ranne into the Romaine army, to finde out some of his friendes, whom he tolde what had befalled him, and prayed them to helpe him to recover his sworde: whereto they agreed. And being a good company of lusty valliant souldiers together, they rushed straight in among their enemies, at the place where he brought them, and so dyd set apon them with suche force and furie, that they made a lane through the middest of them, and with great slaughter and spilling of bloude, even by plaine force, they cleared the waye still before them. Now when the place was voyded, they sought for the sworde, and in the ende founde it with great a doe, amongest a heape of other swords and dead bodies, whereat they rejoyced marvelously. Then singing a songe of victorie, they went againe more fiercely then before to geve a charge upon their enemies, who were not yet broken a sonder: untill suche time as at the length, the three thousand chosen Macedonians fighting valliantly even to the last man, and never forsaking their rancks, were all slaine in the place. After whose overthrowe, there was a great slaughter of other also that fled: so that all the valley and foote of the mountaines thereaboutes was covered with dead bodies. The next daye after the battell, when the Romaines dyd passe over the river of Leucus, they founde it ronning all a bloude. For it is sayed there were slaine at this field, of Perseus men, above five and twentie thousand: and of the Romaines side, as Posidonius sayeth, not above sixe score, or as Nasica writeth, but foure score only. And for so great an overthrowe, it is reported it was

The valliantnes of Marcus Cato.

Æmilius victorie of Perseus.

The battell fought and wonne in one hower.

wonderfull quickly done, and executed. For they beganne to fight about three of the clocke in the after noone, and had wonne the victorie before foure, and all the rest of the daye they followed their enemies in chase, an hundred and twenty furlonges from the place where the battell was fought: so that it was very late, and farre forth night, before they returned againe into the campe. So suche as returned, were receyved with marvelous great joye of their pages that went out with linckes and torches lighted, to bring their masters into their tentes, where their men had made great bonfiers, and decked them up with crownes and garlands of laurell, saving the generalles tent only: who was very heavy, for that of his two sonnes he brought with him to the warres, the younger could not be founde, which he loved best of the twaine, bicause he sawe he was of a better nature then the rest of his brethern. For even then, being newe crept out of the shell as it were, he was marvelous valliant and hardie, and desired honour wonderfully. Now Æmylius thought he had bene cast awaye, fearing least for lacke of experience in the warres, and through the rashnes of his youthe, he had put him selfe to farre in fight amongest the prease of the enemies. Hereupon the campe heard straight what sorowe Æmylius was in, and how grievously he tooke it. The Romaines being set at supper, rose from their meate, and with torche light some ranne to Æmylius tent, other went out of the campe to seeke him among the dead bodies, if they might knowe him: so all the campe was full of sorowe and mourning, the vallies and hilles all abouts dyd ringe againe with the cries of those that called Scipio alowde. For even from his childhood he had a naturall gift in him, of all the rare and singular partes required in a captaine and wise governour of the common weale above all the young men of his time. At the last, when they were out of all hope of his comming againe, he happely returned from the chase of the enemies, with two or three of his familliars only, all bloudied with new bloude (like a swift running greyhownde fleshed with the bloude of the hare) having pursued very farre for joye of the victorie. It is that Scipio which afterwards destroyed both the citties of Carthage and Numantium, who

The valliantnes of Scipio the lesse.

was the greatest man of warre, and valliantest captaine of the Romaines in his time, and of the greatest authoritie and reputation emong them. Thus fortune deferring till another time the execution of her spite, which she dyd beare to so noble an exployte, suffered Æmylius for that time, to take his ful pleasure of that noble victorie. And as for Perseus, he fled first from the cittie of Pydne, unto the cittie of Pella, with his horsemen, which were in manner all saved. Whereupon the footemen that saved them selves by flying, meeting them by the waye, called them traitours, cowards, and villanes: and worse then that, they turned them of their horse backes, and fought it out lustely with them. Perseus seeing that, and fearing least this mutinie might turne to light on his necke, he turned his horse out of the highe waye, and pulled of his purple coate, and caried it before him, and tooke his diademe, fearing least they should knowe him by these tokens: and bicause he might more easely speake with his friends by the waye, he lighted a foote, and led his horse in his hande. But suche as were about him, one made as though he would mende the latchet of his shooe, an other seemed to water his horse, another as though he would drincke: so that one dragging after another in this sorte, they all left him at the last, and ranne their waye, not fearing the enemies furie so muche, as their Kings crueltie: who being greved with his misfortune, sought to laye the faulte of the overthrowe upon all other, but him selfe. Now he being come into the cittie of Pella by night, Euctus and Eudæus, two of his treasorers came unto him, and speaking boldly (but out of time) presumed to tell him the great faulte he had committed, and dyd counsell him also what he should doe. The King was so moved with their presumption, that with his owne handes he stabbed his dagger in them both, and slue them outright. But after this facte, all his servauntes and friendes refused him, and there only taried with him but Evander Cretan, Archedamus Ætolian, and Neo Bœotian. And as for the meane souldiers, there were none that followed him but the Cretans, and yet it was not for the good will they dyd beare him, but for the love of his golde and silver, as bees that keepe their hives for love of the hony. For he

Perseus fled from Pydne to Pella.

Time, and dutie, to be observed to the Prince.

Death, the indignation of the Prince.

The covetousnes of the Cretans.

caried with him a great treasure, and gave them leave to spoyle certen plate and vessell of golde and silver, to the value of fiftie talents. But first of all, when he was come into the cittie of Amphipolis, and afterwards into the cittie of Alepse, and that the feare was well blowen over: he returned againe to his olde humour, which was borne and bred with him, and that was, avarice and miserie. For he made his complainte unto those that were about him, that he had unwares geven to the souldiers of Creta, his plate and vessell of gold to be spoyled, being those which in olde time belonged unto Alexander the great: and prayed them with teares in his eyes that had the plate, they would be contented to chaunge it for ready money. Now suche as knewe his nature, founde streight this was but a fraude and a Cretan lye, to deceave the Cretans with: but those that trusted him, and dyd restore againe the plate they had, dyd loose it every jotte, for he never payed them pennie of it. So he got of his friendes, the value of thirtie talents which his enemies sone after dyd take from him. And with that summe he went into the Ile of Samothracia, where he tooke the sanctuarie and priviledge, of the temple of Castor and Pollux. They saye, that the Macedonians of long continuaunce dyd naturally love their Kings: but then seeing all their hope and expectation broken, their hartes failed them, and broke withall. For they all came and submitted them selves unto Æmylius, and made him lorde of the whole Realme of Macedon in two dayes: and this doth seeme to confirme their wordes, who impute all Æmilius doings unto his good fortune. And surely, the marvelous fortune he happened on in the cittie of Amphipolis, doth confirme it muche, which a man cannot ascribe otherwise, but to the speciall grace of the godds. For one daye beginning to doe sacrifice, lightning fell from heaven, and set all the wodde a fire apon the aulter, and sanctified the sacrifice. But yet the miracle of his fame is more to be wondred at. For foure dayes after Perseus had lost the battell, and that the cittie of Pella was taken, as the people of Rome were at the listes or showe place, seing horses ronne for games: sodainly there rose a rumour at the entring into the listes

Misers whine for their gooddes.

The Macedonians submit them selves to Æmylius.

Wonders.

where the games were, how Æmylius had wonne a great battell of king Perseus, and had conquered all Macedon. This newes was rife straight in every mans mouthe, and there followed upon it a marvelous joye and great cheere in every corner, with showtes and clapping of handes, that continued all the daye through the cittie of Rome. Afterwards they made diligent enquierie, how this rumour first came up, but no certaine authour could be knowen, and every man sayed they heard it spoken: so as in the ende it came to nothing, and passed awaye in that sorte for a time. But shortely after, there came letters, and certen newes that made them wonder more then before, from whence the messenger came that reported the first newes of it: which could be devised by no naturall meanes, and yet proved true afterwards. We doe reade also of a battell that was fought in Italie, nere unto the river of Sagra, wherof newes was brought the very same daye unto Peloponnesus. And of another also in like manner that was fought in Asia against the Medes, before the cittie of Mycala: the newes whereof came the same daye unto the campe of the Græcians, lying before the cittie of Platoees. And in that great jorney where the Romaines overthrewe the Tarquines, and the armie of the Latines: immediatly after the battell was wonne, they sawe two goodly young men come newly from the campe, who brought newes of the victorie to Rome, and they judged they were Castor and Pollux. The first man that spake to them in the market place before the fountaine, where they watered their horse being all of a white fome, tolde them: that he wondred howe they could so quickly bring these newes. And they laughing came to him, and tooke him softely by the beard with both their handes, and even in the market place his heare being blacke before, was presently turned yellowe. This miracle made them beleeve the reporte the man made, who ever after was called Ænobarbus, as you would saye, bearded as yellowe as golde. Another like matter that happened in our time, maketh all suche newes credible. For when Antonius rebelled against the emperour Domitian, the cittie of Rome was in a marvelous perplexitie, bicause they looked for great warres towards Germanie. But

Newes brought to Rome out of Macedon in 4 dayes, of Æmylius victorie there: and no man knewe howe they came.

Ænobarbus why so called.

in this feare, there grewe a sodaine rumour of victorie, and it went currantly through Rome, that Antonius him selfe was slaine, and all his armie overthrowen, and not a man left a live. This rumour was so rife, that many of the chiefest men of Rome beleeved it, and dyd sacrifice thereupon unto the goddes, geving them thankes for the victorie. But when the matter came to sifting, who was the first authour of the rumour: no man could tell. For one put it over still to another, and dyed so in the ende amongest the people, as in a bottomles matter, for they could never boult out any certen grounde of it: but even as it came flying into Rome, so went it flying awaye againe, no man can tell howe. Notwithstanding, Domitian holding on his jorney to make this warre, met with postes that brought him letters for the certen victorie: and remembring the rumour of the victorie that ranne before in Rome, he founde it true, that it was on the very same daye the victorie was gotten, and the distaunce betweene Rome and the place where the field was wonne, was above twenty thousand furlonges of. Every man in our time knoweth this to be true. But againe to our historie. Cn. Octavius, lieutenant of the armie of Æmylius by sea, came to ancker under the Ile of Samothracia, where he would not take Perseus by force out of the sanctuarie where he was, for the reverence he dyd beare unto the goddes Castor and Pollux: but he dyd besiege him in suche sorte, as he could not scape him, nor flye by sea out of the Ilande. Yet he had secretly practised with one Oroandes a Cretan, that had a brigantine, and was at a prise with him for a summe of money to convey him awaye by night: but the Cretan served him a right Cretans tricke. For when he had taken a borde by night into his vessell, all the Kings treasure of golde and silver, he sent him worde that he should not faile the next night following to come unto the peere by the temple of Ceres, with his wife, his children and servauntes, where in deede was no possibilitie to take shipping: but the next night following he hoysed saile, and got him awaye. It was a pittiefull thing that Perseus was driven to doe and suffer at that time. For he came downe in the night by ropes, out of a litle straight windowe upon the walles,

Cn. Octavius, Æmylius lieutenaunt by sea.

The miserable state Perseus was brought unto, by the craft and subtletie of a Cretan.

and not only him self, but his wife and litle babes, who never knewe before what flying and hardnes ment. And yet he fetched a more grievous bitter sighe, when one tolde him on the peere, that he sawe Oroandes the Cretan under saile in the mayne seas. Then daye beginning to breake, and seeing him selfe voyde of all hope, he ranne with his wife for life to the wall, to recover the sanctuarie again, before the Romaines that sawe him could overtake him. And as for his children, he had geven them him selfe into the hands of one Ion, whom before he had marvelously loved, and who then dyd traiterously betraye him: for he delivered his children unto the Romaines. Which parte was one of the chiefest causes that drave him (as a beast that will followe her litle ones being taken from her) to yeld him selfe into their hands that had his children. Now he had a speciall confidence in Scipio Nasica, and therefore he asked for him when he came to yeld him selfe: but it was aunswered him, that he was not there. Then he beganne to lament his hard and miserable fortune every waye. And in the ende, considering howe necessitie enforced him, he yelded him selfe into the hands of Cneus Octavius, wherein he shewed plainely, that he had another vice in him more unmanly and vile, then avarice: that was, a fainte harte, and feare to dye. But hereby he deprived him self of others pittie and compassion towards him, being that only thing which fortune cannot denie and take from the afflicted, and specially from them that have a noble harte. For he made request they would bring him unto the generall Æmylius, who rose from his chayer when he sawe him come, and went to mete him with his friends, the water standing in his eyes, to mete a great King, by fortune of warre, and by the will of the goddes, fallen into that most lamentable facte. But he to the contrarie, unmanly, and shamefully behaved him selfe. For he fell downe at his feete, and embraced his knees, and uttered suche uncomely speache and vile requestes, as Æmylius selfe could not abide to heare them: but knitting his browes against him, being hartely offended, he spake thus unto him: 'Alas poore man, why doest thou discharge fortune of this 'faulte, where thou mightest justly charge and accuse her to

King Perseus yeldeth him self in Samothracia, unto Cneus Octavius.

Perseus unprincely behaviour unto Æmylius.

PAULUS ÆMILIUS

Æmylius oration unto Perseus prisoner.

'thy discharge, doing things, for the which every one judgeth 'thou hast deserved thy present miserie, and art unworthie 'also of thy former honour? why dost thou defame my 'victorie, and blemish the glory of my doings, shewing thy 'self so base a man, as my honour is not great, to overcome 'so unworthie an enemie? The Romaines have ever esteemed 'magnanimitie, even in their greatest enemies: but dastard-'lines, though it be fortunate, yet is it hated of every bodie.' Notwithstanding, he tooke him up, and taking him by the hande, gave him into the custodie of Ælius Tubero. Then Æmylius went into his tent, and caried his sonnes, and sonnes in law with him, and other men of qualitie, and specially the younger sorte. And being set downe, he continued a great space very pensive with him self, not speaking a word: in so much as all the standers by, wondered much at the matter. In the ende, he beganne to enter into discourse and talke of fortune, and the unconstancy of these worldly things, and sayed unto them: 'Is there any man 'living, my friends, who having fortune at will, should there-'fore boast and glorie in the prosperitie of his doings, for 'that he hath conquered a contrie, cittie, or Realme: and 'not rather to feare the unconstancie of fortune? who laying 'before our eyes, and all those that professe armes at this 'present, so notable an example of the common frayeltie of 'men, doth plainely teache us to thincke, that there is nothing 'constant or perdurable in this world. For when is it, that 'men maye thinke them selves assured, considering that when 'they have overcome others, then are they driven to mistrust 'fortune most, and to mingle feare and mistrust, with joye of 'victorie: if they will wisely consider the common course of 'fatall destenie that altereth daylie, somtime favoring one, 'otherwhile throwing down another? you see, that in an 'howers space we have troden under our feete, the house of 'Alexander the great: who hath bene the mightiest and most 'redouted prince of the world. You see a King, that not 'long since was folowed and accompanied, with many thousand 'souldiers of horsemen and footemen: brought at this present 'into such miserable extremitie, that he is inforced to receive 'his meate and drinke daylie at the hands of his enemies.

Æmylius oration touching fortune and her unconstancie.

'Should we have any better hope then, that fortune will 'allwayes favour our doings, more then she doth his now, at 'this present? no out of doubt. Therefore digesting this 'matter well, you young men I saye, be not to bragge nor 'foolish prowde, of this conquest and noble victorie: but 'thinke what maye happen hereafter, marking to what end 'fortune will turne the envie of this our present prosperitie.' Such were Æmylius words to these young men, as it is reported, bridling by these and such like persuasions, the lusty bravery of this youth, even as with the bit and bridle of reason. Afterwardes he put his armie into garrisons to refreshe them: and went him selfe in persone in the meane time to visite Græce, making it an honorable progresse, and also a commendable. For as he passed through their citties, he releved the people, reformed the government of their state, and ever gave them some gifte or present. Unto some he gave corne, which king Perseus had gathered for the warres: and unto other he gave oyles, meeting with so great store of provision, that he rather lacked people to geve it unto, to receyve it at his handes, then wanting to geve, there was so much. As he passed by the cittie of Delphes, he sawe there a great piller, foure square, of white stone, which they had set up, to put king Perseus image of gold upon it. Whereupon he commaunded them to set up his in that place, saying: it was reason the conquered should geve place unto the conquerours. And being in the cittie of Olympia, visiting the temple of Iupiter Olympian, he spake this openly, which ever since hath bene remembred: that Phidias had rightly made Iupiter, as Homer had described him. Afterwardes when the tenne ambassadours were arrived that were sent from Rome to establish with him the realme of Macedon, he redelivered the Macedonians their countrie and townes againe, to live at libertie, according to their lawes, paying yerely to the Romaines for tribute, a hundred talents: where before they were wont to paye unto their Kings tenne times as muche. And he made playes and games of all sortes, and dyd celebrate sumptuous sacrifices unto the goddes. He kept open courte to all commers, and made noble feastes, and defrayed the whole charge thereof, with

Æmylius honorable progresse in Græce.

Æmylius setteth Macedon at a staye.

the treasure Perseus had gathered together, sparing for no coste. But through his care and foresight there was suche a speciall good order taken, every man so curteously receyved and welcommed, and so orderly marshalled at the table according to their estate and calling: that the Græcians wondred to see him so carefull in matters of sporte and pleasure: and that he tooke as great paynes in his owne persone, to see that small matters should be ordered as they ought: as he tooke great regard for discharge of more weighty causes. But this was a marvelous pleasure to him, to see that among such sumptuous sightes prepared to shewe pleasure to the persones invited, no sight or stately shewe dyd so delight them, as to enjoye the sight and company of his persone. So he told them, that seemed to wonder at his diligence and care in these matters: that to order a feast well, required as great judgement and discretion, as to set a battell: to make the one fearefull to the enemies, and the other acceptable to his friendes. But men esteemed his bountie and magnanimitie for his best vertue and qualitie. For he dyd not only refuse to see the Kings wonderful treasure of golde and silver, but caused it to be told, and delivered to the custodie of the treasurers, to carie to the coffers of store in Rome: and only suffered his sonnes that were learned, to take the bookes of the Kings librarie. When he dyd rewarde the souldiers for their valliant service in this battell, he gave his sonne in lawe Æmylius Tubero a cuppe, weying five talents. It is the same Tubero we tolde you of before, who lived with sixteene other of his kynne all in one house, and of the only revenue they had of a litle farme in the countrie. Some saye, that cuppe was the first pece of plate that ever came into the house of the Ælians, and yet it came for honour and reward of vertue: but before that time, neither them selves, nor their wives, would ever have, or weare, any gold or silver. After he had very well ordered and disposed all things, at the last he tooke leave of the Græcians, and counselled the Macedonians to remember the libertie the Romaines had geven them, and that they should be carefull to keepe it, by their good government and concorde together. Then he departed from them, and tooke

Æmylius wordes about the care and good order at feasts.

Æmylius abstinence.

his jorney towardes the countrie of Epirus, having receyved commission from the Senate of Rome, to suffer his souldiers who had done service in the battell, and overthrowe of king Perseus, to spoyle all the citties of that countrie. Wherefore that he might surprise them on a sodaine, and that they should mistrust nothing, he sent to all the citties that they should send him by a certaine daye, tenne of the chiefest men of every cittie. Who when they were come, he commaunded them to goe and bring him by suche a daye, all the golde and silver they had within their citties, aswell in their private houses, as in their temples and churches, and gave unto everie one of them a captaine and garrison with them, as if it had bene only to have receaved and searched for the gold and silver he demaunded. But when the daye appointed was come, the souldiers in divers places (and all at one time) set upon their enemies, and dyd rifle and spoyle them of that they had, and made them also paye ransome every man: So as by this policie, there were taken and made slaves in one daye, a hundred and fiftie thousand persones, and three score and tenne citties spoyled and sacked every one. And yet when they came to devide the spoyle of this generall destruction of a whole Realme by the polle, it came not to every souldiers parte, above eleven silver Drachmes a pece. Which made every one to wonder greatly, and to feare also the terrour of the warres, to see the wealthe and riches of so great a Realme, to amowunte to so litle for every mans share. When Æmylius had done this facte against his owne nature, which was very gentle and curteous: he went unto the sea syde to the citty of Orica, and there imbarked with his armie bownde for Italie. Where when he was arrived, he went up the river of Tyber against the streame, in king Perseus chief galley, which had sixteene owers on a side, richely set out with the armour of the prisoners, riche clothes of purple culler, and other suche spoyles of the enemies: so that the Romaines ronning out of Rome in multitudes of people to see this galley, and going side by side by her as they rowed softely, Æmylius tooke as great pleasure in it, as in any open games or feastes, or triumphe that had bene shewed in deede. But when the

Æmylius cruell acte spoyling of Epirus.

Æmylius tooke shippe at the cittie of Orica, and returned into Italie.

souldiers sawe, that the golde and silver of king Perseus treasure was not devided amongest them according unto promise, and that they had a great deale lesse then they looked for, they were marvelously offended, and inwardly grudged Æmylius in their hartes. Nevertheles they durst not speake it openly, but dyd accuse him, that he had bene to straight unto them in this warre, and therefore they dyd shewe no great desire, nor forwardnes, to procure him the honour of triumphe. Which Servius Galba understanding, that had bene an olde enemie of his, notwithstanding he had the charge of a thousand men under him in this warre: he like an envious viper tolde the people, howe Æmylius had not deserved the honour of triumphe, and sowed seditious wordes against him among the souldiers, to aggravate their ill will the more against him. Moreover, he craved a daye of the Tribunes of the people, to have respit to bring forth suche matter as they determined to object against him: saying the time then was farre spent, the sunne being but foure howers highe, and that it would require lenger time and leysure. The Tribunes made him aunswer, that he should speake then what he had to saye against him, or otherwise they would not graunte him audience. Hereupon he beganne to make a long oration in his dispraise, full of railing wordes, and spent all the rest of the daye in that rayling oration. Afterwardes when night came on, the Tribunes brake up the assembly, and the next morning the souldiers being incoraged by Galbaes oration, and having confedered together, dyd flocke about Galba, in the mount of the Capitoll, where the Tribunes had geven warning they would keepe their assembly. Now being broade daye, Æmylius triumphe was referred to the most number of voyces of the people, and the first tribe flattly dyd denie his triumphe. The Senate, and the residue of the people hearing that, were very sorie to see they dyd Æmylius so open wrong and injurie. The common people sayed nothing to it, but seemed to be very sorie, howbeit they sought no redresse. The lordes of the Senate cried out apon them, and sayd it was to much shame, and exhorted one another to bridell the insolencie and boldnes of these souldiers, who

The envie of Servius Galba unto Æmylius.

Contention about Æmylius triumphe.

would growe in the ende to such tumulte and disorder, that they would commit all mischief and wickednes, if betimes they were not looked to, and prevented, seeing they dyd so openly stand against their generall, seeking to deprive him of the honour of his triumphe and victorie. So they assembled a good company of them together, and went up to the Capitoll, and prayed the Tribunes they would staye to take the voyces of the people, untill they had acquainted them with such needefull matter, as they had to open unto them. The Tribunes graunted to it, and silence was made. Then Marcus Servilius, who had bene Consul, and had fought three and twenty combats of life and death in his owne persone, and had allwayes slaine as many of his enemies as chalenged him man for man: rose up, and spake in favour of Æmylius in this manner: 'I knowe now (sayed he) better 'then before, how noble and worthie a captaine Paulus 'Æmylius is, who hath atchieved such glorie and honorable 'victorie, with so dishonorable and disobedient souldiers. 'And I can but wonder, that the people not long since 'rejoyced, and made great accompt, of the victories and 'triumphes wonne apon the Illyrians and other nations of 'Africke: and that now they should for spite envie his glorie '(doing what lyeth in them to hinder) to bring a Macedonian 'king alive in a triumphe, and to shewe the glorie and great- 'nes of king Philip and Alexander the great, subdued by the 'Romaines force and power. What reason have ye, that not 'long since, apon a flying rumour that Æmylius had wonne 'the battell against Perseus, you straight made sacrifices to 'the goddes with great joye, praying them that you might be 'witnesses of the trothe thereof: and now that the persone 'him selfe whom you made generall is returned home, and 'doth deliver you most assured victorie, you doe frustrate the 'goddes most solemne thankes and honour due to them, and 'doe deprive your selves also of your wonted glorie in such a 'case? as if you were afeard to see the greatnes of your pro- 'speritie, or that you ment to pardone a King, your slave and 'prisoner. And yet of the two, you have more reason to 'hinder the triumphe, as pittying the King: then envying 'your captaine. But the malice of the wicked, through your

Servilius oration for the furtheraunce of Æmylius triumphe.

'pacience is growen to suche an insolent audacitie and boldnes, 'that we see men present here before us, which never went from 'the smoke of the chimney, nor caried away any blowes in the 'field, being crammed at home like women and housedowes: 'and yet they are so impudent and shameles, as they dare 'presume unreverently to your faces, to prate of the office and 'duety of a generall of an armie, and of the desert of triumphe, 'before you I saye, who by experience of many a sore cut and 'wounde apon your bodies in the warres, have learned to 'knowe a good and valliant captaine, from a vile and cowardly 'persone.' And speaking these wordes, he cast open his gowne, and shewed before them all, the infinite scarres and cuttes he had receyved upon his brest: and then turning him behinde, shewed all suche places as were not fitte to be seene openly, and so turned him againe to Galba, and sayed unto him: 'Thou mockest me for that I shewe thee: but I rejoyce before 'my countrie men and cittizens: that for serving my contrie 'night and daye a horse backe, I have these wounds apon me 'which thou seest. Now get thee about thy busines, and re-'ceive their voyces: and I wil come after, noting them that are 'naughtie and unthankfull cittizens, who like to be soothed 'with flatterie, and not stowtely commaunded, as behoveth a 'generall in the warre.' These wordes so reined the harde headed souldiers with the curbe of reason, that all the other tribes agreed in one, and graunted Æmylius triumphe: the order and solemnitie whereof was performed in this sorte.

A notable description of Æmylius triumphe.

First, the people having set up sundrie scaffoldes aswel in the listes and field (called *Circos* by the Latines) where the games and common running of horses and charrets are made, as also about the market place, and in other streetes of the cittie, through the which, the shewe of the triumphe should passe: they all presented them selves in their best gownes to see the magnificence and state thereof. All the temples of the goddes also were set wide open, hanged full of garlands of flowers, and all perfumed within: and there were set through all the quarters of the cittie, numbers of sergeaunts and other officers holding tipstaves in their hands, to order the stragling people, and to keepe them up in corners and lanes endes, that they should not pester the streetes, and hinder the triumphe.

Furthermore, the sight of this triumphe was to continue three dayes, whereof the first was scant sufficient to see the passing by of the images, tables, and pictures, and statues of wonderfull bignes, all wonne and gotten of their enemies, and drawen in the showe, upon two hundred and fiftie charrets. The second daye, there were caried upon a number of cartes, all the fairest and richest armour of the Macedonians, aswell of copper, as also of iron and steele, all glistering bright, being newly furbished, and arteficially layed in order (and yet in such sorte, as if they had bene cast in heapes one upon another, without taking any care otherwise for the ordering and laying of them) fayer burganets upon targets: habergions, or brigantines and corselets, upon greaves: rounde targets of the Cretans, and javelings of the Thracians, and arrowes amongest the armed pykes: all this armour and cariage, being bound one to another so trimly (neither being to lose, nor to straight) that one hitting against another, as they drue them upon the cartes through the cittie, they made suche a sound and noyse, as it was fearefull to heare it: so that the only sight of these spoyles of the captives being overcome, made the sight so muche more terrible to behold it. After these cartes loden with armour, there followed three thousand men, which caried the ready money in seven hundred and fiftie vessels, which wayed about three talents a pece, and every one of them were caried by foure men: and there were other that caried great bowles of silver, cuppes and goblets facioned like hornes, and other pottes to drinke in, goodly to behold, aswel for their bignes, as for their great and singular imbossed workes about it. The third day early in the morning, the trumpets beganne to sound and set forwardes, sounding no marche nor swete note, to beawtifie triumphe withall: but they blewe out the brave alarom they sounde at an assault, to geve the souldiers corage for to fight. After them followed sixe score goodly fat oxen, having all their hornes gylte, and garlands of flowers and nosegayes about their heads, and there went by them certaine yong men, with aprons of nedle worke, girt about their midle, who led them to the sacrifice, and young boyes with them also, that caried goodly basons of gold and silver, to cast and sprinkle the bloud of the sacrifices about. And after these, followed those that caried all coynes of gold devided by basons and vessels, and every one of them waying three talents as they dyd before, that caried the great holy cuppe, which Æmylius had caused to be made of massi gold, set full of precious stones, waying the weight of tenne talents, to make an offering unto the godds. And next unto them went other that caried plate, made and wrought after antike facion, and notable cuppes of the auncient kings of Macedon: as the cuppe called Antigonus, and another Seleucus: and to be shorte, all the whole cubberd of plate of gold and silver of king Perseus. And next them came the charret of his armour, in the which was all king Perseus harnesse, and his royall bande (they call a Diademe) upon his armour. And a litle space betweene them, followed next the Kings children, whom they led prisoners, with the traine of their schoolemasters and other officers, and their servaunts, weeping and lamenting: who held up their hands unto the people that looked apon them, and taught the Kings young children to doe the like, to aske mercie and grace at the peoples hands. There were three prety litle children, two sonnes and a daughter amongest them, whose tender yeres and lacke of understanding, made them (poore soules) they could not feele their present miserie, which made the people so muche more to pittie them, when they saw the poore litle infants, that they knew not the chaunge of their hard fortune: so that for the compassion they had of them, they almost let the father passe without looking upon him. Many peoples harts did melt for very pittie, that the teares ranne downe their cheekes, so as this sight brought both pleasure and sorow, together to the lookers on, untill they were past and gone a good way out of sight. King Perseus the father, followed after his children and their traine, and he was clothed in a blacke gowne, wearing a payer of slippers on his feete after his contrie manner. He shewed by his countenance his troubled minde, opprest with sorow of his most miserable state and fortune. He was followed with his kinsefolks, his familliar frends, his officers and household servants, their faces disfigured by blubbering, shewing to the world by their lamenting teares, and sorow-

Perseus children.

King Perseus.

full eyes cast apon their unfortunate master, how much they sorowed and bewailed his most hard and cursed fortune, litle accompting of their own miserie. The voice goeth, that Perseus sent unto Æmylius to intreate him, that he should not be led through the cittie in the showe and sight of the triumphe. But Æmylius mocking (as he deserved) his cowardly faint hart, aunswered: as for that, it was before, and is now in him, to doe if he wil. Meaning to let him understand thereby, that he might rather chuse to dye, then living to receive such open shame. Howbeit his hart would not serve him, he was so cowardly, and made so effeminate, by a certen vaine hope he knew not what, that he was contented to make one among his own spoiles. After all this, there followed 400 princely crownes of golde, which the citties and townes of Græce had purposly sent by their ambassadours unto Æmylius, to honour his victorie: and next unto them, he came him selfe in his charret triumphing, which was passing sumptuously set forth and adorned. It was a noble sight to behold: and yet the person of him self only was worth the looking on, without all that great pompe and magnificence. For he was apparelled in a purple gowne branched with gold, and caried in his right hand a lawrell boughe, as all his armie did besids: the which being devided by bands and companies, followed the triumphing charret of their captaine, some of the souldiers, singing songes of victorie, which the Romaines use to singe in like triumphes, mingling them with mery pleasant toyes, rejoycing at their captaine. Other of them also dyd singe songs of triumphe, in the honour and praise of Æmylius noble conquest and victorie. He was openly praised, blessed, and honored of every body, and neither hated nor envied of honest men. Saving the ordinary use of some god, whose propertie is allwayes to lessen or cut of some part of mans exceding prosperitie and felicitie, mingling with mans life the sence and feeling of good and evill together: bicause that no living persone should passe all his time of life, without some adversitie or misfortune, but that such (as Homer sayeth) should only thinke them selves happie, to whom fortune hath equally sorted the good with the evill.

Æmylius scorneth Perseus cowardlines.

Foure hundred crownes of gold sent unto Æmylius by the citties of Græce.

Æmylius adversitie.

And this I speake, bicause Æmylius had 4 sonnes, two of the which he gave in adoption unto the families of Scipio and of Fabius, as we have sayed before: and two other which he had by his second wife, he brought up with him in his owne house, and were both yet very young. Of the which the one dyed, being 14 yeres of age five dayes before his fathers triumphe: and the other dyed also, 3 dayes after the pompe of triumphe, at 12 yeres of age. When this sorowfull chaunce had befallen him, every one in Rome did pittie him in their hartes: but fortunes spite and crueltie did more greve and feare them, to see her litle regard towards him, to put into a house of triumphe (full of honour and glorie, and of sacrifices and joye) such a pittiefull mourning, and mingling of sorowes and lamentations of death, amongest such songs of triumple and victorie. Notwithstanding this, Æmylius taking things like a wise man, thought that he was not only to use constancie and magnanimitie, against the sword and pike of the enemie: but a like also against all adversitie and enmitie of spiteful fortune. So, he wisely wayed and considered his present misfortune, with his former prosperitie: and finding his misfortune conterpeased with felicitie, and his private grieves cut of with common joye, he gave no place to his sorowes and mischances, neither blemished any way the dignity of his triumphe and victorie. For when he had buried the eldest of his two last sonnes, he left not to make his triumphant entrie, as you have heard before. And his second sonne also being deceased after his triumphe, he caused the people to assemble, and in face of the whole cittie he made an oration, not like a discomforted man, but like one rather that dyd comforte his sorowfull contrymen for his mischance. 'He told them, that concerning mens 'matters, never any thing dyd feare him: but for things 'above, he ever feared fortune, mistrusting her chaunge 'and inconstancy, and specially in the last warre, doubting 'for so great prosperitie as could be wished, to be payed 'home with an after intollerable adversitie, and sinister 'chaunce. For as I went (sayed he) I passed over the gulfe 'of the Adriatike sea, from Brindes unto Corfu in one daye.

Æmylius fortitude in his great adversitie.

Æmylius oration in his trouble, for the death of his children.

'And from thence in five dayes after, I arrived in the cittie 'of Delphes, where I dyd sacrifice unto Apollo. And 'within five other dayes, I arrived in my campe, where I 'found mine armie in Macedon. And after I had done 'the sacrifice, and due ceremonies for purifying of the same, 'I presently beganne to followe the purpose and cause of my 'comming: so as in 15 dayes after, I made an honorable ende 'of all those warres. But yet, mistrusting fortune allwayes, 'seing the prosperous course of my affaires, and considering 'that there were no other enemies, nor daungers I neded to 'feare: I feared sorely she would chaunge at my returne, 'when I should be upon the sea, bringing home so goodly 'and victorious an armie, with so many spoiles and so many 'Princes and Kings taken prisoners. And yet when I 'was safely arrived in the haven, and seing all the cittie 'at my returne full of joye, and of feastes and sacrifices: I 'still suspected fortune, knowing her manner well enough, 'that she useth not to gratifie men so franckly, nor to 'graunt them so great things clearly, without some certen 'sparke of envie waiting on them. Neither dyd my minde 'being still occupied in feare of some thing to happen to 'the common wealth, shake of this feare behind me: but 'that I sawe, this home mishappe and miserie lighted upon 'me, enforcing me with mine owne hands in these holy dayes 'of my triumphe, to burie my two young sonnes one after 'another, which I only brought up with me, for the succes-'sion of my name and house. Wherefore, me thinkes now 'I may saye, I am out of all daunger, at the least touching 'my chiefest and greatest misfortune: and doe beginne to 'stablish my selfe with this assured hope, that this good 'fortune henceforth shall remaine with us evermore, with-'out feare of other unlucky or sinister chaunce. For she 'hath sufficiently contervailed the favorable victorie she 'gave you, with the envious mishappe wherewith she hath 'plagued both me and mine: shewing the conquerour and 'triumpher, as noble an example of mans miserie and 'weaknes, as the party conquered, that had bene led in 'triumphe. Saving that Perseus yet, conquered as he is, 'hath this comforte left him: to see his children living, and 'that the conquerour Æmylius hath lost his.' And this was the summe of Æmylius notable oration he made unto the people of Rome, proceeding of a noble and honorable disposed minde. And though it pittied him in his harte to see the straunge chaunge of king Perseus fortune, and that he hartely desired to helpe him, and to doe him good: yet he could never obtaine other grace for him, but only to remove him from the common prisone (which the Romaines call *Carcer*) into a more clenly and sweter house: where being straitly garded and looked unto, he killed him selfe by abstinence from meate, as the most parte of historiographers doe write. Yet some writers tell a marvelous straunge tale, and manner of his death. For they saye the souldiers that garded him, kept him from sleepe, watching him straightly when sleepe tooke him, and would not suffer him to shut his eye liddes (only apon malice they dyd beare him, bicause they could not otherwise hurte him) keeping him awake by force, not suffering him to take rest: untill suche time as nature being forced to geve over, he gave up the ghoste. Two of his sonnes dyed also: but the third called Alexander, became an excellent turner and joyner, and was learned, and could speake the Romaine tongue very well, and dyd write it so trimly, that afterwards he was chauncelour to the magistrates of Rome, and dyd wisely and discretly behave him selfe in his office. Furthermore, they doe adde to this goodly conquest of the realme of Macedon, that Æmylius conquered another speciall good thing, that made him marvelously well liked of the common people: that is, that he brought so muche gold and silver unto the treasurie store of Rome, as the common people needed never after to make contribution for any thing, untill the very time and yere that Hircius and Pansa were Consuls, which was about the beginning of the first warres of Augustus and Antonius. And yet Æmylius had one singular good gift in him: that though the people dyd greatly love and honour him, yet he ever tooke parte with the Senate and nobilitie, and dyd never by worde nor dede any thing in favour of the people, to flatter or please them, but in matters concerning government, he dyd ever leane to the nobilitie and good men.

The death of king Perseus.

A straunge kind of death.

The state of Perseus sonnes.

By Æmylius victorie, the people payed no more subsidie.

And this dyd Appius afterwards cast in his sonnes teethe, Scipio Africanus. For both of them being two of the chiefest men of their time, and contending together for the office of Censor: Appius had about him to favour his sute, all the Senate and Nobilitie, as of auncient time the familie of the Appians had ever held on their parte. And Scipio Africanus, though he was a great man of him selfe, yet he was in all times favoured and beloved of the common people. Whereupon when Appius sawe him come into the market place, followed with men of small qualitie and base condition, that had bene slaves before, but otherwise could skilfully handle suche practises, bring the people together, and by oportunitie of cries and lowde voyces (if neede were) obteine what they would in the assemblies of the cittie: he spake out alowde, and sayed: O Paulus Æmylius, now hast thou good cause to sighe, and mourne in thy grave where thou lyest (if the dead doe know what we doe here on earth) to see Æmylius a common sergeant, and Licinius a pratling fellowe, howe they bring thy sonne unto the dignitie of a Censor. And as for Scipio, he was allwayes beloved of the common people, bicause he dyd favour them in all things. But Æmylius also, although he tooke ever the noble mens parte, he was not therefore lesse beloved of the common people, then those that allwayes flattered them, doing all things as the people would, to please them: which the common people did witnesse, aswell by other honours and offices they offred him, as in the dignitie of the Censor which they gave him. For it was the holiest office of all other at that time, and of greatest power and authoritie, specially for inquierie and reformation of every mans life and manners. For he that was Censor, had authoritie to put any Senatour of the counsell, and to disgrade him, if he dyd not worthely behave him selfe according to his place and calling: and might name and declare any one of the Senate, whom he thought to be most honest, and fittest for the place againe. Moreover, they might by their authoritie, take from licentious young men, their horse which was kept at the charge of the common weale. Furthermore, they be the sessours of the people, and the muster masters, keping

Æmylius chosen Censor.

The office and authoritie of the Censor.

bookes of the number of persones at every mustering. So there appeared numbred in the register booke Æmylius made then of them, three hundred, seven and thirtie thousand, foure hundred, and two and fiftie men, and Marcus Æmylius Lepidus named president of the Senate, who had that honour foure times before, and dyd put of the counsell three Senatours, that were but meane men. And the like meane and moderation he and his companion, Martius Philippus kept, upon viewe and muster taken of the Romaine horsemen. And after he had ordered and disposed the greatest matters of his charge and office, he fell sicke of a disease that at the beginning seemed very daungerous, but in the ende there was no other daunger, saving that it was a lingring disease, and hard to cure. So, following the counsell of phisitians, who willed him to goe to a cittie in Italy called Velia, he tooke sea, and went thither, and continued there a long time, dwelling in pleasaunt houses upon the sea side, quietly and out of all noyse. But during this time of his absence, the Romaines wished for him many a time and ofte. And when they were gathered together in the Theaters, to see the playes and sportes, they cried out divers times for him: whereby they shewed that they had a great desire to see him againe. Time being come about when they used to make a solemne yerely sacrifice, and Æmylius finding him selfe also in good perfect health: he returned againe to Rome, where he made the sacrifice with the other priestes, all the people of Rome gathering about him, rejoycing muche to see him. The next daye after, he made another particular sacrifice, to geve thankes unto the goddes for recoverie of his healthe. After the sacrifice was ended, he went home to his house, and sate him downe to dinner: he sodainly fell into a raving (without any perseverance of sicknes spied in him before, or any chaunge or alteration in him) and his wittes went from him in suche sorte, that he dyed within three dayes after, lacking no necessarie thing that an earthly man could have, to make him happy in this world. For he was even honoured at his funeralles, and his vertue was adorned with many goodly glorious ornaments, neither with gold, silver, nor ivorie, nor with other suche sump-

Æmylius sicknes.

Æmylius removed from Rome, and dwelt in the citty of Velia.

The death of Æmylius in Rome.

Æmylius funeralles.

tuousnes or magnificence of apparell, but with the love and good will of the people, all of them confessing his vertue and well doing: and this dyd not only his naturall country men performe in memorie of him, but his very enemies also. For all those that met in Rome by chaunce at that time, that were either come out of Spayne, from Genua, or out of Macedon, all those that were young and strong, dyd willingly put them selves under the coffin where his bodie laye, to helpe to carie him to the churche: and the olde men followed his bodie to accompany the same, calling Æmylius the benefactour, saviour, and father of their countrie. For he dyd not only intreate them gently, and graciously, whom he had subdued: but all his life time he was ever ready to pleasure them, and to set forwardes their causes, even as they had bene his confederates, very friends, and neere kinsemen. The inventorie, of all his goodes after his death, dyd scant amownte unto the summe of three hundred, three score, and tenne thousand silver Drachmes, which his two sonnes dyd inherite. But Scipio being the younger, left all his right unto his elder brother Fabius, bicause he was adopted into a very riche house, which was the house of the great Scipio Africanus. Suche they saye was Paulus Æmylius conditions and life.

Æmylius goodes what they came to.

THE ENDE OF PAULUS ÆMYLIUS LIFE

THE LIFE OF TIMOLEON

BEFORE Timoleon was sent into Sicile, thus stoode the state of the Syracusans. After that Dion had driven out the tyranne Dionysius, he him selfe after was slaine immediatly by treason: and those that ayded him to restore the Syracusans to their libertie, fell out, and were at dissention among them selves. By reason whereof, the cittie of Syracusa chaunging continually newe

The state of the Syracusans before Timoleons comming.

tyrannes, was so troubled and turmoiled with all sorte of evills, that it was left in manner desolate, and without inhabitants. The rest of Sicile in like case was utterly destroyed, and no citties in manner left standing, by reason of the long warres: and those fewe that remained, were most inhabited of forreine souldiers and straungers (a company of lose men gathered together that tooke paye of no prince nor cittie) all the dominions of the same being easely usurped, and as easie to chaunge their lorde. In so muche, Dionysius the tyranne, tenne yeres after Dion had driven him out of Sicile, having gathered a certen number of souldiers together againe, and through their helpe driven out Niseus, that raigned at that time in Syracusa: he recovered the Realme againe, and made him selfe King. So, if he was straungely expulsed by a small power out of the greatest Kingdome that ever was in the worlde: likewise he more straungely recovered it againe, being banished and very poore, making him selfe King over them, who before had driven him out. Thus were the inhabitants of the cittie compelled, to serve this tyranne: who besides that of his owne nature he was never curteous nor civill, he was now growen to be farre more dogged and cruell, by reason of the extreme miserie and misfortune he had endured. But the noblest cittizens repaired unto Icetes, who at that time as lorde ruled the cittie of the Leontines, and they chose him for their generall in these warres: not for that he was any thing better then the open tyrannes, but bicause they had no other to repaire unto at that time, and they trusted him best, for that he was borne (as them selves) within the cittie of Syracusa, and bicause also he had men of warre about him, to make head against this tyranne. But in the meane time, the Carthaginians came downe into Sicile with a great armie, and invaded the countrie. The Syracusans being afrayed of them, determined to send ambassadours into Græce unto the Corinthians, to praye ayde of them against the barbarous people, having better hope of them, then of any other of the Græcians. And that not altogether bicause they were lineally descended from them, and that they had receyved in times past many pleasures at their handes: but also for that

Icetes, tyranne of the Leontines.

they knewe that Corinthe was a cittie, that in all ages and times, dyd ever love libertie, and hate tyrannes, and that had allwayes made their greatest warres, not for ambition of Kingdomes, nor of covetous desire to conquer and rule, but only to defend and mainteine the libertie of the Græcians. But Icetes in another contrarie sorte, he tooke apon him to be generall, with a minde to make him selfe king of Syracusa. For he had secretly practised with the Carthaginians, and openly notwithstanding, in words he commended the counsell and determination of the Syracusans, and sent ambassadours from him selfe also with theirs, unto Peloponnesus: not that he was desirous any ayde should come from them to Syracusa, but bicause he hoped if the Corinthians refused to send them ayde (as it was very likely they would, for the warres and troubles that were in Græce) that he might more easely turne all over to the Carthaginians, and use them as his friendes, to ayde him against the Syracusans, or the tyrante Dionysius. And that this was his full purpose, and intent, it appeared plainely sone after. Now when their ambassadours arrived at Corinthe, and had delivered their message, the Corinthians, who had ever bene carefull to defend such citties as had sought unto them, and specially Syracusa: very willingly determined in counsaill to send them ayde, and the rather for that they were in good peace at that time, having warres with none of the Græcians. So their only staye rested, upon choosing of a generall to leade their armie. Now as the magistrates and governours of the cittie were naming suche cittizens, as willingly offred their service, desirous to advaunce them selves: there stept up a meane commoner, who named Timoleon, Timodemus sonne, a man that untill that time was never called on for service, neither looked for any suche prefarment. And truely it is to be thought it was the secret working of the gods, that directed the thought of this meane commoner to name Timoleon: whose election fortune favored very much, and joyned to his valliantnes and vertue, marvelous good successe in all his doings afterwardes. This Timoleon was borne of noble parents, both by father and mother: his father was called Timodemus, and his mother Demareta. He was naturally inclined to love his

By what voice Timoleon came to be generall.

Timoleons parentage and manners.

countrie and common weale: and was allwayes gentle and curteous to all men, saving that he mortally hated tyrantes and wicked men. Furthermore nature had framed his bodie apt for warres and for paynes: he was wise in his grenest youth in all things he tooke in hande, and in his age he shewed him selfe very valliant. He had an elder brother called Timophanes, who was nothing like to him in condition: for he was a rashe harebraynd man, and had a greedy desire to reigne, being put into his head by a companie of meane men, that bare him in hande they were his friendes, and by certen souldiers gathered together, which he had allwayes about him. And bicause he was very hotte and forward in warres, his cittizens tooke him for a noble captaine, and a man of good service, and therefore oftentimes they gave him charge of men. And therein Timoleon dyd helpe him muche to hide his faulte he committed, or at the least made them seeme lesse, and lighter then they were, still increasing that small good gifte that nature brought forth in him. As in a battell the Corinthians had against the Argives and the Cleoneians, Timoleon served as a private souldier amongest the footemen: and Timophanes his brother, having charge of horsemen, was in great daunger of being cast away, if present helpe had not bene. For his horse being hurte, threwe him on the grounde in the middest of his enemies. Whereupon parte of those that were about him, were affrayed, and dispersed them selves here and there: and those that remained with him, being fewe in number, and having many enemies to fight withall, dyd hardly withstand their force and charge. But his brother Timoleon seeing him in suche instant daunger a farre of, ranne with all speede possible to helpe him, and clapping his target before his brother Timophanes, that laye on the grounde, receyving many woundes on his bodie with sworde and arrowes, with great difficultie he repulsed the enemies, and saved his owne and his brothers life. Now the Corinthians fearing the like matter to come that before had happened unto them, which was to lose their cittie through default of their friends helpe: they resolved in counsell, to entertaine in paye continually foure hundred souldiers that were

Timophanes, Timoleons brother, what he was.

Timoleon saved his brothers life.

straungers, whom they assigned over to Timophanes charge. Who, abandoning all honestie and regarde of the trust reposed in him, dyd presently practise all the wayes he could to make him selfe lorde of the cittie: and having put divers of the chiefest cittizens to death without order of lawe, in the ende, he openly proclaimed him selfe King. Timoleon being very sorie for this, and taking his brothers wickednes would be the very highe waye to his fall and destruction: sought first to winne him with all the good words and persuasion he could, to move him to leave his ambitious desire to reigne, and to salve (as neere as might be) his harde dealing with the cittizens. Timophanes set light by his brothers persuasions, and would geve no eare unto them. Thereupon Timoleon then went unto one Æschylus his friend, and brother unto Timophanes wife, and to one Satyrus a soothesayer (as Theopompus the historiographer calleth him, and Ephorus calleth him Orthagoras) with whom he came againe another time unto his brother: and they three comming to him, instantly besought him to beleeve good counsell, and to leave the Kingdome. Timophanes at the first dyd but laughe them to scorne, and sported at their persuasions: but afterwards he waxed warme, and grew into great choller with them. Timoleon seeing that, went a litle a toside, and covering his face fell a weeping: and in the meane season, the other two drawing out their swordes, slue Timophanes in the place. This murder was straight blowen abroade through the cittie, and the better sorte did greatly commend the noble minde and hate Timoleon bare against the tyrante: considering that he being of a gentle nature, and loving to his kinne, dyd notwithstanding regard the benefit of his countrie, before the naturall affection to his brother, and preferred duety and justice, before nature and kinred. For, before he had saved his brothers life, fighting for defence of his countrie: and now in seeking to make him selfe King, and to rule the same, he made him to be slaine. Suche then as misliked popular government and libertie, and allwayes followed the Nobilitie: they set a good face of the matter, as though they had bene glad of the tyrantes death. Yet still reprov-

The Corinthians enterteined 400 straungers, and made Timophanes captaine of them to keepe their cittie.

Timophanes cruelty, and usurpation of the kingdom.

Timophanes slaine by his brothers procurement.

ing Timoleon for the horrible murder he had committed against his brother, declaring howe detestable it was both to the gods and men: they so handled him, that it grieved him to the harte he had done it. But when it was told him that his mother tooke it marvelous evill, and that she pronounced horrible curses against him, and gave out terrible wordes of him, he went unto her in hope to comfort her: howbeit she could never abide to see him, but allwayes shut her doore against him. Then he being wounded to the harte with sorowe, tooke a conceit sodainly to kill him selfe by absteining from meate: but his friends would never forsake him in this despaire, and urged him so farre by intreaty and persuasion, that they compelled him to eate. Thereupon he resolved thenceforth to give him self over to a solitarie life in the countrie, secluding him selfe from all companie and dealings: so as at the beginning, he dyd not only refuse to repaire unto the cittie, and all accesse of companie, but wandring up and downe in most solitarie places, consumed him selfe and his time with melancholie. And thus we see, that counsells and judgements are lightly caried awaye (by prayse or disprayse) if they be not shored up with rule of reason, and philosophie, and rest confounded in them selves. And therefore it is very requisite and necessarie, that not only the acte be good and honest of it selfe, but that the resolution thereof be also constant, and not subject unto chaunge: to the ende we maye doe all things consideratly. Lest we be like unto likerous mowthed men, who as they desire meates with a greedy appetite, and after are sone weary, disliking the same: even so we do soddenly repent our actions, grounded upon a weake imagination, of the honestie that moved us thereunto. For repentaunce maketh the acte, which before was good, naught. But determination, grounded upon certaine knowledge and truthe of reason, doth never chaunge, although the matter enterprised, have not allwayes happy successe. And therefore Phocion the Athenian having resisted (as muche as in him laye) certen things which the generall Leosthenes dyd, and which contrarie to his minde tooke good effect: and perceyving the Athenians dyd open sacrifice unto the goddes, to geve them

Our acts must be honest, and constant.

thankes for the same, and muche rejoyce at the victorie they had obteined. I would have rejoyced to (sayed he) if I had done this: but so would I not for any thing, but I had geven the counsell. And after that sorte, but more sharpely dyd Aristides Locrian (a very friend and companion of Platoes) aunswer Dionysius the elder, tyrante of Syracusa: who asked his goodwill to marye one of his daughters. I had rather see my daughter deade (sayde he) then maried unto a tyranne. And within a certayne tyme after, the tyranne put all his sonnes to deathe: and then he asked him in derision, to greeve him the more, if he were still of his former opinion for the marying of his daughter. I am very sorye, (sayed he) with all my harte, for that thou hast done: but yet I doe not repent me of that I have sayed. That peradventure proceeded of a more perfect vertue. But to returne againe to Timoleon. Whether that inwarde sorowe strooke him to the harte for the deathe of his brother, or that shame did so abash him, as he durst not abide his mother: twenty yeares after, he never did any notable or famous acte. And therefore, when he was named to be generall of the ayde that shoulde be sent into Sicile, the people having willingly chosen and accepted of him: Teleclides, who was chiefe governor at that time in the citie of Corinthe, standing uppon his feete before the people, spake unto Timoleon, and did exhorte him to behave him selfe like an honest man, and valiant Captaine in his charge. For, sayd he, if you handle your selfe well, we will thinke you have killed a tyranne: but if you doe order your selfe otherwise then well, we will judge you have killed your brother. Nowe Timoleon being busie in leavying of men, and preparing him selfe: letters came to the Corinthians from Icetes, whereby plainely appeared, that Icetes had caried two faces in one hoode, and that he was become a traytor. For he had no sooner dispatched his Ambassadors unto them, but he straight tooke the Carthaginians parte, and dealt openly for them, intending to drive out Dionysius, and to make him selfe king of Syracusa. But fearing least the Corinthians would send ayde before he had wrought his feate: he wrote againe unto the Corinthians, sending them worde, that they shoulde not neede nowe to put

Phocions saying.

Aristides grave saying.

Timoleon chosen generall to go into Sicile.

Icetes tyran of the Leontines, a traytor.

them selves to any charge or daunger for comming into Sicile, and specially, bicause the Carthaginians were very angrie, and did also lye in wayte in the way as they should come, with a great fleete of shippes to meete with their armie: and that for him selfe, bicause he sawe they taried long, he had made league and amitie with them, against the tyranne Dionysius. When they had red his letters, if any of the Corinthians were before but coldely affected to this jorney, choller did then so warme them against Icetes, that they franckly graunted Timoleon what he would aske, and helpe to furnishe him to set him out. When the shippes were ready rigged, and that the souldiers were furnished of all thinges necessary for their departure, the Nunnes of the goddesse Proserpina sayed, they sawe a vision in their dreame, and that the goddesses Ceres and Proserpina did appeare unto them, apparrelled like travellers to take a jorney: and tolde them, that they woulde goe with Timoleon into Sicile. Apon this speache onely, the Corinthians rigged a galley, they called, the galley of Ceres and Proserpina: and Timoleon him selfe before he would take the seas, went into the citie of Delphes, where he made sacrifice unto Apollo. And as he entred within the Sanctuarie where the aunsweres of the Oracle are made, there happened a wonderfull signe unto him. For amongest the vowes and offerings that are hanged uppe uppon the walles of the Sanctuarie, there fell a bande directly uppon Timoleons heade, imbrodered all about with crownes of victorie: so that it seemed Apollo sent him already crowned, before he had set out one foote towardes the jorney. He tooke shippe, and sayled with seven gallyes of Corinthe, two of Corphue, and tenne the Leucadians did set out. When he was launched out in the mayne sea, having a francke gale of winde and large, he thought in the night that the element did open, and that out of the same there came a marvelous great bright light over his shippe, and it was much like to a torche burning, when they showe the ceremonies of the holy mysteries. This torche did accompanie and guide them all their voyage, and in the ende it vanished away, and seemed to fall downe uppon the coast of Italye, where the Shippemasters had determined to

A signe happened to Timoleon.

Timoleon tooke shippe towards Sicile.

A burning torche appeared in the element unto Timoleon.

arrive. The wise mens opinions being asked what this might signifie: they aunswered: That this wonderfull sight did betoken the dreame, the Nunnes of the goddesse Ceres dreamed, and that the goddesses favoring this jorney, had shewed them the waye, by sending of this light from heaven: bicause that the Ile of Sicile is consecrated unto the goddesse Proserpina, and specially for that they reporte her ravishement was in that Ile, and that the whole realme was assigned unto her for her joynter, at the day of her mariage. Thus did this celestiall signe of the goddes bothe encorage those that went this jorney, and deliver them also assured hope, who sayled with all possible speede they coulde: untill such time, as having crossed the seas, they arrived upon the coast of Italie. But when they came thither, the newes they understoode from Sicile put Timoleon in great perplexitie, and did marvelously discourage the souldiers he brought with him. For Icetes having overthrowen the battell of the tyranne Dionysius, and possessed the greatest parte of the citie of Syracusa: he did beseege him within the castell, and within that parte of the citie which is called the Ile, where he had pent him up, and inclosed him in with walles rounde about. And in the meane time he had prayed the Carthaginians, that they would be carefull to keepe Timoleon from landing in Sicile, to the ende that by preventing that ayde, they might easily devide Sicile betwene them, and no man to let them. The Carthaginians following his request, sent twenty of their gallyes unto Rhegio, amonge which Icetes Ambassadors were sent to Timoleon, with testimonie of his doinges: for they were fayer flattering wordes, to cloke his wicked intent he purposed. For they willed Timoleon he shoulde goe him selfe alone (if he thought good) unto Icetes, to counsell him, and to accompanie him in all his doinges, which were nowe so farre onwardes in good towardnes, as he had almost ended them all. Furthermore, they did also perswade him, he shoulde send backe his shippes and souldiers to Corinthe agayne, considering that the warre was nowe brought to good passe, and that the Carthaginians woulde in no case that his men should passe into Sicile, and that they were determined to fight with them, if they made any force to

Icetes beseegeth Dionysius.

Icetes sendeth Ambassadors unto Timoleon.

enter. So the Corinthians at their arrivall into the citie of Rhegio, finding there these Ambassadors, and seeing the fleete of the Carthaginians shippes, which did ryde at ancker not farre of from them: it spyted them on the one side to see they were thus mocked and abused by Icetes. For every one of them were marvelous angrye with him, and were greatly afeard also for the poore Sicilians, whome to playnely they sawe left a praye unto Icetes for rewarde of his treason, and to the Carthaginians for recompence of the tyrannie, which they suffered him to establish. So, on the other side they thought it impossible to concquer the shippes of the Carthaginians, which laye in wayte for them, and so neare unto them: considering they were twyse as many in number as they, and hard for them to subdue the armie also that was in the handes of Icetes in Sicile, considering that they were not come to him, but onely for the mayntenaunce of the warres. Notwithstanding, Timoleon spake very curteously unto those Ambassadors, and captaynes of the Carthaginians shippes, letting them understande that he would doe as much as they would have him: and to say truely, if he woulde have done otherwise, he could have wonne nothing by it. Nevertheles he desired for his discharge, they woulde say that openly, in the presence of the people of Rhegio, (being a citie of Greece, friend and common to both parties) which they had spoken to him in secrete: and that done, he would departe incontinently, alledging that it stoode him very much uppon for the safetie of his discharge, and that they them selves also should more faithfully keepe that they promised unto him touching the Syracusans, when they had agreed upon it, and promised it, before all the people of Rhegio, who should be witnes of it. Now, all this was but a fetche and policie delivered by him, to shadowe his departure, which the Captaines and governers of Rhegio did favor, and seeme to helpe him in: bicause they wished Sicile should fall into the handes of the Corinthians, and feared much to have the barbarous people for their neighbours. For this cause they commaunded a generall assembly of all the people, during which tyme, they caused the gates of the citie to be shut: geving it out, that it was bicause the Citizens

Timoleon craftier then the Carthaginians.

Rhegio a citie of Greece.

should not goe about any other matters in the meane time. Then when all the people were assembled, they beganne to make long orations without concluding any matter: the one leaving alwayes to the other a like matter to talke of, to the ende they might winne time, untill the gallyes of the Corinthians were departed. And staying the Carthaginians also in this assemblye, they mistrusted nothing, bicause they sawe Timoleon present: who made a countenaunce, as though he woulde ryse to say some thing. But in the meane time, some one did secretely advertise Timoleon, that the other gallyes were under sayle, and gone their waye, and that there was but one galley left, which taried for him in the haven. Thereupon he sodainly stale away through the prease, with the helpe of the Rhegians, being about the chayer where the orations were made: and trudging quickly to the haven, he imbarked incontinently, and hoysed saile also. And when he had overtaken his fleete, they went all safe together to lande at the citie of Tauromenion, which is in Sicilie: there they were very well received by Andromachus, who long before had sent for them, for he governed this citie, as if he had bene Lorde thereof. He was the father of Timæus the Historiographer, the honestest man of all those that did beare rule at that time in all Sicile. For he did rule his Citizens, in all justice and equitie, and did alwaies shew him selfe an open enemy of tyrans. And following his affection therein, he lent his citie at that time unto Timoleon, to gather people together, and perswaded his Citizens to enter into league with the Corinthians, and to ayde them, to deliver Sicile from bondage, and to restore it againe to libertie. But the captaines of the Carthaginians that were at Rhegio, when they knewe that Timoleon was under sayle and gone, after the assemblie of the counsell was broken uppe: they were ready to eate their fingers for spyte, to see them selves thus finely mocked and deceived. The Rhegians on the other side, were mery at the matter, to see howe the Phenicians stormed at it, that they had such a fine parte played them. Howbeit in the ende, they determined to send an Ambassador unto Tauromenion, in one of their gallyes. This Ambassador spake very boldely, and barbar-

Timoleon landeth at Tauromenion in Sicile.

Andromachus the father of Timæus the Historiographer, governer of the citie of Tauromenion.

The Carthaginians Ambassador did threaten to destroy the citie of Tauromenion, by shewing Andromachus the palme and backe of his hand.

ously unto Andromachus, and in a choller: and last of all, he shewed him first the palme of his hande, then the backe of his hande, and did threaten him that his citie shoulde be so turned over hand, if he did not quickly send away the Corinthians. Andromachus fell a laughing at him, and did turne his hande uppe and downe as the Ambassador had done, and bad him that he shoulde get him going, and that with speede out of his citie, if he would not see the keele of his galley turned upward. Icetes nowe understanding of Timoleons comming, and being affrayed, sent for a great number of gallyes unto the Carthaginians. Then the Syracusans beganne to despayre utterly, when they sawe their haven full of the Carthaginians galleyes, the best parte of their citie kept by Icetes, and the castell by the tyran Dionysius. And on thother side, that Timoleon was not yet comen but to a litle corner of Sicile, having no more but the litle citie of Tauromenion, with a small power, and lesse hope: bicause there was not above a thowsand footemen in all, to furnishe these warres, neither provision of vittells, nor so much money as woulde serve to entertayne and pay them. Besides also, that the other cities of Sicile did nothing trust him. But by reason of the violent extorcions they had alate suffered, they hated all Captaines and leaders of men of warre to the deathe, and specially for the tretcherie of Calippus and Pharax, whereof the one was an Athenian, and the other a Lacedæmonian. Both of them sayed they came to set Sicile at libertie, and to drive out the tyrans: and yet nevertheles they had done so much hurte unto the poore Sicilians, that the miserie and calamitie which they had suffered under the tyrans, seemed all to be golde unto them, in respect of that which the Captaines had made them to abyde. And they did not thinke them more happy, that had willingly submitted them selves unto the yoke of servitude: then those which they sawe restored, and set at libertie. Therefore perswading them selves, that this Corinthian woulde be no better unto them, then the other had bene before, but supposing they were the selfe same former craftes, and alluring baytes of good hope and fayer wordes, which they had tasted of before, to drawe them to accept newe tyrans: they did sore suspect it, and rejected all the Corinthians perswasions. Saving the Adranitans onely, whose litle citie being consecrated to the god Adranus, (and greatly honored and reverenced through all Sicile) was then in dissention one against an other: in so muche as one parte of them tooke parte with Icetes, and the Carthaginians, and an other side of them sent unto Timoleon. So it fortuned, that bothe the one and the other, making all the possible speede they coulde, who shoulde come first: arrived bothe in manner at one selfe tyme. Icetes had about five thowsande souldiers. Timoleon had not in all, above twelve hundred men, with the which he departed to goe towards the citie of Adranus, distant from Tauromenion, about three hundred and fortie furlonges. For the first dayes jorney, he went no great way, but lodged betymes: but the next morning he marched very hastely, and had marvelous ill way. When night was come, and day light shut in, he had newes that Icetes did but newly arrive before Adranus, where he encamped. When the private captaines understood this, they caused the voward to stay, to eate and repose a litle, that they might be the lustier, and the stronger to fight. But Timoleon did set still forwards, and prayed them not to stay, but to goe on with all the speede they could possible, that they might take their enemies out of order (as it was likely they should) being but newly arrived, and troubled with making their cabbons, and preparing for supper. Therewithall as he spake these wordes, he tooke his target on his arme, and marched him selfe the formost man, as bravely and coragiously as if he had gon to a most assured victorie. The souldiers seeing him marche with that life, they followed at his heeles with like corage. So they had not passing thirty furlonges to goe, which when they had overcomen, they straight set apon their enemies, whome they found all out of order, and began to flye, so soone as they saw they were upon their backes before they were aware. By this meanes there were not above three hundred men slayne, and twise as many moe taken prisoners, and so their whole campe was possessed. Then the Adranitans opening their gates, yelded unto Timoleon, declaring unto him with great feare, and no lesse wonder, how at the very time when he

The god Adranus.

Timoleon overthrew Icetes armie, and made him flye from Adranus.

The Adranitans yeld unto Timoleon.

gave charge apon the enemies, the dores of the temple of their god opened of them selves, and that the Javeling which the Image of their god did hold in his hand, did shake at the very ende where the iron head was, and how all his face was seene to sweate. This (in my opinion) did not onely signifie the victorie he had gotten at that time, but all the notable exploytes he did afterwardes, unto the which, this first encounter gave a happye beginning. For immediatly after, many cities sent unto Timoleon, to joyne in league with him.

Mamercus tyran of Catana.

And Mamercus, the tyran of Catana, a souldier, and very full of money, did also seeke his friendship. Furthermore, Dionysius the tyran of Syracusa, being weary to follow hope any longer, and finding him selfe in maner forced unto it by long continuaunce of seige: made no more reckoning of Icetes, when he knewe that he was so shamefully overthrowen. And contrariwise, much esteeming Timoleons valiantnes, he sent to advertise him, that he was contented to yelde him selfe and the castell into the handes of the Corinthians. Timoleon being glad of this good happe unlooked for, sent Euclides and Telemachus, two Captaines of the Corinthians, to take possession of the castell, with fowre hundred men, not all at a tyme, nor openly (for it was unpossible, the enemies lying in wayte in the haven) but by small companies, and by stelthe, he conveyed them all into the castell. So the souldiers possessed the castell, and the tyrans pallace, with all the moveables and municion of warres within the same. There were a great number of horse of service, great store of staves and weapons offensive of all sortes, and engynes of batterie to shoote farre of, and sundry other weapons of defence, that had bene gathered together of long tyme, to arme threescore and tenne thowsand men. Moreover, besides all this, there were two thowsand souldiers, whome with all the other thinges rehearsed, Dionysius delivered up into the handes of Timoleon: and he him selfe, with his money and a few of his friendes, went his way by sea, Icetes not knowing it, and so came to Timoleons campe. This was the first tyme that ever they sawe Dionysius a private man, in base and meane estate. And yet within fewe dayes after, Timoleon sent him from thence unto Corinthe in a shippe, with litle store of money.

Dionysius the tyran, yeldeth him selfe and the castell of Syracusa, unto Timoleon.

Dionysius the tyran of Syracusa sent to Corinthe.

Who was borne and brought up in the greatest and most famous tyrannie, and kingdome, conquered by force, that ever was in the world: and which him selfe had kept by the space of tenne yeares after the death of his father. Since Dion drave him out, he had bene marvelously turmoyled in warres, by the space of twelve yeares: in which time, although he had done muche mischiefe, yet he had suffered also a great deale more. For he sawe the death of his sonnes when they were men growen, and able to serve and cary armor. He saw his daughters ravished by force, and deflowred of their virginitie. He saw his owne sister (who was also his wife) first of all shamed, and cruelly handled in her person, with the greatest villanies and most vile partes done unto her, that his enemies could devise: and afterwards horribly murdered with his children, and their bodies in the end throwen into the sea, as we have more amply declared in the life of Dion. Now when Dionysius was arryved in the cittie of Corinthe, every Græcian was wonderfull desirous to go see him, and to talke with him. And some went thither very glad of his overthrow, as if they had troden him downe with their feete, whom fortune had overthrowen, so bitterly did they hate him. Other pittiyng him in their heartes, to see so great a chaunge, did behold him as it were with a certaine compassion, considering what great power, secret and divine causes have over mens weakenes and frailtie, and those thinges that daily passeth over our heades. For the world then, did never bring forth any worke of nature, or of mans hand so wonderful, as was this of fortune. Who made the world see a man, that before was in maner Lorde and Kinge of all Sicile, sit then commonly in the cittie of Corinthe, talking with a vitailer, or sitting a whole day in a perfumers shoppe, or commonly drinking in some celler or taverne, or to brawle and scolde in the middest of the streetes, with common whores in face of the world, or els to teach common minstrels in every lane and alley, and to dispute with them with the best reason he had, about the harmony and musike, of the songs they sang in the Theaters. Now some say he did this, bicause he knew not els how he should drive the time away, for that in dede he was of a

The miseries and calamities of Dionysius the tyran.

Dionysius brought to Corinthe.

The Inconstancie of fortune.

base mynde, and an effeminate person, given over to all dishonest lusts and desires. Other are of opinion, he did it to be the lesse regarded, for feare lest the Corinthians should have him in gealouzy and suspicion, imagining that he did take the chaunge and state of his lyfe in grievous part, and that he should yet looke backe, hoping for a tyme to recover his state againe: and that for this cause he did it, and of purpose fained many thinges against his nature, seeming to be a starke nideotte, to see him do those thinges he did. Some notwithstanding have gathered together certaine of his answers, which doe testifie that he did not all these thinges of a base brutish mynde, but to fitte himselfe onely to his present misery and misfortune. For when he came to Leucades, an auncient cittie built by the Corinthians, as was also the citty of Syracusa: he told the inhabitants of the same, that he was like to yong boyes that had done a fault. For as they flye from their fathers being ashamed to come in their sight, and are gladder to be with their brethren: even so is it with me, said he: for it would please me better to dwell here with you, then to go to Corinthe our head citty. Another tyme, being at Corinthe, a stranger was very busie with him, (knowing how familiar Dionysius was with learned men and Philosophers, while he raigned in Syracusa) and asked him in the ende in derision: what benefite he got by Platoes wisedome and knowledge? he answered him againe: How thinkest thou, hath it done me no good, when thou seest me beare so paciently this change of fortune? Aristoxenus a musitian, and other, asking him what offence Plato had done unto him: he answered: That tyrans state is ever unfortunate, and subject to many evills: but yet no evill in their state was comparable to this. That none of all those they take to be their most familiars, dare once tell them truely any thing: and that through their fault, he left Platoes company. Another tyme there commeth a pleasaunt fellow to him, and thinking to mocke him finely, as he entred into his chamber, he shooke his gowne, as the manner is when they come to tyrans, to shewe that they have no weapons under their gownes. But Dionysius encountred him as pleasantly,

Notable sayings of Dionysius Syracusan.

The benefite of Philosophy.

A tyranes state unfortunate.

This agreeth with Æsops wordes to Solon, who wished him comming to princes, to please them, or not to come nere them.

saying to him: Do that when thou goest hence, to se if thou hast stollen nothing. And again, Philip King of Macedon, at his table one day discending into talke of songs, verse, and tragedies, which Dionysius his father had made, making as though he wondred at them, how possibly he could have leisure to do them: he answered him very trimly, and to good purpose. He did them even at such tymes (quod he) as you and I, and all other great Lordes whom they recken happy, are disposed to be drunke, and play the fooles. Now for Plato, he never saw Dionysius at Corinthe. But Diogenes Sinopian, the first tyme that ever he met with Dionysius, sayd unto him: O, how unworthy art thou of this state. Dionysius stayed sodainely, and replied: Truly I thanke thee (Diogenes) that thou hast compassion of my misery. Why sayd Diogenes againe: Doest thou thinke I pitty thee? Nay it spiteth me rather to see such a slave as thou (worthy to dye in the wicked state of a tyrant like thy father) to lyve in such securitie, and idle lyfe, as thou leadest amongst us. When I came to compare these wordes of Diogenes, with Philistus wordes the Historiographer, bewailing the harde fortune of the daughters of the Leptines, saying that they were brought from the toppe of all worldly felicity, honor, and goodes, (whereof tyrannicall state aboundeth) unto a base, private, and humble life: me thinkes they are the proper lamentations of a woman, that soroweth for the losse of her boxes of painting cullers, or for her purple gownes, or for other suche prety fine trimmes of golde, as women use to weare. So, me thinkes these things I have intermingled concerning Dionysius, are not impartinent to the description of our lives, neither are they troublesom nor unprofitable to the hearers, oneles they have other hasty busines to let or trouble them. But now if the tyraunt Dionysius wretched state seeme straunge, Timoleons prosperitie then was no lesse wonderfull. For within fiftie dayes after he had set foote in Sicile, he had the castel of Syracusa in his possession, and sent Dionysius as an exile to Corinthe. This did set the Corinthians in suche a jollitie, that they sent him a supply of two thousand footemen, and two hundred horse-

See Solons life, and his answer to Æsop.

Diogenes saying to Dionysius the tyrane.

Timoleons prosperitie.

men, which were appointed to land in Italie, in the countrie of the Thurians. And perceyving that they could not possiblie goe from thence into Sicile, bicause the Carthaginians kept the seas with a great navie of shippes, and that thereby they were compelled to staye for better oportunitie: in the meane time they bestowed their leysure in doing a notable good acte. For the Thurians, being in warres at that time with the Brutians, they dyd put their cittie into their hands, which they kept very faithfully and friendly, as it had bene their owne native countrie. Icetes all this while dyd besiege the castell of Syracusa, preventing all he could possible, that there should come no corne by sea unto the Corinthians that kept within the castell: and he had hiered two straunge souldiers, which he sent unto the cittie of Adranus, to kill Timoleon by treason, who kept no garde about his persone, and continued amongest the Adranitans, mistrusting nothing in the world, for the trust and confidence he had in the safegard of the god of the Adranitans. These souldiers being sent to do this murther, were by chaunce enformed that Timoleon should one day do sacrifice unto this god. So apon this, they came into the temple, having daggers under their gownes, and by litle and litle thrust in through the prease, that they got at the length hard to the aulter. But at the present time as one encoraged another to dispatche the matter, a third persone they thought not of, gave one of the two a great cut in the head with his sworde, that he fell to the grounde. The man that had hurte him thus, fled straight upon it, with his sworde drawen in his hande, and recovered the toppe of a highe rocke. The other souldier that came with him, and that was not hurte, got holde of a corner of the aulter, and besought pardone of Timoleon, and told him he would discover the treason practised against him. Timoleon thereupon pardoned him. Then he told him howe his companion that was slaine, and him selfe, were both hiered, and sent to kill him. In the meane time, they brought him also that had taken the rocke, who cried out alowde, he had done no more then he should doe: for he had killed him that had slaine his owne father before, in the cittie of the Leontines.

Icetes hiereth two souldiers to kill Timoleon at Adranus.

The treason discovered to Timoleon by one of the souldiers.

And to justifie this to be true, certaine that stoode by dyd affirme, it was so in deede. Whereat they wondred greatly to consider the marvelous working of fortune, howe she doth bring one thing to passe by meanes of another, and gathereth all things together, howe farre a sonder soever they be, and linketh them together, though they seeme to be cleane contrary one to another, with no manner of likenes or conjunction betwene them, making the ende of the one, to be the beginning of another. The Corinthians examining this matter throughly, gave him that slue the souldier with his sworde, a crowne of the value of tenne minas, bicause that by meanes of his juste anger, he had done good service to the God that had preserved Timoleon. And furthermore, this good happe did not only serve the present turne, but was to good purpose ever after. For those that sawe it, were putte in better hope, and had thenceforth more care and regard unto Timoleons persone, bicause he was a holy man, one that loved the goddes, and that was purposely sent to deliver Sicile from captivitie. But Icetes having missed his first purpose, and seeing numbers daylie drawen to Timoleons devotion: he was mad with him self, that having so great an armie of the Carthaginians at hand at his commaundement, he tooke but a fewe of them to serve his turne, as if he had bene ashamed of his facte, and had used their frendshippe by stelth. So he sent hereupon for Mago their generall, with all his fleete. Mago at his request brought an huge army to see to, of a hundred and fiftie sayle, which occupied and covered all the haven: and afterwards landed three score thousand men, whom he lodged every man within the cittie of Syracusa. Then every man imagined the time was now come, which olde men had threatned Sicile with many yeres before, and that continually: that one day it shoud be conquered, and inhabited by the barbarous people. For in all the warres the Carthaginians ever had before in the countrie of Sicile, they could never come to take the cittie of Syracusa: and then through Icetes treason, who had receyved them, they were seene encamped there. On thother side, the Corinthians that were within the castell, founde them selves in great distresse, bicause their

The wonderfull worke of fortune.

Icetes bringeth Mago a Carthaginian with a great army to Syracusa.

vittells waxed scant, and the haven was so straightly kept. Moreover, they were driven to be armed continually to defend the walles, which the enemies battered, and assaulted in sundry places, with all kyndes of engines of batterie, and sundry sortes of devised instruments and inventions to take citties: by reason whereof, they were compelled also to devide them selves into many companies. Nevertheles, Timoleon without, gave them all the ayde he could possible: sending them corne from Catana, in litle fisher botes and small crayers, which got into the castell many times, but specially in storme and fowle weather, passing by the gallyes of the barbarous people, that laye scatteringly one from another, dispersed abroad by tempest, and great billowes of the sea. But Mago and Icetes finding this, determined to goe take the cittie of Catana, from whence those of the castell of Syracusa were vittelled: and taking with them the best souldiers of all their armie, they departed from Syracusa, and sayled towardes Catana. Nowe in the meane space, Leon Corinthian, captaine of all those that were within the castell, perceyving the enemies within the cittie kept but slender warde: made a sodaine salie out apon them, and taking them unwares, slue a great number at the first charge, and drave awaye the other. So by this occasion he wanne a quarter of the cittie, which they call Acradina, and was the best parte of the cittie, that had receyved least hurte. For the cittie of Syracusa seemeth to be built of many townes joyned together. So having found there great plenty of corne, golde, and silver, he would not forsake that quarter no more, nor returne againe into the castell: but fortifying with all diligence the compasse and precinct of the same, and joyning it unto the castell with certen fortifications he built up in haste, he determined to keepe both the one and the other. Now were Mago and Icetes very neere unto Catana, when a post overtooke them, purposely sent from Syracusa unto them: who brought them newes, that the Acradina was taken. Whereat they both wondred, and returned backe againe with all speede possible (having failed of their purpose they pretended) to keepe that they had yet left in their handes. Now for that matter, it is yet

Leon captaine of the Corinthians within the castell.

Leon wanne Acradina.

a question, whether we should impute it unto wisedome and valliancie, or unto good fortune: but the thing I will tell you now, in my opinion, is altogether to be ascribed unto fortune. And this it is. The two thousand footemen and two hundred horsemen of the Corinthians, that remained in the cittie of the Thurians, partly for feare of the gallyes of the Carthaginians that laye in wayte for them as they should passe, Hanno being their admirall: and partly also for that the sea was very rough and highe many dayes together, and was allwayes in storme and tempest: in the ende, they ventured to goe through the countrie of the Brutians. And partly with their good will (but rather by force) they got through, and recovered the cittie of Rhegio, the sea being yet marvelous highe and rough. Hanno the admirall of the Carthaginians, looking no more then for their passage, thought with him selfe that he had devised a marvelous fine policie, to deceyve the enemies. Thereuppon he willed all his men to put garlands of flowers of triumphe upon their heades, and therewithall also made them dresse up, and set forth his gallyes, with targets, corselets, and brigantines after the Græcians facion. So in this bravery he returned backe againe, sailing towards Syracusa, and came in with force of owers, rowing under the castells side of Syracusa, with great laughing, and clapping of hands: crying out alowde to them that were in the castell, that he had overthrowen their ayde which came from Corinthe, as they thought to passe by the coast of Italie into Sicile, flattering them selves, that this dyd muche discorage those that were besieged. But whilest he sported thus with his fonde devise, the two thousand Corinthians being arrived through the countrie of the Brutians in the citie of Rhegio, perceyving the coaste cleare, and that the passage by sea was not kept, and that the raging seas were by miracle (as it were) made of purpose calme for them: they tooke seas forthwith in such fisher boates and passengers as they found readie, in the which they went into Sicile, in suche good safety, as they drue their horse (holding them by the raynes) alongest their boates with them. When they were all passed over, Timoleon having received them, went immediatly to take Messina, and

Contention of fortune and valliancie.

The stratageame of Hanno the admirall of the Carthaginians.

Timoleon marcheth to Syracusa.

marching thence in battell raye, tooke his way towards Syracusa, trusting better to his good fortune, then to his force he had: for his whole number in all, were not above foure thowsand fighting men. Notwithstanding, Mago hearing of his comming, quaked for feare, and dowted the more upon this occasion. About Syracusa are certeyne marishes, that receive great quantitie of sweete fresh water, aswell of fountaynes and springes, as also of litle ronning brookes, lakes, and rivers, which ronne that wayes towards the sea: and therefore there are great store of eeles in that place, and the fishing is great there at all tymes, but specially for such as delite to take eeles. Whereuppon the Græcians that tooke paye on both sides, when they had leysure, and that all was quiet betwene them, they intended fishing. Now, they being all contrey men, and of one language, had no private quarrell one with an other: but when tyme was to fight, they did their duties, and in tyme of peace also frequented familiarly togither, and one spake with an other, and specially when they were busie fishing for eeles: saying, that they marvelled at the scituacion of the goodly places thereabouts, and that they stoode so pleasauntly and commodious apon the sea side. So one of the souldiers that served under the Corinthians, chaunced to say unto them: Is it possible that you that be Græcians borne, and have so goodly a citie of your owne, and full of so many goodly commodities: that ye will give it uppe unto these barbarous people, the vile Carthaginians, and most cruell murderers of the worlde? where you should rather wishe that there were many Sicilies betwixt them and Greece. Have ye so litle consideration or judgement to thinke, that they have assembled an armie out of all Africke, unto Hercules pillers, and to the sea Atlanticke, to come hether to fight to stablish Icetes tyrannie? who, if he had bene a wise and skilfull Captaine, would not have cast out his auncestors and founders, to bringe into his contrye the auncient enemies of the same: but might have received such honor and authoritie of the Corinthians and Timoleon, as he could reasonably have desired, and that with all their favor and good wil. The souldiers that heard this tale, reported it agayne in their campe: Insomuch they made Mago suspect there was treason in hand, and so sought some culler to be gon. But hereuppon, notwithstanding that Icetes prayed him all he could to tary, declaring unto him how much they were stronger then their enemies, and that Timoleon did rather prevayle by his hardines and good fortune, then exceede him in number of men: yet he hoysed sayle, and returned with shame enough into Africke, letting slyppe the conquest of all Sicile out of his handes, without any sight of reason or cause at all. The next day after he was gone, Timoleon presented battell before the citie, when the Græcians and he understoode that the Carthaginians were fled, and that they saw the haven ryd of all the shippes: and then beganne to jeast at Magoes cowardlines, and in derision proclaymed in the citie, that they would give him a good reward that could bringe them newes, whether the armie of the Carthaginians were fled. But for all this, Icetes was bent to fight, and woulde not leave the spoyle he had gotten, but defende the quarters of the citie he had possessed, at the swordes poynt, trusting to the strength and scituacion of the places, which were hardly to be approached. Timoleon perceyving that, devided his armie, and he with one parte thereof did sett upon that side which was the hardest to approache, and did stand upon the river of Anapus: then he appoynted an other part of his armie to assault all at one time, the side of Acradina, whereof Isias Corinthian had the leading. The thirde parte of his armie that came last from Corinthe, which Dinarchus and Demaratus led: he appoynted to assault the quarter called Epipoles. Thus, assault being given on all sides at one time, Icetes bandes of men were broken, and ranne their way. Now that the citie was thus wonne by assault, and come so sodaynely to the handes of Timoleon, and the enemies being fled: it is good reason we ascribe it to the valiantnes of the souldiers, and the captaines great wisedom. But where there was not one Corinthian slayne, nor hurt in this assault: sure me thinkes herein, it was onely the worke and deede of fortune, that did favor and protect Timoleon, to contende against his valiantnes. To the ende that those which should hereafter heare of his

Mago forsaketh Sicile upon suspect of treason.

Anapus fl.

Timoleon wynneth the citie of Syracusa.

TIMOLEON

doings, should have more occasion to wonder at his good happe: then to prayse and commend his valiantnes. For the fame of this great exployte, did in few dayes not onely ronne through all Italye, but also through all Greece. Insomuch as the Corinthians, (who could scant beleeve their men were passed with safetie into Sicile) understoode withall that they were safely arrived there, and had gotten the victorie of their enemies: so prosperous was their jorney, and fortune so spedely did favor his noble actes. Timoleon having now the castell of Syracusa in his hands, did not followe Dion. For he spared not the castell for the beawtie and stately building thereof, but avoyding the suspicion that caused Dion first to be accused, and lastly to be slayne: he caused it to be proclaymed by trompett, that any Syracusan whatsoever, should come with crowes of iron, and mattocks, to helpe to digge downe and overthrow the forte of the tyrans. There was not a man in all the citie of Syracusa, but went thither straight, and thought that proclamacion and day to be a most happy beginning, of the recoverie of their libertie. So they did not onely overthrowe the castell, but the pallace also, and the tombes: and generally all that served in any respect for the memorie of any of the tyrans. And having cleared the place in fewe dayes, and made all playne: Timoleon at the sute of the Citizens, made counsell halls, and places of justice to be built there: and did by this meanes stablish a free state and popular government, and did suppresse all tyrannicall power. Nowe, when he sawe he had wonne a citie that had no inhabitants, which warres before had consumed, and feare of tyrannie had emptied, so as grasse grewe so highe and rancke in the great markett place of Syracusa, as they grased their horses there, and the horsekeepers laye downe by them on the grasse as they fed: and that all the cities, a fewe excepted, were full of redde deare and wilde bores, so that men geven to delite in hunting, having leysure, might finde game many tymes within the suburbes and towne dytches, hard by the walles: and that such as dwelt in castells and stronge holdes in the contrye, would not leave them, to come and dwell in cities,

Timoleon overthroweth the castell of Syracusa.

Timoleon made Syracusa a popular government.

The miserable state of Sicile.

by reason they were all growen so stowte, and did so hate and detest assemblies of counsell, orations, and order of government, where so many tyrans had reigned. Timoleon thereuppon seeing this desolacion, and also so fewe Syracusans borne that had escaped, thought good, and all his Captaines, to write to the Corinthians, to send people out of Greece to inhabite the citie of Syracusa agayne. For otherwise the contrye would growe barren and unprofitable, if the grounde were not plowed. Besides, that they looked also for great warres out of Africke: being advertised that the Carthaginians had honge up the body of Mago their general upon a crosse (who had slayne him selfe for that he could not aunswere the dishonor layed to his charge) and that they did leavy another great mightie armie, to returne againe the next yere following, to make warres in Sicile. These letters of Timoleon being brought unto Corinthe, and the Embassadors of Syracusa being arrived with them also, who besought the people to take care and protection over their poore citie, and that they would once againe be fownders of the same: the Corinthians did not gredily desire to be Lordes of so goodly and great a citie, but first proclaymed by the trompett in all the assemblies, solemne feastes, and common playes of Greece, that the Corinthians having destroyed the tirannie that was in the citie of Syracusa, and driven out the tyrannes, did call the Syracusans that were fugitives out of their contrye, home againe, and all other Sicilians that liked to come and dwell there, to enjoy all freedom and libertie, with promise to make just and equall division of the landes among them, the one to have as much as the other. Moreover they sent out postes and messengers into Asia, and into all the Ilands where they understoode the banished Syracusans remayned: to perswade and intreat them to come to Corinthe, and that the Corinthians would give them shippes, Captaines, and meanes to conduct them safely unto Syracusa, at their owne proper costes and charges. In recompence whereof, the citie of Corinthe receaved every mans most noble praise and blessing, aswell for delivering Sicile in that sorte from the bondage of tyrannes: as also for keeping it out of the handes of the barbarous

Mago slue him selfe, being called to aunswer his departure out of Sicile.

people, and restored the naturall Syracusans, and Sicilians, to their home and contrye againe. Nevertheles, such Sicilians as repayred to Corinthe apon this proclamacion (them selves being but a small number to inhabite the contrye) besought the Corinthians to joyne to them some other inhabitantes, aswell of Corinthe it selfe, as out of the rest of Greece: the which was performed. For they gathered together about tenne thowsand persons, whom they shipped, and sent to Syracusa. Where there were already a great number of other comen unto Timoleon, aswell out of Sicile it self, as out of al Italie besides: so that the whole number (as Athanis writeth) came to three score thowsand persons. Amongst them he devided the whole contrye, and sold them houses of the citie, unto the value of a thowsand talents. And bicause he would leave the olde Syracusans able to recover their owne, and make the poore people by this meanes to have money in common, to defraye the common charges of the citie, as also their expences in time of warres: the statues or images were solde, and the people by most voyces did condemne them. For they were solemly indited, accused, and arraigned, as if they had bene men alive to be condemned. And it is reported that the Syracusans did reserve the statue of Gelon, an auncient tyranne of their citie, honoring his memorie, bicause of a great victorie he had wonne of the Carthaginians, neare the citie of Himera: and condemned all the rest to be taken away out of every corner of the citie, and to be sold. Thus beganne the citie of Syracusa to replenishe againe, and by litle and litle to recover it selfe, many people comming thither from all partes to dwell there. Thereupon Timoleon thought to set all other cities at libertie also, and utterly to roote out all the tyrans of Sicile, and to obteyne his purpose, he went to make warres with them at their owne dores. The first he went against, was Icetes: whome he compelled to forsake the league of the Carthaginians, and to promise also that he would rase all the fortresses he kept, and to live like a private man within the citie of the Leontines. Leptines in like maner, that was tyran of the citie of Apollonia, and of many other litle villages thereabouts: when he saw him

The Corinthians replenished the citie of Syracusa, with three score thowsand inhabitants.

Leptines, tyran of Apollonia, yelded to Timoleon.

selfe in daunger to be taken by force, did yeld him selfe. Whereupon Timoleon saved his life, and sent him unto Corinthe: thinking it honorable for his contrye, that the other Græcians should see the tyrans of Sicile in their chiefe citie of fame, living meanely and poorely like banished people. When he had brought this to passe, he returned forthwith to Syracusa about thestablishment of the common weale, assisting Cephalus and Dionysius, two notable men sent from Corinthe to reforme the lawes, and to helpe them to stablishe the goodliest ordinaunces for their common weale. And now in the meane time, bicause the souldiers had a minde to get some thing of their enemies, and to avoyd idlenes: he sent them out abroade to a contrye subject to the Carthaginians, under the charge of Dimarchus, and Demaratus. Where they made many litle townes rebell against the barbarous people, and did not onely live in all aboundance of wealth, but they gathered money together also to mainteyne the warres. The Carthaginians on thother side, while they were busy about the matters, came downe into Lilybea, with an armie of three score and tenne thowsand men, two hundred gallyes, and a thowsand other shippes and vessells that caried engines of batterie, cartes, vittells, municion, and other necessary provision for a campe, intending to make sporting warres no more, but at once to drive all the Græcians againe quite out of Sicile. For in deede it was an able armie to overcome all the Sicilians, if they had bene whole of them selves, and not divided. Now they being advertised that the Sicilians had invaded their contrye, they went towards them in great furie, led by Asdrubal and Amilcar, generalls of the armie. This newes was straight brought to Syracusa, and the inhabitants were so striken with feare of the report of their armie: that being a marvelous great number of them within the citie, scant three thowsand of them had the hartes to arme them selves, and to goe to the fielde with Timoleon. Now the straungers that tooke pay, were not above foure thowsand in all: and of them, a thowsand of their hartes fayled, and left him in midd way, and returned home againe. Saying, that Timoleon was out of his wittes, and more rashe then his yeares

The armie and shippes of the Carthaginians against Timoleon, Asdrubal and Amilcar being generalls.

required, to undertake with five thowsand footemen, and a thowsand horse, to goe against threescore and tenne thowsand men : and besides, to cary that small force he had to defend him selfe withal, eight great dayes jorney from Syracusa. So, that if it chaunced they were compelled to flye, they had no place whether they might retyre them selves unto with safetie, nor man that woulde take care to burye them, when they were slayne. Nevertheles, Timoleon was glad he had that proofe of them, before he came to battell. Moreover, having incoraged those that remayned with him, he made them marche with speede towards the river of Crimesus, where he understoode he should meete with the Carthaginians. So getting up upon a litle hil, from whence he might se the campe of the enemies on the other side: by chaunce, certen moyles fell apon his armie loden with smallage. The souldiers tooke a conceyt at the first apon sight of it, and thought it was a token of ill lucke: bicause it is a maner we use, to hange garlands of this erbe, about the tombes of the dead. Hereof came the common proverbe they use to speake, when one lyeth a passing in his bed: he lacketh but smallage. Asmuch to say, he is but a dead man. But Timoleon to draw them from this foolish superstition, and discorage they tooke, stayed the armie. And when he had used certen perswasions unto them, according to the time, his leysure, and occasion: he told them that the garland of it selfe came to offer them victorie before hand. For, sayd he, the Corinthians doe crowne them that winne the Istmian games (which are celebrated in their contrye) with garlands of smallage. And at that time also even in the solemne Istmian games, they used the garland of smallage for reward and token of victorie: and at this present it is also used in the games of Nemea. And it is but lately taken up, that they have used braunches of pyne apple trees in the Istmian games. Now Timoleon had thus incoraged his men, as you have heard before: he first of all tooke of this smallage, and made him selfe a garland, and put it on his head. When they sawe that, the Captaines and all the souldiers also tooke of the same, and made them selves the like. The soothsayers in like maner at the very same time,

Timoleon went with 6000 men against the Carthaginians.

Crimesus fl.

Smallage an ill signe.

Proverbe.

Garlandes of smallage.

perceyved two eagles flying towards them: the one of them holding a snake in her talents, which she pearced through and through, and the other as she flewe, gave a terrible cry. So they shewed them both unto the souldiers, who did then all together with one voyce call upon the gods for helpe. Now this fortuned about the beginning of the sommer, and towards the later ende of Maye, the sunne drawing towards the solstyce of the sommer: when there rose a great myst out of the river, that covered all the feilds over, so as they could not see the enemies campe, but onely heard a marvelous confused noyse of mens voyces, as it had come from a great armie, and rising up to the toppe of the hil, they layed their targets downe on the grownd to take a litle breathe: and the sunne having drawen and sucked up all the moyst vapours of the myste unto the toppe of the hills, the ayer began to be so thicke, that the toppes of the mountaynes were all covered over with clowdes, and contrarily, the valley underneath was all cleare and fayer, that they might easily see the river of Crimesus, and the enemies also, how they passed it over in this sort. First, they had put their cartes of warre foremost, which were very hotly armed and well appoynted. Next unto them there followed tenne thowsand footemen, armed with white targets upon their armes: whom they seeing a farre of so well appoynted, they conjectured by their stately marche and good order, that they were the Carthaginians them selves. After them, divers other nations followed confusedly one with an other, and so they thronged over with great disorder. There Timoleon considering the river gave him oportunity to take them before they were halfe past over, and to set upon what number he would: after he had shewed his men with his finger, how the battel of their enemies was devided in two partes by meanes of the river, some of them being already passed over, and the other to passe: He commaunded Demaratus with his horsemen, to geve a charge on the voward, to keepe them from putting them selves in order of battell. And him selfe comming downe the hill also with all his footemen into the valley, he gave to the Sicilians the two winges of his battell, mingling with them some straungers that served under him: and

The order of the Carthaginians armie.

Timoleon geveth charge upon the Carthaginians as they came over the river of Crimesus.

placed with him selfe in the middest, the Syracusans, with all the choyce and best liked straungers. So he taried not long to joyne, when he saw the small good his horsemen did. For he perceyved they could not come to geve a lusty charge apon the battell of the Carthaginians, bicause they were paled in with these armed cartes, that ranne here and there before them: whereupon they were compelled to wheele about continually, (onles they would have put them selves in daunger to have bene utterly overthrowen) and in their returnes to geve venture of charge, by turnes on their enemies. Wherefore Timoleon taking his target on his arme, cried out alowde to his footemen, to follow him coragiously, and to feare nothing. Those that heard his voyce, thought it more then the voyce of a man, whether the furie of his desire to fight did so strayne it beyonde ordinary course, or that some god (as many thought it then) did stretch his voyce to cry out so lowde and sensibly. His souldiers aunswered him againe with the like voyce: and prayed him to leade them without lenger delay. Then he made his horsemen understand, that they should draw on the toneside from the cartes, and that they should charge the Carthaginians on the flanckes: and after he did set the formost rancke of his battell, target to target against the enemies, commaunding the trumpets withall to sownd. Thus with great furie he went to geve a charge apon them, who valiantly receyved the first charge, their bodies being armed with good iron corselets, and their heades with fayer murrions of copper, besides the great targetts they had also, which did easily receyve the force of their dartes, and the thrust of the pyke. But when they came to handle their swordes, where agilitie was more requisite then force: a fearefull tempest of thunder, and flashing lightning withall, came from the mountaynes. After that came darke thicke clowdes also (gathered together from the toppe of the hilles) and fell uppon the valley, where the battell was fought, with a marvelous extreame shower of rayne, fierce violent windes, and hayle withall. All this tempest was upon the Græcians backes, and full before the barbarous people, beating on their faces, and did blindefold their eyes, and continually tormented them with the rayne

The service of the armed cartes.

Timoleons marvelous bigge voyce.

Timoleons order and fight.

A marvelous tempest of thunder, lightning, rayne, winde, and hayle, full in the Carthaginians faces as they fought.

that came full apon them with the winde, and the lightnings so ofte flashing amongest them, that one understoode not another of them. Which did marvelously trouble them, and specially those that were but freshe water souldiers, by reason of the terrible thunderclapps, and the noyse, the boysterous winde and hayle made uppon their harnes: for that made them they could not heare the order of their Captaines. Moreover, the durt did as much annoye the Carthaginians, bicause they were not nimble in their armor, but heavely armed as we have told you: and besides that also, when the playtes of their coates were through wett with water, they did lode and hinder them so muche the more, that they could not fight with any ease. This stoode the Græcians to great purpose, to throwe them downe the easier. Thus when they were tombling in the durte with their heavy armor, up they could rise no more. Furthermore, the river of Crimesus being risen highe through the great rage of waters, and also for the multitude of people that passed over it, did overflowe the valley all about: which being full of ditches, many caves, and hollow places, it was straight all drowned over, and filled with many ronning streames, that ranne overthwart the feild, without any certen channell. The Carthaginians being compassed all about with these waters, they could hardly get the way out of it. So as in the end they being overcome with the storme that still did beate apon them, and the Græcians having slayne of their men at the first onset, to the number of foure hundred of their choycest men, who made the first fronte of their battell: all the rest of their armie turned their backes immediatly, and fled for life. Insomuch, some of them being followed very neare, were put to the sworde in the middest of the valley: other, holding one another hard by the armes together, in the middest of the river as they passed over, were caried downe the streame and drowned, with the swiftnes and violence of the river. But the greatest number did thinke by footemanship to recover the hilles thereabouts, who were overtaken by them that were light armed, and put to the sworde every man. They saye, that of tenne thowsande which were slayne in this battell, three thowsande of them were meere naturall citizens of

Timoleons victorie of the Carthaginians.

 Carthage, which was a very sorowfull and greevous losse to the city. For they were of the noblest, the richest, the lustiest, and valiantest men of all Carthage. For there is no chronicle that mentioneth any former warres at any tyme before, where there dyed so many of Carthage at one feild and battell, as were slayne at that present tyme. For before that time, they did alwayes entertaine the Fibyans, the Spanyards, and the Nomades, in all their warres: so as when they lost any battell, the losse lighted not on them, but the straungers payed for it. The men of accompt also that were slayne, were easily knowen by their spoyles. For they that spoyled them, stoode not trifling about getting of copper and iron together, bicause they found gold and silver enoughe. For the battell being wonne, the Græcians passed over the river, and tooke the campe of the barbarous people, with all their cariages and bagage. And as for the prisoners, the souldiers stole many of them away, and sent them going: but of them that came to short to make common division of the spoyle amonge them, they were about five thowsand men, and two hundred cartes of warre that were taken besides. Oh, it was a noble sight to behold the tent of Timoleon their generall, how they envyroned it all about with heapes of spoyles of every sorte: amongest which there were a thowsand brave corselets guylt, and graven, with marvelous curious workes, and brought thither with them also tenne thowsand targets. So the conquerours being but a small number, to take the spoile of a multitude that were slaine they filled their purses even to the toppe. Yet were they three daies about it, and in the end, the third day after the battel, they set up a marke or token of their victorie. Then Timoleon sent unto Corinthe, with the newes of this overthrow, the fairest armors that were gotten in the spoyle: bicause he would make his countrie and native citie spoken of and commended through the world, above al the other cities of Greece. For that at Corinth only, their chief temples were set forth and adorned, not with spoiles of the Greecians, nor offerings gotten by spilling the blood of their owne nation and contrie: (which to say truely, are unpleasant memories) but with the spoiles taken from the barbarous people their enemies, with inscriptions witnessing the valliancie and justice of those also, who by victorie had obteined them. That is to wit, that the Corinthians and their captaine Timoleon, (having delivered the Greecians dwelling in Sicile, from the bondage of the Carthaginians) had geven those offerings unto the gods, to geve thanks for their victory. That done, Timoleon leaving the straungers he had in pay, in the contrie subject to the Carthaginians, to spoile and destroy it: he retorned with the rest of his army unto Syracusa. Where at his first comming home, he banished the thowsand souldiers that had forsaken him in his jorney, with expresse charge that they should departe the cittie before sunne sette. So these thowsand cowardly and mutinous souldiers passed over into Italie, where, under promise of the countrie, they were al unfortunately slayne by the Brutians: such was the justice of the goddes to paie their juste rewarde of their treason. Afterwards, Mamercus the tyranne of Catana, Icetes (whether it was for the envie they did beare to Timoleons famous dedes, or for that they were affrayde of him) perceiving tyrannes could looke for no peace at his handes: they made league with the Carthaginians, and wrote unto them that they should send another armie and captaine sodainely, if they would not utterly be driven out of Sicile. The Carthaginians sent Gisco thither with threescore and tenne saile, who at his first comming tooke a certen number of Grecian souldiers into pay, which were the first the Carthaginians ever retained in their service: for they never gave them pay until that present time, when they thought them to be men invincible, and the best souldiers of the world. Moreover, the inhabitantes of the territorie of Messina, having made a secret conspiracie amongest them selves, did slay foure hundred men that Timoleon had sent unto them: and in the territories subject unto the Carthaginians, nere unto a place they call Hieres, there was another ambush layd for Euthimus Leucadian, so as him self and al his souldiers were cut in peces. Howbeit the losse of them made Timoleons doings notwithstanding more fortunate: for they were even those that had forcibly entred the temple of Apollo in the cittie of Delphes, with Philodemus Phocian, and with Onomarchus,

Timoleon banisheth the thowsand trayterous souldiers out of Sicile.

Gisco sent from Carthage with 70 saile into Sicile.

Messina riseth against Timoleon.

TIMOLEON

who were partakers of their sacriledge. Moreover, they were lose people and abjectes, that were abhorred of everie body, who vacabondlike wandred up and downe the contry of Peloponnesus, when Timoleon for lacke of other was glad to take them up. And when they came into Sicile, they alwaies overcame in al battells they fought, whilest they were in his company. But in the ende, when the furie of warres was pacified, Timoleon sending them about some speciall service to the ayde of some of his, they were cast away every man of them: and not all together, but at divers times. So as it seemed that Goddes justice, in favor of Timoleon, did separate them from the rest, when he was determined to plague them for their wicked desertes, fearing least good men should suffer hurt by punishing of the evill. And so was the grace and goodwill of the goddes wonderful towards Timoleon, not onely in matters against him, but in those things that prospered well with him. Notwithstanding, the common people of Syracusa tooke the jeasting wordes and writings of the tyrans against them, in marvelous evill part.

Mamercus verses, tyranne of Catana.

For Mamercus amongest other, thinking well of him selfe, bicause he could make verses and tragedies, having in certen battels gotten the better hand of the straungers, which the Syracusans gave pay unto, he gloried very much. And when he offred up the targets he had gotten of them, in the temples of the godds: he set up also these cutting verses, in derision of them that were vanquished:

> With bucklers pot lyd like, which of no value were,
> we have these goodly targets wonne, so richly trymmed here,
> All gorgeously with golde, and eke with Ivorye,
> with purple cullers finely wrought, and dect with Ebonye.

Calauria, a citie of Sicile.

These thinges done, Timoleon led his armie before the citie of Calauria, and Icetes therewhile entred the confines of the Syracusans with a maine army, and caried away a marvelous great spoile. And after he had done great hurt, and spoiled the contry, he returned backe againe, and came by Calauria, to despite Timoleon, knowing wel enough he had at that time but few men about him. Timoleon suffered him to passe by, but folowed him afterwards with his horsemen and lightest armed footemen. Icetes understanding that, passed over the river called Damirias, and so staied on the other side as though he would fight, trusting to the swift ronning of the river, and the height of the bankes on either side of the same. Now the captaines of Timoleons bands fell out marvelously amongest them selves, striving for honor of this service, which was cause of delaying the battel. For none would willingly come behind, but every man desired to lead the voward, for honor to begin the charge: so as they could not agree for their going over, one thrusting another to get before his companion. Wherfore Timoleon fell to drawing of lots, which of them should passe over first, and tooke a ring of every one of them, and cast them all within the lappe of his cloke: so rolling them together, by chaunce he pluckt one at the first, wheron was graven the markes and tokens of a triumph. The young Captaines seeing that, gave a shoute of joy, and without tarying drawing of other lottes, they began every man to passe the river as quickly as they could, and to set apon the enemies as sodainely. But they being not able to abide their force, ranne their wayes, and were faine to cast their armor away to make more hast: howbeit there were a thowsand of them lay dead in the feilde. And within few daies after, Timoleon leading his armie to the citie of the Leontines, tooke Icetes alive there, with his sonne Eupolemus, and the generall of his horsemen, who were delivered into his hands by his owne souldiers. So Icetes and his sonne were put to death, like the traitors and tyrannes: and so was Euthydemus also, who though he was a valliant souldier, had no better mercie shewed him, then the father and the sonne, bicause they did burden him with certaine injurious words he spake against the Corinthians. For they say, that when the Corinthians came first out of their contrie into Sicile to make wars against the tyrannes: that he making an oration before the Leontines, said amongest other things: that they should not neede to be afraide, if

Damirias, fl.

Strife among Timoleons captaines for passing over the river.

Timoleons devise to draw lottes to pacifie the strife.

Timoleon taketh Icetes, and Eupolemus his sonne alive, and did put them to death.

The women of Corinthe were come out of their contrie.

Thus we see, that men do rather suffer hurt, then put up injurious words: and do pardone their enemies, though they revenge by deds, bicause they can do no lesse. But as for injurious words, they seme to proceed of a deadly hate, and of a cancred malice. Furthermore, when Timoleon was returned againe to Syracusa, the Syracusans arrained the wives of Icetes, and his sonne, and their daughters: who being arrained, were also condemned to die by the judgement of the people. Of al the actes Timoleon did, this of al other (in my opinion) was the fowlest dede: for if he had listed, he might have saved the poore women from death. But he passed not for them, and so left them to the wrath of the cittizens, who would be revenged of them, for the injuries that were done to Dion, after he had driven out the tyranne Dionysius. For it was Icetes that caused Arete, the wife of Dion, to be cast into the sea, his sister Aristomache, and his sonne that was yet a sucking child, as we have written in another place in the life of Dion. That done, he went to Catana against Mamercus, who taried him by the river of Abolus, where Mamercus was overthrowen in battel, and above two thowsand men slaine, the greatest part wherof were the Carthaginians, whom Gisco had sent for his reliefe. Afterwards he graunted peace to the Carthaginians, upon earnest sute made unto him, with condition, that they should kepe on thother side of the river of Lycus, and that it should be lawful for any of thinhabitants there that would, to come and dwel in the territory of the Syracusans, and to bring away with them their goodes, their wives and their children: and furthermore, that from thenceforth the Carthaginians should renounce al league, confederacy, and alliance with the tyrannes. Wherupon Mamercus having no hope of good successe in his doings, he would goe into Italye to stir up the Lucanians against Timoleon, and the Syracusans. But they that were in his company, returned backe againe with their gallies in the myd way: and when they were returned into Sicile, they delivered up the cittie of Catana into the handes of Timoleon, so as Mamercus was constrained to save him selfe, and to flye unto Messina, to Hippon the tyranne thereof. But Timoleon followed him, and beseged the cittie both by sea and by lande. Whereat Hippon quaked for feare, and thought to flye by taking shippe, but he was taken startyng. And the Messenians having him in their hands, made all the

Icetes wives and children put to death.

The crueltie of Icetes towards Dion and his.

Mamercus overcome in battel.

Abolus fl.

Timoleon maketh peace with the Carthaginians.

Lycus fl.

Catana yelded up unto Timoleon.

Hippon the tyranne of Messina.

children come from the schole to the Theater, to see one of the goodliest sightes that they could devise: to wit, to see the tyran punished, who was openly whipped, and afterwards put to death. Now for Mamercus, he did yeld him self unto Timoleon, to be judged by the Syracusans, so that Timoleon might not be his accuser. So he was brought unto Syracusa, where he attempted to make an oration to the people, which he had premeditated long before. But seeing that the people cryed out, and made a great noyse, bicause they would not heare him, and that there was no likelyhoode they would pardone him: he ranne overthwart the Theater, and knocked his head as hard as he could drive, upon one of the degrees whereon they sate there to see the sportes, thinking to have dashed out his braynes, and have rid him self sodainely out of his paine. But he was not happy to die so, for he was taken straight being yet alive, and put to death as theves and murderers are. Thus did Timoleon roote all tyrans out of Sicile, and make an end of all warres there. And wheras he found the whole ile, wilde, savage, and hated of the natural contry men and inhabitants of the same, for the extreme calamities and miseries they suffred: he brought it to be so civil, and so much desired of straungers, that they came farre and neare to dwell there, where the naturall inhabitants of the country selfe before, were glad to flye and forsake it. For Agrigentum, and Gela, two great cities, did witnesse this, which after the warres of the Athenians, had bene utterly forsaken and destroyed by the Carthaginians, and were then inhabited againe. The one, by Magellus and Pheristus, two Captaines that came from Elea: and the other by Gorgos, who came from the ile of Ceo. And as nere as they could, they gathered againe together the first auncient Citizens and inhabitants of the same: whom Timoleon did not onely assure of peace and safetie to live there, to settle them quietly together: but willingly did helpe them besides, with all other thinges necessary, to his uttermost meane and abilitie, for which they loued and honored him as their father and founder. And this his good love and favor, was common also to all other people of Sicile whatsoever. So that in all Sicile there was no truce taken

Hippon put to death.

Mamercus the tyranne put to death.

Timoleon quieteth all Sicile.

TIMOLEON

in warres, nor lawes established, nor landes devided, nor institucion of any policie or government thought good or avayleable, if Timoleons devise had not bene in it, as chiefe director of such matters: which gave him a singular grace to be acceptable to the goddes, and generally to be beloved of al men. For in those dayes, there were other famous men in Greece, that did marvelous great thinges: amongest whom were these, Timotheus, Agesilaus, Pelopidas, and Epaminondas, which Epaminondas Timoleon sought to follow in all thinges, as neare as he could, above any of them all. But in all the actions of these other great Captaines, their glorie was alway mingled with violence, payne, and labor: so as some of them have bene touched with reproche, and other with repentaunce. Whereas contrarywise, in all Timoleons doinges (that onely excepted, which he was forced to doe to his brother) there was nothing but they might with trothe (as Timæus sayd) proclayme the saying of Sophocles:

Timoleon compared with the famousest men of Gæce.

> Oh mightie goddes of heaven, what Venus stately dame,
> or Cupid, (god) have thus yput, their handes unto this same?

And like as Antimachus verses, and Dionysius paynting, both Colophonians, are ful of synewes and strength, and yet at this present we se they are things greatly labored, and travelled with much payne: and that contrariwise in Nicomachus tables, and Homers verses, besides the passing workmanship and singular grace in them, a man findeth at the first sight, that they were easily made, and without great payne. Even so in like manner, whosoever will compare the paynefull bloudy warres and battels of Epaminondas, and Agesilaus, with the warres of Timoleon, in the which, besides equitie and justice, there is also great ease and quietnes: he shall finde, waying things indifferently, that they have not bene fortunes doings simply, but that they came of a most noble and fortunat corage. Yet he him self doth wisely impute it unto his good happe, and favorable fortune. For in his letters he wrote unto his familiar frendes at Corinthe, and in some other orations he made to the people of Syracusa: he spake it many times, that he thanked the almighty gods, that it had pleased them to save and deliver

Timoleon attributeth his good successe unto fortune.

Sicile from bondage, by his meanes and service, and to geve him the honor and dignitie of the name. And having builded a temple in his house, he did dedicate it unto fortune, and furthermore did consecrate his whole house unto her. For he dwelt in a house the Syracusans kept for him and gave him in recompence of the good service he had done them in the warres, with a marvelous faire pleasaunt house in the contrie also, where he kept most when he was at leisur. For he never after returned unto Corinthe againe, but sent for his wife and children to come thither, and never delt afterwards with those troubles that fell out amongest the Greecians, nether did make him selfe to be envied of the cittizens: (a mischiefe that most governors and captains do fal into, through their unsatiable desire of honor and authoritie:) but lived al the rest of his life after in Sicile, rejoycing for the great good he had done, and specially to see so many cities and thowsands of people happy by his meanes. But bicause it is an ordinary matter, and of necessitie, (as Simonides saith) that not only al larkes have a tuft upon their heades, but also that in all citties there be accusers, where the people rule: there were two of those at Syracusa, that continually made orations to the people, who did accuse Timoleon, the one called Laphystius, and the other Demænetus. So this Laphystius appointing Timoleon a certen day to come and aunswere to his accusation before the people, thinking to convince him: the cittizens began to mutine, and wold not in any case suffer the day of adjornement to take place. But Timoleon did pacifie them, declaring unto them, that he had taken all the extreame paines and labor he had done, and had passed so many daungers, bicause every cittizen and inhabitant of Syracusa, might franckly use the libertie of their lawes. And another time Demænetus, in open assembly of the people, reproving many thinges Timoleon did when he was generall: Timoleon aunswered never a word, but onely said unto the people, that he thanked the goddes they had graunted him the thing he had so oft requested of them in his praiers, which was, that he might once see the Syracusans have full power and libertie to say what they would. Now Timoleon in all

Timoleon dwelleth still with the Syracusans.

Simonides saying.

Timoleons accusers.

Timoleons great praise.

mens opinion, had done the noblest actes that ever Greecian captaine did in his time, and had above deserved the fame and glory of al the noble exploytes, whiche the rethoricians with all their eloquent orations perswaded the Greecians unto, in the open assemblies, and common feastes and plaies of Greece, out of the which fortune delivered him safe and sound before the trouble of the civill warres that folowed sone after: and moreover he made a great proofe of his valliancie and knowledge in warres, against the barbarous people and tyrannes, and had shewed him selfe also a just and merciful man unto al his frendes, and generally to al the Greecians. And furthermore, seeing he wonne the most part of all his victories and triumphes, with out the sheading of any one teare of his men, or that any of them mourned by his meanes, and also ryd all Sicile of all the miseries and calamities raigning at that time, in lesse then eight yeeres space: he beyng nowe growen olde, his sight first beginning a litle to faile him, shortly after he lost it altogether. This happened, not through any cause or occasion of sicknesse that came unto him, nor that fortune had casually done him that injurie: but it was in my opinion, a disease inheritable to him by his parentes, which by time came to laie hold on him also. For the voyce went, that many of his kin in like case had also lost their sight, which by litle and litle with age, was cleane taken from them. Howbeit Athanis the Historiographer writeth, that during the warres he had against Mamercus and Hippon, as he was in his campe at Mylles, there came a white spott in his eyes, that dimmed his sight somwhat: so that every man perceived that he should lose his sight altogether. Notwithstanding that, he did not raise his seige, but continued his enterprise, untill he tooke both the tyrans at last: and so soone as he returned to Syracusa againe, he did put him self out of his office of general, praying the citizens to accept that he had already done, the rather bicause things were brought to so good passe, as they them selves could desire. Now, that he paciently tooke this misfortune to be blind altogether, peradventure men may somewhat marvel at it: but this much more is to be wondred at, that the Syracusans after he was

Timoleon in his age lost his sight.

The great honor the Syracusans did Timoleon being blind.

blind, did so much honor him, and acknowledge the good he had done them, that they went them selves to visite him oft, and brought straungers (that were travellers) to his house in the city, and also in the contry, to make them see their benefactor, rejoycing and thinking them selves happy, that he had chosen to end his life with them, and that for this cause he had despised the glorious retorne that was prepared for him in Greece, for the great and happy victories he had wonne in Sicile. But amongest many other thinges the Syracusans did, and ordeyned to honor him with, this of all other me thinketh was the chiefest: that they made a perpetuall lawe, so oft as they should have warres agaynst forreyne people, and not agaynst their owne contry men, that they should ever choose a Corinthian for their generall. It was a goodly thing also to see how they did honor him in the assemblies of their councell. For if any trifling matter fell in question among them, they dispatched it of them selves: but if it were a thing that required great counsaill and advise, they caused Timoleon to be sent for. So he was brought through the market place in his litter, into the Theater, where all the assembly of the people was, and caryed in even so in his litter as he sate: and then the people dyd all salute him with one voyce, and he them in lyke case. And after he had pawsed a while to heare the praises and blessinges the whole assembly gave him, they dyd propounde the matter doubtfull to him, and he delivered his opinion upon the same: which being passed by the voyces of the people, his servauntes caryed him backe againe in his litter through the Theater, and the citizens dyd wayte on him a litle way with cryes of joye, and clapping of handes, and that done, they dyd repayre to dispatche common causes by them selves, as they dyd before. So his old age being thus entertayned with suche honour, and with the love and good wyll of every man, as of a common father to them al: in the ende a sicknesse tooke him by the backe, whereof he dyed. So the Syracusans had a certen tyme appoynted them to prepare for his funeralles, and their neighbours also therabouts to come unto it. By reason wherof his funeral was so much more honorably performed in all thinges, and

A lawe made to honor Timoleon.

The death of Timoleon.

Timoleons funeralles.

specially for that the people apoynted the noblest younge gentelmen of the citie to carrie his coffyn upon their shoulders, rychely furnished and set forth, whereon his body laye, and so dyd convey him through the place, where the Palyce and Castell of the tyranne Dionysius had been, which then was rased to the grounde. There accompanied his body also, many thowsandes of people, all crowned with garlandes of flowers and apparreled in their best apparell: so as it seemed it had been the procession of some solemne feast, and all their woordes were praisinges and blessinges of the dead, with teares ronnyng downe their cheekes, which was a good testimonie they dyd not this as men that were glad to be discharged of the honor they dyd him, neither for that it was so ordayned: but for the just sorowe and griefe they tooke for his death, and for very hartie good love they dyd beare him. And lastly, the coffin being put uppon the stacke of wod where it should be burnt, Demetrius one of the heralds that had the lowdest voyce, proclaymed the decree that was ordeined by the people, the effect whereof was this: The people of Syracusa hath ordained, that this present body of Timoleon Corinthian, the sonne of Timodemus, should be buried at the charges of the common weale, unto the summe of two hundred Minas, and hath honored his memorie with playes and games of musicke, with ronning of horses, and with other exercises of the bodie, whiche shalbe celebrated yeerely on the day of his death for evermore: and this, bicause he dyd drive the tyrannes out of Sicile, for that he overcame the barbarous people, and bicause he replenished many great cities with inhabitantes againe, which the warres had left desolate and unhabited: and lastly, for that he had restored the Sicilians againe to their libertie, and to live after their owne lawes. And afterwards, his tombe was built in the market place, about the which a certen time after, they builded certen cloysters and gallaries to exercise the youth in, with exercise of their bodyes, and the places so walled in, was called Timoleontium: and so long as they dyd observe the lawes, and civill policie he stablished amongest them, they lived long tyme in great continuall prosperitie.

An honorable decree of the Syracusans for the memorie of Timoleon.

Timoleons tombe built in the market place.

THE COMPARISON OF PAULUS ÆMYLIUS WITH TIMOLEON

YTHE these two men were suche as the Historiographers have described them to be: it is certayne, that comparing the one with the other, we shall fynde no great oddes nor difference betweene them. For fyrst of all, the warres they made, have been agaynst great and famous enemies: the one against the Macedonians, and the other agaynst the Carthaginians, and both their victories very notable. For the one of them conquered the realme of Macedon, whiche he tooke from the seventh kyng that raigned by succession from the father to the sonne, since the tyme of the great Antigonus: and the other drave al the tyrannes out of Sicile, and restored the whole Ile and Cities therin, unto their former libertie. Unles some wil alledge perhappes that there was this difference betweene them, that Æmylius fought agaynst kyng Perseus, when he had all his power whole and entier, and had fought with the Romans many tymes before, and had the better of them in all conflictes: where Timoleon set uppon Dionysius, when he was in greatest dispayre, and in maner utterly cast away. On the contrarie syde, it may be objected for Timoleon, that he overcame manie tyrannes, and a myghtie great armie of the Carthaginians, with a verie small number of men, and yet men of all sortes: not as Æmylius with a great armie of well trayned and expert souldiers in warres, but with men gathered togeather at adventure of all sortes, being mercenarie hierlings, and fighting men for paie, lose people, and men unruly in warres, that woulde doo but what they listed. For where the goodly deeds are like, and the meanes unequall: there we must confesse that the praise is due unto the generall. Bothe the one and the other kept their handes cleane from corruption,

The comparison of Timoleon and Paulus Æmylius for the warres.

PAULUS ÆMILIUS AND TIMOLEON

in the charge which they tooke upon them. But it seemeth that Æmylius came so facioned and prepared, by the good civill lawe, and moral disciplyne of his countrie: and that Timoleon came rawly thither, and afterwards facioned him selfe to be that he was. And this is to be proved: for that al the Romains in that time were so civilly brought up, and exceeded al other in straight keeping the lawes of their countrie. Where to the contrarie, there was not one of the captaines of the Greecians that came then, or were sent into Sicile, but fell straight to corruption, when he had put his foote in Sicile, Dion onely excepted: and yet they had a certaine suspicion of him, that he aspired to the kingdome, and imagined in his head to stablishe a certaine Empire at Siracusa, like unto that of Lacedæmon. Timæus the Historiographer writeth, that the Siracusans sent Gilippus with shame backe againe into his countrie, for his unsaciable greedy covetousnes, and for his great theftes, and bribes taken in his charge. Divers other have also written the great treasons and falsehoddes Pharax Spartan, and Calippus Athenian did commit, both of them seeking to make them selves lordes of Siracusa: and yet what men were they, and what meanes had they to have suche a foolishe vaine hope and fancie in their heades? Considering that the one dyd folowe and serve Dionysius, after that he was driven out of Siracusa: and the other also was but a private captaine of a bande of footemen, of those that came in with Dion. Timoleon in contrary maner was sent, to be generall of the Siracusans, upon their great instance and sute. And he having no neede to seeke or hunte after it, but onely to keepe the power and authoritie they dyd willingly put into his handes: so soone as he had destroyed and overthrowen all suche as woulde unjustly usurpe the government, he dyd immediately of his owne good wyll, franckly resigne up his office and charge. And sure, so is this a notable thyng to be commended, and estemed in Paulus Æmylius: who having conquered so great and riche a realme, he never increased his goodes the value of one farthing, nether dyd see nor handle any mony at all, although he was very liberall, and gave largely unto others. I meane not in speak-

The wonderful continencie of Æmylius from bribes.

ing this to upbrayde or detect Timoleon, for that he accepted a fayre house the Siracusans gave him in the citie, and a goodly mannor also in the countrie: for in such cases there is no dishonesty in receiving, but so is it greater honesty to refuse, then to take. But that vertue is most rare and singuler, where we see they will receive nor take nothing, though they have justly deserved it. And if it be so, that the body is stronger and better compounded, which best abideth chaunge of parching heate, and nipping cold: and that the mynde is much more stronger and stable, that swelleth not up with pride of prosperitie, nor drowpeth for sorowe in adversitie. Then it appeareth, that Æmylius vertue was so much more perfect, in that he shewed him selfe of no lesse grave and constant a mynde, in the pacience he endured for his losse and sorowe happened unto him: (losyng at one tyme in manner, both his children) then he had done before, in al his triumphe and greatest felicitie. Where Timoleon to the contrarye, having done a worthie act against his brother, could with no reasone suppresse the griefe and sorowe he felt: but overcome with bitter griefe and repentaunce, continued the space of twentie yeeres togeather, and never durst once only shewe his face againe in the market place, nor deale any more in matters of the common weale. Truely, for a man to beware to doo evil, and to shonne from evil, it is a verie good and comely thyng: so also to be sorie, and a fearde of everye reproche, and ill opinion of the worlde, it sheweth a simplenesse of nature, and a good and well disposed minde, but no manly corage.

Not to take giftes, commended for a singuler vertue.

Æmylius Constancie far exceeded Timoleons.

THE ENDE OF TIMOLEONS LIFE

THE LIFE OF PELOPIDAS

> To be to bold and venturous is not good.

CATO the elder, aunswered certaine on a time, that marvelously commended a bolde, a venturous, and desperate man for the warres: that there was great oddes, to esteeme manhodde so muche, and lyfe so litle. And surely it was wisely spoken of him. The report goeth, that king Antigonus gave paye to a souldier among other, that was very hardie and venturous, but he had a noughtie sickly bodye. The king asked him one day, what he ayled to be so pale, and evill cullered? The souldier told him, he had a secret disease upon him, that he might not tell him with reverence. The king hearing him say so, commaunded his Phisitions and Surgeons to looke to him, and if he were curable, that they should heale him with all possible speede: and so they dyd. After the souldier had his health againe, he would venter no more so desperately in the warres, as he dyd before. Insomuch, king Antigonus selfe perceiving his slacknes, and drawing backe, rebuked him, and said unto him: that he wondred to see so great a chaunge and alteration in him. The souldier never shrinking at the matter, told him the troth plainely. Your selfe, and it please your majestie, is cause of my cowardlynes now, by healing my disease, that made my life lothsome to me.

> The aunswere of a souldier to king Antigonus.

Much like were a Sibaritans wordes, towching the life and manner of the Lacedæmonians, that it was no marvaill they had such a desire to die in the warres, seeing they did it to ridde them selves of their troubles, and most miserable and straight life. But we must not wonder though the Sybaritans, being womanish men, and altogeather geven to pleasure, did so thinke: that those men hated their lives, who feared not death, for the desire they had to doo good, and goodwill they had to doo their duetie. Which was contrarie in the Lacedæmonians. For they were of opinion, that to live

> Divers opinions of life and death.

and die willingly, was a vertue: as these funerall verses doo witnesse:

> The dead which here doe rest, did not in life esteeme,
> that life or death were (of them selves) or good or bad to deme.
> But even as life did end, or death was brought to passe,
> so life or death, was good or bad, this their opinion was.

And in deede to flye death, is no shame, so it proceede not of a cowardly hart: nether to desire death is commendable, if it be with contempt and hate of life. This is the reason why Homer saith, the valliantest men are ever best armed, when they come to battaile. The lawe makers among the Greecians, doo ever punishe him that castes away his target, but never him that casteth away his sworde or lawnce. For every man must first thinke to defende him selfe, before he seeke to hurt his enimie, and specially such as have the whole state of a realme in their handes, and be generalles of the feeld. For if the comparison be true, that Iphicrates the Athenian captaine made, that in an armie of men, the light horsemen resemble the handes, the men of armes the feete, the battaill of footemen the stomake and brest, the captaine, the head of a mans body: it seemeth then, that the venturous captaine putting him selfe in daunger with out cause, is not onely careles of his owne life, but also of all theirs whose lives depende upon his saftie. As contrarily, he being carefull of his owne person, cannot but be carefull of his souldiers that serve under him. Therefore Callicratidas a Lacedæmonian captaine, and a woorthie man otherwise, did unwisely aunswere a soothsaier that bad him take hede to him selfe: for the signes and tokens of the sacrifices did threaten his death. Sparta, said he, standeth not upon one man alone. It is true, that to fight by sea or by land man for man, Callicratidas was but one man of him selfe: but as captaine or lieuetenaunt generall, he had the whole power and force of the armie in his person. For he was not a man alone, when so manie mens lives were lost with his. Now olde Antigonus was of a contrary minde. For he being redie to geve battell by sea, about the Ile of Andros, made a better aunswer to one that said unto him: his enemies had moe shippes then

Why the Greecians do punish him that casteth away his target.

Iphicrates comparison of an armie of men.

A lieuetenant of an armie must be careful to save him selfe.

PELOPIDAS

him selfe. For how many shippes doest thou recken then my selfe? said he. Therein he did wisely to make great accompt of the worthines of a generall, specially when it is joyned with hardines, and experience. For the chiefest poynte of service, is to save him, that saveth all other. For when Chares on a time shewed the Athenians openly, the sundrie woundes and cuttes he had received apon his body, and his target also thrust through with many piks: Timotheus straight said unto him, Chares, I am not of thy minde. For when I did besege the citie of Samos, I was ashamed to see a darte throwne from the walles, light hard by me, for that I shewed my selfe a rashe young man, and more venturous then became a generall of so great an armie. For when it standeth much apon the whole armie, and that it is necessarie the generall thereof doo put him selfe in daunger: then he should put him selfe forwarde, and occupie both handes and body without respect, not regarding their wordes that say, a good wise captaine shoulde die for age, or at the least old. But where there is smal honor to be woone by very good successe, and contrariewise muche losse and distruction by great misfortune: no man of wisedome or judgement would wish a generall, to fight as a private souldier, to hazard the losse of a generall. I thought good therefore to make this preface before the lives of Pelopidas, and of Marcellus, both which were woorthie men, and died otherwise then they shoulde. For they both were valliant souldiers in the fielde, and did both of them honor their contrie with famous victories, and specially against great and dreadfull enemies. For the one was the first (as they saie) that overthrewe Hanniball, who was never overcome by any before. And the other also overcame the Lacedæmonians in battell, that ruled al Greece at that time both by sea and by land. Yet they both carelesly lost their lives, by venturing to boldely: when their contrie stoode in greatest neede of suche men and captaines, as they were. This is the cause, why we folowing the resemblaunce that was betweene them, have compared their lives together. Pelopidas, the sonne of Hippoclus, came of one of the noblest houses of the citie of Thebes, as Epaminondas did. He being brought up in great wealth, his father left him heire of all

Timotheus saying.

Pelopidas and Marcellus lost both their lives, by to much venturing.

Pelopidas stock and liberalitie.

his landes and goodes, being but a young man. So he straight shewed him selfe willing to doo good with his monie, to those that needed helpe, and were worthie: to let the worlde see, that his monie was not his maister. For as Aristotle saith, of these rich men, the most part of them do not use their goods, for extreame covetousnes: other againe doo abuse them, as being geven to overmuche pleasures. So riche men became slaves all their life time, some to pleasure, other to profit. Now, al Pelopidas other frendes woulde be beholding to him, and take very thanckfully his curtesie and liberalitie towardes them. But Epaminondas could never be brought to any thing at his handes. Howbeit Pelopidas selfe folowed Epaminondas maner: for he tooke a pride and pleasure to goe simply appareled, to fare meanely, to labor willingly, and to make warres openly as he did. He was even such another, as Euripides the Poet described Capaneus to be: when he said of him:

Aristotles saying of rich men.

> He rich and welthie was, yet was he therewithall,
> no wight that purchast worldly hate, nor insolent at all.

For he would have been ashamed, that the poorest man of the cittie of Thebes, shoulde have worne meaner apparell apon his backe, then him selfe. As for Epaminondas, his povertie was not daintie to him, bicause his parentes were ever poore: and yet for all that he passed it over more easely, by studie of Philosophie, which he gave him selfe unto, and for that from his youth he liked to leade a spare life without excesse. Where Pelopidas matched in a noble house, and maryed highly, and had two children by his wife: neverthelesse he had no minde to keepe or increase his goodes the more for that, but gave him selfe altogeather to serve the common weale as long as he lived. By reason whereof his wealth decaied, and his best frendes grewe angrie with him, telling him how he did not well to make no more reckoning of a thing that was so necessarie, as to have goodes. And he aunswered them: In dede they are necessarie, I doo confesse it, but yet for suche a one, as this poore, lame, and blynd man that standeth by. They both were a like borne to all vertue, saving that Pelopidas tooke most pleasure in exercise

Pelopidas saying for the necessitie of monie.

of his body and strength, and Epaminondas in the exercise of his wit and learning. So as the pastyme eche of them tooke when they were at leasure, was, that the one delighted to wrastle, and to hunte, and liked any kinde of exercise of his body: and the other to heare, to studie, and alwaies to learne some thing of Philosophie. But among all the excellent giftes and good partes in either of them, and that most wanne them honor and estimation in the world, they were onely commended, and singulerly noted of wise men, for the perfect love and frendshippe that was ever invyolably kept betwene them, until their deathes: having been joyned togeather in so many battels, warres, charges of armies, and otherwise in matters of state and government. For if a man will consider, and looke into the doinges of Aristides, Themistocles, and Cimon, of Pericles, Nicias, and Alcibiades, how full of dissentions, envies, and suspicions they were one against another in governing the common weale: and againe will consider the love, honour, and kindnesse, that continued alwaies betwext Pelopidas and Epaminondas: no doubt they will saie these two are more worthie to be called brethren in warre, (as they saie) and companions in government, then any of them we have named before, whose care and studie was alwaies rather to overcome one another, then to overcome their enemies, and the onely cause thereof was their vertue. For their actes shewed they did not seeke glorie, nor riches for them selves (the covetousnes whereof doth allwaies breede quarrelles and envy) but both of them from the begining fell one in love with an other, with a great kindenes and estimation of them selves, to see their contrie florishe, and growe to great honor through their service, and in their time: and so they reckoned all the good exploytes both of the one and the other, that tended to that ende, as their owne. The most part of writers thinke, this great and earnest love thone did beare to an other, did growe first betwene them, in a jorney they made togeather unto Mantinia, to ayde the Lacedæmonians, that were at that time confederates of the Thebans. For they being both set in battell raye, one hard by another among the footmen, against the Arcadians that stoode before them: it fortuned that the point of the

The perfit frendshippe betwixt Pelopidas and Epaminondas.

The true cause of frendshippe.

battell of the Lacedæmonians in the which they were, gave backe, and many of them ranne away. But they determyning to die rather then to flye, stoode close together, and fought with the enemies that came apon them: untyll such time as Pelopidas being hurt in seven places before, fell downe at the last upon a heape of dead bodies, aswell of their owne souldiers, as of their enemies, even one apon an other. Then Epaminondas thinking he had ben slaine, stept notwithstanding before him to defend his body and armor, and he alone fought against many, being willing to die, rather then to forsake Pelopidas lying amongest the dead bodies: untyl him selfe being thrust into the brest with a pyke, and sore cut on his arme with a swoorde, was even ready to geve over, when Agesipolis (king of the Lacedæmonians,) came with the other poynt of the battell in happie howre, who saved both their lives past all hope. Now after this battell, the Lacedæmonians both in wordes and deedes did curteously intreate the Thebans, as their frendes, and cònfederates. Notwithstanding, in troth they beganne to feare the power and great corage of that cittie, and specially the faction and associates Ismenias and Androclidas had set up, whereof Pelopidas also was a companion: bicause they thought it was populer, and inclined muche to desire libertie. Whereupon Archias, Leontidas, and Philip, al three great welthie men of the cittie of Thebes, and misliking to be equall with other cittizens: did perswade Phœbidas, a captaine of the Lacedæmonians, that going and comming through the contrie of Bœotia with an armie, he would one day assaie to take the castell of Thebes called Cadmea, and driving those out of the cittie that would resist him, he would put the government of the state into the hands of a fewe of the noblest persones, who would be at the devotion of the Lacedæmonians, and obey them in all thinges. Phœbidas brought it to passe, and did worcke his feate before the Thebans mistrusted any thing, apon a holy day called Thesmophoria. After he had wonne the castell, he apprehended Ismenias, and sent him to Lacedæmon, where shortly after they put him to death. Pelopidas, Pherenicus, and Androclidas, with many other, saved them selves by flying, and were banished Thebes by

Agesipolis, king of the Lacedæmonians.

Cadmea, the castel of Thebes, taken by Phœbidas captaine of the Lacedæmonians.

Ismenias death.

Pelopidas, Pherenicus and Androclidas, banished from Thebes.

sounde of Trompet. Epaminondas taried stil in Thebes, and no man tutched him, for they made small accompt of him, bicause he was altogether geven to his booke: and though his goodwill had served him to have done some feate, his povertie made him unable to doo any thing. The Lacedæmonians understanding of the taking of the castel, did straight put Phœbidas out of his charge, and set a fine of a hundred thowsand Drachmes apon his head: but yet they kept still the castell of Cadmea in their handes with a great garrison. All the other citties and people of Greece did wonder much at it, that they should allowe the fact, and punishe notwithstanding the doer. So the Thebans having lost their auncient libertie, and being made subject by both these, Archias, and Leontidas, so as all hope was taken from them ever to winde out of this tyrannie, or at any time to overthrowe it, seing it was maintained and defended by the Lacedæmonians, and that they coulde not possibly take from them all the seigniorie and dominion they had throughout Greece, aswell by sea as by lande: Leontidas and his followers notwithstanding, when they understoode that they who were banished from Thebes, were very wel received and entertained of the people at Athens, and much made of also of the nobilitie, they sought secretly by treason to have them kylled. To do this feate, they sent certaine men unknowen unto Athens, who by treason slue Androclidas, howbeit they missed the kylling of the other. Furthermore, the Lacedæmonians wrote to the Athenians, that they should not receive suche as were banished from Thebes, nor that they shoulde favor them, but drive them out of their cittie, as those which by their allyes were justly proclaimed common enemies. The Athenians notwithstanding, being men alwaies civilly geven, and inclined in nature to humanitie, as being borne and bred up withall, and very desyrous besides to requite the Thebans curtesy, who had bene the chiefest meanes and doers in restoring againe the populer state and government at Athens: they would by no meanes offer the Thebans any such injurie, seing they had stablished a lawe and decree, that if any Athenian passing to and fro through the contrie of Bœotia, did beare armor against the thirtie

Archias and Leontidas, governers of Thebes, under the Lacedæmonians.

Androclidas slayne.

The thanckfulnes of the Athenians unto the Thebans.

tyrannes, that were governors and oppressors of the libertie of Athens, there should no Bœotian seeme to see, or knowe any thing therof. In the meane time Pelopidas, though he were of the younger sort, did procure still every one that was banished, to seeke the libertie of his contrie, and openly made an oration to them all, declaring, that it were not onely a cowardly part, but also a wicked offence to the goddes, if they would suffer their contrie to remaine so in continuall bondage, and straungers to inhabite it with a garrison, to make them subject to the yoke: and they in the meane time to be contented to save them selves, to live delicately and idely at Athens, to studie to doe what shal please the Athenians to commaund them, and to be affraide of the orators, and those which through eloquence can perswade the common people to doo what they lust. Therefore he perswaded them that they should hazard all, being a matter of so great weight, and take example of Thrasybulus noble corage and hardynes: who departing from Thebes, did drive out the tyrannes that did oppresse Athens: and even so, we departing from Athens, should seeke to deliver Thebes also from bondage. When he had by these perswasions drawen them to his opinion, they secretely sent unto their frendes that remayned still in Thebes, to let them understand their minde and determination: who all lyked very well of their purpose. Insomuche, Charon that was the chiefest man among them, promised to lende them his house to assemble in. Philidas also founde meanes to be secretarie to Philip and Archias, who were governers and captaines of the city at that time for the Lacedæmonians. Epaminondas on thother side making no shewe of any thing, had of longe time practised to styrre up the corage of the younge men of Thebes. For when they were at any games or exercises of bodye, he woulde ever procure them to wrastle with the Lacedæmonians. And after he sawe them rejoyce when they had cast them, and that they were the stronger: he would chide them, and tell them they might be ashamed, for lacke of corage, to suffer the Lacedæmonians to hold their noses to the gryndstone, that were nothing like to them in strength. Now, the confederates appointed a day certen, to breake the

Pelopidas counsel for the libertie of the Thebans.

Conspiracie against the Lacedæmonians, for the libertie of Thebes.

ise of their pretended enterprise, and agreed that Pherenicus, with other that were banished, shoulde tarie at the village of Thriasium, and that they should sende the valliauntest and lustest young men before, to geve the venter to enter the cittie: adding this therewithall, that if the enemies fortuned to surprise them, all the other of the conspiracie joyntly togeather, should be ready to geve order, that their fathers, mothers, and children, should lacke nothing necessarie for them. Pelopidas was the first man offered him selfe to undertake the enterprise: and after him Melon, Damoclidas, and Theopompus, all three, men of the greatest houses of Thebes, who loved marvelously togeather, and for no respect would ever offend one another, although from the beginning there was ever emulation among them for honor and glory, by striving who should exceede other in vertue and valliantnes. Now they were twelve of them, who taking leave of the rest, sent a foote post before to Charon, to advertise him of their comming: and they them selves went on their jorney casting litle short clokes apon them, and taking houndes with them, and hunters staves in their handes, bicause their enterprise should not be mistrusted by those that met them on the way, and that they should thinke them hunters up and downe the feildes for their pleasure. So, when their messenger they sent came to the cittie, and had tolde Charon that they were comming: he never shronke from his worde, though the daunger towarde was great, but like a stowt and honest man did abide by his promise he made, and tolde him they should be most hartely welcom to his house. But another man called Hipposthenidas, very honest otherwise, and one that loved his contry and the preservation thereof, and a good frend of those also that were banished: fainting straight apon the sodaine report of these newes, and his minde was troubled, and his hart fayled him so, as his nose fell a bleeding, to thinke apon the greatnes of the instant daunger he was like to fal into, having never cast before with him selfe, how by this enterprise they shoulde put all the empire of the Lacedæmonians in hazard of utter destruction, and laye a plat besides to overthrowe all their owne common weale and state, by laying al their hope apon

Charon kept promise, with daunger of life.

a fewe banished men, hardly able to wade through with their enterprise. Whereupon, so sone as he was come home, he secretly dispatched a messenger, one of his familliar frends, unto Melon and Pelopidas, to will them they should deferre their enterprise for better oportunitie, and so to returne backe again to Athens. Chlidon was the man he sent of this message, who presently went home to his house: and taking his horse out of the stable, bad his wife fetche him the brydell quickly. The brydell not being readily to be founde, she told him she had lent it out to one of their neighbours. Then they fell a chiding together about it, and at length brake out to fowle wordes, and lastely his wife fell a cursing of him, and prayed the goddes he might have ill lucke in his jorney, and those that sent him. Chlidon having spent the most part of the day, chiding and brawling with his wife about the brydell, and furthermore misliking the tokens of his wives cursing and banning of him: he determined not to goe a foote out of the dores of that arrant, and so went about some other busines. Thus had this noble enterprise in manner bene altogeather dashed, before it was fully begonne. Nowe those that were in Pelopidas companie, chaunged apparell with the contrie men, bicause they woulde not be knowen, and did devide them selves, for that they would not come into the cittie all together, but at divers gates, beinge day light. At that time it was a mervelous winde and great snowe, and the weather was so boysterous, that every man got him within dores: which fell out happily for the conspirators, that they were not knowen when they came into the cittie. So their frendes and confederates within the citie receaved them as they came, and brought them to Charons house: where were assembled together, with those that were banished, eight and forty persones only. Now for the tyrans, thus stoode the matter with them. Philidas their secretary was of the conspiracy, as we have told you before, and he knewe all the practise. Wherefore he had longe before solemnely bidden Archias and his companie, to supper to his house that verie night, to be mery together, and had promised to entertaine them with women to welcome them with all: of purpose,

Pelopidas commeth into Thebes disgised in cloynes apparel.

Philidas secretary to the tyrans.

 that when they had in their full cuppes, and were in the middest of all their pleasure, the conspirators might then use them as they woulde. So they beinge sette at table, before they were sped of their cuppes, one came to them, and told them truely of the treason (not particularities, neither as a thinge certaine, but of a rumor onely that ranne abroade in the towne) howe the banished men were hidden in Charons house. Philidas woulde have passed the matter over. Howbeit Archias would nedes sende one of his garde straight for Charon, to commaunde him to come to him presently. It was within night, and Pelopidas and his company prepared themselves to worke their feate, being armed every man, and their swords in their hands, when apon a sodaine they heard one knocke at the gate. And one of the house runninge straight to the gate, came backe againe afearde to tell them that it was one of Archias garde that came for Charon, to come immediatly to the governours. Then were they in doubt that their practise was discovered, and that they were all cast away, before they coulde make any proofe of their valliantnes: notwithstanding, they were all of opinion, that Charon should obey the message, and that he should present himselfe before the governors, to take away all suspition from them. Charon of him selfe was a stout man, very constant, and resolute in daunger for his owne persone: yet it greved him much at that time, for feare the confederates shoulde suspect him he hadde bewrayed them, if so many honest citizens whom he had lent his house unto, should unfortunately miscarie. Therefore before he went out of his house, he went into his wives chamber to fetch his sonne, that was a goodly boy, but strong as any boy of his age could be: so he brought him to Pelopidas, and prayed him, if he understoode that he had betrayed them any way, or otherwise had sought their hurt, they shoulde then use his sonne as an enemie without any compassion towardes him. When the confederates saw the good zeale and true noble mind of Charon, they all fell a weping, and were angrie with him, that he should thinke any of them so faint harted, or timerous, for any daunger coulde come to them, that they shoulde suspect or accuse

Pelopidas daunger.

him for any thinge: and therewith all they prayed him, not to leave the boye with them, but rather to convey him into some place out of the tyrans daunger, where he might be brought up, that one day he might be revenged of the wrong and injurie they had done to them, and to their contrie. Charon aunswered them, he woulde not take him away, and that he saw no life nor health more happy for him, then to dye with his father without infamy, and with so many honest men his frends. So after he had besought the goddes to prosper them, and hadde encouraged and embraced everie one of the confederators one after an other: He went to the governors, and studied by the way so to frame his wordes and countenance, as though he shoulde seeme to thinke of any thinge else, then of that he purposed to do. When he came to Philidas dore that made the feast, Archias and Philidas him selfe came unto him, and asked him: Charon, what are they (sayd they) that are come into the city, and hidden in some house, with certaine citizens that do accompany them? Charon was somewhat abashed at the first, and asked them againe: What men be they? who are they that hides them in the citie? But when he perceived that Archias coulde tell nothinge of certaintie, then he thought straight that some man hadde informed them that was not privie to the practise, but hadde hearde some thinge of it. Thereupon he willed them to take heede it was no false alarome, to make them afrayed: Neverthelesse (sayd he) I will enquire further of it: for at all adventure it is good to be circumspect in such a case to be sure. Philidas aunswered him, he said truely: and so he brought Archias backe againe into the hall, where he made him drinke deeper than before, still entertaining the company with hope of the womens comming. Charon returning home againe, found all the confederats ready to attempt their enterprise, not as men that reckened of their lives, nor that had any hope to prevaile: but as those that were determined to dye valliantly, and to sell their lives dearly. Now he truely tolde unto Pelopidas onely, what was said unto him and the rest: he told that Archias had sent for him to speake with him, of other matters. The storme of the former daunger was scant

PELOPIDAS

blowen over, but fortune sent them an other. For immediatly uppon talke had with Charon at the first, came a messenger from Athens, that brought a letter to the same Archias, written by the Bishop of Athens at that time, called Archias also as him selfe, and was his old hoste and frende: wherein he wrote not of simple conjecture, nor surmised suspition, but the plaine conspiracy in every degree, as afterwards it fell out. So the messenger was brought to Archias that was dronke, and deliveringe him the letter, he said unto him: Sir, he that sendeth you this letter, straightly charged me to tel you, that you should presently read the contents thereof, because it is a matter of great importance. Archias laughing sayd unto him: Waighty matters to morrow. So he tooke the letter and put it up, and then fell againe to his tale he had begonne with Philidas. But ever after, the Greecians made this a common proverbe among them: Waighty matters to morrow. Now when the conspirators spied their time to go about their businesse, they devided them selves in two companies. Pelopidas and Damoclidas went with one company, to sette upon Leontidas and Hypates, because they dwelt nere together: Charon and Melon with the rest, went against Archias and Philip, beinge disguised in womens apparell they had put upon their privy cotes, and wearing garlands of pyne apple and fyrre trees on their heads, that covered all their faces. So when they came to shew them selves at the hall dore where the bancket was made, they that were in the hall at the first sight, thinking they had beene the women they looked for, beganne to showte, and made great noyse and joye. But when the conspirators cast their eyes rounde about the hall to knowe those which were at the table, they drew out their swordes, and set uppon Archias and Philip overthwart the table: then they shewed them selves what they were. Then Philidas bad his guestes he hadde bidden to the bancket with them, that they shoulde not stirre, for they shoulde have no hurt: so some of them sate still. But the greatest nomber of them woulde needes from the borde, to defende their governours. Howebeit bicause they were so dronke that they knewe not what they

Archias Bishop of Athens, bewraieth the treason to Archias in a letter.

Waighty matters to morrow, Prov.

Pelopidas killeth the tyrans.

did, they were soone slaine with them. Now Pelopidas enterprise was not so easie. For they went against Leontidas, that was a sober discrete man, and withall, hardy of his handes: and they found he was gone to bed, his dores were shut up, and they knocked long before any man came to the dore. At the length, one of his men that hearde them rappe so hard, with much a do came to open the dore: but he had no sooner thrust backe the bolt of the dore, and beganne to open it, but they pushed it from them with such a force apon him altogether, that they layed him on the grounde, and went straight to his maisters chamber. Leontidas hearinge the noyse of them that ranne uppe to him in such hast, presently mistrusted the matter: and leaping out of his bed, tooke his sworde in his hande, but did forget to put out the lampes that burned in his chamber all night, for if they hadde beene out, they might easily have hurt one an other in the darke. But the lampes givinge cleare light in the chamber, he went to the chamber dore, and gave Cephisodorus, the first man that pressed to enter apon him, such a blowe with his sword, that he dropped downe dead at his feete. Havinge slaine the first man, he dealt with the seconde that came after him, and that was Pelopidas. The fight went hard betwene them two, bothe for that the chamber dore was verie straight, as also for that Cephisodorus body lying on the ground, did choke the comming in at the chamber. Notwithstandinge, Pelopidas overcame him in the ende, and slue him: and went from thence with his companie, straight to Hypates house, where they got in, as they did into Leontidas house before. But Hypates knewe presently what it was, and thought to save him selfe in his neighbours houses. Howbeit the conspirators followed him so hardė, that they cutte him of before he coulde recover their houses. Then they gathered together, and joyned with Melons company, and sent immediatly with all possible speede to Athens, to the banished Thebans there, and cried through the city, Liberty, liberty, arming those citizens that came to them, with the armor and spoyles of their enemies, that were hanged up in common vawtes, and armorers shops about Charons house, which they brake

The liberty of the Thebans restored.

 open, or caused to be opened by force. On the other side, Epaminondas, and Gorgidas, came to joyne with them, with a company of young men and honest olde men well appointed, whom they had gathered together. Hereupon, the whole citie was straight in an uprore and tumult, and every house was full of lights, one running to an other to know what the matter was. Nevertheles the people did not yet assemble together, but every one being amazed, musing at this stur, not understanding the troth, staied untill day came on, that they might call a counsell. But truely herein, me thinkes the Captaines of the garrison of the Lacedæmonians were greatly in fault, that they did not sturre betimes, and set upon them incontinently: consideringe they were xv. hundred souldiers, besides a great number of citizens that would have come, one after an other to take their partes. But the great noyse they heard, made them afeard, and to see lights in every mans house, and the people running up and down the streets in great multitudes to and fro: wherupon they stirred not, but only kept them within the castel of Cadmea. The next morninge by breake of day, came the other banished Thebans from Athens very wel armed, and al the people of Thebes drew together in counsail. Thither did Epaminondas and Gorgidas bring Pelopidas, and his consorts, and presented them before the people, compassed about with priests and the professed of the city, offering them crownes to put upon their heads, and they praied the assembly of the citizens, that they would help their gods, and their contrie. Al the people that were present, when they saw them, rose up, and stoode on their feete, and with great showtes and clapping of hands received them, as their saviours, that had delivered their contry from bondage, and restored them again to liberty: and therupon, before them al, even in the market place, by the whole voice and consent of the people, they chose Pelopidas, Melon, and Charon, governors and captaines of all Bœotia. Pelopidas then immediatly made them besiege the castell of Cadmea about, with trenches, and force of wod, doing al he could possible to winne it, and to expulse the Lacedæmonians, before any supply and aide came to them from Sparta. So he did, and prevented it so sodainly,

Pelopidas receiveth the Castell of Cadmea by Composition.

that the garrison being departed out of the castel by composition, as they returned towards Lacedæmonia, they found Cleombrotus king of Sparta in the contry of Megara, comming towards them with a great army to help them. Afterward, of the three captaines which had charge of their garrison that lay at Thebes, the Spartans condemned two of them to death: Hermippidas, and Arcissus, were presently executed: and the third captaine, Dysaoridas, they set so greevous a fyne on his head, that he went out of Peloponesus. This enterprise being attempted, and executed with the like valiantnes, and the same daunger and trouble, that Thrasybulus practise was, when he delivered Athens from the slavery of the thirty governors and tyrans, and having the like fortune, and happy ende: the Græcians termed it cosyn german to Thrasybulus act. And in deede it were a harde matter to find two other such, besides them two, that with so few men overcame their enemies, being many moe in nomber then them selves, or that with so small help did overcome those that were of so great force, or that performed their enterprise with their only valiantnes and wisedom, and were cause besides of so great blessing and benefit to their contry, as Pelopidas and Thrasybulus attempt was. But the great chaunge and alteracion of the state afterwards, did make their actes farre more noble and famous. For the warre that overthrew the majestie of Sparta, and that tooke away al the seigniorie and rule of the Lacedæmonians bothe by sea and by land, beganne the very same night, when Pelopidas him self making the twelvt person, and entring into a private house, (taking nether citie, nor castel, nor stronge hold) to tel truly by figurative speach, did breake and cut in sonder the linkes and chaynes that lincked straight together, and strengthened the Lacedæmonians whole empire and monarchie over al Greece: who until that present time were thought so strong, as no possibilitie could breake or sonder them. Now the Lacedæmonians fortuning afterwards to invade the contry of Bœotia with a mighty army: the Athenians trembling for feare of their great power, did utterly leave to protect them, and renownced the league and alliance they had made before with them. And moreover,

Pelopidas overthrewe the seigniorie of the Lacedæmonians.

Pelopidas policy to make the Athenians fall out againe with the Lacedæmonians.

they did straightly prosecute law against those, that were accused to take part with the Bœotians: wherof some of them were put to death, other were banished from Athens, and the rest condemned in great summes of money. To be short, every man sayd the Thebans were but undone, considering they had no help, and were beloved besides of none. At that present time it fel out Pelopidas and Gorgidas were generals over al Bœotia for that yere, who devising to throw a bone betwixt the Athenians and the Lacedæmonians again, to make them square, they used this policie. There was a captaine of the Lacedæmonians called Sphodrias, a valliant man, but else of smal capacity, and vainly given, having a certen fond ambition and humor, perswading him selfe he had done some notable good service in his time. This Sphodrias was left in the city of Thespies, with a great band of souldiers, to receave and favor al the Bœotians, that had a minde to revolte from the Thebans. Pelopidas of him selfe sent a marchaunt, (a very frende of his) unto Sphodrias, with a great some of money from him, and certaine perswasions withall, which prevailed more then the money, wishinge him to attempt some greater matter, and to seke to winne the haven of Pirae: a thing soone wonne, if he came to assault it on the sodaine, and the rather, for that the Athenians mistruste nothinge, neither keepe watch nor ward there. Moreover, that he might assure him selfe, nothinge coulde be better welcome to the lords of Lacedæmonia, then to make them lords of the city of Athens also. And againe, that the Thebans, being at deadly foode with the Athenians, for that they had betraied and forsaken them in their nede, would not aide nor succor them in any respect. Sphodrias giving to light eare to this vaine perswasion, tooke the souldiers he had with him, and marching away by night, entred the realme of Attica, and went on to the city of Eleusin: but when he came thither, his souldiers were afeard, and would go no further. So his purpose beinge discovered, he was forced to returne backe to Thespies, having raised such a warre to the Lacedæmonians, as fel out to be of no small importance to them, nor easie to be pacified. For after that time, the Athenians sought league and amity againe with the Thebans, and did aide them very lovingly: and moreover, putting them selves to sea, they sailed up and downe, procuring and drawing to their league all such, as were willing to rebell against the Lacedæmonians: and the Thebans besides, had many prety skirmishes with the Lacedæmonians in the meane time, in their own contry of Bœotia. It is true they came to no great battels, but yet it was such a great learning and continual training of them in marshall discipline, as the Thebans stil increased in corage and valliantnes, and waxed stronger and better souldiers: for by those skirmishes they grewe not onely expert souldiers, but waxed more skilfull in using their weapons, then before. As we read, that Antalcidas a Spartan said one day to king Agesilaus, comminge home sore hurt from Bœotia: Surely the Thebans have given you a worthy reward, for teaching them to be souldiours against their wils. But to say truly, Agesilaus was not their maister to teache them to make wars, but they were the good and wise leaders of the Thebans, who like good wod men in choosing their game, could skilfully choose both time and place to give their enemies battel, and make them retire again with safety, after they had bin fleshed, giving them a litle tast of the frutes and commodity of victory: but among them, Pelopidas was he that deserved most honor and glory. For, since the first time they gave him charge of men of warre, they never failed, but chose him continually every yeare, either Captaine of the holy bande, or governor of Bœotia so long as he lived: so that Pelopidas only did the most things in this warre. The Lacedæmonians were overthrowen in sundry jorneis, that they were distressed by the cities of Platees, and of Thespies, where Phœbidas himselfe (that had before taken the castell of Cadmea) was slaine amongst other. An other great power of theirs also was overthrowen nere to the city of Tanagra, where Panthoidas governor of the same, was also slaine. Now all these victories, though they much encoraged the hearts of the conquerors, and made them hardy: yet did they not therby altogether conquer the mindes of the vanquished. For the Lacedæmonians were not overcome in any pitched field, nor set battel, where they had their whole army together: but

The Thebans exercise in armes.

Antalcidas saying to king Agesilaus.

The victory of the Thebans against the Lacedæmonians.

Pelopidas victory of the Lacedæmonians at the battaile of Tegyra.

Melas fl.

Latona brought to bed betwene two springes called the Palme, and the Olive.

they were light rodes, and skirmishes properly laid of purpose, where somtime flying, somtime driving them againe, they bickered very oft, and put them to the worst. But the battell of Tegyra, which was but a florish and profe to the journey of Leuctres, wan Pelopidas great honor. For he had no companion to chalenge any part of his glory and victory, neither did he leave his enemies any lawful excuse, to shadow or cover their overthrow. For he spied al occasion he might possible, how to take the city of Orchomene, that tooke part with the Lacedæmonians, and had received two ensignes of footemen of theirs to kepe it. Pelopidas being advertised one day, that the garrison of Orchomene was gone abroad to make a rode into the contrey of the Locrides, hoping he shuld finde Orchomene without garrison: he marched thither with his holy band, and certaine number of horsemen. But when he drew neere the city, he had intelligence there was another garrison comming from Sparta, to supply the place of the garrison that was abroad: wherupon he returned backe againe by the city of Tegyra, for he could have passed no other way, but to have turned down by the foote of the mountaine. For al the valley that lay betwen both, was drowned with the overflowing of the river of Melas, which even from his very hed carieth ever such bredth with it, as it maketh the marishes navigable, so as it is unpassable for any shallow it hath. Not far from these marishes, standeth the temple of Apollo Tegyrian, where was an oracle in old time, but left of at this day, and had never long continuance, but only untill the time of the warres of the Medes, when Echecrates was maister and chiefe priest there. And some holde opinion, that Apollo was borne there: for they cal the next mountaine to it, Delos, at the foote wherof the marishes of the river of Melas doo end, and behinde the temple are two goodly springes, from whence commeth great abowndance of good sweete water: whereof the one of them is called to this day the Palme, and the other the Olive. And some say also, that the goddesse Latona was not brought to bed betwene two trees, but betwene these two springes. For mownt Ptoum is hard by it also, from whence the wilde bore came on a sodaine that flighted her. And the tale that is tolde of the serpent Pytho, and of the gyaunt Tityus, doo both confirme it, that Apollo was borne in the same place. I passe over manie other conjectures confirming the same, for that we doo not beleve in oure contrie that Apollo is among the nomber of those, who from mortall men have beene translated to immortall goddes, as are Hercules and Bacchus, that through the excellencie of their vertue, did put of mortalitie, and tooke immortality apon them: but we rather take him for one of those that never had beginninge nor generation, at the least if those thinges be to be credited, which so many grave and auncient writers have left in writing to us, touching so great and holy things. The Thebans returning backe from Orchomene, and the Lacedæmonians on the other side returning also from Locride, both at one time, they fortuned both armies to mete about the citty of Tegyra. Now, so sone as the Thebans had discovered the Lacedæmonians passing the straite, one of them ranne sodainely to Pelopidas, and tolde him: Sir, we are fallen into the handes of the Lacedæmonians. Nay, are not they rather fallen into ours, aunswered Pelopidas againe? with these wordes, he commaunded his horsemen that were in the rereward, to come before, and sett apon them: and him selfe in the meane time put his footemen immediately into a pretie squadron close togeather, being in all, not above three hundred men, hoping when he should come to geve charge with his battell, he should make a lane through the enemies, though they were the greater nomber. For the Lacedæmonians devided them selves in two companies, and every company, as Ephorus writeth, had five hundred men: and as Callistenes sayed, seven hundred. Polybius, and divers other authors saye, they were nyne hundred men. So, Theopompus and Gorgoleon, the Captaynes of the Lacedæmonians, lustely marched agaynst the Thebans: and it fell out so, that the first charge was geven, where the chiefetaynes or generalles were of either side, with great furie on eyther parte, so as both the generalls of the Lacedæmonians which sett uppon Pelopidas together, were slayne. They being slayne, and all that were about them, being either hurt or killed in the fielde: the rest of the

Pelopidas victorie.

 armie were so amased, that they devided in two, and made a lane on either side, for the Thebans to passe through them if they would. But when they saw Pelopidas ment not to take the passage they offred him, and that he came on still with his men to set apon those that were yet in battel raye, and slue all them that stoode before him: then they turned tayle, and tooke them to their legges. Howbeit the Thebans did not chase them farre, fearing the Orchomenians who were not farre from them, and the new garrison besides, that were come from Lacedæmon not long before. And this was the cause they were contented that they had overcomed them by force, and had passed through their armie in despite of them, and broken and overthrowen them. So when he had set up markes of triumphe, and spoyled their slayne enemies, they returned home againe, glad men for their obteyned victorie. For in all the warres the Lacedæmonians ever made, aswell with the Græcians, as with the barbarous people also, there was never chronicle mencioned at any tyme, that their enemies being so fewe, did overcome them that were so many, nor that they were overcome also by any number equall in battell. Whereuppon they grewe so coragious and terrible, that no man durst once abyde them: for their onely fame did so terrifie their enemies that came to fight agaynst them, that they thought with no equall force to be able to performe asmuche as they had done. But this battell of Tegyra was the first that made both them and the other Greecians knowe, that it was not the ryver of Eurotas alone, nor the valley that lyeth betweene the ryvers of Cnacion, and of Babyce, that breedeth the valiant and hardy fighting men: but that it is in all places else, where they learne young men to be ashamed of dishonest and vyle thinges, and to venter their lives for honest causes, fearing more dishonorable reproche, then honorable daunger. These are the people most to be feared, and are most terrible also to their enemies. And for the holy band we mencioned before, it is saide, Gorgidas was the first erector of the same. They were three hundred chosen men entertained by the state, and they alwaies kept within the castell of Cadmea, and the bande was called the

What enemies are moste terrible and to be feared.

The first institution of the holie bande.

townes bande: for at that time, and specially in that part of Greece, they called the castels and great holdes in citties, the townes. Other say it was a bande of footemen that were in love one with another. And therefore Pammenes pleasaunt wordes are noted, saying, that Nestor coulde no skyll to set an armie in battell raye, seeing he gave the Greecians counsell, in the Iliades of Homer, that they should set them in battel raye, every countrie and tribe by them selves:

That by affections force, and lynkes of kyndly love:
that one might alwaise helpe at hande, that other to behove.

For, saide he, one frende should rather be set by another that loves togeather: bicause in daunger, men commonly do litle regarde their contrie men, or suche as are of their tribe. But men that doo love one another, can never be broken nor overcome: for the passion of love that entertaineth eche others affection, for affection sake, dothe kepe them from forsaking one another. And those that are beloved, being ashamed to doo any vyle or dishonest thing before those that love them, for very love will sticke one by another to the death. And sure the reason is good, if it be true that lovers doo in deede more regard them they love, though they be absent: then other that be present. As appeareth by the example of hym, that being striken downe to the ground, his enemie lifting up his swoorde to kyll him, he praied him he woulde geve him his deathes wounde before, lest his frende that loved him, seeing a wounde on his backe, shoulde be ashamed of him. It is reported also, that Iolaus being beloved of Hercules, did helpe and accompanie him in all his labors and quarrels. Whereupon Aristotle writeth, that unto his time, such as loved hartily togeather, became sworne brethren one to another, apon Iolaus tombe. And therefore me thinkes it is likely, that this bande was first called the holy bande, by the selfe same reason that Plato calleth a lover, a divine frende by goddes appointment. It is written also, that this bande was never broken, nor overthrowen, before the battel of Chæronea: After that battel, Philip taking vewe of the slaine bodies, he stayed in

Men loving together, fight desperately against their enemies.

Hercules and Iolaus love.

Platoessaying of a lover.

 that place where the foure hundred men of that bande laye all dead on the grounde, one harde by another, and all of them slayne and thrust through with pikes on their brestes, whereat he wondred muche: and being tolde him that it was the lovers bande, he fel a weeping for pittie, saying: Wo be to them that thinke these men did, or suffered any evyll or dishonest thing. And to be short, the misfortune of Laius, that was slaine by his owne brother Oedipus, was not the first originall cause of this custome, that the Thebans beganne to be in love one with an other as the Poets write: but they were their first lawmakers, who perceiving them to be a stout and fierce nation of nature, they sought even from their youthe to make them gentell and civill, and therefore in all their actions both of sport and earnest, they continually acquainted them with playing of the flute, being highly estemed of them in those dayes. They brought in the use also to make love, in the middest of all their youthefull sportes and exercises of their bodies, to frame the young mens manners, and to bring them to a civil lyfe. And therfore they had reason that gave the goddesse Harmonia to the Thebans, for defender and patronesse of their cittie, who was begotten (as they say) betwene Mars and Venus. For that geveth us to understande, that where force and warlike corage is joyned with grace, to winne and perswade: all thinges by this union and accorde are brought, to a goodly, proffitable, and most perfect government. Now, to returne againe to the matter of this holy bande of the Thebans. Gorgidas deviding it in the former ranckes, and placing it all alongest the fronte of the battell of the footemen, it did not appeare what they were able to doo of them selves, for that he brought them not all into one body: so as thereby they might see what service the whole companie coulde doo, being togeather, considering that it was devided and mingled amongest manie other, that were a great deale of lesse value then them selves. But Pelopidas that had made good proofe of their valliauntnes before, when they fought about him of them selves, without others by them, at Tegyra: would never after devide nor seperat them one from the other, but keeping them together as one entier body that had al

The Goddesse Harmonia.

his members, he would alwaies beginne with them to geve a charge, in his most daungerous battels. For, as we see in running of coches at games, that horses being tyed all together in a fronte, doo runne faster and stronger, then they doo when they are lose, and put to it alone: and not for that they being many togeather doo breake through the ayer better, but for that the contention and envy betweene them to outronne one another doth in dede set their hartes and stomakes a fyre. Even so he thought, that valliaunt men geving one another a desire and envie to doo well, shoulde have the more corage, and woulde be of greater force, when they fought one in anothers sight. But the Lacedæmonians afterwardes being at peace and league with all the other Greecians, proclaymed open warres against the Thebans onely: and kyng Cleombrotus went to invade them with an army of tenne thowsande footemen, and a thowsande horsemen. Wherupon, the Thebans were not only in the like daunger they stoode in before to lose their libertie, but the Lacedæmonians did openly threaten they would utterly destroy them for ever: so that all the contrie of Bœotia stoode in greater feare, then ever they did before. And one day as Pelopidas went out of his house to goe to the warres, his wife bringing him out of the doores to take her leave of him, weeping, she praied him hartely to looke well to him selfe. But he aunswered her againe: My good wife, it is for private souldiers to be carefull of them selves, but not for captaines, for they must have an eye to save others lives. And when he came to the campe, he founde the captaines and the Lieuetenantes of the armie, in sundrie opinions: and he was the first that agreed with Epaminondas opinion, who thought it best they shoulde geve battell to the enemies. Pelopidas at that time was neither governor of Bœotia, nor general of the armie, but onely captaine of the holy bande: notwithstanding they had great affiance in him, and gave him great authoritie in counsaile concerning their affaiers: such as became a man that had made so good testimonie of his naturall love and affection to his contrie, as he had done. Now, being determined in counsaile that they shoulde geve the enemie battell, they all mustred together in the valley of Leuctres,

Cleombrotus king of the Lacedæmonians.

Pelopidas princely aunsweare.

where he had a vision in his dreame, that troubled him verie muche. In that valley there are the tombes of the daughters of one Scedasus, whiche by reason of the place, they call the Leuctrides, for that they were buried there, after they had bene defyled and ravished, by certaine guestes of the Spartans that laye in their house, travayling that way. This act being so horrible and wicked, the poore father of these defiled virgines, coulde neither have justice, nor revenge of the Lacedæmonians, and therefore after he had bande and cursed the Lacedæmonians with most horrible and execrable raylinges and curses as might be possible, he kylled him selfe upon the graves of his daughters. The Lacedæmonians had many sundrie oracles, prophecies and signes of the goddes to warne them, to take heede of the wrathe of the Leuctrides: howbeit everie man understoode not the signification of this prophecie, but were deceived by the equivocation of the name. For there was a litle towne in the contrie of Laconia, standing apon the sea, called Leuctrum: and in Arcadia also by the cittie of Megalipolis, there was another towne called by the same name. This misfortune chaunced longe before the battell of Leuctres: but then Pelopidas dreaming in his tente, thought he sawe in a vision the daughters of Scedasus weeping about their graves, and cursing the Lacedæmonians: and that he sawe their father also, commaunding him to sacrifice a red mayden to his daughters, if they woulde obtaine the victorie. This commaundement at the first, seemed verie cruel and wicked: whereuppon when he rose, he went to the Prognosticators and generalles of the armie, and tolde them his dreame. So, some of them saide, this was no matter to be lightly passed over, but to be considered of, alledging manie examples in the like cases. As of Menecius the sonne of Creon in olde time, and of Macaria the daughter of Hercules. And yet of later memorie, the wise Pherecydes, whome the Lacedæmonians slue, and whose skynne their kynges doo keepe at this daye, by commaundement of an oracle. And Leonidas, who following a prophecie of the goddes, did as it were sacrifice him selfe, for the safetie of Greece. And furthermore, the younge boyes which Themistocles did sacrifice to Bacchus Omestes (to say, eating rawe

Se what plagues folowe where justice is denied.

Pelopidas dreame and vision in the fieldes of Leuctres.

flesh) before the battell of Salamina. And all these sacrifices were acceptable to the goddes, as the victories following did plainely shewe. In contrarie manner also kinge Agesilaus, comminge from those very places, from whence king Agamemnon came in the time of the warres of Troia, and going also against the same enemies: dreamed one night in the cittie of Aulide, he sawe the goddesse Diana, asking him his daughter for sacrifice. But he tenderly loving her, would by no meanes perfourme it: and thereupon was compelled to breake of his jorney, before he had executed his enterprise, and departed with small honor. Other to the contrarie stoode to it stowtely, and saide it was not to be done. For, so cruell, abhominable, and brutish a sacrifice, could not be acceptable to any of the goddes, nor to any god, better or mightier than ours: considering that they be no impressions in the ayre, nor gyants that rule the world, but the one onely mightie and eternall God father of gods and men. And, to beleve that either goddes or demy goddes doo delite in murder, or sheading of mans blood, it is a meere mockery and folly. But admit it were so, they were no more to be regarded therein, then those that have no power at all: yet it is a manifest token of a wicked spirite, when they have suche damnable and horrible desires in them, and specially if they abide styll with them. Now, the generalles and heads of the armie of the Thebans being of sondry opinions, and Pelopidas being more afraid then before, by reason of their disagreement: a young mare colte, or fyllie, breaking by chaunce from other mares, ronning and flynging through the campe, came to staye right against them. Then every man beganne to looke apon her, and to marke what a faire fyllie it was, and red colored every where, and what a pride she tooke with her selfe to heare her owne neying. Theocritus then the soothesayer being amongest them, did beholde her, and knew straight what the fyllie ment, and so cried out foorthwith: O happie Pelopidas, loe here is the sacrifice thou lookest for, seeke no other virgine for thy sacrifice, but take this that God him selfe doth send thee. When Theocritus had saide so, they tooke the fyllie, and laide her apon the tombe of Scedasus dawghters, and put garlandes of flowers about her,

Agesilaus dreame.

as they handled other sacrifices: and then after their praiers made to the gods, they did sacrifice her with great joye, and told Pelopidas vision in his dreame the night before through all the campe, and the sacrifice they had made also according to the signification thereof. Moreover, when they came to joyne battell, Epaminondas being generall, drew all his army on the left hande, bicause he woulde bring the right winge of the enemies army (where they had placed the naturall Spartans) further from the other Greecians their frendes and allyes, that were set in the other wing of their battell: that he comming with his whole power together to geve a charge uppon Cleombrotus their king (being in a corner by him selfe) might be distressed or overthrowen. The enemies fynding Pelopidas intent, beganne to chaunge their order, and having men enowe, ment to thruste out their ryght winge at length to compasse in Epaminondas. But Pelopidas in the meane time sodainely prevented them, and ronning with great furie with his squadron of three hundred men, he set apon Cleombrotus before he coulde disorder his men to put furth the right winge, and joyne them together againe. And so he founde the Lacedæmonians not yet setled in their rankes, and brake them in this disorder, thrusting one in anothers place to put them selves againe in order: notwithstanding the Lacedæmonians of all other men were the only captaines, and most expert souldiers in marshal discipline, as men so trained and practised, that no sodaine altering of forme, or order in their rankes, coulde either trouble or disorder them. For they were men so trained, that they could turne head or side upon any sodaine occasion offered, and coulde fight and order them selves in battell every way alike. So Epaminondas going to geve thonset apon them alone, with the whole force of his battaile togeather, not tarrying for others: and Pelopidas also with an incredible corage and readines, presenting him selfe in battell before them, did put them into such a terrible feare, that they cleane forgotte their skill in fightinge, and their wonted courage fayled them. For they cowardly turned their backes, and there were moe Lacedæmonians slaine that day, than ever were before in any former battell. Pelopidas therefore, being neither

The battell at Leuctres.

The cause of the overthrow of the Lacedæmonians.

Pelopidas and Epaminondas victorie, at the battaile of Leuctres.

governor of Bœotia, nor general of all the army, but onely captaine of the holy band: did notwithstanding winne as muche honor and glorie of this victorie, as Epaminondas, that was governor of Bœotia, and generall of all the armie. In dede afterwardes they were both governors of Bœotia together, when they invaded the contrey of Peloponnesus: where they made most parte of the cities and people rebell against the Lacedæmonians, and take their parte. As the Elians, the Argives, and all Arcadia, and the best parte of Laconia selfe, notwithstandinge it was in the hart of winter, and in the shortest dayes of the yeare, and towardes the latter ende also of the last moneth of their yeares authority and rule, having not many dayes to continew in office, being forced to leave their authority, apon paine of death if they did refuse, unto other officers new chosen, the beginning of the next moneth following. Whereupon their other companions, and governors also of the contrie of Bœotia, what for feare to incurre the daunger of the lawe, as also to avoyde the trouble to lye in campe in the sharpest of winter: they did urge and perswade them to bring the armie backe againe into their contrie. But Pelopidas was the first that yeelded to Epaminondas opinion, and wanne the other Thebans also to consent unto it, to be contented to be led by them, to geve assault to the city selfe of Sparta. So, through their perswasion they passed over the river of Eurotas, and tooke many litle townes of the Lacedæmonians, and wasted and destroyed all the contrie to the sea side, leading under their ensignes an armie of threescore and ten thowsande fightinge men, and all Greecians, the Thebans not making up the twelvt parte of them. Now, the honor and great reputacion of these two persones, Epaminondas and Pelopidas, brought their frendes and confederates, that they followed them, without any resolution of counsell or publike order, and never opened their mouthes against them, but willingly marched under their conduction. And in my opinion, truely me thinkes it is the first and chiefest point in the lawe of nature, that he that is weake, not able to defend himselfe, should leane to one that is strong, and able to defende bothe. Even much like to freshe water souldiers, and rawe sea men,

Pelopidas and Epaminondas jorney into Peloponesus, being both governors of Bœotia.

A penall lawe at Thebes, for resigning up of offices at the yeers end.

Pelopidas and Epaminondas went over the river of Eurotas, with 70 thowsand men.

PELOPIDAS

that lying at sea in calme weather, and in safe harber, are as lusty and bragge with the masters and boteswaines as may be: and let a litle storme of weather come apon them sodainely, and that they be in any daunger, then they looke on the masters, hoping for no life but at their handes. And even in like maner the Elians and Argives, who though in all assemblies of counsel they woulde ever jarre and strive with the Thebans, for honor and superioritie in the armie: yet when any battell came to be fought, wherin they saw there was daunger, then their pecockes braverie was gone, and they were glad to obey their generalles commaundement. In this journey they brought all the cities of the province of Arcadia to be in league with them, and tooke all the contrie of Messenia from the Lacedæmonians, which they peaceably enjoyed: and called home againe all the auncient inhabitantes of the same, and restored them to their contrie, and replenished the citie of Ithome: Then returninge afterwardes into their contrie by the citie of Cenchrees, they overthrew the Athenians that came to trouble them, in entringe into the straight of Peloponnesus, supposinge to have stopped their passage. Thus was the valliantnes of these two worthy men greatly commended and honored of every body, for so many notable exployts and victories as they had wonne, and their marvelous good successe greatly wondered at. But as their glory and renowne increased abroade, so did their contrie mens malice and envie encrease against them at home: who had prepared such a welcome home for them, as was to bad and vile for so honorable service as they had done. For Epaminondas and Pelopidas bothe, at their returne, were accused of treason. For there was a speciall law at Thebes, that commaunded all such as should happen to be governors of Bœotia, to resigne their office immediatly to the new officers elect, at the beginning of the first moneth of the yeare, which in Bœotia they call Boucation: and they had kept it foure whole moneths above their tearme appointed, in which time they had done all that we have spoken of before, as well in the province of Messenia and of Arcadia, as also in the contrie of Laconia. Pelopidas was the first of the two that was called in by processe, ther-

The ingratitude of the Thebans, toward Pelopidas and Epaminondas.

The Lawe Boucation.

fore he stoode in the greater daunger: howbeit in the end, they were both discharged again. As for Epaminondas, he tooke his accusation and the attempt of his enemies (wherby they sought to have cast them both away) quietly enough: judging, that pacience to those that deale in state and government, is a great shew of force and magnanimitie. But Pelopidas being of a hotter nature, and more chollericke, and set on besides by some of his friendes, did take this occasion to be revenged. Meneclidas the orator was one of those that came into Charons house with Pelopidas, and Melon, but notwithstandinge the Thebans did nothing honor him, as they did the rest. He taking this ill at their handes, being marvelous eloquent of speeche, but vitiously geven otherwayes, and a man of a vile and mischievous nature: did fondly abuse his eloquence, falsely accusinge those that were his betters, in honesty and credit. And not beinge contented with this first accusation, he practised so commonly, that he put Epaminondas one yeare from being governor of Bœotia, which he sued for: and moreover he was ever against him in all matters of state he tooke in hande. But he coulde never bring Pelopidas out of favour with the people: and therefore he sought to make bate betwixt him and Charon. For it is the common tricke of all spitefull persones, when they can not be thought so honest men as those whome they envie: to go about to prove that they are not so honest and meete men, as those whome they preferre and commende. So, in all his orations he made to the people, he continually extolled and commended Charons noble actes and victories, and specially that victory above other, which the Thebans wanne before the jorney of Leuctres, in a skirmish of horsemen, that was before the city of Platees, he havinge charge of the same: of the which he woulde leave this memory. Androcydes a Cyzicenian and painter, was at a price with the Thebans to painte them some other battell in a table, and he did drawe this worke in the citie selfe of Thebes: but as he was in hand with all, the rebellion of the Thebans fell out against the Lacedæmonians, and warre followed on the necke of that, whereuppon the painter forsooke Thebes, leavinge his worke in manner done and perfitte. The Thebans

Epaminondas patience.

Pelopidas condemneth Meneclidas, a seditious orator and accuser.

The practise of spitefull men.

Our forefathers did paint and set forth their battailes.

 kept this table by them, and this Meneclidas moved the people they woulde hange it up in some temple or publicke place with an inscription apon it, sayinge thus: This was Charons victorie, of purpose to deface and obscure the glorie of Pelopidas and Epaminondas. To vaine and fond was his ambition, to set before so many noble battells and victories, one simple overthrowe of Charon, in the which Gerandas, one of the meanest gentlemen of all Sparta was slayne, and forty other with him: and this was all he did. Pelopidas misliked Meneclidas motion, maintaining that it was directly against the lawes of Thebes, which did expresly forbid that no private person should be honored with the title of common victorie, but willed the glory thereof should be attributed to all the people generally. In dede Pelopidas in all his orations did greatly praise and commend Charon, notwithstandinge, he made open proofe, howe Meneclidas was an envious and spitefull detractor, and a naughty wicked man, oftentimes askinge the Thebans, if they them selves were worthy of no honor? so as in the end he caused Meneclidas to be condemned in a great summe of money. But he finding him selfe unable to pay it, beinge so great a summe: practised afterwardes to alter the whole state and government. I thought good to dilate this at large, bicause me thinkes it doth somewhat declare Pelopidas nature, and maners, what they were. Now about that time, Alexander, the tyran of Pheres, was at open warres with many people of Thessalie, and did use all policie he coulde, to bringe them all to his obedience. Whereupon the free cities sent their Ambassadors unto Thebes, to pray them to send them a captaine, with an armie to aide them. Then Pelopidas seeinge Epaminondas occupied about the warres of Peloponnesus, did offer himselfe to the Thessalian Ambassadors, beinge lothe to drowne his experience and sufficiency in warres, with unprofitable and tedious idlenes, knowing that in those partes where Epaminondas lay, there neded no other captaine. Now when he came with his armie into Thessalie the citie of Larissa yelded presently unto him: where the tyran Alexander came to mete with him, and to pray him to treate a peace betwixt him and the Thessalians.

Alexander the tyran of Pheres.

Larissa, a city.

Pelopidas attempted to bring it to passe, seeking in steade of a tyran, to make him a gentle, just, and lawefull governor of Thessalie. But when he saw no perswasions could take place with the tyran, and that he grewe more stubborne and untractable, and woulde not heare reason: and moreover that he heard many grevous complaintes of his great cruelties, and how they accused him to be a marvelous dissolute and unruly person in all his doinges, and extreamely covetous besides: then he beganne to speake roundly to him, and to handle him roughly. But the tyran thereupon stole away secretely from him, and fled with his gard and souldiers about him. So Pelopidas leavinge the Thessalians out of all feare and daunger of the tyran, and furthermore in good peace and amity one with the other, he went into Macedon: where Ptolomy made warre at that time with Alexander, beinge kinge of Macedon, they bothe having sent for him to heare and determine the quarrell betwixt them, and also to helpe him that had the right, against him that did the wrong. So when he came thither, he pacified them bothe, and restored the banished men of either side, to their landes and goodes againe. For assurance of the peace, he tooke the kinges brother in ostage, whose name was Philip, and thirtie other children of the noblest mens sonnes of Macedon, whom he brought away with him to Thebes, to let the Greecians see, that the reputacion of the Thebans power stretched farre, and the renowne also of their manner of government and justice. It is the same Philip, that made warre afterwardes with the Greecians, to take their libertie from them: howbeit being but a boy at that time, he was brought up at Thebes in Pammenes house. And this is the cause, why some thought Philip did followe Epaminondas manner: and it might be paradventure, he did learne of him to be quicke and ready in the warres, which in deede was but a peece of Epaminondas vertue. But as to the continency, justice, magnanimitie, and clemencie, which were the speciall pointes that made Epaminondas of great fame: Philip coulde neither by nature, education, nor studie ever attaine unto. The Thessalians havinge sent afterwardes to Thebes, to complaine of Alexander the tyran of

Philip of Macedon, delivered for ostage unto Pelopidas.

 Pheres, that did againe molest and trouble the free cities of Thessalie: Pelopidas was sent thither Ambassador with Ismenias, carying no power with him from Thebes, litle thinking he shoulde have needed to have made warres: whereupon he was compelled to take men of the contrie selfe, uppon the instant necessitie offered. At the very same time also, all Macedon was up in armes. For Ptolomy had slaine the king, and usurped the kingdom, and the servaunts and frendes of the dead king called upon Pelopidas for aide: who desiring to come even uppon the fact, and having brought no men of warre out of his owne contrie with him, did presently leavie certaine men where he was, and so marched forward with them against Ptolomy. Nowe Ptolomy when bothe their powers met, did corrupt the souldiers Pelopidas had brought with money, to take his parte. But notwithstandinge this policy he had practised, yet he was afeard of the name onely, and greatnes of Pelopidas reputacion: wherefore he went unto Pelopidas, as to a better man than him selfe, and making marvelous much of him, and intreating of him, he made promise, and bounde it by othe, that he would keepe the realme for the brethren of the dead king, and that he woulde take all those for his frendes or enemies, whom the Thebans did either love or hate. And for assurance of his promise, he gave him his sonne Philoxenus in ostage, and fifty other of his frendes, all the which Pelopidas sent unto Thebes. But in the meane time, beinge marvelously offended with the treason of the souldiers against him, understandinge that the most parte of their goodes, their wives and children, were in the citie of Pharsale, he thought if he coulde winne that, it were a marvelous good way for him to be revenged of the trechery of the souldiers against him: whereupon he leavied certaine Thessalians, and went to that citie. Pelopidas was no sooner come thither, but Alexander the tyran arrived also with his armie. Pelopidas supposing he had come to justifie him selfe, clearing the complaintes of the Thessalians made against him: went to him, though he knew him to be a very wicked man, and one that delited in murder and sheading of blood. Nevertheles, he hoped he durst not have attempted any thing against him, for the authority and seigniories sake of Thebes, by whom he was sent thither, as also for his owne reputacion. But the tyran seeing him slenderly accompanied, and without traine of souldiers: tooke him prisoner, and wanne the city of Pharsale at that present time. But this act of his put his subjects in a great feare, who seeing him commit so shamefull a deede against all equity, did thinke straight he ment to spare no man, but would use men, and all thinges else that came in his handes, like a desperate man, and one that reckned him self cast away. But when the Thebans understoode this newes, they were marvelous sorie, and straight sent an army thither appointinge other Captaines then Epaminondas, bicause then they had some misliking of him. Alexander the tyran having brought Pelopidas in the meane time to Pheres, did suffer any man that woulde, at the first to come and see him, and speake with him: supposinge his imprisonment had killed his hart, and had made him very humble. But when he was tolde the contrary, how Pelopidas did comforte the citizens of Pheres, and willed them to be of good cheare, tellinge them the hower was now come that the tyran should smarte for al the mischiefes he had done: and that he sent him word to his face, he had no reason to hang and put his poore citizens daily to death as he did, with sundry kindes of cruell torments, who had in nothing offended him, and did let him alone, knowinge that if ever he got out of his hands, he would be revenged of him. The tyran wondering at this great stomake of his, and at his marvelous constancy fearing nothing: asked what he ment to long for hasty death? Pelopidas beinge tolde what he sayd, aunswered him againe: Mary, sayd he, bicause thow shouldest dye the sooner, beinge more odious to the goddes and men, then yet thou art. After this answere, the tyran would never suffer any man to come and speake with him againe. But Thebe, that was the daughter of the tyran Iason deceased, and wife at that time of Alexander the tyran, hearinge reporte of Pelopidas noble minde and corage by his keepers: she hadde a mervelous desire to see him, and to speake with him. But when she came to see him, like a woman she could not at the first discerne the greatnesse of his noble heart, and

Pelopidas taken prisonner by the tyran Alexander at Pharsale.

Pelopidas stoutnes.

Thebe the wife of Alexander the tyran.

 excellent hidden vertue, findinge him in such misery: yet conjecturing by exterior show, notinge his simple apparell, his heares and beard growen very long, and how poorely he was served, and worse entertained: she thought with her selfe his case was to be pittied, and that he was in no state mete for the glory of his name, wherewith she fell a weepinge for compassion. Pelopidas that knewe not what she was, beganne to muse at the first: but when it was tolde him she was Iasons daughter, then he curteously saluted her for her father Iasons sake, who while he lived was his very good frend. So Thebe said unto him: My Lord Pelopidas, I pittie thy poore Lady and wife. Truely so do I pitty thee, quod Pelopidas againe to her: that thou beinge no prisoner, canst abide such a wicked Alexander. This aunswere tickled Thebe at the heart, who with great impacience did beare the cruelty, violence, and villany of the tyran her husband: that besides all other infamous actes of his detestable life, committed Sodomy with her youngest brother. So she oft visitinge Pelopidas, and boldly makinge her mone to him, telling him closely all the injuries her husbande offered her: through Pelopidas talke with her, by litle and litle she grew to abhorre him, and to conceive a hate in heart against him, desiring revenge of him. But now the Captaines of the Thebans that were sent to deliver Pelopidas, beinge entred into Thessalie with their armie: (whether it was through default of ignoraunce, or their mishap) they returned home with shame, and did nothing. Whereupon the Thebans at their returne home, condemned them everie man in the summe of tenne thousande Drachmes, and sent Epaminondas thither againe with an other armie: at whose comming, all Thessalie rose incontinently, for the reputation of so great a captaine. And his fortune was so good, that he had in a manner utterly overthrowen all the whole state of the tyran: his frends and captaines were so much afraid, and his subjectes on the other side so well disposed to rebell, and marvelous glad for the hope they had, quickely to see the tyran have his deserved hyer, for all his former wicked deedes he had committed. Notwithstanding, Epaminondas preferring the deliverie and safety of Pelopidas, before the consideration of his owne

Epaminondas sent into Thessalie with an army.

honor and glorie, and fearinge least Alexander seeinge him selfe in daunger to be turned out of all he had, falling in despayre like a bedlem beast, woulde bende all his desperation and fury against Pelopidas: he drew these warres out in length, compassinge him rounde about, but not fiercely setting apon him, with culler to prepare his way the better by delaying still, therby to soften the cruell minde of this tyran, goinge on in this gentle sorte, and partely to cutte his combe and extreme pride, but specially to preserve Pelopidas, from the daunger and crueltie of his beastly rage. For he knew right well he was a cruel man, and one that neither regarded reason, nor justice in any sorte, consideringe howe he made some man to be buried alive, and others to be put in the skinnes of beares and wilde bores, and then to set houndes apon them to teare them in peeces, or else him selfe for his pastime would kill them, with shootinge or throwinge of dartes at them. And in the cities of Melibæa and of Scotusa, bothe of them beinge in league and frendshippe with him, he spying a time one day when the citizens were assembled in counsaill together, sodainely compassed them in with his gard and souldiers, and put them every one to the sword, even to the litle children. And he consecrated the darte also wherwith he had slaine his owne uncle Polyphron, and having put garlandes apon it, he did sacrifice to it, as to a god, and called it Tychon, as one woulde say, happy killer. And an other time being in a Theater, where the tragedy of *Troades* of Euripides was played, he went out of the Theater, and sent word to the players notwithstandinge, that they shoulde go on with their playe, as if he had bene still amonge them: saying, that he came not away for any misliking he had of them or of the play, but bicause he was ashamed his people shoulde see him weepe, to see the miseries of Hecuba and Andromacha played, and that they never saw him pity the death of any one man, of so many of his citizens as he had caused to be slaine. The gilty conscience therefore of this cruell and heathen tyran, did make him tremble at the only name and reputacion of Epaminondas: and as the common proverbe sayth:

The brutishe cruelty of Alexander the tyran.

He lett his winges downe fall, not much unlike the cocke,
which doth refuse the pit preparde, and lyst not bide the shocke.

So he sent straight unto Epaminondas to excuse him selfe. But Epaminondas woulde in no wise suffer the Thebans, through his meanes, to make league with such an hell hounde: only he yelded to abstinence of armes for thirty daies, apon delivery of Pelopidas and Ismenias into his handes, with whom he straight returned unto Thebes. Now the Thebans being advertised that the Lacedæmonians and the Athenians did sende Ambassadors to Artaxerxes the mighty king of Persia, to make league with him: they sent to him Pelopidas for them also, being wisely considered of them to sende a man of such fame and reputacion. For Pelopidas passing first through contries subject to the kinge of Persia, his fame was such where he came, that the peoples talke was onely of him. For the reporte of the famous battells he had wonne of the Lacedæmonians, was not only caried into the next regions and contries of Asia: but since the first newes of the journey of Leuctres was brought thither, Pelopidas havinge after that wonne victorie apon victorie, his estimacion grewe so great, as it was blowen abroade through the worlde, even to the highest and furthest partes of the East contries. And when he came to the king of Persiaes court, the princes, great Lordes, and captaines of Persia that sawe him, had him in great admiration, sayinge: loe this is he that conquered the Lacedæmonians, and tooke all their seigniorie, and authority from them, bothe by sea and by land, and drave the Spartans beyond the river of Eurotas, and from mount Taugetum, who not longe before made warres with the great kinge of Persia, beinge ledde under their kinge Agesilaus, even to the middest of Asia, for the realmes of Suse, and of Ecbatane. So king Artaxerxes selfe was very glad of his comminge, and praised him above them all, and made his estimacion greater then it was before, by his great and honorable entertaininge of him, meaninge thereby to returne the honor to him selfe againe: bicause menne shoulde thinke that the most famous men of the worlde came to honor him, and to see his court, as esteeminge bothe him, and his greatnesse, the onely happines of

Epaminondas delivered Pelopidas out of prison.

Artaxerxes king of Persia.

Pelopidas sent Ambassador to the king of Persia.

Pelopidas greatly honored of the king of Persia.

the worlde. But when he had seene his face, and heard him speake, and perceived that his wordes were much graver then the Athenians, and plainer then the Lacedæmonians: he then was further in love with him then before, and without disguising he did honor and favor him above all the other Ambassadors, who found that he made more estimacion of him, then of them all. Notwithstanding, he seemed to beare greater good will unto Antalcidas Lacedæmonian, then to any other of the Greecians: for that one day beinge at the table, he tooke a garlande of flowers from his owne head, and washed it in perfuming water, and sent it unto him. In dede he did not use Pelopidas with that open familiaritie, yet did he send him the goodliest and richest presentes he could devise, and graunted him besides al his requestes he made unto him: which were, that all the people of Greece should be free: that the city and contrie of Messina, should be inhabited againe: and that the citizens of Thebes by their successors should be taken, as ancient frends and allyes of the kings of Persia. So when he had receaved these aunswers, he returned home againe, and would by no meanes accept any of the great presents the king had offred him: which caused the other Ambassadors of the Greecians to be so ill welcome home to their cities. For among other, Timagoras was accused to the Athenians, and condemned to dye, and was executed: which if they did in respect of the great presents he had taken of the kinge, truely they had reason, and it was worthily done of them. For he tooke not only gold and silver enough, as much as they would give him: but receaved a very rich bed also, and Persian chamberlains to make and dresse it up, as if no Greecian servauntes of his could have served that turne. Moreover he receaved foure score milche kine to the paile, and neateheards to keepe them, having neede of cowes milke belike, to heale a disease that fell upon him: and woulde needes be caried in a litter apon mens armes from the kings court, unto the Mediterranian sea, the king rewarding them for their paines that caried him, with foure Talents. Yet it seemeth the gifts he tooke did not offende the Athenians so much, considering that Epicrates (a drudge or tanckerd bearer) did

Pelopidas refused the great giftes of the kinge Artaxerxes.

Timagoras Ambassador for the Athenians, put to death for taking great giftes of the kinge of Persia.

 not onely confesse before the people, howe he had taken giftes of the king of Persia: but sayd furthermore, that he would have a law made, that as they did yerely choose nine officers to rule the whole city: so that they would choose nine of the poorest and meanest citizens, and sende them Ambassadors unto the king of Persia, that they might returne home rich men with his giftes. The people laughed to heare him, but yet were they very angry the Thebans had obtained all that they demaunded: not considering that Pelopidas estimacion and worthinesse did more prevaile, and take better effect, then all the orations the other could make, and specially to a Prince that sought alwaies to enterteine those Græcians, which were of greatest force and power in the warres. This Ambassade did greatly increase every mans love and good will unto Pelopidas, bicause of the replenishinge againe of Messina with inhabitants, and the infranchesing setting at liberty of all the other Greecians. But the tyran Alexander of Pheres, returning againe to his old accustomed cruelty, and having destroied many cities of Thessalie, and placed his garrisons through al the contry of the Phthiotes, Achaians, and Magnesians: the cities being advertised of Pelopidas returne againe to Thebes, they sent Ambassadors immediatly to Thebes, to pray them to sende them an army, and namely Pelopidas for Captaine, to deliver them from the miserable bondage of the tyran. The Thebans willingly graunted them, and put all things in readines very sodainely. But Pelopidas being ready to set forward in his iorney, there fel a sodain eclipse of the sunne, so as at none daies it was very darke in Thebes. Pelopidas seing every man afraid of this eclipse above, he would not compell the people to depart with this feare, nor with so ill hope to hazard the losse of seven thowsande Thebans, being all billed to go this jorney: but notwithstanding, he put him selfe alone into the Thessalians handes, with three hundred horsemen of straungers, that were glad to serve with him, with whom he tooke his jorney against the soothsayers mindes, and against the good will of all his citizens, who thought this eclipse did threaten the death of some great persone like him selfe. But Pelopidas though he needed no spurre to be revenged

Pelopidas second jorney against the tyran Alexander of Pheres.

The eclipse of the sunne made the Thebans afraid.

apon the tyran Alexander, being by nature hotte, and desirous of him selfe to revenge the spite and villany he had offred him: yet he had a further hope to finde the tyrans house devided against himselfe, by the former talke he had with his wife Thebe, in time of his imprisonment there. Nevertheles, the fame and reputacion of the jorney undertaken, did wonderfully increase his noble corage, and the rather, bicause he was desirous (all he coulde) the Greecians should see, that at the very same time when the Lacedæmonians did sende governors and captaines to Dionysius, the tyran of Sicile, to serve and aide him, and that the Athenians as hyerlings tooke pay of the tyran Alexander of Pheres, in whose honor they had set up a statue of brasse in their city, as unto their savior: the Thebans only at the selfe same time tooke armes against them, to deliver those whom the tyrans oppressed, and sought to roote out all tyrannical government over the Greecians. So, when he came to the city of Pharsale, and had gathered his army together, he went presently into the field to mete with the tyran, Alexander, perceaving Pelopidas had very fewe Thebans about him, and that he had twise as many moe Thessalians with him, then the other had: he went to the temple of Thetis, to mete with Pelopidas. There one telling Pelopidas, that Alexander was comminge against him with a great power: Pelopidas answered him straight, al the better, we shal kil the more. Now, in the middest of the valley, there are certaine round hils of a good prety height, which they commonly call the dogges heads: they both strived which of their footemen should first get those hils. Pelopidas having a great number of horsemen, and good men at armes in the fielde, sent them before to give charge apon the enemies, that preased to winne the vantage of the place: and having overthrowen them, they followed the chase all the valley over. But in the meane time, Alexander having his footemen hard by, marched forwards, and got the hils, bicause the Thessalians that were further of came to late: notwithstandinge, when they came to the hilles, they sought forcibly to clime them up, being very high and steepe. But Alexander comming downe the hil, gave charge apon them

Battaill geven by the temple of Thetis, unto the tyran Alexander.

PELOPIDAS to their disadvantage, and slue the first that gave the attempt to get up against the hil: and the residue beinge sore hurt, retyred againe without their purpose. Pelopidas seeing that, sounded the retreate for the horsemen that followed the chase, to repayre to the standard, and commaunded them they should set apon the footemen of the enemies that were in battell raye: and him selfe ranne to helpe those that fought to winne the hilles. So he tooke his target on his arme, and passing through the rereward, got to the formest ranckes: to whome, the sight of his persone did so redouble their force and corage, that the enemies them selves thought it hadde beene a freshe supply of newe mens hartes and other bodies, then theirs with whom they hadde fought before, that came thus lustely to sette againe apon them. And yet they did abide two or three onsettes. Howebeit in the ende, perceiving those men did still more fiercely force to gette up the hill, and moreover how their horsemen were come in from the chase: they gave way, and left them the place retyring backe by litle and litle. Then Pelopidas havinge wonne the hilles, stayed on the top of them, viewinge the army of his enemies, which were not yet returned from their flying, but waved up and downe in great disorder. And there he looked all about, to see if he coulde spye out Alexander: and at the length he founde him out amongest others, in the right winge of his battell, settinge his men againe in order, and incoraging of them. After he had set eye on him, it was no holding of him backe, his hart so rose against him apon sight of him, that gevinge place to wrath, he neither regarded his persone, nor the intent of his jorney, but runninge farre before his men, he cried with a lowde voyce to the tyran, and chalenged the combat of him. The tyran woulde not abide him, nor come out to fight with him, but fled, and hid him selfe amongest his souldiers. But for his souldiers, the first that thought to set apon Pelopidas, were slaine by him, and many left dead in the fielde. The residue standing stowtly to it, and close together, did passe his curaces through with their long pykes, and thrust him into the brest. The Thessalians seeinge him thus sore handled and distressed, for pities sake came runninge from the toppe of those hilles, to the place where Pelopidas was, to helpe him. But even as they came, he fell downe deade before them. Then did they together with their horsemen so fiercely sette apon them, that they made the whole battell of the enemies to flye: and followinge them in chase a great waye from that place, they covered the valley with deade bodies, for they slue above three thowsande men. It is no marvell, if the Thebans that were at Pelopidas death, tooke it very heavilie, and lamented bitterly: callinge him their father, their saviour, and maister, as one that hadde taught them the worthiest thinges that might be learned of any. But the Thessalians and other frendes and confederates also of the citie of Thebes, besides their excedinge in setting out their common proclamations and edictes in prayse of his memorie, and doing him all the honor that could be due to the most rare and excellent persone that ever was: they did yet more shewe their love and affection towardes him, by their passinge great sorowe and mourning they made for him. For it is sayed, that they that were at the battell, did not put of their armor, nor unbridle their horses, nor woulde dresse their woundes, hearinge tell of his death: before they went first and sawe his body not yet colde with fightinge, laying great heapes of the enemies spoyles about it, as if he coulde have tolde what they had done, nor before they had clipped of their owne heares, and the heare of their horses, in token of sorowe. And many of them also, when they were come into their tentes and pavilions, woulde neither have fier, eate, nor drinke: and all the campe was full of sorowe and mourninge, as if they hadde not wonne a notable victorie, but hadde beene overthrowen and made subject by the tyranne. Afterwardes when the newes of his deathe was spread through all the contrie, the Magistrates of everie cittie through which Pelopidas bodie was conveyed, went to receave it verie honorablie, accompanied with all the younge menne, Priestes, and children, caryinge tokens and crownes of triumphe, and other ornamentes of golde. And when his funerall daye came, that his bodie shoulde be caried to be buried, the oldest and noblest persones of the Thessalians went to the Thebans, and prayed them that they might have the bury-

Pelopidas slaine.

The great lamentacion and mourning for Pelopidas death.

The oration of the Thessalians to the Thebans.

inge of him: and one amonge them beinge the mowthe of the reste, spake in this manner to the Thebans. 'My Lordes 'of Thebes, our good beloved frendes, and confederates, we 'onely crave this good turne at your handes, wherin you 'shal much honor us, and in our great calamity somwhat 'also comfort us. For we shall never more accompany 'Pelopidas alive, nor requite his honorable deserts to us, 'that he shal ever know them. But if it please you to let 'us handle his body with our handes, and that we may bury 'him, and set forth his obsequies: we will imagine then at 'the least that you doe thinke that, which we our selves do 'certainly beleve: that we Thessalians, not you Thebans, 'have received the greatest losse of both. For you have lost 'in deede a worthy Captaine, and we have not only receaved 'that like losse with you, but the hope also of recoveringe 'of our liberty. For how dare we againe sende to you 'for an other Captaine, when we can not redeliver you 'Pelopidas?' The Thebans hearing their peticion, graunted their desire: and in mine opinion, no funeralles could be done with greater pompe and honor, then the Thessalians performed his: being men that recken not dignity, magnificence, and pompe, to consist in ornaments of Ivory, nor of purple. As Philistus doth set it out, who praiseth to the moone the buryinge of Dionysius the tyran of Syracusa, which was the ende of his tyranny, as a sumptuous conclusion of a stately tragedy. And Alexander the great, at the death of Ephestion, did not only clippe his horse heares and mules, but plucked downe also the battellments of the wals of the city: bicause it shoulde appeare, that the very walles them selves did mourne for his death, shewinge that deformitie, in steede of their former beawtie. But all such thinges are done only by force and compulsion, apon the Lordes commaundementes, which doe but raise up envy against their memorie for whom they are done, and hatred of them that are against their willes constrained to do the thing they misliked: and are no just proofes of honor nor good will, but rather vaine showes of barbarous pompe, and pride in him, that disposeth his authority and plenty of goodes, in trifling toyes not to be desired. Where contrariwise it

The strange manner of sorowe, of Alexander the great, for the death of Ephestion.

plainely appeareth, that a private man dying in a foreine contry, by reason should be accompted most happy of all other creatures, that having neither his wife, kinne, nor his children by him, he should be conveyed to his funerals, accompanied with such multitudes of crowned people and number of cities, envying one an other who should most honor the funerals, as being unrequested, and least of all compelled. For saith Esope, the death of a happy man is not grevous, but most blessed, seeing it bringeth all good mens doinges to happines, and leaveth fortune to her fickle chaunge, and sportinge pleasure. But in my judgement, a Lacedæmonian spake better, when he sayd to Diagoras an old man, that had him selfe in old time gotten victory in the games Olympicall, and had sene besides, his own children, and his childrens children (both sonnes and daughters) crowned with victories also in the self same games: O Diagoras, die presently, els thou shalt never come to heaven. But these victories of the Olympicall and Pythian games, whosoever should put them al together, are not to be compared with one of the battels only, that Pelopidas hath foughten and wonne: having spent the most parte of his time in great calling and dignity, and lastly ended the same, beinge governor of Bœotia the third time (which was the highest office of state in all his contry) when he had distroied the tyrans that kept the Thebans in bondage, and was also slaine himselfe, valiantly fighting for the recovery of the Thessalians liberty. But as Pelopidas death was grevous to the Thebans frends and confederats: so fell it out very profitable for them. For the Thebans hearinge of Pelopidas death, did not delay revenge, but sent an army forthwith of seven thowsande footemen, and seven hundred horsemen, under the conduct of Malcitas, and of Diogiton. They findinge Alexanders army overthrowen, and that he had lost the most parte of his strength, did compel him to geve up the Thessalians townes he kept by force against them, and to set the Magnesians, the Phthiotes, and the Achaians at liberty, withdrawinge his garrisons he had placed in their strong holdes: and therewithall to sweare, that from thence forth he would marche under the Thebans, against any enemy they should

Pelopidas happines.

Esops sayinge of the happines of the dead.

Death a blessed thing.

The Thebans revenged Pelopidas death.

leade him, or commaunde him to go against. So, the Thebans were pacified apon these conditions. Now will I tell you how the gods plagued him soone after for Pelopidas death, who (as we have tolde you before) had pretily instructed Thebe his wife, that she shoulde not feare the outward appearance nor power of his tyranny, although she were environed with souldiers of banished men, whom the tyran enterteined to gard his person. Her self on the other side, fearing his falshode, as also hating his cruelty, conspired her husbands death with her three brethren, Tisiphomus, Pytholaus, and Lycophron, and executed her conspiracy after this sorte. The tyrans palice where he lay, was straightly garded every where with souldiers, who nightly watched his persone: but their bed chamber which they commonly used to lie in, was in the top of al his palice, where they kept a dog tyed at the chamber dore, to give warninge, which was a terrible dog, and knewe none but the tyran and his wife, and his keeper that gave him meate. Nowe when Thebe purposed to worke her feate, she locked up her three brethren a whole day neere unto their bed chamber. So when night was come, and being bed time, she went her selfe alone according to her maner, into Alexanders chamber: and finding him a sleepe, she stale out straight againe, and bad the keeper of the dogge to cary the dogge away, for her husbande was disposed to take rest, and would have no noyse. There was no way to get up to this chamber but by a ladder, which she let downe: and fearing least her brethren should make a noyse, she had covered the ladder staves with wolle before she let it fall downe. When she had gotten them up with their swordes, and had set them before the dore, she went first her selfe into the chamber, and tooke away the tyrans sword that hong at his beds head, and showed it them, as a token geven them that he was a sleepe. When it came to the pinche to do the deede, these young men were afrayed, and their heartes beganne to faile them. But she tooke on with them and called them cowardly boyes, that would not stande to it, when it came to the point, and with all, sware in her rage, that she woulde goe wake the tyran, and open all the treason to him. So partely

Alexander the tyran of Pheres slaine by his wife.

for shame, and partely for feare, she compelled them to come in, and to step to the bed, her selfe holding a lampe to light them. Then one of them tooke him by the feete, and bounde them hard: an other caught him by the heare of his head, and pulled him backewards: and the third thrust him through with his sword. So by chaunce he dyed sooner then he should have done, and otherwise then his wicked life deserved, for the maner of his death. So Alexander was the first tyran that was ever slaine by the treason of his wife, whose body was most villanously and dispitefully used after his death. For when the townes men of Pheres had drawen him through the city in myer and durt, they cast him out at length to the dogs to devoure.

Alexander the tyran of Pheres was the first tyran that wasslaine by his wife.

THE ENDE OF PELOPIDAS LIFE

THE LIFE OF MARCELLUS

MARCUS CLAUDIUS that was five times Consull at Rome, was the sonne (as they say) of an other Marcus: and as Posidonius wryteth, he was the first of his house surnamed Marcellus, as who would say, a marshall and warlike man by nature. For he was cunninge at weapons, skilfull in warres, stronge and lusty of body, hardy, and naturally geven to fight. Yet was he no quarreller, nor shewed his great corage, but in warres against the enemy: otherwise he was ever gentle, and fayer condicioned. He loved learning, and delited in the Greeke tongue, and much esteemed them that could speake it. For, he him selfe was so troubled in matters of state, that he could not study, and follow it, as he desired to have done. For if God (as Homer sayth) did ever make men

Marcellus kinred.

Marcellus condicions.

> To use their youth in warres, and battells fierce and fell,
> till crooked age came creeping on, such feates for to expell:

They were the noblest and chiefest men of Rome at that time. For in their youth, they fought with the Carthaginians in Sicile: in their middle age, against the Gaules, to kepe them from the winning of all Italie: and againe in their old age, against Hanniball and the Carthaginians. For their age was no priviledge for them to be dispenced with, in the service of their warres, as it was else for common citizens: but they were bothe for their nobilitie, as also for their valliantnes and experience in warres, driven to take charge of the armies delivered them, by the Senate and people. Now for Marcellus, there was no battell could make him give grounde, beinge practised in all fightes: but yet he was more valliant in private combate man for man, then in any other fight. Therefore he never refused enemie that did chalenge him, but slue all those in the fielde that called him to the combat. In Sicile he saved his brother Octacilius life, being overthrowen in a skirmishe: for with his shielde he covered his brothers body, and slue them that came to kill him. These valliant partes of him, being but a young man, were rewarded by the generalles under whom he served, with many crownes, and warlike honors, usually bestowed apon valliant souldiers. Marcellus increasing still his valliantnes and good service, was by the people chosen Ædilis, as of the number of those that were the worthiest men, and most honorable: and the Priestes did create him Augure, which is a kinde of Priesthoode at Rome, having authority by law, to consider and observe the flying of birds, to divine and prognosticate thinges thereupon. But in the yere of his office of Ædile, he was forced against his wil to accuse Capitolinus, his brother in office with him. For he being a rash, and dissolute man of life, fell in dishonest love with his colleagues sonne Marcellus, that bare his owne name: who beinge a goodly young gentleman, even freshly come to mans state, was as well thought of, and taken of every man for his manhoode and good qualities, as any way for his beawty and personage. The first time Capitolinus moved this dishonesty to him, he did of him selfe repulse his shameles offer, without any others privitie: but when he saw he came againe to tempt him the seconde time, he

The Romaines troubled with warres.

Marcellus saved his brother Octacilius.

Marcellus chosen Ædilis and Augure.

Marcellus accuseth Capitolinus.

straight revealed it to his father. Marcellus his father beinge marvelously offended withall, (as he had good cause) went and accused Capitolinus before the Senate. Capitolinus at the first, layed in many exceptions and fained excuses, to kepe him from appearing, and in the end he appealed to the Tribunes of the people: but they declared plainely they would not receive his appeale, nor take any knowledge of the matter. At the length he was forced to aunswere the matter before the Senate, and denied flatly that he attempted ever any such thinge, bicause there were no witnesses to prove it against him. Whereupon the Senate thought good to sende for young Marcellus who comminge before them, bothe blushed, and wept together. The Senate seeinge shamefastnesse in him, mingled with teares, and a malice that coulde not be pacified without seeking other proofe: they tooke it a cleare case, and so condemned Capitolinus presently in a great summe of money, which Marcellus converted into silver vessell, to serve at sacrifices, and so did consecrate them to the service of the goddes. Now when the Romaines had ended their first warre against the Carthaginians, which held them fully the space of two and twenty yeares: Immediatly after that, they beganne a newe warre against the Gaules. For the Insubrians, beinge a people derived from the Gaules, and dwelling at the foote of the mountaines of the Alpes on Italie side, being able to make a good power of them selves, did notwithstanding pray aide of the other Gaules inhabiting on the other side of the mountaines: and they caused the Gessates, a mercenary people and hierlings to them that woulde give pay, to bring great numbers with them. Truely me thinkes it was a marvelous matter, and wonderfull good happe for the Romaines, that this warre of the Gaules came not apon them, while they were at wars with the Carthaginians: and that the Gaules also had lien quiet all that while (as if they had purposely sworne to set apon the conquerors) expecting still an end betwene them, and then to set apon the conquerors, when they had nothing to say to any other. Yet the scituacion of their contry did trouble the Romaines much, bicause they were so nere neighbours unto them, and had

The Romaines had warres with the Carthaginians two and twenty yeres together.

The warre of the Gaules.

Gessates mercenary Gaules.

warres as it were at their owne dores. And so did the auncient reputacion of the Gaules somewhat appawle the Romaines, who as it shoulde seeme they did feare more, then any other nation whatsoever: bicause Rome had bene taken before by the Gaules. Since which time, a law was made, that Priestes and ecclesiasticall persones should be dispenced with, from going to the warres, onles the Gaules did rise against them. The preparacion they made for this warre at that time, did plainly show the feare they had then of the Gaules. For the world thinkes, that never before, nor since, there were so many naturall Romaines assembled together in fielde, as were then at that present. Moreover, the new come cruelty they used in their sacrifices, doth recorde this to be true. For before, they never used any straunge maner in their sacrifice, or barbarous facion, but were favorable in their opinions about the ceremonies of religion, and agreeable to the Greecians, touching the service of the goddes. But then, they were compelled to obey certaine oracles, and auncient prophecies they found wrytten in Sibylles bookes: and they buried two Greecians alive in the oxe market, a man and a woman, and likewise two Gaules, a man and a woman. Unto them they doe yet continew certaine secret anniversaries in November, that are not to be sene of every body. The Romaines in their first battels of this warre, were often overcommen, and did overcome: but these battels were to litle purpose, for ending of the warres. In the yere that C. Quintius Flaminius, and P. Furius Philo were Consuls, and sent with great armies to make warres apon the Insubrians, people subject to the state of Milane: newes were brought to Rome, that there was a river seene in the contry of Romania, red as blood, and three moones also at the very same time in the city of Rimini. Furthermore, the Priestes and Soothsayers, that had observed and considered the tokens, and significations of birdes on that day, when these two were chosen Consuls: they tolde plainly there was error in their election, and that they were directly chosen against all signes and tokens of the birdes. Thereupon the Senate wrote immediatly to the campe to them, and willed them to come home to depose themselves of their

A lawe to exempt ecclesiastical persons from the wars.

The Romaines did feare the warre of the Gaules.

Men and women buried alive.

Flaminius and P. Furius Consulls.

Newes brought to Rome, of strange things seene in Romania.

Consulshippe, before they did attempt any thing as Consuls against the enemies. The Consul Flaminius receaved the letters in time: but bicause he was ready to give battell, he woulde not open them, before he had first overthrowen his enemies, and spoyled their contrie, as in dede he did. But when he was come backe to Rome againe, and had brought marvelous great spoyles with him, the people for all that woulde not goe out to meete him, bicause he did not presently obey the letters they wrote unto him, nor returned apon it as they commaunded him, but contemptuously, without any regard of their displeasure, followed his owne phantasie: whereupon they had almost flatly denied him the honor of triumphe. For his triumphe was no sooner ended, but they compelled him to give over his Consulship, and made him a private man with his companion. The Romaines therein were so religiously bent, as they would all things shoulde be referred unto the gods good grace and pleasure, and would suffer none to contemne the observations and prognosticatinge of the soothsayers, nor their auncient uses and customes, for any prosperity and felicity that could happen. For they thought it more necessary and profitable for benefit of the common weale, that the Senate and magistrates should reverence the ceremonies and service of the goddes: then that they should overcome their enemies in battell. As for example Tiberius Sempronius, a man as much honored and esteemed of the Romaines for his justice and valliantnes, as any other of his time: beinge one yeare Consul, did nominate and elect two other for Consuls the yeare following, Scipio Nasica, and Caius Martius. These two being entred into their Consulship, and sent from Rome also to their severall provinces appointed them by lot: Sempronius by chaunce tooke certen litle bookes in his hande, where were briefly written the rules appertaining to the ceremonies of publike sacrifice, and reading in them, he found a certaine ordinaunce he never heard before. And this it was. That if a magistrate were set in any tent or hyred house without the citie, to beholde and observe the prognostications of birdes, and that upon any sodaine occasion he were driven to come againe

Flaminius overcame the Gaules in battayle.

The great religion of the Romaines.

An ordinance for publike sacrifice.

into the citie, before the birdes had given any certaine signes: the second time when he returned againe to ende his observations, there was no remedy, but he must leave his tent or first hyred house, and take an other, and beginne new observations againe. Tiberius utterly ignoraunt of this ordinaunce before, had kept his observations twise in one selfe house, and had chosen there, Nasica and Martius, Consulls to succeede him. But when he knew he had offended, he told the Senate of it: who would not let slippe so litle a fault: but wrote to the newe Consulls, and they straight left their provinces, and returned againe to Rome, willingly resigninge up their offices. That was a prety while after. Againe also, about the very present time we write of nowe, there were two Priestes of noble houses (and noble persones also) the one called Cornelius, and the other Cethegus, bothe which were disgraded of their Priesthoode, bicause they had not given the intrayles of the sacrificed beast in order, as they should have done. Quintus Sulpitius in like maner, was disgraded of his Bishopricke, bicause his miter which the Flamines doe weare, fell of his head in his sacrificing. Minutius being Dictator also, and havinge chosen Caius Flaminius generall of the horsemen: bicause they heard the noyse of a ratte at the election of Flaminius, they were bothe put out of their authoritie, and other chosen in their place. Now, though they were thus precise even in trifles, it was not by reason of any supersticion mingled with their religion: but bicause they woulde not breake any jotte of the auncient institucions and ceremonies of their contrie. But to our storie againe. Flaminius beinge deprived of his Consullshippe, Marcellus was created Consull in his place, by the regents at that time called Interreges. Marcellus being invested in his office, chose Cneus Cornelius for his companion: and they say, that the Gaules beinge inclined to peace, and the Senate of Rome also willinge to harken to peace, Marcellus did stirre up the people, and made them rather desire warre. Notwithstandinge, they concluded peace at that time: but the Gaules Gessates immediatly after renued the wars againe. For there came over the mountaines of the Alpes, a thirty thowsand of them, and they joyned with the Insubrians,

Marcellus and Cneus Cornelius Consulls.

which were many moe in number then them selves. Now, they being in a marvelous jolity, went incontinently to lay siege to the city of Acerres, that standeth apon the river of Po: and during the siege, king Britomarus taking ten thowsande Gessates with him, went and destroyed all the countrie about the Po. Marcellus hearing that, left with his companion Cneus Cornelius, al the armed footemen, and the third parte of the horsemen, in his campe by Acerres: and he him selfe with the residue of the horsemen, and six hundred footemen light armed, marched towards the enemy, travelling night and day, until he met with the ten thowsand Gessates, nere unto a village of Gaule on this side the mountaines, called Clastidium, which was subject not long before to the Romaines. So he had no leasure to take rest, nor to refresh his men a litle: for the barbarous people knew straight he was come, and tooke him for no better then by and by overcome, bicause he had so fewe footemen. And for his horsemen, the Gaules made no reckening of them: for besides themselves are very good men at armes, and excell all other in that fight, yet were their number of horsemen farre above Marcellus. Therefore they straight marched towardes him in a marvelous furie, and with thunderinge showtes, as if they would have devowred them at their comminge. Britomarus their king, advaunced him selfe before all his company. Marcellus fearing to be compassed in behinde, being so small a number: he put out the winges of his horsemen as much as he could, to have the contrie at large, so that his two wings were very slender, untill he came nere his enemies. And being ready to gallop towardes the enemie, it fortuned his horse beinge afraid with the noyse of his enemies, turned about, and caried Marcellus backe againe in spite of his teeth. But he fearing the Romaines supersticion, in taking this for an evill token, and that they woulde take a conceite apon the same: plucking the bridle with his left hande, turned his horse head againe uppon the enemie, and then he worshipped the sunne, as though he had not turned his horse by chaunce, but purposely for that cause. For it is the Romaines manner to turne about so, when they do honor their goddes. So when they beganne to joyne battell, he made a vowe to Iupiter Feretrian,

The Gaules Gessates make warres with Rome, and come over the Alpes.

Acerres, a city apon the river of Po.

Clastidium, a village on this side the mountaines.

The maner of the Romaines when they worship.

The combat on horsebacke betwixt Britomarus king of the Gaules, and Marcellus.

Marcellus slue king Britomarus at Clastidium.

Marcellus prayer unto Iupiter Feretrian.

The Gaules overcome by Marcellus.

to offer him uppe the goodliest spoyles of his enemies, if he did overcome. The kinge of the Gaules seeinge him at that instant, imagined by the markes and tokens he saw, that he should be the general of his enemies: So he set spurres to his horse, and gallopped towardes him from all his company geving him defiance, and chalenged him, shaking his staffe in his hande. He was the goodliest persone and strongest man of all the Gaules, and his armor was all guilt and silvered, and so set foorth with sundry workes and colours, that it shined as the sunne. Marcellus on the other side havinge viewed all the army of his enemies through out, and perceavinge none so richely armed as the king: thought straight it was against him, that he had made his prayer and vowe to Iupiter. Then he put his horse in full cariere against him, and came with such a force and fury to him, that he pearced his armor with his staffe, and overthrew him, but yet he killed him not dead: wherupon he sodainly redoubled two or three strokes besides apon him, and so slew him right out. Then he lighted from his horse, and taking the dead kinges armor in his hande, he lift up his eyes to heaven, and said: O Iupiter Feretrian, thou that doest from heaven beholde and direct, all marshall feates and Captaines deedes: thy selfe I call to witnes, that I am the third Romaine Captaine, that being generall of the army, have slaine with my owne handes, the king and generall of the enemies: and I promise here to thee, to offer thee up the richest spoyles of mine enemies, so thy godheade will vowchesafe to graunt us the like good fortune in all this warre besides. His prayer ended, the men of armes of the Romaines ranne in among the horsemen and footemen of the Gaules, one being unparted from an other: and fortune did so favor them, that they wanne a passing victory, in such a straunge and wonderfull maner, as was incredible. For it was never seene before nor since, that so fewe horsemen did overthrow, so great a number of men of armes and footemen ranged together. Now when Marcellus hadde slaine the greater number of them, and had gotten their spoyles and all their baggage: he returned againe to his companion Cneus Cornelius, whom he founde makinge warres unfortunately with the Gaules, before the greatest and most populous city they had, called Millaine, which the Gaules on this side the mountaines take for their chiefe city, and from whence all other had their first originall. Whereupon they did all their possible endevor to defende it, and did as straightly besiege the Consull Cornelius, as he did them. Now, when Marcellus was come to the campe againe, the Gessates understanding that their king Britomarus was slaine in battel, returned backe againe into their contry, and the city of Millaine was taken. After that, all the other cities there about yelded of them selves, without force of siege, and the Gaules wholly submitted them selves and all that they had, to the mercy of the Romaines, who graunted them peace uppon easie condicions. For these famous victories, the Senate of Rome gave all the honor of triumphe unto Marcellus only, and that was as wonderfull and worthy a sight, as any that ever past before him: what for the infinite spoyles, and the numbers of great men taken prisoners, and also for the exceeding sumptuousnes and stately shew thereof. But the goodliest sight of all for the rarenes, was to behold Marcellus selfe, carying on his shoulders the whole spoyle of the barbarous king, to offer up to Iupiter Feretrian. For he had cut downe a goodly younge oke of the mountaine, straight, and shut up very long, which he had trimmed up in forme of triumphe, hanging all the armed peces he had wonne of the king, very orderly rounde about it. Then, when all the show of his triumphe was past, he him selfe tooke the oke on his shoulders, and gotte up upon his triumphing charet, and so marched through the city, carying these signes thereupon: which was the noblest sight, and honorablest show, of the whole triumphe. His army followed after the charet, singing verses and songes of victory, in praise of the goddes and their Captaine: and when he had passed through the whole city, and was come to the temple of Iupiter called Feretrian, there he set up this young oke, and token of triumphe. This Marcellus is the third and last Romaine Captaine, to whom happened this honor in our age. For the first man that ever offred up to Iupiter the spoyles of the general of their enemies, was king Romulus, who wanne the like spoyles of Acron, king of

Marcellus wanne the city of Millaine.

Marcellus triumphe.

Marcellus offeringe up of his rich spoiles.

MARCEL-LUS

The three persones that offered up *Spolia opima* in Rome: Romulus. Cossus. Marcellus.

Iupiter Feretrian why so called.

Spolia opima: what they be.

the Cæninians. The second was Cornelius Cossus, who slue Tolumnius, generall of the Thuscans. And the third was Marcellus, who slue with his owne handes Britomarus, king of the Gaules: and after him, no man ever since could obtaine the like good fortune. The god to whom these maner of spoyles are consecrated thus, is called Iupiter Feretrian, so tearmed as some write, bicause they do cary this token of triumphe to him, following the derivation of this Greeke word, *Ferin*, which signifieth to cary: for in those former times, many Greeke words were mingled with the Latine. Other affirme it is one of the surnames of Iupiter, signifying as much as lightening: for *Ferire* in the Latine tonge, signifieth to strike. And some say also, in warres it is properly to hurt or kill with his owne handes: for the Romaines do use at this day when they geve a charge apon their enemies in battell, or that they have them in chase flying, to crie, incoraging one an other, *Feri, Feri*: which is as much, as kill, kill. And the spoyles taken from the enemies also, are generally called *Spolia*: but those which Lieutenantes generall, or generalles, do take from the generalles of their enemies, when they have slaine them, they are called particularly *Spolia opima*. Yet some hold opinion, that kinge Numa Pompilius mencioning the rich spoyles, or *Spolia opima* in his commentaries, speaketh of the first, the second, and the third: and commaundeth that the first spoyles which are wonne, should be consecrated to Iupiter Feretrian: the second unto Mars: and the third unto Quirinus. And that they should give to him that had wonne the first spoyles, three hundred Asses: the second, two hundred: and the third a hundred. But notwithstanding, the best opinion and usuall taking of *Spolia opima*, referreth them to be the first spoyles wonne in a foughten field, and those which the Lieutenant of an army, or a general, doth take from the general of the enemies, after he hath slaine him with his owne handes. And thus much for declaracion of this matter. Furthermore, the Romaines were so joyfull of this victory, and of their good successe in this warre, that they caused a massie cuppe of golde to be made of the spoyle they had gotten, weyinge a hundred pounde weight, which they sent to offer up in the temple of Apollo Pythias, in the city of Delphes, in token of thankes: and they made liberall division besides of the spoyles unto their frendes and confederates, and sent a great parte of it unto Hieron king of Syracusa, who was their confederate. Not long after, Hanniball being entred Italie, Marcellus was sent with an army by sea, into Sicile. And after the great overthrow was given at the battel of Cannes, wherin there died so many thowsande Romaines, and that very few of them saved them selves by flyinge, into the city of Cannusium: they looked that Hanniball havinge overcome the flower of all the Romaines youth, and their greatest force, woulde not fayle to come straight to Rome. Wherefore Marcellus first sent fifteene hundred of his men by sea, to help to defende Rome: and havinge afterwardes receaved commaundement from the Senate, he came to Cannusium, where he tooke such as were fled thither for succor after the battell, and so brought them out to the fielde, to defende the contrie. Now the Romaines having lost the most parte of all their best Captaines, in diverse sundry battells before: of all those that remained, Fabius Maximus was the onely able and reputed man for commendacion of his honesty and wisedom, yet they misliked of him notwithstanding, for a timerous man, and of no corage, as a man to ful of doubts and consideracion, and loth to put any thing in hazard: saying, he was a good Captaine to defende, but not to offende the enemy. Whereupon they thought good to joyne Marcellus lively youth and corage, with Fabius feminine feare and wisedom: and therefore some yeares they chose them both Consulls together, or else they sent one of them as Consull, and the other as Proconsull, eche in his turne, to the contrie where they hadde warres. And for proofe hereof, Posidonius wryteth, that the Romaines at that time called Fabius Maximus their target, and Marcellus their sword. Therefore Hanniball him selfe sayed, he feared Fabius Maximus as his governor, and Marcellus as his enemy: bicause the one kept him from hurting of others, and the other did hurt to him selfe. Immediatly after this great victory at Cannes, Hannibals souldiers became so bolde, so carelesse, and disordered, that

Marcellus sent into Sicile with an army.

Posidonius wordes of Fabius and Marcellus.

MARCELLUS

they kept the fielde without feare of any thing, and dispersed them selves farre from their campe: wherefore Marcellus setting apon those stragglers, he slue them every man, and so by litle and litle did still lessen the power and strength of his enemy. Afterwardes he aided the cities of Bizantium and of Nola, and stablished the true devotion and love of the Bizantines towardes the Romaines: from thence he went to Nola, and found great sedition there betwixt the Senate and people, bicause the Senate coulde not keepe the people in obedience, but they woulde needes take Hannibals parte. The cause of the peoples stubbornnesse grewe, by occasion of a gentleman of the city called Bandius, a noble gentleman to the people, and a valliant man of his hands. This Bandius having fought valliantly at the battell of Cannes, after he hadde slaine many a Carthaginian, was him selfe in the ende striken downe, and founde lyinge amonge deade bodies, sore wounded and mangled: whereupon Hanniball greatly commending his valliantnes, did not onely let him go without ransome, but furthermore presented him, and made him his hoste and frende. Hereupon Bandius at his comming home, to requite Hannibals honor and curtesie, became one of those that most favored Hannibal, and most perswaded the people of Nola to take his parte. Notwithstandinge this, Marcellus thinking it to great a sinne against the goddes, to put a man to death that had made so great proofe of his valliantnes, and had served with the Romaines in their greatest warres, and extremest daunger, and who besides the goodnes of his nature, hadde a marvelous gift also, to winne mens good wills by his great curtesie: when this Bandius came one day to do his duety to him, Marcellus of purpose asked him what he was, though he had knowen him long before, only to take occasion to talke with him. The other aunswered him, his name was Lucius Bandius. Then Marcellus seeming to be marvelous glad, and to wonder at him, sayed: And art thou that Bandius they speake of so much at Rome, whom they say did so notable service in persone at the battel of Cannes, and never forsooke Paulus Æmilius the Consull, but receaved so many woundes uppon thy body in defence of him? Bandius aunswered, that he was the man, and therewith

Lucius Bandius, of Nola: a valliant man.

Marcellus gentlenes.

shewed him many woundes he had apon his body. Marcellus then replyed: Alas, thou that cariest such notable markes of thy unfained love towards us, what diddest thou meane, that thou camest not straight againe unto us? art thou perswaded we are so miserable and unthankefull, that we will not worthily reward the vertue and valliantnesse of our frendes, whom our enemies selves do honor? After Marcellus had used this curteous speach unto him, and had imbraced him, he gave him a goodly horse for service in the warres, and five hundred Drachmes of silver besides. So after that time, Bandius did ever take Marcellus parte, and alwayes followed him, being very faithfull to him, and shewed him selfe very seveare and earnest to accuse them, that tooke Hannibals parte in the city: which were many in number, and had conspired among them selves, that the first time the Romaines should go into the fielde to skirmishe with the enemies, they woulde shut the gates after them, and take the spoyle of al their cariages. Marcellus being informed of this treason, did set his men in battell raye within the city, hard by the gates, and behind them he placed al the sumpters and cariage in good order: besides that, he made proclamation by trompet, that no citizen apon paine of death shoulde approch the walles. This occasion drew Hanniball to come hard to the city, seeinge no watche apon the walles, and made him the bolder to come in disorder, imagininge there had bene some mutinie or sedition within, betwene the noble men and the people. But in the meane time, Marcellus set open the gates being hard by, and sayling out apon the sodaine with the best men of armes he had, he gave a charge upon Hanniball in the voward. Immediatly after came out his footemen at an other gate, running straight upon Hanniball, with a wonderfull crie and showte: so as Hanniball to withstand them, was driven to devide his men in two companies. But as he was devidinge of them, sodainely a third gate opened apon them, from whence all the residue of the Romaines issued out, who sette uppon the Carthaginians on every side, they beinge marvelously amazed to be so sodainely set on, which they looked not for: so having their handes full with those that came first apon them,

Reward made Bandius a true subject.

Marcellus victorie of Hanniball at Nola.

beinge scant able to defende them selves against them, and seeinge this newe and last charge also: they were forced to retyre. This was the first time, that ever Hannibals souldiers beganne to give place to the Romaines, who drave them backe unto their campe, and slewe a great number of them, and did hurt diverse of them besides. For some wryte, there were slaine of the Carthaginians at that conflict, above five thowsande: and of the Romaines there died not past five hundred men. But Titus Livius doth not set out the overthrow so great, and yet confesseth that Marcellus wanne great honor by it, and that it made the Romaines marvelous valliant againe, after so many and sundry battells as they had lost one after an other: for then they were perswaded that they fought not with an enemy altogether unvincible, but that he might somtime also, as well as them selves, receive both losse and hurt. Therefore, one of the Consulls dyinge about that time, the people caused Marcellus to be sent for, and placed him in his roome: and in spite of the Senate they deferred all deputacion untill his returne from the campe. Marcellus came no sooner to Rome, but he was chosen Consull in the deade mans roome, by all the voyces of the people. Notwithstandinge, when they went to choose him, it thundered marvelously: which the Priestes and Augures tooke for an ill token, but yet they durst not openly speake against his election, bicause they feared the people. Howbeit Marcellus of him selfe did willingly give up his Consullshippe, and yet was it no exception to him for his service in the warres: for they created him Proconsull, and sent him againe to the campe at Nola, where he did severely punishe such as tooke Hannibals parte. Who being advertised thereof, came thither with all possible spede to helpe them: and even at his first comming, he offered Marcellus battell, which refused it at that time. Nevertheles, he tooke his time, when Hanniball hadde sent the best parte of his army to forrage, as meaning to fight no more battels: and then he set apon him, having given his footemen long pykes, such as they use in fight apon the sea, and taught them also, howe to hurt the enemy a farre of, keping them still in their handes. But the Carthaginians having no skill of their

Marcellus proconsull.

pykes, and fighting with shorte javelings in their hands, did strike downe right blowes: which was the cause, that they being set apon by the Romaines, were driven to turne their backes, and flee before them. So there were five thowsande of the Carthaginians left dead in the field, foure elephants slaine, and two taken alive: and furthermore, three dayes after the battell, there came a three hundred horsemen, some of them Spaniards, and other Numidians, that submitted them selves to the Romaines. Never came there such a misfortune before to Hanniball: who had of long time kept together in great love and amity, an army assembled of sundry barbarous nations and people. Howbeit these three hundred continued ever after faithfull to the end, both to Marcellus, and to all other Lieutenants and generals of the Romaines. Shortely after, Marcellus beinge againe chosen Consull the thirde time, went into Sicile. For Hannibals prosperous successe and victories had so incoraged the Carthaginians, as they sought againe to conquer this Ilande: and specially bicause that after the death of Hieronimus the tyran, there rose some tumult at Syracusa. Uppon which occasion, the Romaines had sent an army thither before, and a Prætor called Appius: at whose handes Marcellus having received the army, a great number of the Romaines became humble suters to him, to pray him to aide them in their calamity, which was this. Of those that scaped from the battell of Cannes, some saved them selves by flying, other were taken prisoners, of which there were such a number, as it appeared that Rome had not people enough left onely to keepe the walles. Nevertheles, those few that remained, their hartes were so great, that they woulde never redeeme the prisoners, which Hannibal was contented to deliver them uppon small ransome, but made a decree they should not be redeemed: and so suffered some of them to be killed, others to be solde for slaves out of Italie. And moreover, those that saved them selves by flying, they sent straight into Sicile: commaunding they should not once set foote againe in Italie, whilest they had warres with Hanniball. These were the men that came altogether, and fell downe at Marcellus feete, so soone as he arrived in Sicile, and humbly

Certaine Spanyards and Numidians revolted from Hanniball.

Marcellus the third time Consull, sent into Sicile.

The severity of the Romaines to cowardly souldiers.

besought him, to appoint them to serve under some ensigne, that they might fight to do their contrie honor and service: promising him with teares running downe their cheekes, that their faithfull service then should witnesse for them, that the overthrow they had at Cannes, fell apon them rather by misfortune, then through lacke of corage. Whereupon Marcellus having compassion on them, wrote to the Senate in their favor, and prayed them that they would graunt him licence to supply the bands of his army, as they diminished, with those poore Romaines his contrymen. Many reasons passed to, and fro, against this sute: nevertheles, it was concluded in the ende by the Senate, that the common wealth made no reckening of the service of faint harted men like women: wherefore if Marcellus thought good of their service, yet it shoulde not be lawfull for him to give them any crownes or rewards of honor, for any notable service soever they did, as all generalles are wont to give to honest men that serve valliantly. This order of the Senate misliked Marcellus very much, who at his returne home out of Sicile, made his complaint in open Senate, and told them they did him manifest wrong, to deny him that favor, that having done his common wealth such faithful service diverse times, as he had done, he might not restore so many poore Romaines to their honor againe. Nowe, when Marcellus was in Sicile, he received great hurtes and injuries by Hippocrates, generall of the Syracusans: who, to pleasure the Carthaginians, and by their meanes to make him selfe chiefe Lord of Syracusa, did put many Romaine citizens to death. Wherupon Marcellus went and layed siege to the city of the Leontines, and when he had taken it by assault, he hurt never a townes man, nor naturall citizen of the same: but such traytors as he founde there, and had fled from his campe, and yelded to the enemies, them he caused to be whipped, and then hanged. But notwithstanding, Hippocrates had before caused it to be bruted at Syracusa, that Marcellus had put all the Leontines to the sword, not sparing litle children: and afterwards Hippocrates comming thither on the sodaine, in the feare and garboyle of this false brute, he easily tooke the city. Marcellus hearing Hippocrates had taken Syracusa, left forth-

Cowardes detested of the Romaines.

Hippocrates generall of the Syracusans.

Marcellus wanne the city of the Leontines.

with the Leontines, and went with his whole army, and camped hard by Syracusa: and sent his Ambassadors to tell the Syracusans truely, what he had done in the city of the Leontines, and quite contrarie to that they were informed of. Howbeit that prevailed not, for they beleved not Marcellus, bicause Hippocrates being the stronger, had wonne the city. Wherupon he beganne then to approch the walles, and to assault in every quarter, as well by sea as by lande. Appius tooke charge of them that gave assault by lande. Marcellus him selfe, with three score galleyes of five owers at every bancke, well armed, and full of all sortes of artillery and fire works, did assault by sea, and rowed hard to the walle, having made a great engine and devise of battery, uppon eight galleyes chained together, to batter the walle: trusting in the great multitude of his engines of battery, and to all such other necessarie provision as he had for warres, as also in his owne reputacion. But Archimedes made light accompt of all his devises, as in deede they were nothinge comparable to the engines him selfe had invented: and yet were not his owne such, as him selfe did recken of, to shew singularity of worke and devise. For those he had made, were but his recreations of Geometry, and thinges done to passe the time with, at the request of king Hieron: who had prayed him to call to minde a litle, his geometricall speculation, and to apply it to thinges corporall and sencible, and to make the reason of it demonstrative, and plaine, to the understanding of the common people by experiments, and to the benefit and commodity of use. For this inventive arte to frame instruments and engines, (which are called mechanicall, or organicall, so highly commended and esteemed of all sortes of people) were first set forth by Architas, and by Eudoxus: partely to beawtifie a litle the science of Geometry by this finenes, and partly to prove and confirme by materiall examples and sencible instruments, certeine Geometrical conclusions, wherof a man can not finde out the conceiveable demonstrations, by enforced reasons and proofes. As that conclusion which instructeth one to searche out two lynes meane proportionall, which can not be proved by reason demonstrative, and yet notwithstandinge is a principall and

Marcellus besiegeth Syracusa.

Archimedes a notable mathematician.

Architas and Eudoxus, famous Mathematicians.

an accepted grounde, for many thinges which are conteined in the arte of portraiture. Both of them have facioned it to the workemanship of certeine instruments, called Mesolabes or Mesographes, which serve to finde these meane lines proportionall, by drawing certaine curve lines, and overthwart and oblike sextions. But after that, Plato was offended with them, and mainteined against them, that they did utterly corrupt and disgrace, the worthines and excellency of Geometry, making it to discende from things not comprehensible, and without body, unto things sencible and materiall, and to bringe it to a palpable substance, where the vile and base handie worke of man is to be employed: since that time I say, handy craft, or the arte of engines, came to be separated from Geometry, and being long time despised by the Philosophers, it came to be one of the warlike artes. But Archimedes havinge tolde king Hieron, his kinseman and very frende, that it was possible to remove as great a weight as he would, with as litle strength as he listed to put to it: and boasting him selfe thus (as they reporte of him) and trusting to the force of his reasons, wherewith he proved this conclusion, that if there were an other globe of earth, he was able to remove this of ours, and passe it over to the other: kinge Hieron wondering to heare him, required him to put this devise in execution, and to make him see by experience, some great or heavy weight removed, by litle force. So Archimedes caught hold with a hooke of one of the greatest carects, or hulkes of the king (that to draw it to the shore out of the water, required a marvelous number of people to go about it, and was hardly to be done so) and put a great number of men more into her, than her ordinary burden: and he himselfe sittinge alone at his ease farre of, without any straining at all, drawing the ende of an engine with many wheeles and pullyes, fayer and softly with his hande, made it come as gently and smoothly to him, as it had floted in the sea. The king wondering to see the sight, and knowing by proofe the greatnes of his arte: he prayed him to make him some engines, both to assault and defend, in all maner of sieges and assaultes. So Archimedes made him many engines, but kinge Hieron never occupied any of

Why Plato reproved Eudoxus and Architas.

Archimedes with an engine drew one of the greatest hulkes Hieron the king had a shore.

them, bicause he raigned the most parte of his time in peace, without any warres. But this provision and munition of engines, served the Syracusans turne marvelously at that time: and not only the provision of the engines ready made, but also the enginer and worke maister him selfe, that had invented them. Now, the Syracusans seeing them selves assaulted by the Romaines, both by sea and by land, were marvelously perplexed, and could not tel what to say, they were so afrayed: imagining it was impossible for them to withstande so great an army. But when Archimedes fell to handle his engines, and to set them at liberty, there flue in the ayer infinite kindes of shot, and marvelous great stones, with an uncredible noyse and force on the sodaine, apon the footemen that came to assault the city by land, bearing downe, and tearing in peeces all those, which came against them, or in what place soever they lighted, no earthly body beinge able to resist the violence of so heavy a weight: so that all their ranckes were marvelously disordered. And as for the gallies that gave assault by sea, some were soncke with long peeces of timber like unto the yards of shippes, whereto they fasten their sailes, which were sodainly blowen over the walles with force of their engines into their gallies, and so soncke them by their overgreat weight. Other being hoysed up by the prooes with handes of Iron, and hookes made like cranes billes, plonged their poupes into the sea. Other being taken up with certaine engines fastened within, one contrary to an other, made them turne in the ayer like a whirlegigge, and so cast them apon the rockes by the towne walles, and splitted them all to fitters, to the great spoyle and murder of the persons that were within them. And sometimes the shippes and gallies were lift cleane out of the water, that it was a fearfull thing to see them hang and turne in the ayer as they did: untill that casting their men within them over the hatches, some here, some there, by this terrible turning, they came in the end to be empty, and to breake against the walls, or else to fall into the sea againe, when their engines left their hold. Now for Marcellus engine, which he brought against the walles, uppon a bridge made of gallies joyned together: that was called

The wonderful force of Archimedes engines at Marcellus siege of Syracusa.

Marcellus Sambuca.

Sambuca, by reason of the facion it had like to an instrument of musicke of the same name, which is a harpe. The same being yet a good prety way of from the walls, there fell a great stone apon it sent from the walls, weying ten talents. Then, a seconde after that, and a third one after that, the which falling all into this engine with such a thunder and terrible tempest, brake the fundacion of the engine, and tare all the bridge of the gallies joyned together in peeces, that susteined it. So that Marcellus being amazed with all, not knowing well what it ment: was glad to retyre quickely, and sent to make his trompet sound the retreate to those that gave assault by land. Hereupon they sate in counsaille to determine what was to be done, and they resolved, that the next morninge before day they shoulde approche the walles if it were possible: bicause that Archimedes engines, which were very strong and hard wounde up, should by this meanes sende all the force and furie of their stones and shot over their heades, and that neere hande also he coulde do no good with them, for that they had not the scope of their leavel and cariage they should have. But Archimedes had prevented this devise by long preparation before, having made provision of engines for farre and neere, the leavell and cariage whereof was proportioned for all distances: their shot shorte, the arrowes not very long, many holes and arches in the walles one harde by an other, where there were store of crosbowes to kill neere hande, sette in such places, as the enemies coulde not see them without. Wherefore, when the Romaines thought to approche, thinking they had bene safe and close, that no man saw them: it amazed them all when they were receaved againe with infinite shot, and striken to the ground with stones that fell apon their heades like leade (for there was no parte of all the walles, from whence they had not the like shotte). Whereupon they were forced againe to retyre from the walles. And yet when they were further of from them, the arrowes, stones, and other kinde of shotte that flue in every place amonge them, killed a great nomber of them, scattered farre from thence: so that many of them were slaine and sore wounded, and diverse of their shippes splitted, and they not once able to be revenged, nor to hurt their enemies, bicause Archimedes had placed his engines very closely behinde the walles, and not apon the walles in sight of the enemy. So that it appeared the goddes fought against the Romaines, they were so slaine and wounded, and yet they coulde not tell how, nor by whom. Notwithstanding, Marcellus escaped with life, safe from hurt, and mocking his workemaisters and enginers, he had in his campe, he sayd unto them: What, shall we not leave to make warres with this Briarian enginer and Geometrician here? who sitting still apon the wharfe, in sporting manner hath with shame overthrowen our navy, and exceeded all the fabulous hundred handes of the Gyants, discharginge at one instant so many shot among us? For in deede, all the residue of the Syracusans were, as the body and members of Archimedes preparacion: and he him selfe was the only creature that moved and did all, all weapons else being quiet, and his engines only occupied, to assault and defend. At the length, Marcellus seeing his men thus afeard, as if they did but see the ende of a rope, or any peece of timber upon the walle, they ranne away, crying out, that Archimedes was letting loose some of his engines apon them: he would no more approche the walles, nor geve assault, determininge to see if he coulde winne it by longe siege. Notwithstanding, Archimedes had such a great minde, and was so profoundly learned, having hidden in him the onely treasure and secrets of Geometricall inventions: as he would never set forth any booke how to make all these warlicke engynes, which wanne him at that time the fame and glory, not of mans knowledge, but rather of divine wisedom. But he esteminge all kinde of handy craft and invention to make engines, and generally all maner of sciences bringing common commodity by the use of them, to be but vyle, beggerly, and mercenary drosse: employed his witte and study onely to write thinges, the beawty and subtiltie whereof, were not mingled any thinge at all with necessitie. For all that he hath written, are geometricall proposicions, which are without comparison of any other writings whatsoever: bicause the subject whereof they

Marcellus wondred at Archimedes engynes.

Archimedes profowndely learned.

treate, doeth appeare by demonstracion, the matter giving them the grace and the greatnes, and the demonstracion proving it so exquisitely, with wonderfull reason and facilitie, as it is not repugnable. For in all Geometry are not to be founde more profounde and difficulte matters wrytten, in more plaine and simple tearmes, and by more easie principles, then those which he hath invented. Now some do impute this, to the sharpnes of his wit and understanding, which was a naturall gift in him: other do referre it to the extreame paines he tooke, which made these things come so easily from him, that they seemed as if they had bene no trouble to him at all. For no man livinge of him selfe can devise the demonstracion of his propositions, what paine soever he take to seeke it: and yet straight so soone as he commeth to declare and open it, every man then imagineth with him selfe he could have found it out well enough, he can then so plainly make demonstracion of the thing he meaneth to shew. And therfore that me thinks is like enough to be true, which they write of him: that he was so ravished and dronke with the swete intysements of this Sirene, which as it were lay continually with him, as he forgate his meate and drinke, and was careles otherwise of him selfe, that oftentimes his servants got him against his will to the bathes, to washe and annoynt him: and yet being there, he would ever be drawing out of the Geometricall figures, even in the very imbers of the chimney. And while they were annointing of him with oyles and swete savors, with his finger he did draw lines apon his naked body: so farre was he taken from himself, and brought into an extasy or traunse, with the delite he had in the study of Geometry, and truely ravished with the love of the Muses. But amongst many notable things he devised, it appeareth, that he most estemed the demonstracion of the proportion betwene the Cylinder (to wit, the round colomne) and the Sphære or globe conteined in the same: for he prayed his kinsemen and frends, that after his death they would put a Cylinder apon his tombe, conteining a massie Sphære, with an inscription of the proportion, wherof the continent excedeth the thing conteined. So Archimedes being as you have heard,

Archimedes Siren.

Archimedes demonstracion of the Cylinder.

did asmuch as lay in him, both save him selfe and Syracusa from taking. But now againe to Marcellus. Marcellus during the siege at Syracusa, wanne the city of Megares in Sicile, one of the auncientest cities in all the Ilande: and he tooke besides, the campe of Hippocrates, lying by Aciles, where he slue above eight thousand men, surprising them apon the sodaine, even as they were preparing to lodge, and to fortifie their campe. Then he overcame a great parte of the champion contrie of Sicile, and made the cities to rebel that tooke the Carthaginians parte: and in al the battels he fought, he ever overcame them that durst bid him battell. It chaunced afterwards, that he tooke a Lacedæmonian Captaine prisoner, called Danippus: even as he came out of Syracusa by sea. The Syracusans desirous to redeme him, sent to him to pray he might be ransommed. They made many parlees about his raunsome, and drew out this practise to diverse meetings: until Marcellus had taken good markes of a certeine tower, that had no great watch kept upon it, and into the which he might secretly convey a certeine number of men, the walle of the city in that place being no very hard thing to skale. Therefore when he had geven a good gesse by estimacion at the height of that tower, by often approching to it, having parled many a time hard by it: he provided skaling ladders, and tooke the oportunity of a feast which the Syracusans solemnised in the honor of Diana, on which day they gave them selves to al feasting, sporting, and playes. So he tooke not only the tower, but filled all the walls round about with armed men before day, and brake open the maine gate and entry of the citie called Hexapyle. And as the Syracusans began to stirre, perceiving the Romaines on the wals: Marcellus made his men sound their trompets on every side. Whereupon the Syracusans were so afraid and amazed, that they beganne to flie, thinkinge all the city besides had bene taken, where in deede the greatest and strongest quarter of the city called Acradina, was not yet touched: bicause it is walled in rounde about, and separated from the rest of the citie, which is devided into two other partes, the one called the newe citie, and the other fortune. The two partes whereof

Marcellus victories in Sicile.

Danippus a Lacedæmonian Captaine taken prisoner.

Marcellus winneth Syracusa.

Acradina.

beinge wonne, Marcellus by the breake of the daye forced in by the gate or entrie of the Hexapyle. And when his Captaynes tolde him he was happie, to winne so goodly a citie, so easely: they say, that he lookinge about him, and consideringe the greatnesse and statelinesse of the same, he wept for verie pitie, foreseeinge whereto it shoulde come, thinking with him selfe what a sodayne chaunge it shoulde have, when his armie came to spoyle and sacke the same. For there was not a Captaine that durst denie the souldiers when they demaunded the spoyle, and yet were there many that would nedes have it burnt and rased to the ground. But Marcellus would not agree to that in any case, and besides, it was sore against his minde to graunt them the spoyle of the goodes and slaves: straightly commaunding them notwithstanding, not to lay handes of any free man, and not to kill, hurt, nor to make any Syracusan slave. Wherein, though he shewed great favor and mercy, yet it greved him to see so famous a citie, brought to that miserable state: and in the middest of all the joy he had for his victorie, he could not refraine from weeping for pity to see so rich and wealthie a citie, in the turning of a hand, spoyled, and brought to nought. For it is sayd, that the riches and goodes taken away at the sacke of Syracusa, were nothinge inferior to the spoyles of Carthage, which was also sacked not longe after that: for the other parte of the city of Syracusa called Acradina, was soone after also taken by treason, and spoyled against the Captaines willes, savinge the kinges treasure, which was reserved to be caried to the common treasure of Rome. Syracusa beinge taken, nothinge greved Marcellus more, than the losse of Archimedes. Who beinge in his studie when the citie was taken, busily seekinge out by him selfe the demonstracion of some Geometricall proposition which he hadde drawen in figure, and so earnestly occupied therein, as he neither sawe nor hearde any noyse of enemies that ranne uppe and downe the citie, and much lesse knewe it was taken: He wondered when he sawe a souldier by him, that bad him go with him to Marcellus. Notwithstandinge, he spake to the souldier, and bad him tary untill he had done his conclusion, and brought it to

Marcellus gentlenes.

Rich spoyles at Syracusa.

Archimedes mathematician slaine in his study.

demonstracion: but the souldier being angry with his aunswer, drew out his sword, and killed him. Other say, that the Romaine souldier when he came, offered the swords poynt to him, to kill him: and that Archimedes when he saw him, prayed him to hold his hand a litle, that he might not leave the matter he looked for unperfect, without demonstracion. But the souldier makinge no reckening of his speculation, killed him presently. It is reported a third way also, sayinge, that certeine souldiers met him in the streetes going to Marcellus, carying certeine Mathematicall instrumentes in a litle pretie coffer, as dialles for the sunne, Sphæres and Angles, wherewith they measure the greatnesse of the body of the sunne by viewe: and they supposing he hadde caried some golde or silver, or other pretious Iuells in that litle coffer, slue him for it. But it is most true, that Marcellus was marvelous sorie for his death, and ever after hated the villen that slue him, as a cursed and execrable persone: and howe he made also marvelous much afterwards of Archimedes kinsemen for his sake. The Romaines were estemed of at that time by all nations, for marvelous expert souldiers, and taken for verie vallyant and daungerous men to be dealt with: but they never shewed any example of their clemencie and curtesie, and least of all of any civill manner to any straungers, untill Marcellus taught the way, whose actes did shewe the Greecians then, that the Romaines were more gratious and mercifull, then they. For he did so curteouslie intreate those that hadde to do with him, and shewed such favour to private persones, and also to whole citties: that if there were any crueltie shewed in the citties of Enna, or at Megares, or against the Syracusans, it was rather through their owne fault and follie that were hurt, then theirs that didde them the hurte. And for profe hereof, I will recite you one example onely amongest many. There is a citie in Sicile called Engyium, it is no great thinge, but a verie auncient citie of name, by reason of the trafficke thither, for that there are certeine goddesses to be seene, whome they worship, called the mothers. Some say the Cretans were the first builders and founders of the temple there, where you shall see speares and helmets of copper, and

Divers opinions of Archimedes death.

Marcellus clemency.

Engyium a city in Sicile.

MARCELLUS apon them are graven the name of Meriones: and apon others, Ulysses name also, which are consecrated to these goddesses. This citie stoode altogether at the devotion of the Carthaginians: and Nicias beinge the chiefest man of the same, was all he might against it, and perswaded them openlie in all their counsailles to take parte with the Romaines, provinge it by many reasons, that his enemies counsaylinge the contrarie, were unprofitable members of the common wealth. Whereuppon Nicias enemies fearinge his greatnesse and authoritie, they did conspyre amonge them selves to apprehende him, and to deliver him to the Carthaginians. But Nicias hearinge of suche a matter, and findinge that they laye in wayte to take him: used this pollicie to prevent their treason. He gave out openlie very ill speeches against the goddesses, and did many things in derogation of their honor: and sayd the sight of them (which was a matter of great credit) was but devise, and that there was no credit to be geven to them. These words tickled his enemies, imagining that the common people would lay the mischiefe they pretended against him, to him selfe, as the only causer of his owne hurt. So they havinge appointed a day to apprehende him, by chaunce a common counsaill was kept that day they hadde determined of: where Nicias speaking to the people about matter of counsaill, in the middest of his oration fell to the grounde, to the great wonder of the whole assembly, as every man may conjecture. Howbeit never a man sturred, and a prety while after he beganne to lift uppe his head a litle, and to looke gastely about him, with a faint trembling voyce, which he still gathered higher and lowder by litle and litle, untill he sawe all the people wonderously afrayed and amazed, that not one of them durst speake. Then throwing his gowne from him, and renting his coate, he got upon his feete halfe naked, and ranne towardes the gate of the Theater, cryinge out that the goddesses mothers did torment him: and not a man durst once come neere him, nor offer to stoppe him, they were so supersticious and foolishly afrayed of the goddesses, imagining it was some divine punishment. But by this meanes he easily got to the gates of the city, and fled from

Nicias craft.

them all: and he was never seene after that time, to do, or speake, like a madde man in any thing. His wife that was made privy to his devise, and furthered his intent, went first and fell downe on her knees before the goddesses mothers in their temple, as she had hartily prayed unto them: and faining afterwards she would go seeke her husbande, that ranne up and downe the fieldes like a madde man, she went out of the city with her litle children, and no body troubled her. Thus did they escape without daunger, and went unto Marcellus to Syracusa. The Engienians afterwards played such insolent partes, that Marcellus in the ende went thither, and caused them all to be taken and bounde, as though he woulde have put them to execution. But Nicias came to him with the teares in his eyes, and embracing his knees, and kissinge his handes, besought him to take pitie of his poore citizens, beginning first with those that were his greatest enemies. This good nature of Nicias so pacified Marcellus wrath, that he pardoned them all, and did no hurt to the city, and gave Nicias certeine land, besides many other rich giftes he bestowed apon him. Thus it is reported in the history of Posidonius the Philosopher. Now Marcellus being sent for home by the Romanes, bicause they had warres in their owne contrie, and even at Rome gates: he departed out of Sicile, returning towardes Rome, and caried the goodliest tables, pictures, and statues, and other such ornamentes as were in Syracusa, meaning first to beautifie his triumphe with them, and to leave them afterwardes for an ornament to Rome, which before that time never knewe what such curious workes ment. For, this finenes, and curious tables and imagery, never came into Rome before, but was throughly set out with armor and weapons of barbarous people, and with bloody spoyles, and was also crowned with monumentes of victories and triumphes of diverse enemies, which were no pleasaunt, but rather fearefull sightes to looke apon, farre unfitte for feminine eyes. But even as Epaminondas did call the plaine of Bœotia, Mars scaffolde, where he kept his games: and Xenophon also called the city of Ephesus, the armorers shoppe: even so me thinkes (as Pindarus said) they might rightly have tearmed Rome,

Marcellus the first that brought in finenes and curious tables and pictures into Rome, of the spoyles of Syracusa.

the temple of Mars fighting. And this wanne the peoples good willes much more to Marcellus, bicause he did so passingly set foorth Rome, with such excellent fine toyes of Greece. But Fabius Maximus on the other side, was better beloved of the old men: bicause he brought no such toyes with him from the city of Tarentum, when he wanne it. In deede he brought away golde and ready coyne, and much other goodes that were profitable: but for images and tables, he left them standing in their places, speaking a thing of great note. Let us leave the Tarentines their goddes offended with them. And furthermore the noble men were angry with Marcellus, saying, that by this act he had purchased Rome great malice and hate. First, bicause he did not onely leade men prisoners in his triumphe, but the gods also: and secondly, bicause he had filled the people full of pritle pratle, and idle curiosity, spending all the whole day in gasinge, and wondering at the excellency of the workemen, and of their workes, where before they woulde fall to their labor, or else they went to the warres, not being acquainted with curiosity, nor idle life as Euripides sayd, speaking of Hercules:

In wicked practises, he simple was to see,
but he excelld in vertuous dedes, and feates that worthy be.

Notwithstandinge, Marcellus did glory amongest the Greecians them selves, sayinge: that he had taught the Romaines to esteeme the wonderfull workes of Greece, which they knewe not before. But at his returne out of Sicile, his enemies procured, that his honor of triumphe was denied him. So Marcellus knowing that he had yet left somewhat to do in Sicile, and that the warre was not altogether ended, and fearing besides least a third triumphe would make him to much envied: he was contented with good will to have the honor of the great triumphe, in the mountaine of Alba only: and of the litle triumphe, in the city of Rome. This maner of litle triumphe is called in Greeke, *Evan*, and the Romaines call it *Ovatio*. And this difference there is betwene them: that in the *Ovation* triumphe, the party to whom it is graunted, doth not enter into the city

Marcellus entreth into Rome with Ovation triumphe.

apon triumphing charet drawen with foure horses, nor doth cary any lawrell apon his head in token of triumphe, nor hath any trompettes or hornes blowen before him, but doth marche a foote with a payer of slippers on his fete, having flutes and howboyes playing before him, and wearing a garlande of fyrre tree apon his heade : so as this maner of entry is nothing warlike, and is rather a pleasaunt then fearefull sight. And that reason doth flatly drawe me to beleve, that these two kindes of entries they graunted to the Captaines, returning from the warres with victorie: were devided in the olde time, rather for the maner, then for the greatnes of the doings. For such as had overcomen their enemies by great slaughter and bloody battells, they did make their entry with pompe of triumphe, that was altogether marshall and terrible, followed with their souldiers armed, and crowned with lawrell garlandes, as their custome was in musteringe their campe in the warres. But they on the contrary side, that without any exployte of armes returned home with victorie, either by peaceable meanes, or by force of their eloquence: the law graunted them the honor of Ovation triumphe,which was quiet, and full of all joy and mirth. For the flute is an instrument of pleasure belonginge to peace, and the fyrre tree is a tree consecrated to Venus, which goddesse, above all goddes and goddesses doth most detest warres. This second kinde of entry was called *Ovatio*, not as many Greecians have taken it, comming of this word *Evan*, which is a voyce and song of joy, although they did use also to accompanie the Captaines making their entry in this sorte, crying and singing *Evan*: but there were certeine Greecians that would have fetched the derivation of this word, from an old common custome they had: and were of opinion besides, that parte of this honor did apperteine to god Bacchus, whose surname we cal Evius, and somtimes Thriambus. Howbeit this is not the true derivation of the name, but after this sorte. At the great triumphe and entry made, the Captaine or generall that triumpheth as a conqueror, did offer and sacrifice (by the old orders and ancient customes of Rome) one, or divers oxen: where at the seconde triumphe called the Ovation, he onely sacrificed

What the Ovation triumphe is.

Ovation whereof it is called.

The sacrifice of the quiet triumphe.

MARCELLUS

The sacrifices of the litle triumphe Ovation.

The difference betwixt the Spartans and Romaines in their sacrifices for victorie.

The Syracusans accuse Marcellus.

a mutton, which the Romaines call in their tongue *Ovem*, and thereof was it called Ovation. And here by the way is to be noted, the difference betwixt the lawe maker of the Romaine lawes and customes, and the law maker of the Lacedæmonians: how both of them were contrary to the other, in appointinge their sacrifices for victorie. For at Sparta, the Captaine or generall that had done his feate by policy or frendshippe, the sacrifice he did offer uppe to the goddes, was an oxe: and he that by force, and bloody battell had obtained victory, only offred up a cocke for sacrifice. For though they were very good souldiers, yet they thought better of his service, that by his wisedom and wise perswasions obteined victory: then of his, that wanne it by valliantnes, and force of armes. Thus may you see which of these two lawemakers hadde best reason in his ordinaunces. But nowe to Marcellus againe. He beinge chosen Consull the fourth time, his enemies and evill willers did stirre uppe the Syracusans against him, and perswaded them to complayne to the Senate of him, that he had cruelly, and uncurteously used them, contrary to the auncient league and allyances made long time before with the Romaines. Marcellus beinge sacrificinge one day in the Capitoll, while the Senate were sette in counsaill: the Syracusans deputies came before them, and kneeling downe, besought them to give them audience, and that they would do them justice. The other Consull that was present rebuked them, being angry they had so maliciously spyed the occasion of Marcellus absence. But when Marcellus hearde of it, he straight left of all, and came to the Senate, and first satte him downe in his Consulls chayer, where he gave audience as Consull, and dispatched diverse causes: when he had done so, he rose out of his chayer, and came downe among them, standinge as a private persone to aunswere at the barre, as other offenders and men accused, suffering the Syracusans to alleadge and say against him what they would. Then were the Syracusans blancke, when they saw the majesty of Marcellus, and his stayed countenance in all thinges: so that having founde him before a very valliant man in warres and unconquerable, they found him then a man no lesse dreadful in his Consuls robe: that they hong downe their eyes, and durst not looke him in the face. Notwithstanding, they being suborned by his enemies, beganne at the length boldely to accuse him, and yet with sorow and lamentacion, the effect whereof was this. That they beinge the Romaines frendes and confederates, had abidden such injuries at Marcellus handes, as all other generalles never offred their very enemies. Whereto Marcellus straight aunswered againe to the contrary. That for many injuries the Romaines had received of them, they suffred nothing but that, which was unpossible they should not suffer, that resisted untill they were taken by force: and yet they might thanke them selves for any thing they suffered, bicause they would not obey nor consent, to reasonable capitulacions and articles of peace, which he had oftentimes offered them. And againe, they could not alleage for their excuse, that the tyrans had compelled them to make warres: when they to the contrary, bicause they would enter into warres, were contented to be subject to a tyran. So, when both parties hadde spoken their mindes, the Syracusans (as the maner is) went out of the Senate house, and Marcellus also, leavinge his fellowe Consull in his place in the Senate, and taried without the dore, attending the sentence of the Senate, never altering his countenaunce nor wonted looke, neither for feare of sentence, nor for malice or anger against the Syracusans, quietly looking for his judgement. Afterwards when the Senators voyces were gathered together, and that Marcellus was cleared by the most voyces: then the Syracusans fell downe at his feete weeping, and besought him not to wreake his anger apon them that were present, and moreover that he would have compassion of the residue of the citizens, who did acknowledge his great grace and favor extended to them, and confessed them selves bound to him for ever. Marcellus moved with pity by their intreaty, he pardoned them, and ever after did all the Syracusans what pleasure he coulde possible. For through his intreaty and request, the Senate did confirme and ratifie his graunt unto them, which was: that they might use the liberty and benefit of their owne lawes, and quietly enjoy their goodes also which were left them. To requite this special grace

Marcellus being Consull, aunswered the Syracusans accusations as a private man.

Marcellus constancy.

Marcellus curtesie to the Syracusans.

MARCEL-
LUS

procured them by Marcellus, the Syracusans gave him many honors, and among others they made a law, that ever after, as oft as any of Marcellus name or house came into Sicile, the Syracusans should kepe a solemne feast, with garlands on their heades, and should also sacrifice unto the goddes. After this, Marcellus went against Hanniball. And where all the other Consuls almost, and generalles, after the overthrow at Cannes, had used this only policie with him, not to come to battell: he tooke a contrarie course to them all, thinkinge that tract of time, (whereby they thought to eate out Hannibals force) was rather a direct consuming and destroying of all Italie: and that Fabius Maximus standinge to much upon safety, tooke not the way to cure the disease and weakenes of the common weale of Rome, looking to ende this warre, consuming by litle and litle the strength and power of Rome, committing a fearefull phisitions fault and error, being afraid to heale their pacient sodainly, imagining that to bring them low, doth lessen the disease. So, first of all he went to besiege certeine great cities of the Samnites, which were revolted from obedience of the Romaines: and those he wanne againe with a great provision of corne and money he founde in them, besides three thousande souldiers Hanniball left in garrison there, whome he tooke prisoners. Hanniball after that, havinge slaine the viceconsul Cneus Fulvius in Apulia, with eleven *Tribunis militum* (to wit, Colonels, every one havinge charge of a thousande footemen) and overthrowen the greatest parte of his armie: Marcellus wrote letters to Rome, hoping to comforte the Senate and people, telling he would go thither, and did warrant them he woulde drive Hanniball out of Apulia. When the Romaines had red his letters, they were nothing the more comforted, but rather (as Livie writeth) more afraid and discouraged: bicause they doubted the daunger to come woulde be greater, then the losse past, takinge Marcellus to be a farre greater and better generall, then ever was Fulvius. Neverthelesse, Marcellus performing the contentes of his letters wrytten to Rome, drave Hanniball out of Apulia, and made him retyre into Lucania. And Marcellus finding him in that contry, by a city called Numistron, lodged

Marcellus actes against Hanniball in his fourth Consullship.

Cneus Fulvius viceconsull slaine in Apulia by Hanniball.

apon hilles, and in places of strength and advantage: he camped hard by him in the valley, and the next morninge he was the first that presented his enemy battell. Hanniball on the other side, came downe into the valley, and they joyned battell: which was so cruelly fought, and so long time, as it coulde not be discerned who had the better. For the battell being begonne at nine of the clocke in the morning, it was darke night ere they gave over. The next morning by pepe of day, Marcellus set his men againe in battell raye, in the middest of all the dead bodies that lay slaine in the fielde, and chalenged Hanniball, to prove who should have the field. But Hanniball refused, and marched his way thence: so as Marcellus thereby had good leasure left him to strippe his slaine enemies, and also to bury his owne souldiers. When he had finished that, he presently followed his enemie by the foote, who layed many ambushes for him, but he coulde never trappe him in any: and in every encounter or skirmishe they had together, Marcellus hadde ever the better, which wanne him great fame and credit. Nowe time beinge commen about to choose newe Consulls, the Senate thought good to sende rather for the other Consul that was in Sicile, then to remove Marcellus thence, who had fought with Hanniball. So when the other Consull was come to Rome, the Senate commaunded him to name Quintus Fulvius Dictator, bicause the Dictator was neither chosen by the people, nor by the Senate: but one of the Consuls or Prætors, in open assembly of the people, nameth such a one Dictator, as he liketh of. Wherefore it seemeth, that this word Dictator, came apon that word naming: for, *Dicere* in the Romaine tongue, signifieth to name. Howbeit other holde opinion, that he was called Dictator, bicause he commaundeth of him selfe what he will, without the counsell of the Senate, and the voyces of the people: and this seemeth to be true, bicause the commaundements of the Senate of Rome are called *Edicta*, which we Greecians call *Diatagmata*. Now the other Consull and companion of Marcellus being come out of Sicile, he would nedes name an other Dictator, then him whom the Senate offred him: and bicause he would not be compelled to do

Marcellus fought a battell with Hanniball at Numistron in Apulia.

The Dictator chosen by the Consull or Prætor, not by the people nor Senate.

Whereof Dictator commeth.

Quintus Fulvius chosen Dictator, by the people.

Marcellus Proconsull.

Hannibals oration to his souldiers.

Marcellus stratageame.

Marcellus overcome in battell by Hanniball.

that he was unwilling to do, he stale away one night, and returned againe into Sicile. Hereupon the people did name and appoint Quintus Fulvius Dictator, and the Senate wrote their letters to Marcellus, to confirme him: which Marcellus did, and authorised the peoples election. So he him selfe was chosen againe Proconsul, for the next yeare following: in the which he having conferred with Fabius Maximus about the warres, they were agreed, that Fabius should prove if he could winne the city of Tarentum againe: and that Marcellus in the meane time shoulde keepe Hannibal occupied, that he might not come to aide it. This resolution being taken betwene them, Marcellus went to meete Hannibal by the city of Cannusium: who as he still chaunged and shifted lodginge, bicause he woulde not come to the battell against his will, found Marcellus ever in his eye before him. Insomuch as Hannibal removinge thus his campe, Marcellus plyed him so one day with continuall alaroms and skirmishes, that he brought him to a battell that held all day long till night, and compelled them both to leave of til the next morning: where Marcellus shewed againe in field by breake of the day, in battell ray. Whereat Hannibal being in a marvelous rage, he called his souldiers together, and made an oration to them, earnestly movinge them once againe to fight with Marcellus, if ever they had heretofore fought for his sake. You see, sayd he, that having fought so many battells, and gotten such victories as we have done, we can not yet take breath as we would, nor be in quiet, how much soever we winne, if we drive not away yonder fellow Marcellus. When Hannibal had ended his oration to the Carthaginians, he led them on to the battell: where Marcellus, to no purpose, and out of time, would nedes shew Hanniball a stratageame of warre, that turned him selfe to the worst. For Marcellus perceiving the right wing of his army distressed, made one of his legyons that was set in ray in the rereward of his hoste, to marche to the fronte of his battell, to helpe those that needed ayde. But this removing of the legyon, troubled them that fought, and gave the enemies the victorie: who slue that day two thousand seven hundred of the Romaines. So, when Marcellus was come againe into his campe, he straight called his souldiers before him, to whome he spake in this maner: that he saw a great deale of armor, and bodies of men, but he coulde see no Romaines. The Romaines hearing him say so, besought him to pardon the fault they had committed. Marcellus aunswered, he woulde never pardon them, so long as they were overcome: but when they overcame againe, he was content to remit all. So the next morning he agreed to bringe them againe to fight with the enemy, that such as were at Rome should rather heare newes of their victorie, then of their running away. When he had sayed, he appointed they shoulde geve those bandes that first turned their backes to Hanniball, barley for wheate. So, as there were many of them in great daunger of their lives, for the sore woundes they hadde geven them in the battell: yet was there not a man of them, but Marcellus words did more greve them, then the grevous woundes they had. The next morning betimes was set out of the generalles tent, the coate armor died in skarlet, which is the ordinary signe of battell: and the bandes that had received dishonor the day before, were placed at their owne request in the fronte of the battell. The other Captaines besides, that were not overthrowen: did leade their bandes also to the fielde, and did set them in battell raye. Hanniball hearing of that, cried out: O gods, what a man is this, that can not be quiet, neither with good nor ill fortune? for he is the only odde man, that never giveth rest to his enemy, when he hath overcommed him: nor taketh any for him selfe, when he is overcome. We shal never have done with him, for any thing that I see: sith shame, whether he winne or loose, doth still provoke him to be bolder and vallianter. After orations made of bothe sides, bothe armies marched forwardes to joyne battell. The Romaines being as strong as the Carthaginians, Hanniball put his Elephants in the voward and fronte of his battell, and commaunded his men to drive them apon the Romaines: and so they did. Which in deede did somewhat trouble and disorder the firstranckes of the Romaines: untill such time as Flavius, Tribune of the souldiers, tooke an ensigne in his hande, and marched before the beastes, and

Marcellus hard wordes unto his souldiers.

Hannibals wordes of Marcellus.

Battell betwixt Hanniball and Marcellus.

The worthy act of Flavius, *Tribunus militum.*

gave the first of them such a thrust with the poynt of his ensigne, that he made her turne backe. The first beast being turned backe thus, ranne apon the seconde that followed her, and the second made the third go backe also, and so from one to an other, untill they all turned. Marcellus perceiving that, commaunded his horsemen to set apon the enemies with all the fury they coulde, in that place where he sawe them, somewhat troubled with these beastes, that turned backe againe upon them: and that they should drive them further in amongest them. Which they did, and gave so hotte a charge apon the Carthaginians, that they made them turne their backes, and runne away, and they pursued them still, killing them downe right, even to their campe side: where was the greatest slaughter of all, by reason their Elephants that were wounded, fell downe starke deade within the gate of their campe. And they saye of the Carthaginians there were slaine at this battell, above eight thowsande, and of the Romaines, onely three thowsande: howbeit all the rest of them for the most parte were very sore hurt. Which fell out very well for Hanniball, that he might march away at his pleasure, as he did that night, and got him away farre of from Marcellus, as knowing he was not in state to follow him oversodainely, bicause of his great number of hurt men in his campe: and so by small jorneys he went into Campania, where he lay in garrison all the sommer, in the city of Sinuesse, to heale the woundes of his sore mangled souldiers. Hanniball having now gotten him selfe at the length out of Marcellus hands, and having his army free to serve him as he thought good: he burned and destroyed all Italie where he went and stoode no more in feare of any thing. This made Marcellus ill spoken of at Rome, and caused his enemies to take holde of such a matter against him: for they straight raised Publius Bibulus Tribune, to accuse him, who was a hotte harebrained man, but very eloquent, and coulde deliver his minde very well. So this Bibulus called the people oft to counsaill, and tolde them there, that they must nedes call home Marcellus, and appoint some other to take charge of the army: for as for him, sayd he, bicause he hath fought a litle with Hanniball (and as a man might say, wrestled a litle

Marcellus victory of Hanniball.

Hanniball lay in garrison in the city of Sinuesse in Campania.

P. Bibulus Tribune of the people accuseth Marcellus.

with him) he is now gotten to the bathes to solace him selfe. But Marcellus hearing this, left his Lieutenantes in the campe, and went him selfe to Rome, to aunswer to the untrue accusations layd against him, and there he perceived at his comming, how they intended to prosecute the matter against him apon these informations. So a day of hearinge was appointed for his matter, and the parties came before the people assembled in counsaill, in the great listes or show place, called Circus Flaminius, to give judgement. There Publius Bibulus the Tribune, sitting in his chayer, layd open his accusation with great circumstance: and Marcellus, when Bibulus had tolde his tale, aunswered him in few wordes, and very discretely, only touchinge his purgation. But the noble and chiefest men of the citie, rose uppe, and spake on Marcellus behalfe, telling the people plainely, that they did Marcellus wrong, to recken worse of his valliantnes, then their enemy did: and to judge of him as a coward, considering Hanniball only fled from him, of all other Captaines, and would by no meanes fight with him, never refusinge to fight with any other whatsoever. These perswasions tooke such effect, as where Marcellus accuser looked for his condemnation: Marcellus to the contrary, was not only cleared of his accusation, but furthermore they chose him Consull againe the fift time. So beinge entred into his office, he went first into Thuscan: where visiting the good cities one after an other, and quietinge them, he pacified a great sedition in the contry, when they were all ready to rise and rebell. Afterwards at his returne, he thought to consecrate the temple of honor and vertue, which he had built with the spoyles he gotte in the warres of Sicile. But the Priestes were against it, saying, two goddes might not be in one church. Thereupon he built an other temple, and joyned it to the first, being very angry the Priestes denied so his consecration: and he did take it for an evill token, besides diverse other signes in the element that afterwards appeared, and troubled him much. For there were many temples set a fire with lightening at one time: and the rattes and mise did knawe the golde, that was in the chappell of Iupiter Capitoline. And it is reported also, that an oxe did speake: and a childe came out of the

Circus Flaminius.

Marcellus chosen Consul the fift time.

The temples of honor and vertue built by Marcellus.

Wonderfull signes were seene in Rome unfortunate to Marcellus.

heade of an Elephant, and that the child was alive. Furthermore, the Priestes and Soothsayers sacrificing to the goddes, to withdraw this evill from them these sinister tokens did threaten: they could never finde any favorable signes in their sacrifices. Whereuppon they sought to keepe Marcellus still at Rome, who had a marvelous earnest desire to be gone with speede to the warres: for never man longed for any thing so much, as Marcellus did, to fight with Hanniball. Insomuch he never dreamed other thing in the night, nor spake of any matter els in the day to his frendes and companions, nor prayed to the goddes for any other thinge, but that he might fight with Hanniball in the fielde: and I thincke he woulde willingliest have fought a private combat with him, in some walled city or inclosed lystes for the combat. And had it not bene that he had already wonne him selfe great fame, and shewed him selfe to the worlde, (by sundry great proofes and experience of his doings) a grave, skilfull, and a valliant Captaine as any man of his time: I would have said it had bene a pange of youth, and a more ambitious desire, then became a man of his age, who was three score yere old at that time, when they made him Consull againe the fift time. Nevertheles, after he had ended all his propitiatory sacrifices and purifications, such as the Soothsayers had appointed: he departed from Rome with his fellow Consul Quintus Crispinus to the warres. He found Hanniball lying betwene the cities of Bancia, and Venousa, and sought all the meanes he could to procure him to fight, but he could never get him to it. Howbeit Hanniball being advertised by spyalles, that the Consulls sent an army to besiege the city of the Locrians, surnamed Epizephyrians: (as ye would say, the occidentals, bicause the Greecians, in respect of the Italians, are called the orientals:) he layd an ambush for them that went, under the hill of Petelium, which was directly in their way, where he slew about two thowsand five hundred Romaines. That overthrow did sette Marcellus on fire, and made him more desirous of battell: whereupon he removed his campe from the place he lay in, and marched nearer to his enemy. Betwene their two campes, there was a prety litle hill, strong of scituacion, a wilde thing overgrowen with wod, and there

Marcellus three score yeare olde beinge chosen Consull the fift time.

Q. Crispinus Consull.

Hanniball lay betwixt the cities of Bancia and Venousa.

Mons Petelium.

were high hillocks. From whence they might discerne a great way, both the one and the others campe, and at the foote of the same ranne prety springs: Insomuch as the Romaines wondered, that Hannibal comminge thither first, did not take that place, but had left it to his enemies. Howbeit Hannibal was crafty enough, leaving it of purpose: for as it was commodious to lodge his campe in, so it served his turne better for an ambush. So he filled the wodde, the hollow places, and the valleys there about, with store of shot and spearemen, assuringe him selfe that the place woulde intyse the Romaines thither: and in deede he gessed rightly, for so fell it out. Straight, there flew a rumor abroade in the Romaines campe, that there was a passing place to lodge in, and every man tooke apon him like a skilfull souldier, to tell what vantage they should have apon their enemies, by taking that place, and specially if they did lodge there, or otherwise built a fort upon it. Whereupon Marcellus determined to goe see the place him selfe, taking a few horsemen with him. Notwithstanding, before he would take horse, he called for his Soothsayer to sacrifice to the goddes. The first beast that was sacrificed, the Soothsayer shewed Marcellus the liver of it without a head. The second beast sacrificed, had a fayer great head of a liver, and all the other partes were also sounde, and very newe: that by them it appeared al the feare of the first ill signes and tokens were taken away. Yet the Soothsayers on the other side sayd, it did make them worse afraid then before: for these so favorable and lucky tokens of the sacrifice, followinge immediatly after the first fowle and nawghty signes, made them doubt them much by reason of so straunge and sodaine an alteracion. But as the Poet Pindarus sayth,

An ambush layd by Hanniball.

Ill signes to Marcellus.

> Nor force of burning fire, nor wall of steele nor stone,
> nor whatsoever other thing, is here this earth upon:
> Can kepe abacke the course of fatall desteny,
> nor yet resist the due decrees, which come from heaven on high.

So Marcellus tooke his horse, with Quintus Crispinus his fellow Consull, and his sonne one of the Tribunes of the souldiers, having onely two hundred and twenty horsemen with him, of the which there was not one Romaine among them,

Quintus Crispinus fellowe Consull with Marcellus.

but all were Thuscans, saving forty Fregellanians, who from the beginning of these warres had alwayes shewed them selves very faithfull and loving to Marcellus. The hill we spake of before, being thicke covered with wodde and bushes, the enemies hadde set a skowte to watche on the toppe of it, to geve warning if they saw any comming towardes it. The Romaines coulde not see him, and he on the other side might see even into their campe, and perceive what was done, as he did advertise those at that time that lay in ambushe for Marcellus comminge: and they suffered him to passe on, untill he came directly against them. Then they shewed upon the sodaine, and compassing in Marcellus, they both shot and strake at him, some following them that fled, and other fighting with the forty Fregellanians which only stucke to it: who came roundly in together (notwithstanding the Thuscans were fled) apon the first crie they heard, to defend the two Consulls, untill such time as the Consull Crispinus havinge two woundes on his body with a dart, did turne his horse to flie. And with that, one of the enemies gave Marcellus such a sore blowe with a speare havinge a broade iron head, that he ranne him quite through. The Fregellanians that were left alive, beinge but a few in number, seeinge Marcellus slaine, left him lyinge on the grounde, and tooke his sonne away with them that was very sore hurt, and by the swiftnes of their horses recovered their campe, and saved them selves. At this overthrowe, there were not slayne above fortie men, and five and twentie taken prisonners, of which, five of them were the Consulls sergeauntes, and their officers that caried axes before them, and the other were all horsemen. Within few dayes after, the other Consull Crispinus died also of his hurtes, which was such a misfortune, as never came before to the Romaines, that both their Consulls were slaine at one battell. Now Hanniball made no great reckeninge of all that were slaine, or taken at this fielde: but when he heard that Marcellus selfe was slaine at this overthrow, he went him selfe straight to the place to see him. So when he had viewed his body a great while, standing hard by it, and considering his strength, his stature, and countenance, having taken full view of all the partes of

Marcellus slaine in an ambush at the hill of Petelie.

The Consull Crispinus slaine.

him, he spake no proude word against him, nor shewed any glad countenance, as some other would have done, that had slaine so valliant and daungerous an enemy: but wondering how he came to be slaine so straungely there, he tooke of his ring from one of his fingers that sealed his letters, and geving his body buriall according to his estate, made it to be honorably burnt, and then put all his bones and ashes into a silver potte, on which he him selfe put a crowne of golde, and sent it unto Marcellus sonne. It fortuned so, that certaine light horsemen of the Numidians mette with them that caried this silver pot, and would have taken it from them by force: but they stood to it, and woulde not parte withall, and so fightinge and striving together for it, the bones and ashes were scattered all about. Hanniball hearinge this, sayed to them that were about him: See, howe nothinge can be, which the goddes will not. So he punished the Numidians, and cared no more to gette Marcellus bones together, but perswaded him selfe it was the will of the goddes he shoulde dye so straungely, and that his body shoulde have no buriall. Cornelius Nepos and Valerius Maximus wryte it thus: but Livie, and Augustus Cæsar say, that the pot was caried unto his sonne, and honorably buried.

Marcellus funerall honored by Hanniball.

Marcellus did consecrate many monumentes in diverse places, besides those at Rome. As at Catana in Sicile: a place for young men to exercise them selves in. In the Ile of Samothracia, in the temples of the gods called Cabires: many images and tables he brought from Syracusa. And in the Ile of Lindos, in the temple of Minerva, where among other, there is a statue of his, and this epigramme graven under it, as Posidonius the Philosopher wryteth.

Marcellus monuments.

O thou my frend (I say) which passest forth by me,
  of Claudius Marcellus here, the image mayest thou see:
  whose family at Rome, was of the noblest name.
Seven times he Consull chosen was, in which he overcame,
  great numbers infinite, (in open fielde and fight)
  of such as sought his contries spoyle, and put them all to flight.

The author of this epigramme reckeneth, the two times of his being viceconsull, for two whole Consullshippes: but his posteritie continued alwayes in great honor, unto Marcellus,

Marcellus posterity.

MARCELLUS

the sonne of Octavia, (Augustus Cæsars sister) and of Caius Marcellus. He dyed a young man, being Ædilis of Rome, and maried unto Iulia, Augustus daughter, with whom he lived no long time. But to honor the memory of him, Octavia his mother built the library, and Augustus Cæsar the Theater, which are called to this day, Marcellus Theater and library.

THE COMPARISON OF MARCELLUS WITH PELOPIDAS

Pelopidas and Marcellus actes in wars.

THESE are the greatest thinges and best worthy of memory (in my opinion) of all Pelopidas and Marcellus doinges: and for their maners and naturall condicions otherwise, they were all one, bicause they were both valliant, painefull, and noble minded: saving that this difference onely was betwene them. That Marcellus in many cities he tooke by assault, did cruelly murder them, and spilt much bloode: where Epaminondas and Pelopidas contrarily did never put any to the sword they overcame, neither did they take away the libertie from any citie they tooke: and it is thought the Thebans woulde not have handeled the Orchomenians so cruelly as they did, if one, or both of them had bene present. Nowe for their actes, it was a noble and wonderfull peece of service that Marcellus did, with so small a company of horsemen as he tooke with him, to overthrow so great a number of horsemen and footemen both, of the Gaules: a thinge that never Generall but him selfe did, and specially that slewe with his owne handes in the fielde, the Generall of his enemies. Which Pelopidas could never attaine unto: for he seeking to kill Alexander the tyran of Pheres, was slaine first him selfe, and suffered that, which he desired to have done to an other. And yet for that service may be objected, the battells of Leuctres, and of Tegyra,

Marcellus actes preferred before Pelopidas.

which were both famous and notable. But to encounter with those, there was no notable ambushe or secrete practise done by Marcellus, that was any thing like comparable to that Pelopidas did at his returne from exile, when he slew the tyrans that kept Thebes in bondage. For that was as notable a policy and sodaine an enterprise stolen apon, as none was ever greater, or more famous. It is true Marcellus was yoked with Hanniball, who was a dreadfull and a violent enemy: so were the Thebans also at that very time with the Lacedæmonians, who notwithstanding were overcome of Pelopidas, at the battells of Tegyra, and of Leuctres. Wheras Marcellus did never so much as once overcome Hanniball, as Polybius wryteth, but remained unconquered alwayes, untill that Scipio overcame him in battell. Notwithstandinge, we do geve best credit to the reportes of Cæsar, Livie, Cornelius Nepos, and of king Iuba among the Greecians: who wryte, that Marcellus otherwhile did overthrow certaine of Hanniballs companies, howebeit they were never no great overthrowes to speake of, and it seemeth rather, it was through some mockerie or deceite of that African, then otherwise. Yet sure it was a great matter, and worthy much commendacion, that the Romaines were brought to that corage, as they durst abide to fight with the Carthaginians, having lost so many great overthrowes, and having so many generalls of their armies slaine in battell, and having the whole Empire of Rome in so great daunger of utter destruction. For it was Marcellus only of all other generalls, that put the Romaines in hart againe, after so great and longe a feare thorowly rooted in them: and incoraged the souldiers also to longe to fight with their enemy, and not onely to hope, but to assure them selves of victory. For, where by reason of their continuall losses and fearefull overthrowes they hadde, they thought them selves happy men to escape Hannibals handes by runninge away: he taught them to be ashamed to flie like cowardes, to confesse they were in distresse, to retyre, and leave the fielde, before they had overcome their enemies. And where Pelopidas was never overcome in battell beinge generall, and Marcellus did overcome more then any generall in his time: it might seeme

The maner of Marcellus and Pelopidas deedes.

Marcellus made the Romaines coragious.

therefore that the great number of the victories of the one, should compare with the good happe of the other that was never overcome. It is true that Marcellus tooke the city of Syracusa, and Pelopidas failed of taking the city of Sparta: but yet do I thinke, that it was more valliantly done of Pelopidas, to come so neere Sparta as he did, and that he was the first that passed the river of Eurotas with an army, which never enemy did before him, than it was of Marcellus to winne all Sicile. Unles some paradventure will say againe, this was Epaminondas, not Pelopidas acte, as also in the victorie of Leuctres: where no man living can pretend any parte of glory to the doinges of Marcellus. For he tooke Syracusa, being onely generall alone, and did overthrow the Gaules without his fellow Consull, and fought with Hanniball, without any mans helpe or incoragement: (for all other were against it, and perswaded the contrary) and he was the first that altered the maner of warres the Romaines used then, and that trained his souldiers, that they durst fight with the enemy. For their death, I neither commend the one nor the other, and the straungenesse of either of their deathes doth greve me marvelously: as I do greatly wonder also, how Hanniball in so many battells as he fought (which are innumerable) could alwayes scape unhurt. I can not but greatly commende also the valliantnes of one Chrysantas, whom Xenophon speaketh of in his booke of the institucion of Cyrus, saying: that he having lift up his sword in his hand ready to kill one of his enemies, and hearing the trompet sound the retreate, he softly retyred, and would not strike him. Howbeit it seemeth Pelopidas is more to be excused: for beside that he was very hot and desirous of battel, yet his anger was honorable and just, and moved him to seeke revenge. For as the Poet Euripides sayth:

Rashnes in a Captaine deserveth blame.

The valliantnes and obedience of Chrysantas a souldier.

The best that may betyde, is when a captaine lives,
and doth survive the victories, which he with force achieves.
But if he needes must fall, then let him valliantly
even thrust amid the thickest throng, and there with honor dye.

For so becometh his death famous, and not dishonorable. But now, besides Pelopidas just cause of anger, yet was there an other respect that most pricked him forward, to do that he did: for he saw his victorie ended, in the death of the tyran. Otherwise he shoulde hardly have founde so noble an occasion to have shewed his valliantnesse, as in that. And Marcellus contrarily, without any instant necessity, and havinge no cause of heate or choller, (which putteth all men valliant in fight besides them selves, that they know not what they do) did rashly, and unadvisedly thrust him selfe into the middest of the daunger, where he dyed not as a generall, but as a light horseman and skowt, (forsakinge his three triumphes, his five Consullshippes, and his spoyles and tokens of triumphe, which he had gotten of kinges with his owne hands) among venturous Spaniards and Numidians, that solde their blood and lives for pay unto the Carthaginians: so that I imagine they were angry with them selves (as a man would say) for so great and happy a victory, to have slaine amongest Fregellanian skowtes, and light horsemen, the noblest and worthiest person of the Romaines. I would no man should thinke I speake this in reproch of the memory of these two famous men, but as a griefe onely of them and their valliantnes: which they imployed so, as they bleamished all their other vertues, by the undiscrete hazarding of their persones and lives without cause, as if they woulde and shoulde have dyed for them selves, and not rather for their contry and frendes. And also when they were dead, Pelopidas was buried by the allies and confederats of the city of Thebes, for whose cause he was slaine: and Marcellus in like maner, by the enemies selves that hadde slaine him. And sure the one is a happy thing, and to be wished for in such a case: but the other is farre above it, and more to be wondered at. That the enemy him selfe shoulde honor his valliantnesse and worthinesse that hurt him, more then the office of frendshippe performed by a thankefull frende. For nothing moveth the enemy more to honor his deade enemy, then the admiration of his worthines: and the frende sheweth frendeship many times, rather for respect of the benefit he hath received, then for the love he beareth to his vertue.

Plutarch excuseth his free speech and Iudgement of these famous men.

Pelopidas and Marcellus funeralls unlike.

THE ENDE OF MARCELLUS LIFE

THE LIFE OF ARISTIDES

Aristides wealth.

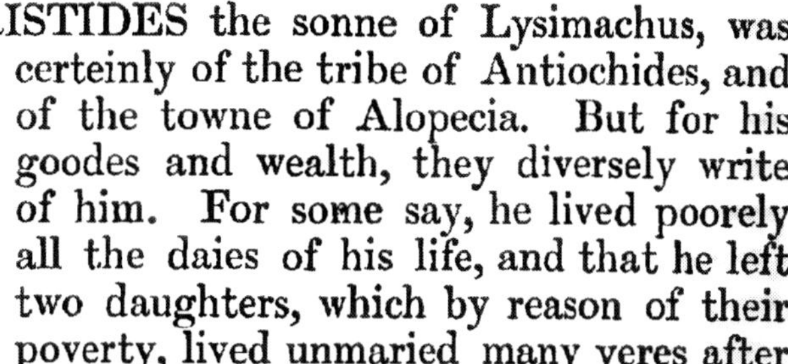

RISTIDES the sonne of Lysimachus, was certeinly of the tribe of Antiochides, and of the towne of Alopecia. But for his goodes and wealth, they diversely write of him. For some say, he lived poorely all the daies of his life, and that he left two daughters, which by reason of their poverty, lived unmaried many yeres after their fathers death. And many of the oldest writers do confirme that for troth. Yet Demetrius Phalerius, in his booke intituled *Socrates*, wryteth the contrary: that he knew certeine landes Aristides had in the village of Phaleria, which did yet beare the name of Aristides lands, in the which his body is buried. And furthermore, to shew that he was well to live, and that his house was rich and wealthy, he bringeth foorth these proofes. First, that he was one yeare mayer or provost of Athens, whom they called, Archon Eponymos, bicause the yeare tooke the name of him that hadde it yearely. And they say he came to it, by drawing of the beane, according to the auncient use of the Athenians, and their wonted manner of makinge their election of the said office: In which election none were admitted to drawe the beane, but such as were highest set in their subsidie bookes, according to the value and rate of their goodes, whom they called at Athens, *Pentacosiomedimnes*, as you would say, those that might dispend five hundred bushels of wheate by the yere, and upwards. Secondly, he alleageth he was banished by the Ostracismon, which banisheth the nobilitie and great rich men onely, whom the common people envie, bicause of their greatnesse, and never dealeth with poore men. The third and last reason he makes is, that he left of his gift, three footed stooles in the temple of Bacchus, which those do commonly offer up, as have won the victory in comedies, tragedies, or other such like pastimes, wherof they them selves had borne the charge. And those threefooted stooles remaine there yet, which they say were geven by Aristides, and have this inscription uppon them: The tribe of Antiochides wanne the victorie, Aristides defrayed the charges of the games, and Archestratus the Poet taught them to playe his comedies. This last reason, though it seeme likeliest of them all, yet is it the weakest of the rest. For Epaminondas (whome every man knoweth was poore even from his birth, and alwayes lived in great povertie) and Plato the Philosopher, tooke apon him to defraye the charges of games that were of no small expence, the one having borne the charges of flute players at Thebes, and the other the dawnce of the children which dawnced in a rounde at Athens: towards the furnishing of which charges, Dion the Syracusan gave Plato money, and Pelopidas also gave Epaminondas money. Now, this is not spoken that vertuous men should alwayes refuse the gifts of their frends, and that they might not in some sorte accept their frendes curtesie offered them: but bicause they should thinke it uncomely and dishonorable for them, to take any thing to enrich them selves, or to spare and hourde up. Howebeit where there is any honorable act to be done, or any publike show to be made, not tending to their private benefit: in such a case they should not refuse their frendes loving offer, and goodwill towardes them. And where Demetrius saith the three footed stoole was offered up in the temple of Bacchus, Panætius declareth plainely, that Demetrius was deceaved by the semblance of the name. For since the time of the warres of the Medes, unto the beginninge of the warre of Peloponnesus, in all the registers and recordes kept of the defrayers of the charges of common playes, there were founde but two men bearinge name of Aristides, that obteined victory: and neither of them both was sonne unto Lysimachus, whom we wryte of at this present. For the one is expresly named the sonne of Xenophilus, and the other was long after the same Aristides we now speake of: as appeareth easily by the wrytinge and orthographie, which is according to the grammer rules, we have used in Greece ever since Euclides time. Moreover it is easie to be knowen, by the

Good men may take giftes, but after a sorte.

name of the Poet Archestratus that is adjoyned to it. For there is no man that maketh mencion of a Poet of this name, in all the warres of the Medes: but in the time of the warres of Peloponnesus, many doe put him in for an author and maker of rymes and songes that were song in common daunces. Yet for all Panætius objections, the matter is to be better looked into, and considered of. But for the Ostracismon banishment, it is true, that such as were great men in estimacion above the common people, either in fame, nobility, or eloquence, they onely were subject unto this banishment. For Damon him selfe, beinge Pericles schoolemaister, was banished: onely bicause the common people thought him to wise. Moreover, Idomeneus wryteth, that Aristides was their provost for a yeare, not by lot of beanes, but by voyces of the Athenians that chose him. And if he were provost since the jorney of Platees, as Demetrius wryteth: it is likely enough that they didde him this honor, for his great vertue and notable service, which other were wont to obteine for their riches. But this Demetrius doth not only defende Aristides, but also Socrates poverty, as if it were a fowle vyce and reproche to be poore. For he wryteth, that he had not only a house of his owne, but also three score and ten Minas at usery, which Criton gave him interest for. But now to our story againe. Aristides was Clisthenes very frend, he that restored the government at Athens after the expulsion of the thirty tyrannes, and did reverence Lycurgus the Lawmaker of the Lacedæmonians for his lawes, above all the men in his time: and therefore he ever favored the state of Aristocratia, that is, where the noble men rule, and have the soverainty. Howbeit he ever had Themistocles (Neocles sonne) his continuall adversary, as takinge parte with the contrary, and defending the popular state of government. Some say, that being schollers, and brought up together, they were ever contrary one to an other in all their actions and doinges, were it in sporte, or in matters of earnest: and ever after, men beganne to see the naturall inclination of them both, by their contrary affections. For Themistocles was quicke, nimble, adventurous, and subtill, and would venter on any thing, apon light

Damon banished bicause he was to wise.

Socrates was not poore.

Aristocratia what it signifieth.

Aristides and Themistocles enemies in the common wealth.

Themistocles disposition.

occasion. Aristides contrariwise was very quiet, temperate, constant, and marvelous well stayed, who woulde for no respect be drawen away from equity and justice, neither would lye, flatter, nor abuse any body, though it were but in sporte. Notwithstanding, Aristus of Chio wryteth, that their malice beganne first of light love, and that it grewe to greatnesse by processe of time betwene them: for (sayeth he) both the one and the other of them fell in love with Stesileus, borne in the Ile of Ceos. This fond light love of theirs, fell not easily from them, nor the envy they conceived one against an other, but continued against eche other in matters of state: such was their malice towardes one an other. In which calling, Themistocles sought the way to winne frendes, by whose meanes he came to great preferment in shorte time, and had made him selfe very strong by them. Therefore, when a frende of his tolde him one day, he was worthy to governe the city of Athens, and were very fitte for it, if he were indifferent, and not partiall. The goddes forbid (quod he) I should ever occupie the place of a governour, where my frendes shoulde not finde more favor then straungers, that doe me no pleasure. But Aristides taking an other course by him selfe, would not stande apon his frendes in government. First, bicause he woulde do no man wrong, with pleasuring his frendes: nor yet would anger them, by denying their requestes. Secondly, bicause he saw many rulers and men of authority bolde to do injustice, and manifest wrong, bearinge them selves apon their frendes: but he caried this opinion, that no honest man, or good citizen, shoulde trust to any bolstring of frendes, but to his owne just and upright doings. Notwithstanding, Aristides perceivinge that Themistocles did rashly alter many thinges, and ever encountered all his wayes, and hindered his doings: he was enforced somtime to crosse Themistocles againe, and to speake against that he preferred, partely to be even with him, but most to hinder his credit and authority, which increased still through the peoples favor and goodwilles towardes him: thinking it better by contrarying him a litle to disapoint sometime a thing that might have fallen out well for the common wealth, rather then by geving him the head, to suffer

Aristides nature.

Themistocles saying for partiality.

Aristides manner of dealing in the common wealth.

ARISTIDES

him to grow to great. To conclude, it fortuned on a time that Themistocles having preferred a matter very profitable for the common wealth, Aristides was so much against it, as Themistocles purpose tooke no place. Moreover Aristides was so earnest against him, that when the counsaill brake up after Themistocles motion was rejected, he spake it openly before them all: that the common wealth of Athens would never prosper, untill they both were laid in Barathrum, which was a prison or hole, wherein they put all theeves and condemned men. An other time, Aristides moved a matter to the people, which diverse were against, but yet it went with him. And when the judge or president of the counsaill did put it to the people, to knowe their allowance of it: Aristides perceiving by the argumentes made against it, that the matter he preferred was hurtfull to the common wealth, he gave it over, and would not have it passe. Many times also Aristides spake by other men, when he would have a thing go forward, for feare least Themistocles spight towardes him, woulde hinder the benefitte of the common wealth. They founde him very constant and resolute in matters of state, whatsoever happened: which wanne him great commendacion. For he was never the prouder for any honor they gave him, nor thought him selfe disgraced for any overthrow he received: being alwayes of this minde, that it was the duety of an honest citizen, to be ever ready to offer his body and life to doe his contry service, without respect and hope of reward of money, or for honor and glory. Therefore when certeine verses were repeated in the Theater, of one of the tragedies of Æschilus, made in commendacion of the auncient Soothsayer Amphiaraus, to this effect:

Barathrum a prison or dungeon.

Aristides constancy.

> He will not only seeme, a just man by his face,
> but just indede he will be founde, and vertue still embrace:
> With all his thought and soule, from whence there may procede,
> grave counsells for to beawtifie, his contries crowne in dede.

All the people straight cast their eyes upon Aristides, as uppon him, that in troth above all other most deserved the praise of so great a vertue. For he was so stoute and resolute, not only to resist favor and frendshippe: but to

Aristides justice.

reject hate and anger also. For in case of justice, neither coulde frendshippe make him go away for his frendes sake: nor envy coulde move him to do injustice, to his very enemy. For proofe hereof it is wrytten, that he had an enemie of his in sute of law, and did prosecute it to judgement: insomuch as after the plaint was red, the judges were so angrie with the offendor, that without any more hearinge of him, they woulde have geven sentence against him. But Aristides rising from his place, went and kneeled at the judges feete with the offendor his enemy, and besought them to geve him leave to speake, to justifie and defende his cause, according to the course of the law. An other time he being judge betwene two private men that pleaded before him, one of them sayd unto him: Aristides, this fellow mine adversary here, hath done you great injurie. My frende (quod Aristides againe) I pray thee tell me onely the injury he hath done thee, for I am judge here to do thee right, and not my selfe. Moreover, he beinge chosen high treasorer of all the revenues of Athens, did declare that all the officers before him, and other his late predecessors, hadde greatly robbed and spoyled the common treasure, but specially Themistocles: who was a wise man, and of great judgement, but yet somewhat light fingered. Therefore when Aristides was to geve uppe his accompt, Themistocles, and many other suborned by him, were against him, and accused him for abusing his office, and followed him so hard, that through their practise they condemned him, as Idomeneus wryteth. Yet the noblest citizens seeing what injury they offered Aristides, tooke his cause in hande, and founde meanes to procure the people not onely to release the fine imposed upon him, but to restore him againe to his office of high treasorer for the yeare following: in the which he seemed to repent his former straightnes and government the yere before, and so dealt more favorably with those he hadde to do, and would not examine every thing so straightly as he did before. Whereupon such as were theeves and stealers of the treasure of the common wealth, did marvelously praise and like him, and became suters for him to continew in the office. But when the day

Aristides wise saying.

Aristides chosen treasorer. Themistocles covetously geven.

Aristides accused and condemned, for abusing his office.

Aristides fine released, and he made treasorer againe.

of election came, that the Athenians woulde choose him againe, Aristides selfe reproved them, and sayd: When I faithfully discharged the duety of mine office committed to me by you, I then received shame and reproche at your handes: and now that I have dissembled, not seeminge to see the theftes and robberies done apon your treasure, ye claw me, and say I am an honest man, and a good citizen. But I would you knew it, and I tell you plainely, I am more ashamed of the honor you do me now, then I was of the fine you did set apon me, when you condemned me the last yeare: and I am sorie to speake it, that you shoulde thinke it more commendation to pleasure the wicked, then to preserve the common wealth. After he had spoken these words, and had bewrayed the common theftes the officers of the city did commit: he stopped the theeves mouthes that so highly praised and commended him for so honest a man, but yet of the noble and honest citizens he was much commended.

Aristides openly reproveth close theeves in the common wealth, and detesteth their praise.

Furthermore, on a time when Dathis Lieutenant to Darius king of Persia, was come with all his navy to go a lande about Marathon, in the contrie of Attica, apon pretence (as he sayd) to be revenged onely of the Athenians that had burnt the city of Sardis, but in dede of minde to conquer all Greece, and to destroy the whole contrie before him: the Athenians chose tenne Captaines to go to the warres, amonge whom Miltiades was the chiefest man of authority. But Aristides drew very neere him in reputacion and creditte, bicause he did very good service in obtaining the victorie, specially when he agreed with Miltiades in counsaill, to geve battell apon the barbarous people: and also when he willingly gave Miltiades the whole rule and order of the army. For every one of the tenne Captaines did by turnes leade the whole army for one whole day: and when Aristides turne came about, he gave his preferment thereof unto Miltiades, teaching his other companions, that it was no shame, but honor for them, to be ruled by the wisest. Thus by his example, he appeased all strife that might have growen amonge them, and perswaded them all to be contented to follow his direction and counsaill, that had best experience in warre. And so he did much advaunce Miltiades honor.

Miltiades chiefe of the ten Captaines that went against Dathis the king of Persiaes Lieutenant.

Miltiades victory of the Persians.

For, after that Aristides had once yelded his authority unto him, every one of the rest did the like when it came to their turne: and so they all submitted them selves unto his rule and leading. But on the day of the battel, the place where the Athenians were most combred, was in the middest of the battell, where they had set the tribes of the Leontides, and of Antiochides: for thither the barbarous people did bend all their force, and made their greatest fight in that place. By which occasion, Themistocles and Aristides fighting one hard by an other, for that the one was of the tribe Leontides, and the other of Antiochides, they valiantly fought it out with the enemies, envying one an other: so as the barbarous people at the last being overthrowen, they made them flie, and drave them to their shippes. But when they were imbarked and gone, the Captaines of the Athenians perceiving they made not towardes the Iles which was their direct course to returne into Asia, but that they were driven backe by storme of winde and pyrries of the sea, towardes the coast of Attica, and the city of Athens, fearinge least they might finde Athens unfurnished for defence, and might set apon it: they thereupon sent away presently nine tribes that marched thither with such speede, as they came to Athens the very same day, and left Aristides in the campe at Marathon, with his tribe and contry men, to looke to the prisoners and spoyle they hadde wonne of the barbarous people. Who nothing deceived the opinion they had of his wisdom. For notwithstanding there was great store of golde and silver, much apparell, moveables, and other infinite goodes and riches in all their tentes and pavillions, and in the shippes also they had taken of theirs: he was not so covetous as once to touch them, nor to suffer any other to medle with them, unlesse by stealth some provided for them selves. As amongst other, there was one Callias, one of Ceres Priestes, called Dadouchos, as you woulde saye the torche bearer: (for in the secret sacrifices of Ceres, his office was to holde the torche) whom when one of the barbarous people saw, and how he ware a bande about his head, and long heare, he toke him for some king, and falling on his knees at his feete, kissed his hand, and shewed him great

The wicked parte of Callias the torche bearer.

store of golde he hadde hidden and buried in a ditche. But Callias, like a most cruell, and cowardly wretch of all other on the earth, tooke away the gold, and killed the poore soule that had shewed him the place, bicause he shoulde not tell it to others. Hereof it commeth, that the comicall Poets do call those that came of him in mockery, Laccoplutes, as made rich by a ditch: bicause of the golde that Callias founde in it. Immediatly after this battell, Aristides was chosen provost of Athens for the yeare: albeit Demetrius Phalerius writeth, that it was a litle before his death, after the jorney of Platees. For in their Chronicles, where they set in order their provosts of Athens for the yere, since Xanthippides time, there appeareth no one name of Aristides in that yeare, that Mardonius the kinge of Persiaes Lieutenant was overthrowen by Platees, which was many yeares after. But contrariwise they finde Aristides enrolled amonge the provostes immediatly after Phanippus, in the yeare the battell was fought at Marathon. Now the people did most commende Aristides justice, as of all other his vertues and qualities: bicause that vertue is most common and in use in our life, and delivereth most benefitte to men. Hereof it came, that he beinge a meane man, obteined the worthiest name that one coulde have, to be called by the whole city, a just man. This surname was never desired of kinges, princes, nor of tyrannes, but they alwayes delited to be surnamed, some Poliorcetes, to say, conquerors of cities: other Cerauni, to say, lightening or terrible: other Nicanores, to say, subduers: and some other, Aeti and Hieraces, to say Eagles or Fawcons, or such like birdes that praye: desiringe rather (as it should appeare by those surnames) the praise and reputacion growinge by force and power, then the commendacion that riseth by vertue and goodnes. And notwithstanding, God whom men desire most to be likened to, doth excell all humaine nature in three speciall thinges: in immortality, in power, and in vertue, of which three, vertue is the most honorable and pretious thing. For as the naturall Philosophers reason, all the foure elements and Vacuum, are immortall and uncorruptible, and so are force and power, earthquakes, lighteninge, terrible stormes, runninge rivers,

Aristides chosen provost of Athens.

Aristides called the Iust.

and inundacions of waters: but as for justice and equity, no man is partaker of them, save onely God, by meanes of reason and understandinge. Therefore, bicause men commonly have three sundry honors to the gods: the first, that they thinke them blessed: the second, that they feare them: the third, that they reverence them: it appeareth then that they thinke them blessed, for the eternitie and immortality of their godhead: that they feare them, bicause of their omnipotency and power: and that they love and worshippe them, for their justice and equitie. And yet notwithstanding, of those three, men do covet immortality, which no flesh can attaine unto: and also power, which dependeth most uppon fortune: and in the meane time they leave vertue alone, whereof the goddes of their goodnes have made us capable. But here they shewe them selves fooles. For justice maketh the life of a noble man, and of one in great authority, seeme divine and celestiall: where without justice, and dealinge unjustly, his life is most beastly, and odious to the worlde. But now againe to Aristides. This surname of a just man at the beginning, made him beloved of all the people: but afterwardes it turned him to great ill will, and specially by Themistocles practise. Who gave it out every where, that Aristides had overthrowen all justice, bicause by consent of the parties he was ever chosen Arbitrator to ende all controversies: and how by this meanes he secretly had procured the absolute power of a kinge, not needing any gard or souldiers about him. The people moreover beinge growen very dissolute and licentious, by reason of the victorie of Marathon, who sought that all thinges should passe by them, and their authoritie: beganne nowe to mislike, and to be greatly offended, that any private man should go before the rest in good fame and reputacion. Whereupon, they came out of all shyeres of Attica into the city of Athens, and so banished Aristides with the Ostracismon: disguising the envy they bare to his glory, with the name of feare of tyranny. For this maner of banishment called Ostracismon, or Exostracismon, was no ordinary punishment for any fault or offence committed: but to geve it an honest cloke, they sayd it was onely a pulling downe and tying shorte, of to

The praise of justice.

Authority would be without corruption.

Themistocles envieth Aristides justice.

Aristides banished with the Ostracismon.

The nature of the Ostracismon.

ARISTIDES

much greatnesse and authority, exceeding farre the maner and countenance of a popular state. But to tell you truly, it was none otherwise, then a gentle meane to qualify the peoples envy against some private person: which envy bred no malice to him whose greatnes did offende them, but onely tended to the banishing of him for tenne yeares. But afterwardes that by practise, this Ostracismon banishment was layed apon meane men, and malefactors, as upon Hyperbolus that was the last man so banished: they never after used it any more at Athens. And by the way, it shall not be amisse to tell you here, why, and wherfore this Hyperbolus was banished. Alcibiades and Nicias were the chiefest men of Athens at that time, and they both were ever at square together, a common thing amongest great men. They perceiving now by the peoples assembling, that they went about to execute the Ostracismon, were marvelously afrayed it was ment to banishe one of them: wherefore they spake together, and made both their followers frends with eche other, and joyned them in one tribe together, insomuch, when the most voyces of the people were gathered to condemne him that should be banished, they founde it was Hyperbolus. The people therewith were much offended, to see the Ostracismon so embased and scorned, that they never after woulde use it againe, and so left it of for ever. But briefely to let you understande what the Ostracismon was, and after what sorte they used it, ye are to know: that at a certaine day appointed, every citizen caried a great shell in his hande, whereupon he wrote the name of him he woulde have banished, and brought it into a certeine place railed about with wodden barres in the market place. Then, when every man hadde brought in his shell: the magistrates, and officers of the city, did count and tell the number of them. For if there were lesse then sixe thowsand citizens, that had thus brought these shels together: the Ostracismon was not full and perfect. That done, they layd a parte every mans name written in these shels: and whose name they founde wrytten by most citizens, they proclaimed him by sounde of trompet, a banished man for tenne yeares, during which time notwithstanding, the party did enjoy all his goodes. Now

Hyperbolus the last man banished with the Ostracismon.

The cause of Hyperbolus banishment.

A description of the Ostracismon.

every man wryting thus his name in a shell, whom they would have banished: it is reported there was a plaine man of the contry (very simple) that coulde neither wryte, nor read, who came to Aristides (being the first man he met with) and gave him his shell, praying him to wryte Aristides name upon it. He beinge abashed withall, did aske the contrie man, if Aristides had ever done him any displeasure. No, sayed the contrie man, he never did me hurt, nor I know him not: but it greeves me to heare every man call him a just man. Aristides hearing him say so, gave him no aunswere, but wrote his owne name upon the shell, and delivered it againe to the contrie man. But as he went his way out of the citie, he lift uppe his handes to heaven, and made a prayer contrary to that of Achilles in Homer, besechinge the goddes that the Athenians might never have such troubles in hande, as they shoulde be compelled to call for Aristides againe. Notwithstandinge, within three yeares after, when Xerxes king of Persia came with his army through the contries of Thessalie and Bœotia, and entred into the heart of the contrie of Attica: the Athenians revoking the law of their Ostracismon, called home againe all those they had banished, and specially, bicause they were afrayd Aristides would take parte with the barbarous people, and that his example should move many other to do the like, wherin they were greatly deceived in the nature of the man. For before that he was called home, he continually travelled up and downe, perswading and incoraginge the Greecians to mainteine and defende their liberty. After that lawe was repealed, and published, and that Themistocles was chosen the only Lieutenant generall of Athens, he did alwayes faithfully aide and assist him in all thinges, as well with his travell, as also with his counsaill: and thereby wanne his enemy great honor, bicause it stoode apon the safetie and preservation of his contrie. For when Eurybiades, generall of the armie of the Greecians, had determined to forsake the Ile of Salamina, and that the gallyes of the barbarous people were come into the middest of the seas, and had environned the Iles all about, and the mouth of the arme of the straight of Salamina, before any man knew they were thus inclosed in: Aristides

A tale of a plaine man that came to Aristides with his shell, to pray him to write Aristides name in it.

Aristides called from exile.

Aristides acts and councells against kinge Xerxes.

departing out of the Ile of Ægina with a marvelous boldenes, ventred through the middest of all the barbarous shippes and fleete, and by good happe gotte in the night into Themistocles tent, and calling him out, spake with him there in this sorte: Themistocles, if we be both wise, it is high time we shoulde nowe leave of this vaine envie and spite we have longe time borne eche other, and that we should enter into an other sorte of envy more honorable and profitable for us both. I meane, which of us two should do his best indevor to save Greece: you, by ruling and commaunding all like Lieutenant generall: and I, by counselling you for the best, and executing your commaundement: consideringe you are the man alone that will roundliest come unto the point that is best: which is in my opinion, that we shoulde hazard battell by sea within the straight of Salamina, and that as soone as might be possible. But if our frendes and confederates do let this to be put in execution, I do assure you, your enemies do helpe it forward. For it is sayd, that the sea, both before and behinde us, and rounde about us, is covered all over with their shippes, so as they that would not before, shall be now compelled of force, and in spite of their heartes, to fight and besturre them like men: bicause they are compassed in all about, and there is no passage left open for them to escape, nor to flie. Whereunto Themistocles aunswered: I am sory, Aristides, that herein your honesty appeareth greater then mine: but since it is so, that you have deserved the honor in beginning, and procuring such an honorable and commendable strife betwene us, I will henceforth indevor my selfe to excede you in continuing this your desire. After which aunswere, he told Aristides, how he purposed to mocke the barbarous kinge, and prayed him to intreate Eurybiades to yelde to his devise, and to perswade him that there was no other way to save Greece, but to fight by sea: for Eurybiades gave more creditte to Aristides perswasions, then he did to Themistocles wordes. For when all the Captaines were called to counsell, to determine whether they should geve battell or not: one Cleocritus Corinthian sayd to Themistocles, that his counsell did not like Aristides at all, as it seemed, bicause he spake never a worde to it being present. Aristides answered him straight, that he utterly mistooke him. For, quod he, if I did not thinke his counsell good, I would not hold my peace as I do: but now I am mute, not for any good will I beare him, but bicause I finde his counsell wise and sounde. While the Captaines of the Greecians were reasoning in this sorte, Aristides seeing Psyttalea (a litle Ilande before Salamina within the straight) full of men of warre of their enemies: imbarked immediatly the valliantest and lustiest souldiers he hadde of all his contry men, into the least foystes or pynnasies he had among all his gallyes: and went with them, and landed in that Ile, and overthrewe all the barbarous people he founde there, and put them to the sworde every man, taking the chiefest of them only prisoners, among which, were three sonnes of Sandauce, the kinges sister, whome he sent unto Themistocles. These three Lordes were all slaine by the commaundement of Euphrantidas the Soothsayer, and sacrificed to Bacchus Omestes, as to say, the cruell Bacchus, and eater of raw flesh, and all upon an oracle they had received. That done, Aristides dispersed his souldiers about the Ile, to receive all such as were by fortune of warre, or of the sea, cast into the Ilande: to the end that no enemy of theirs should scape their hands, nor any of his frendes should perish. For the greatest fleete of all their shippes, and the sharpest encounter of the whole battell, was about this litle Ilande: and therefore the tokens of triumphe were set there. After the battell was wonne, Themistocles to feele Aristides opinion, sayed unto him: We have done a good peece of service, but yet there is an other behinde of greater importance, and that is this: We must bringe all Asia into Europe, which we may easily do, if we saile with all speede to the straight of Hellespont, and go breake the bridge the king hath made there. Then Aristides cried out, Stay there, never speake of that: but I pray you let us rather seeke al the wayes we can, how to drive this barbarous king out of Greece, least if we kepe him in still with so great an army (and he shall see no way before him to escape out) we drive him then to fight like a desperate man, and perill our selves, we can not tell to what. When Themistocles had hearde his opinion, he

Aristides wordes of Themistocles.

Aristides victory at Psyttalea.

Aristides wise counsell for Xerxes flying out of Greece.

A stratageame of Themistocles.

secretely sent the euenuke Arnaces his prisoner, unto kinge Xerxes, to advertise him from him, that he had altered the Greecians purpose, which was fully bent to have broken up the bridge he hadde made at the straight of Hellespont, to passe over his army: and that he was the willinger to let him understande it, that he might the better provide for the safety of his person. King Xerxes being netled with this advertisement, tooke straight his jorney, and with all speede went to recover the straight of Hellespont, and left Mardonius his Lieutenant general in Greece, with three hundred thowsand of the best souldiers of his army. This Mardonius was marvelously dreaded of all the Greecians, for the wonderfull great army he hadde by lande, and he did threaten them also by his letters he wrote unto them. You have, (sayed he) with your shippes by sea, overcome men acquainted to fight by lande, and that never handeled ower: but now, the plaines of Thessalie, or the fieldes of Bœotia, are very fayer and large for horsemen and footemen to make proofe of their valliantnes, if you will come to the battell in the field. He wrote letters to the Athenians, by the kinge his maisters commaundement, of other effect, and offered them from him, to builde up their city againe, to geve them a great pencion, and furthermore to make them Lordes of all Greece, so they woulde geve over, and leave of these warres. The Lacedæmonians beinge forthwith advertised of his letters wrytten to the Athenians, and fearing least they would have bene perswaded by them: sent their Ambassadors with al speede to Athens, to pray them to send their wives and children unto Sparta, and also to offer them vittailles, to relieve their poore olde people, bicause of the great scarcity that was at Athens, for that their city was burnt and rased, and all their contry besides destroyed by the barbarous people. The Athenians having heard the offers of the Ambassadors of Lacedæmon, made them a marvelous answer through Aristides counsell, and this it was. That they bare with the barbarous people, though they thought all thinges were to be sold for gold and silver, bicause they esteemed nothing more pretious, nor better in this world, then to be riche and wealthy: but on the other

Xerxes left Mardonius his Lieutenant in Greece with 300000 men.

The noble minde of the Athenians.

side, they were greatly offended with the Lacedæmonians, that they only regarded the present poverty and necessity of the Athenians, and did forget their vertue and noble corage, thinking to make them fight more valliantly for the preservacion of Greece, by offering them vittells to live withall. The people approving this aunswere, Aristides then caused the Ambassadors of Sparta to come to the assembly, and commaunded them to tell the Lacedæmonians by worde of mouth, that all the golde above, or under the grounde, coulde not corrupt the Athenians, to make them take any summe of money or reward, to leave the defence of the liberty of Greece: and to the herauld that came from Mardonius, he shewed him the sunne, and sayd unto him: so long as yonder sunne keepeth his course about the worlde, so long will the Athenians be mortall enemies unto the Persians, bicause they have spoyled and destroyed all their contry, and have defiled and burnt the temples of their goddes. Besides, he willed that the Priestes, by commaundement of the people, shoulde excommunicate and curse him that woulde procure them to sende unto the Persians to make peace with them, and to breake their league and allyance with the other Greecians. Hereupon, when Mardonius came againe the seconde time to overrunne the contry of Attica: the Athenians got them againe into the Ile of Salamina, and then they sent Aristides Ambassador unto the Lacedæmonians. He sharpely tooke them up, and reproved their sloth and negligence, bicause they had againe forsaken Athens, and left it to the spoyle of the barbarous people: and prayed them yet they woulde looke to save the rest of Greece. The Ephori (which were certeine officers that ruled all things within the city of Sparta) when they had hearde Aristides perswasions: straight tooke order for ayde, though it appeared they did nothing all day but play, and make good cheere, keeping that day one of their solemne feastes they called Hyacinthia. Howebeit the next night following, they sent out five thowsande citizens borne in Sparta, into the fielde, all proper men and valliant souldiers, every one of them carying with him, seven Ilotes (which are the contry men and slaves in the contrie of Lacedæmonia) not making the Ambassadors of Athens privy to it at all. Wherefore Aristides came againe an other time into their counsell, to complaine of their negligence. But they fell a laughinge, and sayd he dreamed, or else he mocked them: for their army which they had sent against the straungers (for so they called the Persians) was already at the city of Orestion in Arcadia. Aristides hearing their aunswere, replyed, that they were to blame to mocke them in that sorte, to sende away their men so secretly, that they might not knowe of it: and that it was no time for them now to go about to deceive their frendes, but their enemies rather. Idomeneus in his story reporteth the matter thus in every point. Notwithstanding, in the decree that was made to sende Ambassadors to Sparta, Aristides is not named for Ambassador, but there are other appointed: as Cimon, Xanthippus, and Myronides. Afterwardes Aristides was chosen by voyces of the people, Lieutenant generall of the army of Athens, in this warre against the Persians, and went unto the campe of the Greecians by the citie of Platæes, with eight thousande footemen wel armed and appointed. There he found king Pausanias the only general of all the whole power and army of the Greecians, who brought with him the force of Sparta: and there came daily into his campe one after an other, a marvelous great multitude of other Greecians. Now touching the army of the barbarous people, they incamped all alongest the river of Asopus: but bicause their campe stretched out a marvelous way in length, they were not intrenched at all, but had onely fortified a peece of grounde foure square with a walle about, which was ten furlonges on every side, to place all their cariage and chiefest thinges in. And for the Greecians againe, the soothsayer Tisamenus, borne in the city of Elide, had told Pausanias, and all the Greecians together, that they should have the victory, so they did not assault at all, but only defend. And Aristides, that had sent to the oracle of Apollo at Delphes, in the name of the Athenians, had aunswer: they should overcome their enemies, so they did sacrifice and make speciall prayers, unto Iupiter and Iuno of mount Cithæron, unto Pan, and unto the Nymphes Sphragitides, and also unto the demy

Aristides Lieutenant generall of the Atheni-ans against Mardonius.

Pausanias king of Lace-dæmon, gene-rall of all Greece.

Asopus flu.

Oracles of the victory of Platæes.

gods, Androcrates, Leucon, Pisander, Damocrates, Hypsion, Actæon, and Polyidus: and so that they did hazard battel also within their owne territories, and in the plaine of Ceres Eleusinian, and of Proserpina. This oracle troubled Aristides marvelously, bicause the demy goddes whome they had commaundement to do sacrifice unto, were the fownders and auncesters of the Platæians: and the cave of the Nymphes Sphragitides, is one of the toppes of mount Cithæron, looking towards the west, where the sunne setteth in sommer. They say there was an oracle there in old time, whose spirit possessed many inhabitants thereabouts, and bestraught them of their wittes: whereupon, they called those so possessed, Nympholepty, as who would say, taken with the Nymphes. And againe to tel the Athenians they shoulde have the victory, so they did hazard battell in the plaine of Ceres Eleusinian, and within their owne territorie: it was even to sende them backe againe into the contry of Attica. Aristides being thus perplexed, Arimnestus Captaine of the Platæians, hadde such a vision in the night in his sleepe. Him thought that Iupiter the savior did appeare unto him, and asked him what the Greecians intended to do? and that he answered: my Lord, we must to morrowe remove our campe into the territories of Eleusin, and there we will fight with the barbarous people, accordinge to the commaundement the oracle Apollo hath geven us. Then that Iupiter replyed, that they were greatly deceaved: for all that Apollo had declared by his oracle was ment within the territorie of the Platæians, and that they shoulde finde it true, if they considered it well. Arimnestus havinge plainely seene this vision in his sleepe, when he did awake in the morning, he straight sent for the oldest citizens, and consideringe with them where this place shoulde be, he founde at the length, that at the foote of mount Cithæron, by the city of Nysia, there was an olde temple they called the temple of Ceres Eleusinian, and of her daughter Proserpina. When he hearde them say so, he went straight and tolde Aristides of it, and founde that it was an excellent place to set an army in battell raye, that hadde but fewe horsemen: for that the foote of mount Cithæron did lette the horsemen, they

The Nymphes Sphragitides.

Arymnestus dreame.

ARISTIDES

coulde not goe to the place where the temple stoode, and where the playne and valley did ende: besides also, that the chappell of Androcrates was even in that place, which was all hidden with thicke wodde rounde about it. And bicause they shoulde lacke nothing to hinder the expresse commaundement of the oracle for hope of victory: the Platæians (through Arimnestus counsell and advise) made a common decree, that the confines of the city of Platææs should be taken away towardes Athens side, and that the lande thereof shoulde be geven clearely unto the Athenians, bicause they shoulde fight with the barbarous people in their owne lande, for the defence and preservation of Greece, accordinge to the commaundement of the oracle. This noble gift and present of the Platæians was so famous, as many yeares after, king Alexander the great having conquered the Empire of Asia, built up the walles againe of the city of Platææs, and when he had done, made a heraulde openly proclaime it at the games Olympicall: that Alexander hadde done the Platæians that honor and dignitie, for a memoriall and honor of their magnanimity. Bicause in the warre against the Persians, they had freely and liberally geven away their lande unto the Athenians, for the safetie of the Greecians: and had shewed them selves of a noble corage also, and very willinge to defende the state of Greece.

The magnanimity of the Platæians.

Alexander the great doth honor the Platæians for their noble mindes.

Now when the army of the Greecians came to be sette in order of battell, there fell a strife betwene the Athenians and the Tegeates, bicause the Athenians would nedes (according to their old custome) have the left wing of the battell, if the Lacedæmonians had the right winge: and the Tegeates on the contrary parte, woulde have the preheminence before the Athenians, alleaging the famous acts and notable service of their auncesters in former warres, whereupon the Athenians did mutine. But Aristides stept betwene them, and told them, that it was no time now to contende with the Tegeates about their nobility and valliantnesse: and as for you, my Lords of Sparta, sayed he, and you also my maisters of Greece: we tell you, that the place neither geveth nor taketh vertue away, and we doe assure you that wheresoever you place us, we will so defend and

Strife betwene the Athenians and Tegeates.

Aristides wisely pacifieth the mutinie.

kepe it, as we will not impayre nor blemish the honor we have wonne in former foughten battells, and gotten victories. For we are not come hither to quarell and fall out with our frends, but to fight with our common enemies: nor to bragge of our ancesters doings, but to show our selves valliant in defence of al Greece. For this battail wil make good proofe to all the Greecians, how much estimacion every city, every Captaine, and particular person wil deserve for his parte. When Aristides had spoken, the Captaines and all other of the counsel concluded in favor of the Athenians, that they should have one of the winges of the battell. But by this meanes, all Greece stoode in marvelous garboyle at that time, and the state of the Athenians specially in great daunger. For a number of the noblest citizens of Athens. And that brought great substance with them to the warres, being now at low state, and in poverty, their goods being spent and gone, and seeing them selves discountenanced, not bearing that rule and authority in the common wealth they were wont to do, bicause other were called to authority, and preferred to the offices of the citie: they gathered together, and met at a house in the city of Platæes, and there conspyred to overthrow the authority of the people at Athens: and if they could not obtaine their purpose, then that they would rather loose all, and betray their contry unto the barbarous people. While these thinges were practised in the campe, many beinge of the conspiracy, Aristides came to an Incklinge of it, and was marvelously afrayed, bicause of the time: wherefore he beganne to be carefull of the matter, being of such importance as it was, and yet would not be curious to understand the whole conspiracy, litle knowing what a number might be drawen into this treason, if it were narrowly looked into, but rather respected that which was just, then what was profitable for the time. So he caused eight persones only of the great number to be apprehended, and of these eight, the two first whom they would have indited as principalles, and were most to be burdened for the conspiracy, Æschines of the towne of Lampra, and Egesias of the towne of Acharna, they founde meanes to flie out of the campe, and to save themselves.

The conspiracy of the rich noble men of Athens.

And for the other, Aristides set them at liberty, and gave them occasion that were not discovered, to be bold, and to repent them of their follies: saying, that the battell should be their judge, where they should purge them selves of all accusations layed against them, and show the world also, that they never had any other intencion but honest, and good, towards their contry. Mardonius, to prove the corage of the Greecians, had sent all his horsemen, (wherein he was farre stronger then the Greecians) to skirmish with them. Who were lodged at the foote of mount Cithæron, in strong places and full of stones, saving the three thowsande Megarians, that camped in the plaine: by reason whereof, they were sore troubled and hurt, by the horsemen of the barbarous people that sette uppon them on every side, for they might charge them where they woulde. Insomuch, in the ende, perceivinge they alone could no longer resist the force of so great a multitude of the barbarous people: they sent with all speede possible to Pausanias, to pray him to send them present aide. Pausanias hearing this newes, and seeing in his owne sight the campe of the Megarians almost all covered with shot and dartes which the barbarous people threw at them, and that they were compelled to stand close together in a litle corner: he wist not what to do. For, to go thither in person with the Lacedæmonians that were footemen heavy armed, he thought that was no way to help them. So he proved to put some ambitious desire and envy of honor, among the private Captaines and generalls of the army of the other Greecians, which were then about him: to see if he coulde move any mans corage and desire, to offer him selfe willingly to goe aide the Megarians. Howebeit they had all deafe eares, but Aristides: who promised to go in the name of the Athenians, and brought Olympiodorus into the fielde, (one of the valliantest Captaines that served under him) with his company of three hundred chosen men, and certaine shot mingled amongest them. These souldiers were ready in a moment, and marched straight in battell ray, a great pace towards the barbarous people. Masistius, that was generall of the horsemen of the Persians, a goodly tall man, perceiving their comming towards him: turned his

Mount Cithæron.

Masistius generall of the horsemen of the Persians.

horse, and gallopped to them. The Athenians taried him, and kept their ground, and the encounter was very hotte, bicause both the one and the other side did the best they could at this first onset to put the rest of the battell in jeopardy: and they fought so long, that Masistius horse was shot through the body with an arrow, that put him to such paine, as he never lin flinging, till he cast his maister on the ground, armed as he was at all peces. So being on the ground, he could not rise againe, as well for the waight of his armor, as for that the Athenians came so sodainely upon him. And notwithstanding there were many about him to hew him in peces, yet they could find no way how to kill him, he was so throughly armed and loden with gold, copper, and iron, not only uppon his body and his heade, but also on his legges and armes: untill at the length there was one that thrust the head of his dart through his bever, and so killed him. The Persians perceiving that, fled immediatly, and forsooke the body of their generall. Shortly after it appeared to the Greecians that they had sped well at this skirmishe, not bicause they had slaine many enemies, but for the great lamentacion the barbarous people made for the losse of Masistius. For his death did so greve them, that they powled themselves, they clipped of their horse and moyles heares, and filled besides all the field therabouts with pitiefull cries and shreekes, as those that had lost the valliantest and chiefest man of authority of all their campe, next unto Mardonius the kings Lieutenant. After this first skirmish, both the one and the other side kept their campe, and would not come into the field many dayes after: for the Soothsayers did promise both sides the victory, as much the Persians, as the Greecians, so they did but onely defend: and contrarywise, they did threaten them to be overthrowen, that did assault. But Mardonius finding vittells waxed scant, and that they were stored but for few dayes, and moreover how the Greecians daily grewe stronger by continuall repayre to their campe, the lenger he delayed: in the end he resolved to tary no lenger, but to passe the river of Asopus the next morning by breake of day, and sodainly to set apon the Greecians. So he gave the Captaines warn-

Masistius slaine by the Athenians.

Alexander kinge of Macedon, revealeth the Persians secrete counsell unto Aristides.

ing the night before what they should do, bicause every man should be redy: but about midnight there came a horseman without any noyse at all, so neere to the Greecians campe, that he spake to the watche, and told them he would speake with Aristides, generall of the Athenians. Aristides was called for straight, and when he came to him, the horseman said unto Aristides: I am Alexander king of Macedon, who for the love and great good will I beare you, have put my self in the greatest daunger that may be, to come at this present time to advertise you, that to morrow morning Mardonius will give you battel: bicause your enemies sodaine comming apon you, should not make you afrayd, being sodainly charged, and should not hinder also your valliant fightinge. For it is no new hope that is come to Mardonius, that makes him to fight: but only scarcety of vittells that forceth him to do it, considering that the prognosticators are all against it that he should geve you battel, both by reason of the il tokens of their sacrifices, as also by the aunswers of their oracles, which hath put all the armie in a marvelous feare, and stande in no good hope at all. Thus he is forced to putte all at adventure, or else if he will needes lye still, to be starved to death for very famine. After king Alexander hadde imparted this secrete to Aristides, he prayed him to keepe it to him selfe, and to remember it in time to come. Aristides aunswered him then, that it was no reason he shoulde keepe a matter of so great importance as that, from Pausanias, who was their Lieutenant generall of the whole armie: notwithstandinge, he promised him he woulde tell it no man else before the battell, and that if the goddes gave the Greecians the victorie, he did assure him, they should all acknowledge his great favor and good will shewed unto them. After they hadde talked thus together, kinge Alexander left him, and returned backe againe: and Aristides also went immediatly to Pausanias tent, and tolde him the talke kinge Alexander and he hadde together. Thereupon the private Captaines were sent for straight to counsaill, and there order was geven, that every manne shoulde have his bandes ready, for they shoulde fight in the morninge. So Pausanias at that time (as Herodotus wryteth) sayed unto

Aristides, that he woulde remove the Athenians from the left to the right winge, bicause they shoulde have the Persians them selves right before them, and that they shoulde fight so much the lustier, both for that they were acquainted with their fight, as also bicause they hadde overcommed them before in the first encounter: and that him selfe would take the left winge of the battell, where he shoulde encounter with the Greecians that fought on the Persians side. But when all the other private Captaines of the Athenians understoode it, they were marvelous angrie with Pausanias, and sayed he did them wronge, and hadde no reason to lette all the other Grecians keepe their place where they were alwayes appointed, and onely to remove them, as if they were slaves, to be appointed at his pleasure, now of one side, then of the other, and to sette them to fight with the valliantest souldiers they had of all their enemies. Then sayed Aristides to them, that they knewe not what they sayed, and how before they misliked, and did strive with the Tegeates, onely for havinge the left wing of the battell, and when it was graunted, they thought them selves greatly honored that they were preferred before them, by order of the Captaines: and nowe where the Lacedæmonians were willing of them selves to geve them the place of the right winge, and did in maner offer them the preheminence of the whole armie: they do not thankefully take the honor offered them, nor yet doe recken of the vantage and benefitte geven them to fight against the Persians selves, their auncient enemies, and not against their natural contry men anciently discended of them. When Aristides had used all these perswasions unto them, they were very well contented to chaunge place with the Lacedæmonians: and then all the talke amonge them was to encorage one an other, and to tell them that the Persians that came against them, had no better hartes nor weapons, then those whom they before hadde overcome, in the plaine of Marathon. For sayed they, they have the same bowes, the same riche imbrodered gownes, the same golden chaines and carcanettes of womanishe persones, hanging on their cowardly bodies and faint hartes: where we have also the same weapons and bodies we hadde, and our hartes more lively and coragious then before, through the sundrie victories we have since gotten of them. Further, we have this advantage more. That we doe not fight as our other confederates the Greecians do, for our city and contry onely, but also to continewe the fame and renowme of our former noble service, which we wanne at the jorneys of Marathon and of Salamina: to the ende the worlde shoulde not thinke that the glory of these triumphes and victories was due unto Miltiades onely, or unto fortune, but unto the corage and worthinesse of the Athenians. Thus were the Greecians throughly occupied to chaunge the order of their battell in hast. The Thebans on the other side that tooke parte with Mardonius, receiving intelligence of the alteringe of their battell, by traytors that ranne betwene both campes: they straight tolde Mardonius of it. He thereupon did sodainly also chaunge the order of his battell, and placed the Persians from the right winge to the left winge of his enemies: either bicause he was afrayed of the Athenians, or else for greater glorie that he hadde a desire to fight with the Lacedæmonians, and commaunded the Greecians that tooke his parte, that they shoulde fight against the Athenians. This alteracion was so openly done, that everie manne might see it: whereuppon Pausanias removed the Lacedæmonians againe, and sette them in the right winge. Mardonius seeinge that, removed the Persians againe from the left winge, and brought them to the right winge (where they were before) against the Lacedæmonians: and thus they consumed all that day in chaunginge their men to and fro. So the Captaines of the Greecians sate in counsel at night, and there they agreed, that they must nedes remove their campe, and lodge in some other place where they might have water at commaundement: bicause their enemies did continually trouble and spoyle that water they had about them, with their horses. Now when night came, the Captaines woulde have marched away with their men, to go to the lodginge they had appointed: but the people went very ill willinge to it, and they hadde much a do to keepe them together. For they were no sooner out of the trenches and fortification of their campe, but the most parte of them ranne to

The treason of the Thebans.

the citie of Platæes, and were marvelously out of order, dispersing them selves here and there, and set up their tents where they thought good, before the places were appointed for them: and there were none that taried behinde, but the Lacedæmonians onely, and that was against their willes. For one of their Captaines called Amompharetus, a marvelous hardie man, that feared no daunger, and longed sore for battell: he was in such a rage with these triflinge delayes, that he cried it out in the campe, that this removinge was a goodly runninge away, and sware he woulde not from thence, but woulde there tary Mardonius comminge with his companie. Pausanias went to him, and tolde him he must doe that the other Greecians hadde consented to in counsell, by most voyces. But Amompharetus tooke a great stone in his handes, and threw it downe at Pausanias feete, and told him there is the signe I geve to conclude battel, and I passe not for all your cowardly conclusions. Amompharetus stubbornnesse did so amaze Pausanias, that he was at his wittes ende. So he sent unto the Athenians that were onwardes on their way, to pray them to tary for him, that they might goe together: and therewithall made the rest of his menne to marche towardes the citie of Platæes, supposinge thereby to have drawen Amompharetus to have followed him, or else he ment to remaine alone behinde. But in triflinge thus, the day brake: and Mardonius understandinge that the Greecians did forsake their first lodging, he made his army presently marche in battell ray to sette apon the Lacedæmonians. So the barbarous people made great showtes and cries, not thinking to goe fight, but to goe sacke and spoyle the Greecians flyinge away, as in deede they did litle better. For, Pausanias seeinge the countenaunce of his enemies, made his ensignes to stay, and commaunded every man to prepare to fight: but he forgate to geve the Greecians the signall of the battell, either for the anger he tooke against Amompharetus, or for the sodayne onset of the enemies, which made them that they came not in straight, nor altogether to the battell after it was begonne, but stragglinge in small companies, some here, and some there. In the meane time, Pausanias was busie in sacrificinge to the goddes, and seeinge

The stubbornnes of Amompharetus Captaine of the Lacedæmonians.

The battell of the Greecians, with the Persians, at the city of Platæes.

that the first sacrifices were not acceptable unto them, by the Soothsayers observations they made: he commaunded the Spartans to throwe their targettes at their feete, and not to sturre out of their places, but onely to doe as he bad them, without resistinge their enemies. When he hadde geven this straight order, he went againe and did sacrifice, when the horsemen of the enemies were at hande, and that their arrowes flewe amongest the thickest of the Lacedæmonians, and did hurte diverse of them, and specially poore Callicrates amonge the rest, that was one of the goodliest menne in all the Greecians hoste and armie. He having his deathes wounde with an arrow, before he gave uppe the ghost, sayed his death did not greve him, bicause he came out of his contrie to dye for the defence of Greece: but it greved him to dye so cowardly, havinge geven the enemie never a blowe. His death was marvelous lamentable, and the constancy of the Spartans wonderfull: for they never stirred out of their places, nor made any countenaunce to defende them selves against their enemies that came apon them, but suffred them selves to be thrust through with arrowes, and slaine in the field, lookinge for the houre the goddes would appoint them, and that their Captaine would commaunde them to fight. Some wryte also, that as Pausanias was at his prayers, and doing sacrifice unto the goddes a litle behinde the battell, certeine of the Lydians came apon him, and overthrew and tooke away all his sacrifice: and how Pausanias, and those that were about him, (havinge no other weapons in their handes) drave them awaye with force of staves and whippes. In memorie whereof, they saye there is a solemne procession kept at Sparta on that daye, which they call the Lydians procession, where they whippe and beate younge boyes about the aulter. Then was Pausanias in great distresse, to see the Priestes offer sacrifice uppon sacrifice, and that not one of them pleased the goddes: at the last he turned his eyes to the temple of Iuno, and wept, and holdinge up his handes, besought Iuno Cithæron, and all the other goddes, (patrones and protectors of the contry of the Platæians) that if it were not the will of the goddes the Greecians shoulde have the victorie, yet that the

Callicrates slaine without fighting.

Note the obedience of the Spartan souldiers unto death.

conquerors at the least should buie their deathes dearely, and that they shoulde finde they fought against valliant men and worthy souldiers. Pausanias had no sooner ended his prayer, but the sacrifices fell out very favorable, insomuch the Priestes and Soothsayers came to promise him victory. Thereupon, he straight gave commaundement to march toward the enemy, which flew from man to man incontinently how they shoulde march. So as he that hadde seene the Squadron of the Lacedæmonians, would have said it had bene like the body of a fierce beast raising up his bristels, preparing to fight. Then the barbarous people saw they shoulde have a hotte battel, and that they should mete with men that would fight it out to the death: wherefore they covered their bodies with great targets after the Persian facion, and bestowed their arrowes lustely apon the Lacedæmonians. But they keeping close together, and coveringe them selves with their shieldes, marched on stil apon them, untill they came to joyne with the enemy so lustely, that they made their targets flie out of their hands, with the terrible thrustes and blowes of their pikes and speares apon their breastes, and overthwart their faces, that they slew many of them, and layed them on the grounde. For all that, they dyed not cowardly, but tooke the Lacedæmonians pikes and speares in their bare hands, and brake them in two by strength of their armes: and then they quickely pluckt out their cimeters and axes, and lustely layed about them, and wrong the Lacedæmonians shields out of their hands by force, and fought it out with them a great while hand to hand. Now, whilest the Lacedæmonians were busily fighting with the barbarous people, the Athenians stoode still imbattelled farre of, and kept their ground. But when they saw the Lacedæmonians tary so long, and that they came not, and heard a marvelous noyse of men as though they were fighting, and besides that there came a speedy messenger unto them sent from Pausanias, to let them understand they were fighting: then they marched with all speede they could to help them. But as they were comming on a great pace over the playne, unto that parte where they heard the noyse: the Greecians that were on Mardonius side came against them. Aristides

Battaill betwixt the Greecians and Persians.

ARISTIDES

seeing them comming towards them, went a good way before his company, and cried out as loude as he could for life, and conjured the Greecians in the name of the gods, the protectors of Greece, to leave of these warres, and not to trouble the Athenians that were going to helpe them that ventured their lives, to defend the common wealth and safety of all Greece. But when he saw they would nedes fight for any request and conjuration he could use, and that they came still apon him, bending them selves to give charge: then he stayed his going to relieve the Lacedæmonians, and was compelled to make head against those that set apon him and his company, they beinge about fifty thousand men, of the which, the most parte notwithstanding went their waies, and left the army, specially when they understoode the Persians were overthrowen and fled. The fury of the battell, and cruellest fight (as they say) was where the Thebans were: bicause the nobility and chiefest men of the contry fought very earnestly for the Persians, but the people refused, being led by a smal nomber of the nobility that commaunded them. So they fought that day in two places, the Lacedæmonians being the first that overthrew the Persians, and made them flie: and they slue Mardonius the kings lieutenant, with a blow of a stone one Arimnestus a Spartan gave him apon his head, rightly as the oracle of Amphiaraus had prophecied before unto him. For Mardonius before the battel had sent thither a Lydian, and a Carian, unto the oracle of Trophonius, of the which, the prophet made answere unto the Carian, in the Carian tonge: and the man of Lydia lay within the sanctuary of Amphiaraus, where he thought in his dreame that one of the priestes of the temple willed him to go out of the place he was in, and he denying it, the Priest tooke up a great stone and threw it at his head, and so thought he was slaine with the blow. And thus it is written. And furthermore, the Lacedæmonians did chase the Persians flying, into their fortification they had in a wodde: and the Athenians also shortly after overthrew the Thebans wherof they slue in the field, a three hundred of the noblest and chiefest of them. For even as the Thebans began to turne tayle, newes came unto the Athenians, that the Persians had

The Greecians victorie of the Persians at Platæes.

Mardonius slaine of Arimnestus a Spartan, with a blow of a stone.

intrenched them selves within their forte and strength in the wodde, where the Lacedæmonians did besiege them. The Athenians suffered the Greecians that fled to save them selves, and they went to help the Lacedæmonians, to take the forte of the barbarous people: who went before but slenderly about it, bicause they had no experience to make an assault, nor force upon a walle. But so soone as the Athenians came into them, they straight tooke it by assault, and made great slaughter of the Persians and barbarous people. For of three hundred thowsand fighting men that Mardonius had in his campe, there were saved only but forty thowsand led under Artabazus: and of the Greecians side, there were not slaine above thirtene hundred and three score in all, amongst which also there were two and fifty Athenians, all of the tribe of Æantides, the which had done more valliantly that day, then any other tribe, as Clidemus writeth. And this is the cause why the Æantides made a solemne sacrifice unto the Nymphes Sphragitides, at the common charge, according to the order geven them by the oracle of Apollo, to geve them thankes for this victorie. Of the Lacedæmonians there dyed foure score and eleven: and of the Tegeates, sixteene. But I marvell Herodotus sayth, that none but these people onely fought in that jorney against the barbarous nation, and no other Greecians besides: for the number of the dead bodies, and their graves also do shewe, that it was a generall victorie and exployte of all the Greecians together. And moreover, if there had beene but these three people onely that hadde fought against them, and that all the rest had stoode and looked on, and done nothinge: sure there had bene no such epigramme as this, engraven apon the alter or tombe that was set up in the place of the battell.

Two hundred and three score thousand Persians slain.

A thowsande three hundred and three score Greecians slaine.

When the victorious Greekes, had driven out of their lande,
the Persians by force of armes, which long did them withstande,
they built to mighty Iove, this holy aulter here,
and made it common for all Greece, as plainly may appeare.
in Guerdon of the good, which he did them restore,
in Guerdon of their liberty, which liked them evermore.

This battell was fought the fourth day of the moneth

which the Athenians call Boedromion, that is, about the moneth of Iuly, or after the Bœotians accompt, the six and twenty of the moneth, they call Panemus, on which day there is yet kept a common assembly of the estates of Greece, in the cities of Platæes, where the Platæians make a solemne sacrifice unto Iupiter, protector of their libertie, to geve him thankes alwayes for this victorie. It is no marvaill that there was such difference then betwixt the monethes and dayes, consideringe that even nowe when astronomie is more perfectly understanded, then it was then: some do yet beginne and ende their monethes at one day, and some at an other. After this great battel and overthrow of the barbarous people, there rose great strife betwixt the Athenians, and the Lacedæmonians, touching the reward and honor of the victorie. For the Athenians would not geve place unto the Lacedæmonians, nor suffer them to set up any tokens or signes of triumphe. Whereupon the Greecians running to armes in mutinie together, by this occasion they had almost spoyled one an other: had not Aristides through his wisedom and wise perswasions, stayed, and quieted the other Captaines his companions, and specially one Leocrates and Myronides, whom he wanne with such discrete and gentle words, that they were contented to referre it wholly unto arbitrement and judgement of the other people of Greece. So the Greecians met in the same place together, purposely to decide their controversie. In this counsell holden there, Theogiton a Captaine of the Megarians, sayd for his opinion, that to avoide the civill warre might growe betwene the Greecians apon this quarrell: he thought it very requisite, to appoint over the reward and honor of this victorie, unto some other city, then to any of the two that fell out about it. After him rose up Cleocritus, Corinthian, seeming to every man there that he woulde have requested this honor for the cittie of Corinthe, beinge in deede the thirde cittie in estimacion of all Greece, next unto Sparta and Athens: howbeit he made an oration in commendacion of the Platæians, which was marvelously liked, and well thought of of every man. For his opinion went flatly with the Platæians, that to ende this strife, they should geve the honor of this

Strife betwixt the Athenians and Lacedæmonians for honor of the victory.

Corinthe the third city of estimation in Greece.

Sparta.

Athens.

Corinthe.

The Grecians graunt the honor of the victory unto the Platæians.

victorie unto the citie of Platæes, and so woulde neither of both parties be angrie that they shoulde be honored. Apon his wordes, Aristides first agreed on the Athenians behalfe, and then Pausanias for the Lacedæmonians, that the Platæians should have the reward. Now they both beinge agreed, before the spoyle was devided betwene them, they sette aside foure score talentes that were geven to the Platæians, with the which they built a temple unto Minerva, and gave her an image, and sett out all her temple with pictures that remaine whole untill this day: and the Lacedæmonians notwithstanding, did set up their tokens of victorie by them selves, and the Athenians theirs also by them selves. So, they sending unto the oracle of Apollo in the city of Delphes, to know unto what gods, and how they should do sacrifice: Apollo aunswered them that they shoulde builde up an aulter unto Iupiter, protector of their libertie, howbeit that they shoulde put no sacrifice upon it, untill they had first put out all the fier through the whole contrie, bicause it had bene polluted and defiled by the barbarous people: and then, that they shoulde fetche pure and cleane fyre at the common aulter, whereon they doe sacrifice unto Apollo Pythias, in the city of Delphes. This aunswer being delivered, the great Lords and officers of Greece went through all the contrie, to put out the fyre every where. And there was a man of the same city of Platæes at that time called Euchidas, that came and offered him selfe, and promised he woulde bringe them fyre from the temple of Apollo Pythias, with all possible speede that might be. So when he came to the city of Delphes, after he hadde sprinckled and purified his body with cleane water, he put a crowne of lawrell apon his heade, and went in that manner to take fyre from the aulter of Apollo. When he had done, he hyed him againe as fast as he coulde ronne for life, unto the citie of Platæes, and came thither before the sunne was set, having commen and gone that day a thowsande furlonges. But after he hadd saluted his citizens, and delivered them the fyre he brought: he fell downe dead at their feete, and gave up the ghost. The Platæians lift him up starke deade, and buried him in the temple of Diana Euclia, to say, of

The wonderfull speede of Euchidas the Platæian, a foote.

Diana Euclia.

good renowme: and caused afterwards this Epitaphe following to be graven upon his tombe:

Euchidas death.

Engraved here doth lye, Euchidas speedy man,
who in one day both to and fro, to Delphes lightly ranne.
Even from this selfe same place, which thou doest here behold,
such hast, post hast, he swiftly made, thereof thou mayest beholde.

Many thinke that this goddesse Euclia is Diana, and so they call her. But other holde opinion she was the daughter of Hercules, and of Myrto the Nymphe, Menætius daughter, and Patroclus sister, that dyed a virgine, and was honored afterwardes as a goddesse, of the Bœotians, and of the Locrians. For in all their cities and townes in open places, they finde an aulter and image dedicated unto her: and all that are maried, doe sacrifice to her apon that aulter. Afterwards there was a generall counsell holden by all the Greecians, in the which Aristides made a motion, that all the cities of Greece shoulde yearely sende their deputies at a certeine day appointed, unto the city of Platæes, there to make their prayers and sacrifices unto the goddes: and that from five yeares, to five yeares, they shoulde celebrate common games, that should be called the games of liberty: and that they should also leavy through all the provinces of Greece, for maintenance of the warres against the Persians and barbarous people, tenne thowsand footemen, a thowsand horsemen, and a flete of a hundred sayle. Item that the Platæians thencefoorth should be taken also for devoute and holy men, and that no man should so hardy hurt or offende them, and that they shoulde onely tende the sacrifices unto the goddes, for the health and prosperitie of Greece. All which articles were enacted in forme and maner aforesayed, and the Platæians bounde them selves yearely to kepe solemne sacrifices and anniversaries for the soules of the Greecians that were slaine in their territories, fightinge for defence of the libertie of the Greecians. And this they observe yet unto this daye in this sorte. The sixteenth day of the moneth of Mæmacterion (which the Bœotians call Alalcomenies, and is about the moneth of Ianuary) they goe a procession, and before the procession there goeth a trom-

A generall counsell holden at the city of Platæes.

Solemne sacrifices and funeralls kept by the Platæians yerely for the Greecians that were slaine at the battaill of Platæes.

petor that soundeth the alarom. Then there follow certeine charrettes loden with braunches of fyrre tree, and with nosegayes and garlandes of triumphe: then a blacke bul, and certeine yong gentlemen noble men sonnes, that cary great cawdrons with two eares full of wine and milke, such as they use to powre apon the graves of deade men for propiciatory oblations, and other young boyes free borne, that cary oyles, perfumes, and other sweete odours in vyoll glasses. For no servaunt or bonde man may lawfully be admitted to have any office about this mistery, for that they whose memory they honor, dyed all fighting for defence of the liberty of Greece. After all this shew, followeth the provost of the Platæians for that time being, last of all: who may not all the rest of the yeare besides so much as touch any iron, nor weare any other coloured gowne but white. Howebeit then he weareth on a purple coloured coate, and holdeth a funerall potte in one of his handes, which he taketh in the towne house, and a naked sworde in the other hande, and so goeth through the cittie in this sorte after all the pompe aforesayed, unto the church yarde where all their graves be that were slaine at that battell. So when he commeth thither, he draweth water out of a well that is there, and with the same he washeth the fouresquare pillers and images that stand apon those tombes, and then annointeth them with oyles and sweete savors: afterwardes, he sacrificeth a bulle, and layeth him apon a heape of wodde hard by him, as they do when they burne the bodies of dead men, and making certaine praiers and peticions unto Iupiter, and Mercurie, goddes of the earth, he doth solemnely invite the soules of those valliant men that dyed, fightinge for the liberty of Greece, unto the feast of this funerall sacrifice. Then he taketh a cuppe full of wine in his hande, and spilling it all upon their tombes, he speaketh these wordes aloude: I drinke to the worthy and valliant men, that dyed sometime in defence of the liberty of Greece. This solemne ceremony and anniversarie, the Platæians doe duely observe unto this present day. Nowe when the Athenians were returned to Athens, Aristides perceiving the people were bent to stablish a populer state, where the people might beare the whole rule and authoritie,

ARISTIDES

judginge them well worthy to be considered of, in respect of their noble service and valiant courage they had shewed in this warre: and considering also that they would hardly be brought to like of any other government, being yet in armes, and very stowte, by reason of the famous victories they had obteyned: he caused a law to be made, that all authority of government should runne in equality among the citizens, and that thencefoorth all burgesses (as well poore as rich) should be chosen by voyces of the people, and promoted to offices within the city. And moreover, when Themistocles tolde in open assembly, that he had a thing in his heade woulde be greatly to the profit and commodity of the state, but yet it was not to be spoken openly for diverse respects: the people willed him to tell it unto Aristides onely, and to take his advise in it, to knowe whether it was meete to be done or not. Then Themistocles tolde him secretly betwene them, that he thought to sette the arcenall afyre, where all the Greecians ships lay: alleaging, that by this meanes the Athenians should be the greatest men of power in all Greece. Aristides hearinge that, without any more, came presently to the people againe, and tolde the whole counsell openly: that nothinge coulde be more profitable in deede for the whole common wealth, and withal more wicked and unjust, then that Themistocles thought good to do. When the people heard Aristides aunswere, they willed Themistocles to lette his devise alone whatsoever it were: so great justicers were the Athenians, and so much did they trust Aristides wisedom and equitie besides. So they made Aristides afterwards generall of the army of the Athenians together with Cimon, and sent them to make warre against the barbarous people. Aristides at his comming thither, seeing Pausanias, and the other Captaines that were generals over the whole army, dealinge hardly, and churlishely with people their confederates: he on the contrary side, spake gently unto them, and shewed him selfe as curteous and familiar to them as he coulde possible, making his companion also familiar to all, and just to every body, not oppressing one to ease other, in defraying the charges of the warres. Aristides takinge this course, it was not noted howe by litle and litle he cutte of

Aristides preferreth the popular state.

A wicked devise of Themistocles.

Aristides sentence apon Themistocles devise.

The justice of the Athenians.

Aristides and Cimon generalls of the Athenians against the barbarous people.

the rule and authoritie of the Lacedæmonians in Greece, not by force of armes, nor by shippes, nor by numbers of horses, but onely by his grave and wise government. For if the justice and vertue of Aristides, and the myldenes and curtesy of Cimon made the government of the Athenians to be liked of, and accepted of all the other people of Greece: the covetousnes, pride, and fiercenesse of Pausanias, made it much more to be desired. For Pausanias never spake unto the other Captaynes of the people, allyes, and confederates, but it was ever in choller, and he was to sharp with them: and for the poore private souldiers, he woulde cause them to be cruelly whipped for every small offence, or else to make them stande a whole day together on their feete, layinge a heavy iron ancker apon their shoulders. No man durst goe forrage, neither for strawe nor reedes to make them couches of, nor durst water their horse before the Spartans: for he had sette skowtes for them to whippe them home, that went out before them. And one day when Aristides thought to have spoken to him, and to have tolde him some thinge: he frowned apon him, and sayed he hadde no leasure to speake with him now, and so would not heare him. Whereupon the Captaines of the other Greecians, and specially those of Chio, of Samos, and of Lesbos, did afterwardes follow Aristides, and perswaded him to take apon him the charge and authority to commaunde the other people of Greece, and to take into his protection the allyes and confederats of the same, who long sithence wished to revolt from the government of the Lacedæmonians, and onely to submitte them selves unto the Athenians. Aristides aunswered them thus: that they had not only reason to doe that they sayd, but that they were also constrained to do it. Notwithstanding, bicause the Athenians might have good grounde and assurance of their undoubted fidelitie and good service, they shoulde deliver them manifest testimony and assurance thereof, by some famous act attempted against the Lacedæmonians, whereby their people hereafter durst never fall from the league of the Athenians. Vliades Samian, and Antagoras of Chio hearing him say so, both Captaines of galleys confedered together: they went one day to set apon the

Aristides justice and vertue tooke from the Lacedæmonians all their rule and authority in Greece.

Pausanias proude and covetous.

Pausanias cruell punishing of his souldiers.

Aristides fine triall of traytors.

The rebellious act of Vliades and Antagoras against Pausanias.

ARISTIDES

admirall galley of Pausanias, hard by Bizantium, the one of the one side of her, and the other on the other side, as she was rowing before all the fleete. Pausanias seeinge them, stoode uppe straight in a marvelous rage against them, and threatned them that before it were longe he woulde make them knowe they had bene better to have assaulted their owne naturall contrie, then to have set upon him as they had done. But they aunswered him, and bad him get him away quickely and he were wise, and let him thanke fortune hardly, that graunted the Greecians victory at the battell of Platæes under his leading: and that it was nothing else but the onely reverence and respect of the same, that had made the Greecians hold their hands till now, from geving him that just punishment his pride and arrogancy had deserved. So the end was, they left the Lacedæmonians, and stacke unto the Athenians: wherin was easily discerned the great corage, and wonderfull magnanimity of the Lacedæmonians. For when they sawe their Captaines were marred and corrupted, through the overgreat authority, and liberty they had, they willingly gave up their commaundement over the other Greecians, and did no more sende their Captaines to be generalls of the whole army of Greece: thinking it better for their citizens, that they should be obedient, and in every point observe the discipline and law of their contrie, then if they had bene otherwise the only rulers and Lords over the whole contrie. Now at what time the Lacedæmonians did commaunde all Greece, as Lordes: the cities and people of Greece did pay a certeine summe of money, towardes defrayinge of the charges of the warres against the barbarous people. But after that their seigniorie and rule was taken from them, the Greecians were contented a taxe should be leavied, and that every city should be reasonably sessed, accordinge to their wealth and abilitie: bicause every citie might know what they shoulde pay. And for this purpose, they prayed the Athenians they would appoint Aristides to take order for it, unto whom they gave full power and authoritie to taxe and sesse every citie indifferently, considering the greatnes of the territory, and the revenues of the same, as every one was reasonably able to beare it. But if

The temperance of the Lacedæmonians.

Aristides did sesse the cities of Greece.

Aristides were poore when he entred into that great charge and office of authoritie, wherein all Greece in manner did referre them selves unto his discretion: he came out of that office more poore, and had made this assessement and taxacion not only justly and truely, but also so indifferently accordinge unto every mans abilitie, that there was no man coulde finde fault with his doinges. And like as the auncient men in olde time did celebrate, and sing out the blessednes of those that lived under the raigne of Saturne, which they called the golden age: even so did the people and confederates of the Athenians afterwardes honor the assessement made by Aristides, calling it the fortunate and blessed time of Greece, and specially, when shortly after it did double, and treble on the sodaine. For the taxe Aristides made, came to about foure hundred and three score talents: and Pericles raised it almost unto a third parte. For Thucydides wryteth, that at the beginninge of the warres of Peloponnesus, the Athenians leavied sixe hundred talentes yearely uppon their confederates. And after the death of Pericles, the orators and counsellers for matters of state did raise it up higher by litle and litle, until it mounted unto the summe of thirteene hundred talentes. And this was not, bicause the warres did rise to so great a charge, by reason of the length of the same, and of the losses the Athenians had received: but for that they did accustome the people to make distributions of money by hand unto every citizen, to make them set up games, and make goodly images, and to builde sumptuous temples. Thus was Aristides therefore justly honored, praised, and esteemed above all other, for this just imposition of taxes, saving onely of Themistocles: who went up and downe flering at the matter, sayinge it was no mete praise for an honest man, but rather for a cofer well barred with iron, where a man might safely lay up his gold and silver. This he spake to be even with Aristides, which was nothing like the sharpe girde Aristides gave him openly, when Themistocles talking with him, tolde him it was an excellent thing for a Captaine to be able to know, and to prevent the counsells and doinges of the enemies: and so is it, sayed Aristides againe, not onely a needefull, but an

Aristides a true cesser.

Tauntes betwixt Themistocles and Aristides.

honest thinge, and mete for a worthy generall of an army, to be cleane fingered, without bribery or corruption. So Aristides made all the other people of Greece to sweare, that they woulde truely keepe the articles of the allyance, and he him selfe as generall of the Athenians, did take their othes in the name of the Athenians: and so pronouncing execrations and curses against them that should breake the league and othe taken, he threw iron wedges red hotte into the sea, and prayed the gods to destroy them even so, that did violate their vowed faith. Notwithstandinge, afterwardes (in my opinion) when there fell out great alteracion in the state, and that the Athenians were forced to rule more straightly then before: Aristides then willed the Athenians to let him beare the daunger and burden of perjury and execration, and that they should not let for feare thereof to do any thing whatsoever they thought mete or necessary. To conclude, Theophrastus wryteth, that Aristides was not only a perfect, an honest, and just man, in private matters betwixt party and party: but in matters of state, and concerning the common weale, he did many thinges oftentimes accordinge to the necessitie of the time, and troubles of the citie, wherein violence and injustice was to be used. As when the question was asked in open counsell, to know whether they might take away the gold and silver that was left in the Ile of Delos safely layed up in the temple of Apollo to beare out the charges of the warres against the barbarous people, and to bring it from thence unto Athens, apon the motion of the Samians, although it was directly against the articles of the allyance, made and sworne amonge all the Greecians. Aristides opinion beinge asked in the same, he aunswered: it was not just, but yet profitable. Now, notwithstanding Aristides had brought his citie, to rule and commaund many thousandes of people: yet was he still poore for all that, and untill his dying day he gloried rather to be praised for his povertie, then for all the famous victories and battells he had wonne: and that plainely appeareth thus. Callias Ceres torche bearer, was his neere kinseman, who through enemies came to be accused, and stoode in hazard of life: so when the day came that his matter was to be heard

Aristides preferred necessity of time, before law and reason.

Aristides gloried in his poverty.

before the Iudges, his accusers very faintly, and to litle purpose, uttered the offences whereof they accused him, and running into other byematters, left the chiefest matter, and spake thus to the Iudges: My Lords, you al know Aristides the sonne of Lysimachus, and you are not ignoraunt also that his vertue hath made him more esteemed, then any man else is, or can be, in all Greece. Howe thinke ye doth he live at home? when you see him abroade uppe and downe the city, in a threde bare gowne all to tattered? Is it not likely, trow ye, that he is ready to starve at home for lacke of meate and reliefe, whom we all see quake for very colde, beinge so ill arrayed and clothed? And yet M. Callias here his cosin germaine the richest citizen in all Athens, is so miserable: that notwithstandinge Aristides hath done much for him, by reason of his great credit and authoritie among you, he suffereth him, and his poore wife and children readie to begge, to starve for any helpe he geveth him. Callias perceiving the Iudges more angryer with him for that, then for any matter else he was accused of: he prayed Aristides might be sent for, and willed him to tel truely whether he had not offered him good rounde summes of money, many a time and oft, and intreated him to take it, which he ever refused, and aunswered him alwayes, that he coulde better boast of his poverty, then him selfe coulde of his riches: (which he sayd many did use ill, and few coulde use them wel) and that it was a hard thing to finde one man of a noble minde, that could away with povertie, and that such onely might be ashamed of poverty, as were poore against their willes. So Aristides confirmed all he spake to be true: and every man that was at the hearinge of this matter, went wholly away with this opinion, that he had rather be poore as Aristides, then rich as Callias. This tale is written thus by Æschines the Socratian Philosopher: and Plato reporteth of him also, that notwithstandinge there were many other famous and notable men of Athens, yet he gave Aristides praise above them all. For others, sayd he, (as Themistocles, Cimon, and Pericles) have beautified the citie with stately porches, and sumptuous buildinges of golde and silver, and with stone of other fine superfluous devises:

A hard thing to away with poverty.

Who may be ashamed of poverty.

Aristides commended of Plato.

but Aristides was only he, that vertuously disposed him selfe and all his doinges, to the furtherance of the state and common weale. His justice and good nature appeared plainely, in his doinges and behaviour towardes Themistocles. For though Themistocles was ever against Aristides in all things, and a continuall enemy of his, and that by his meanes and practise he was banished from Athens: yet when Themistocles was accused of treason to the state, having diverse sharpe enemies against him: as Cimon, Alcmæon, with diverse other: Aristides sought not revenge, when he had him at his advantage. For he neither spake nor did any thinge against him at that time to hurt him: neither did he rejoyce to see his enemie in misery, no more then if he had never envied him in his prosperity. And touching Aristides death, some write he dyed in the realme of Pontus, being sent thither about matters of the state: and other thinke he dyed an old man in the citie of Athens, greatly honored and beloved of all the citizens. But Craterus the Macedonian wryteth of his death in this sorte: After that Themistocles (sayeth he) was fled, the people of Athens became very stubborne and insolent: whereupon, many lewde men grew to be common appeachers and accusers of the noble men and chiefest citizens, and to stirre up the malice and ill will of the common people against them, who were waxen proude by reason of their prosperity, and dominion that was enlarged. Amonge the rest, Aristides was condemned for extorcion and ill behaviour in the common wealth, apon one Diophantes accusation, of the village of Amphitrope: who burdened him, that he tooke money of the Ionians, to make the annuell tribute cease which they payed unto Athens: and so Craterus sayth, that bicause Aristides was not able to pay the fine they set apon his heade (which was five Minas) he was driven to forsake Athens, and to gette him into Ionia where he dyed. Yet doth not Craterus bring foorth any probable matter to prove this true he wryteth: as his pleadinge, his sentence and condemnation, or any decree passed against him, although he used great diligence else in collectinge all such matters, and vowchinge his authors. Furthermore, all other wryters that have specially noted the faultes and offences, committed

Aristides temperance unto Themistocles.

Aristides death.

Aristides condemned for extorcion.

by the people of Athens in former times against their Captaines and governors: they do declare Themistocles exile, Miltiades captivity that dyed in prison, Pericles fine wherein he was condemned, and Paches death that slue him selfe in the pulpit for orations, when he sawe he was condemned: and tell diverse such stories, addinge to also Aristides banishment: but yet they make no maner of mencion of the condemnation which Craterus speaketh of. Moreover, Aristides tombe is to be seene at this day apon the haven of Phalerus, which was set up for him at the charge of the common wealth, as it is reported, bicause he dyed so poore a manne, as they founde nothing in his house to bury him with. Other go further, and say that his daughters were maried by decree of the people, at the charge of the common wealth, and that the citie gave every one of them three thowsande Drachmas: and his sonne Lysimachus, a hundred Minas of silver, and a hundred Iugera, and at Alcibiades request, who was the author of the decree, they gave him foure Drachmas a day besides, of ordinarie allowance. Furthermore, when this Lysimachus dyed, he left alive one onely daughter called Polycrite, whom the people appointed, as Callisthenes wryteth, as much provision to live withall, as they gave to any that wanne the Olympian games. And sithence, Demetrius Phalerian, Hieronymus Rhodian, Aristoxenus the musitian, and Aristotle the Philosopher, at the least if the booke intituled of Nobilitie be any of Aristotles workes: all these agree together, that one Myrto, Aristides daughters daughter, was maried to the wise Socrates, who tooke her to his wife (having a wife already) bicause she was a poore widdow, and could not be maried for her poverty, having much a do to live. Yet Panætius doth wryte against them, in his booke of Socrates life. But Demetrius Phalerian wryteth in his booke he intituled *Socrates*, that he could remember very well he had seene one Lysimachus, Aristides sonnes sonne, or his daughters sonne, that was very poore, and lived of that he could get to interpret dreames, by certaine tables, wherin was wrytten the arte to interpret the signification of dreames: and that he kept commonly about the temple of Bacchus called Iacchion, unto whom, together with his mother and

Aristides tombe.

The Athenians thankefulnes unto Aristides children.

Myrto, Aristides daughters daughter maried unto Socrates.

his sister, he sayd he had caused the people to geve them a Triobolum a peece, every day towards their livinge. It is very true that the selfe same Demetrius Phalerian, when he reformed the state of Athens, ordained that his mother and sister should have ech of them a Drachma by the day to finde them withall, out of the common chamber of the city. And it is no new, nor straunge thing, that the people of Athens were so carefull to helpe, and to relieve, the women that dwelt in the citie: considering that in times past, Aristogiton having a litle daughter in the Ile of Lemnos, in very hard and poore state, and that coulde not be bestowed in mariage for her poverty, they caused her to be brought to Athens, and maried her in one of the noblest houses of the city, and made her a joynter besides in the village of Potamos. Which great curtesy and humanity of theirs, hath ever deserved great fame and commendacion, and yet continueth even until this day, in that noble city of Athens, in the mouth of every man there.

The Athenians commended for their liberality.

THE END OF ARISTIDES LIFE

EDINBURGH

T. & A. CONSTABLE

Printers to Her Majesty

1895

CPSIA information can be obtained at www.ICGtesting.com
Printed in the USA
LVOW062017120313

323921LV00022B/1243/P

9 781179 001395